Culture, Religion, and the Reintegration of Female Child Soldiers in Northern Uganda

Bible & Theology in Africa

Knut Holter
General Editor

Vol. 10

PETER LANG
New York • Washington, D.C./Baltimore • Bern
Frankfurt • Berlin • Brussels • Vienna • Oxford

Culture, Religion, and the Reintegration of Female Child Soldiers in Northern Uganda

Edited by
Bård Mæland

PETER LANG
New York • Washington, D.C./Baltimore • Bern
Frankfurt • Berlin • Brussels • Vienna • Oxford

Library of Congress Cataloging-in-Publication Data

Culture, religion, and the reintegration of female child
soldiers in northern Uganda / edited by Bård Mæland.
p. cm. — (Bible and theology in Africa; v. 10)
Includes bibliographical references.
1. Children and war—Uganda. 2. Child soldiers—Uganda.
3. Women soldiers—Uganda. 4. Soldiers—Rehabilitation—Uganda.
5. Lord's Resistance Army. I. Mæland, Bård.
HQ784.W3C85   303.6'4083096761090511—dc22   2010002620
ISBN 978-1-4331-0951-5
ISSN 1525-9846

Bibliographic information published by **Die Deutsche Nationalbibliothek**.
Die Deutsche Nationalbibliothek lists this publication in the "Deutsche
Nationalbibliografie"; detailed bibliographic data is available
on the Internet at http://dnb.d-nb.de/.

Cover photo © Christine Mbabazi Mpyangu

The paper in this book meets the guidelines for permanence and durability
of the Committee on Production Guidelines for Book Longevity
of the Council of Library Resources.

© 2010 Peter Lang Publishing, Inc., New York
29 Broadway, 18th floor, New York, NY 10006
www.peterlang.com

Printed in the United States of America

To you who shared
from your costly experiences

Table of Contents

List of Contributors

TOR ARNE BERNTSEN is a chaplain to the Royal Norwegian Air Force Academy, Trondheim, Norway. He is also a doctoral student at the School of Mission and Theology, Stavanger, Norway, currently working on a dissertation on the peace and reconciliation process in northern Uganda.

CHRIS COULTER is a researcher and project manager at Uppsala University, Sweden, but also works as a consultant. She works mainly with human rights and gender in conflict and post-conflict settings and has published widely on the subject, including the recent book *Bush Wives and Girl Soldiers: Women's Lives through War and Peace in Sierra Leone.*

RAGNHILD DYBDAHL is head of the Department for Education and Research in Norad, the Norwegian Agency for Development Co-operation. She has also worked as a researcher and practitioner, particularly related to refugees and survivors of potentially traumatising events, and has published several articles on the effects of war on mental health and psychosocial support.

KJETIL FRETHEIM is associate professor of social science at MF Norwegian School of Theology, Oslo, Norway. He is the author of *Rights and Riches: Exploring the Moral Discourse of Norwegian Development Aid.* He has published articles on ethics, development and intercultural communication.

KNUT HOLTER is professor of Old Testament studies at the School of Mission and Theology, Stavanger, Norway. He is author or editor of more than ten books on Old Testament interpretation and African biblical hermeneutics, most recently *Contextualized Old Testament Scholarship in Africa* and (co-ed.) *Global Hermeneutics? Reflections and Consequences.*

MAGNAR KARTVEIT is professor of Old Testament studies at the School of Mission and Theology, Stavanger, Norway. He is the author of *The Origin of the Samaritans*. He has published a number of articles on various Old Testament topics.

NERMINA KRAVIĆ is a neuro-psychiatrist and assistant in the Medical School, University of Tuzla, Bosnia and Herzegovina. She also works at the Psychiatry Department, University Clinical Center Tuzla. Her clinical and research work and interests are focused on children and adolescents, especially on the effects war has had on children and families.

MARTA HØYLAND LAVIK is adjunct professor of Old Testament studies at the School of Mission and Theology, Stavanger, Norway, and a postdoctor fellow at Stavanger University Hospital. She is the author of *A People Tall and Smooth-skinned: The Rhetoric of Isaiah 18*. She has published articles on the African aspect of the Old Testament, and is currently doing research in the field of theology and health.

SUSAN MCKAY is a psychologist, nurse, and professor of Women's and International Studies at the University of Wyoming in Laramie, Wyoming, USA. For more than two decades, she has taught and researched issues focused upon women, girls, and armed conflict, women and peacebuilding, and feminist issues in peace psychology. She is coauthor of *Where Are the Girls? Girls in Fighting Forces in Northern Uganda, Sierra Leone, and Mozambique, Their Lives During and After War.*

CHRISTINE MBABAZI MPYANGU is currently a doctoral student at the School of Mission and Theology Stavanger, Norway, researching on the use of rituals in the reintegration of formerly recruited females in northern Uganda. She also lectures in the Department of Religious Studies, Makerere University.

BÅRD MÆLAND is professor of systematic theology at the School of Mission and Theology, Stavanger, Norway. He is the author of *Enduring Military Boredom: 1750 to the Present* (with Paul Otto Brunstad). He has published articles and books on interreligious hermeneutics, military ethics, and systematic and practical theology, and is currently working on the role of imagination in theology.

HELEN NKABALA NAMBALIRWA is a lecturer in the Department of Religious Studies, Makerere University, and is currently a doctoral student at the

School of Mission and Theology Stavanger, Norway, researching on the Old Testament rhetoric of the Lord's Resistance Army.

EMELINE NDOSSI is a lecturer at Makumira University College, Tumaini University, Tanzania. She is currently a doctoral student at the School of Mission and Theology, Stavanger, Norway, where she researches the needs of female returnees who are returning from the Lord's Resitance Army, and the role played by the Church in the reintegration process. She has published several articles in practical Theology.

DEUSDEDIT R. K. NKURUNZIZA is a senior lecturer in systematic theology, religion, and peace studies, Department of Religious Studies, Makerere University, Uganda. He is the editor of African Peace Series (Konrad-Adenauer Stiftung, Kampala) and Executive Director, East African Institute of Governance and Conflict Management (EAIGCM). He is the Author of *Bantu Philosophy of Life in the Light of the Christian Message: A Basis for an African Vitalistic Theology.*

FIONA SHANAHAN is a doctoral student at the Department of Applied Psychology, University College Cork, Ireland, examining the use of cultural resources in post-conflict social reintegration. Her research interests are in sociocultural psychology, indigenous psychologies, creative participatory methodologies, youth and armed conflict, and the gender dimensions of post-conflict cultural transitions.

KISHOR SHRESTHA is a professor of education at the Research Centre for Educational Innovation and Development, Tribhuvan University in Kathmandu, Nepal. He is a member of the International Working Group on Peace Building with Children (IWGPB) created by the World Forum Foundation, US in 2004. He has published several articles on effects of conflict on children and families.

THOR STRANDENÆS is professor of missiology at the School of Mission and Theology in Stavanger, Norway. His research focuses on missiology, Christianity and culture, Church and society in China, bible translation, and children and worship.

THERESE TINKASIIMIRE is a senior lecturer in the Department of Religious Studies at Makerere University, Kampala, and a religious sister of the Daughters of St. Therese, Uganda. She has published several articles on religion and gender, the Biblical understanding of poverty, and the Church's responses to HIV/AIDS.

MILFRID TONHEIM is a researcher at the Centre for Intercultural Communication (SIK), Stavanger, Norway, and currently researching reintegration of
former girl soldiers in the DR Congo. Her research interests are in delibe-
rative democracy and communicative rationality, the rights and well-being of
the child, children's participation in decision-making processes, and the
social and economic reintegration of children and youth associated with
armed forces or groups.

ANGELA VEALE is a lecturer in the Department of Applied Psychology,
University College Cork, Ireland. Her research and publications focus on
families and child-raising in transnational migration, post-conflict social
reintegration and juvenile justice. She is currently working on sociocultural
approaches to agency/activism of women and children in refugee and post-
conflict populations.

MICHAEL WESSELLS is a psychologist and Professor at Columbia University
in the Program on Forced Migration and Health. He is author of *Child
soliders: From violence to protection* (Cambridge: Harvard University Press,
2006).

MIRANDA WORTHEN is doctoral candidate in the Division of Epidemiology
at University of California, Berkeley. Her research is with vulnerable populations in conflict and post-conflict communities. She is currently researching
psychosocial reintegration of U.S. Veterans returning from combat in Iraq
and Afghanistan.

GERD MARIE ÅDNA is an associate professor of religious studies at the
School of Mission and Theology, Stavanger, Norway. Her research focus has
been on the role of sacrifice in early Islam. She is currently working on
topics connected to memory and forgetfulness within an Islamic setting,
especially in Germany and Norway.

INTRODUCTION

1

Culture, Religion, and the Reintegration of Female Child Soldiers in Northern Uganda

Bård Mæland
School of Mission and Theology, Stavanger, Norway

Introduction

The reintegration of thousands of young persons and young adults back to the society of northern Uganda, from which they were abducted in order to serve as soldiers for the Lord's Resistance Army (LRA) in various capacities, represents tremendous practical, social, and cultural challenges. This is not least the case with regard to the return of females, whose background and experience prove particularly challenging for fragmented and fragile communities to handle.

The main aim of this book is to ponder some of the social, cultural, and religious complexities that surround young females who once were part of the Lord's Resistance Army, and who now are right in the midst of their return and reintegration into families and communities in northern Uganda. Situated in a culturally, religiously, and ritually rich environment, understanding this context may strengthen the ongoing reintegration process.

In order to ponder these complexities, this edited volume has recruited researchers from as diverse fields as anthroplogy, psychology, ethics, religious studies, and theology. Based on papers presented at a conference in Stavanger, Norway, in May 2009, as part of a research project funded by The

Norwegian Programme for Development, Research and Education (NUFU), this book brings scholars from various home turfs together. The overall aim is to examine and discuss major challenges of social, cultual, religious, and moral nature.

To examine the conditions of female youths and young women and mothers, often forced ones, in the midst of this process, is indeed challenging, primarily because of the exacting situation the females themselves face. First, it is challenging because there is not always a family to return to. Family members may have been killed or displaced. The social counterpart of this is that most people have been living in IDP camps, and hence much of civil society has been destroyed. For both reasons, the "reintegration into what?" question becomes a pressing one. Also, sometimes ex-soldiers who return do not necessarily wish to return to their family and community of origin. Secondly, to settle with one or more children, when there is hardly any network or resources to rely on, and when, most often, the father of the children is absent, is in itself a difficult task. Let alone that these women are often exposed to mechanisms of shame and stigma. Lastly, it is indeed challenging for a researcher to justify to do research with vulnerable people who too often have hosted researchers without seeing any significant improvement of their lives. "Why do you come—again?," and, "When will our situation eventually improve?" have been asked more than once by our informants.

It is our conviction that there is hope for those who have been both victims and co-actors of this lengthy (since 1986) and dreadful chapter of human misery and history; hope that the children may be empowered through respect, education, and cooperation. As humans, we are not merely what we did and were subjected to in the past. We are also what diginity, self-respect, and empowerment may help us become. This is the idea behind making their autonomy an issue throughout a discussion of research ethics as well as their level of autonomy in carrying out their duties within the strict, yet not fully determined, LRA orders and "code of conduct." This perspective is reflected in the majority of the articles of the book.

In the continuation of this idea, one may also view the resources of religion and culture: They may either prevent reintegration and produce stigmatization, or they may prove powerful in helping young females return to their families, their villages, and communities, and become active, esteemed, and empowered members of the northern Ugandan society.

Perception, politics, and peace

Part I of the book is concerned with some general issues that may be seen as framing the book from rather diverse angles. In short, issues related to the perception of who the child soldiers are, as well as the overall framework of politics and peace are examined.

In a rare kind of article, Milfrid Tonheim reviews the research status on the field of reintegration of former girl soldiers in an African context. Her contribution is based on a vast body of literature (scholarly books and articles; research and evaluation reports; doctoral dissertations; a few Master theses; as well as working papers) and will likely be a future "must read" for people working in this field. Due to the limited literature on girls' reintegration, she has also taken a side-glance to the challenges of women and boys. Although the area of reintegration of girl soldiers is increasingly researched these days, it "is still in its infancy" (Michael Wessels). As she rightly states, "Until relatively recently, the term child soldier meant in reality a 'boy soldier'." Tonheim reviews and identifies areas that have been well covered by research so far, as well areas where more research-based knowledge is needed, as well as additional programming. The areas where she identifies that more research should be directed, is (a) on self-demobilised girl soldiers, who have long been excluded from Demobilization Rehabilitation and Reintegration (DDR) programmes, and (b) on the experiences and prospects of forced mothers and their children. As to the latter, simply put: the particularities of former girl soldiers require a stronger focus on their children, often having been born, and having lived with armed groups for years. According to Tonheim, "Undoubtedly, the needs of forced mothers and their children have been largely neglected by researchers and reintegration programmes alike, maybe especially the needs of the children born in captivity."

Another topic Tonheim touches, is the issue of terminology and qualitative categories. How should the persons we are writing about, and have been talking to, be denoted? Are they 'child soldiers,' which is often used (cf. the Cape Town principles, 1997), but which may be limiting the various positions and experiences children, especially girls, may have had in armed forces or armed groups? Or should the long-winded 'a child associated with an armed force and armed group' be used, as recommended in the Paris Principles (2007)? And, what about the age issue when you interview a woman who have been with the LRA for more than ten years? With the particularities of females' experience, one should consider a variety of other notions as well, such as 'forced wives', 'forced mothers', 'girl mother' and 'forcibly involved girls'. Yet, this conceptual discussion should primarily reflect contextual matters. If so, and that is one important message conveyed through our book, stereotypes should be abandoned. The choice many of the articles of the book have employed, however, are versions of 'formerly abducted children/girls'. As for the nothern Ugandan situation, this term covers well the actual experiences of the persons (whether children, youths, or adults) many of our researchers have been talking to and are writing about.

Concepts and perceptions are not innocent, they may connect with important issues that are at stake. The article by Tor Arne Berntsen examines the role of child soldiers in the discourse by various political actors in order to end the conflict in northern Uganda. He demonstrates how the child soldier issue has been a discursive site of power struggle between the Government and the Uganda People's Defence Forces (UPDF), on the one hand, and local initiatives to justice and reconciliation, such as the Acholi Religious Leaders Peace Initiativ (ARLPI), on the other. Disparate amd contradictory notions were discovered in the discourse analysis. Hence the connection between the overall peace process and the concept and view of formerly abducted children, is a contested one, making the involvement of children in this prolonged conflict a delicate matter. It is Berntsen's contention that analysing such mechanisms may enable us to "acknowledge the complex moral and political reality of children in armed conflicts and thereby gain a deeper understanding of the war itself and develop a framework for effective resolution and peace building."

One of Tonheim's findings is an emphasis on the resilience and coping abilities of children in a context of war and armed conflict, as found in recent research. Again, this pertains to the perception of what a 'child soldier' is, and, accordingly, how the process of reintegration is viewed. According to her, "Scholars and professionals do no longer only view the child as a victim of war but also as a survivor of war and an agent who actively seek to cope with the adversities s/he faces." Departing from this perspective, Bård Mæland is writing about the issue of moral agency among formerly recruited children. Should they be viewed as victims, not to say supervictims, or are they somehow agents, also in moral terms? This contribution connects both to a legal discussion of perpetrator versus victim, and to a theory of decision-making. Mæland's discussion shows how distinctive moral agency, although confined by a number of constraining factors, can be traced in child soldiers narratives from the African continent. It is his contention that this is an important insight to use in how we approach young persons who have been with armed groups for shorter or longer periods, often also having committed the worst forms of atrocities. It may also prove an important resource for the sake of individual reintegration as well as social reconstruction and restoration.

In the last article of this first part of the book, Deus Nkurunziza argues that "child soldiering is a new form of slavery that targets the exploitation of humanity starting with the child," an "attack on the most ethical foundations of society." According to him, the intentional and strategic use of children by the Lord's Resistance Army as well as the Uganda People's Defence Forces (UPDF) represents a problem that must be tackled by focusing on the root causes of war, such as poverty, insecurity, and bad governance. Also Nkurunziza emphasises the importance and social potential of a successful reintegration of formerly abducted children. They need to be empowered with productive skills to counter the risk of resorting to taking up arms as a means of livelihood and thus contributing to a resurgence of war. Consequently, peace depends directly on an effective reintegration of children once abducted in northern Uganda.

Culture, rituals and stigmatization
Acholiland is a region very rich in traditional rituals. Embedded in a distinctive cosmology, often combined with a Christian or Muslim faith, rituals are for most Acholis seen as a necessary act of healing, purification, crossing of boundaries, returning back to the village, reconciliation, or otherwise bringing the youth and the community in harmony with their ancestors. To understand the acts and the social and cosmological impacts of conducting these rituals may indeed open our eyes to the depths of the reintegration processes that are taking place right now in the northern Uganda. But we also ask: Can culture, tradition, and social norms also make it more difficult for formerly recruited girls to return to their families and villages?

In Part II of the book, issues such as stigmatization and traditional rituals are examined in order to see how culture and religion may prevent or support reintegration. It is our general conviction that the cultural factor is important for the reintegration, both when when cultural norms provide productive resources and when they provide obstacles for female youths and forced mothers who wish to return and reintegrate into their families and communities (some do not wish to).

Based on her book, *Bush Wives and Girl Soldiers* (Cornell University Press 2009), Chris Coulter invites the reader into the diversity—not the generalised picture—of experiences and strategies of abducted women in the postwar society of Sierra Leone. To give but two examples: First, toward the end of the war many abducted girls and women were released, some escaped, and many were abandoned by their bush husbands. Others stayed with their bush husbands and commanders, either out of fear or by choice, or by lack of choice. Secondly, some were welcomed back to their families and communities while others, in fact the majority, were ostracized and expelled, often based on presumptions and rumors about what happened in the bush. Yet, given the diverse experiences, who were the most successful ones to return? One of Coulter's findings is that former girl soldiers who conformed to traditional norms and expectations increased the chances for being well received and reintegrated into their families and communities. Those who were not 'tamed' and 'domesticated' into the town or village, soon experienced stigmatisation, and, at worst, social death. Paradoxically, some of the survival skills acquired during the time of conflict, such as strength and independence, prevented some of these females from successful reintegration.

Based on extensive fieldwork in northern Uganda, Christine Mbabazi Mpyangu examines the use of traditional rituals, such as stepping on an egg (*nyono tongweno*) upon the return of returnees, or cleansing of the land (*moyo cer*). Her focus is the interconnectedness between Acholi beliefs, practices, and social structure; how the Acholi worldview and beliefs frame the rituals, and how the rituals depend on the clan system in the Acholi culture. She also recognises the role of the family as an integrated part of the the religious, cultural, and social contexts for conducting such rituals that may support the process of reintegration.

In another article based on field studies in northern Uganda, Fiona Shanahan and Angela Veale examine the importance of cultural resources for the social reintegration, complementing an individualistic perspective of resilience and strength of formerly abducted girls and young women. They find that culture is important as to the interpretation of what happened with abducted girls and their original societies during the war, as well as to how culture impacts on communal practices during the reintegration.

One of the cultural issues that Shanahan and Veale identify in their study—stigmatisation—is the single topic for Emeline Ndossi's explorative article on stigmatisation and how churches in northern Uganda may mediate and constructively contribute when stigma are enacted by local communities. She finds that there are a number of causes for stigmatisation, and that the churches have played an important role in counteracting stigma. Yet, as long as difficult issues such as breaking of cultural norms are involved, some of which are clearly oppressive to formerly abducted young mothers, one should not be too optimistic about the prospects of eradicating stigmatisation. In this situation, the churches have a role to play.

Miranda Worthen and her coauthors (Susan McKay; Angela Veale; Michael Wessells) take marginalisation and stigmatisation as a point of departure for their study on how young women and young mothers may be empowered to stand up against the prejudices and less generous reception as they return. Based on a multi-year participating action research model, they show how a distinctive research methodology may produce a very positive effect throughout the research: that those non-researchers involved may be empowered by experience of care, respect, and self-esteem. This may in turn help them face various obstacles as they return to their families and local communities.

Whereas Worthen et al. have based their article on a human rights framework, Therese Tinkasiimire uses a liberation-theological framework ("woman defined theology") to counter stigmatisation and to provide empowerment and an inclusive theology for accepting not only females who have taken part in the LRA, but also males and the entire God's creation. Her perspective is deeply ambiguous. Although she presents narratives that witness the darkest hours a human can go through, she still affirms that women because of their involvement in the war have discovered hidden talents, which they would never have known under normal circumstances. In turn, this may in some instances give them the freedom and the independence to live in their communities without interference, which may ultimately accord them their rightful and God-given dignity.

The force of the Old Testament, and the power of interpretation
Tinkasiimire's claims remind me of what the theologian Garrett Green says at the very end of his book *Imagining God: Theology and the Religious Imagination,* making a twist of the Marxist dichotomy of interpretation and social change. He says, "that the most powerful way to change the world is precisely by interpreting it" (Green 1989, 152). In the conflict of northern Uganda it is no hidden secret that the interpretation of the world is one that is heavily informed by a rather distinctive interpretation of both it and of the Bible. Promoting the enforcement of the Ten Commandments among the civilian population of the North, the Lord's Resistance Army has terrified local people as well as the international society. Hence, the religious dimension of the indoctrination, as well as the life within the LRA, needs to be taken seriously in order to prepare the reception and reintegration of youths who participated with and have been exposed to such a religious community. In Part III of this book, the reading of religious text such as the Old Testament texts, has been subjected to exegetical and hermeneutical examination. Based on the difference between modern Biblical scholarship and the "LRA way" of reading the Old Testament, is there such a thing as a correct way of reading the Bible?

Helen Nkabala Nambalirwa shows in her article in an exemplary way how such a task needs to be twofold: First, the religious discourse of LRA needs to be established by empirical tools, for example, as in her case, by interviewing former commanders and soldiers in the LRA. Thus, one sees in her contribution how the LRA has been using the Sodom/Gomorrah narrative in Genesis 18 and 19 to justify their retributive actions against the northern Ugandan population. What Nambalirwa does next, is to work as a Biblical scholar, i.e. by critically comparing the "LRA way" of reading the Old Testament with historical and textual analyses. What she finds, *inter alia,* is that LRA reads this narrative in a selective way, ignoring important aspects of the narrative, and hence using it in a legitimizing way.

Marta Høyland Lavik takes the LRA use of the Old Testament passages as a point of departure for asking how "texts of terror" such as Psalm 137 could and should be read. Through a rhetorical analysis of difficult, not to say terrifying expressions by the psalmist, which includes destruction of children, she concludes that such texts can be read, but need not to, as expressions of hurt religious feelings, and that such texts can be employed for religious justification of acts of hatred and revenge. It is therefore necessary, she maintains, that texts with this kind of devastating potential are (a) read with an ethical consciousness, (b) situated within the history of interpretation as well as not read in isolation from other texts, and (c) discussed with regard to the issue of the authority of the Bible.

In his article about the interpretive role of the academia, Knut Holter draws attention to Lavik's second criterion for approaching texts, texts that seem to open somehow up for actions that are prohibited by international law and which runs counter all moral intuition. Holter's point of departure is whether other kinds of texts may provide a constructive and comforting potential for girls and young women who have been exposed to experiences as formerly recruited young persons. His answer is indeed that there are such texts that may have a potential for hope and empowerment. The texts he draws on are taken from the Book of Lamentations, where the experiences of women (i.e., suffering, starvation, and rape in the context of war and conflict) may liken the experiences of females in northern Uganda. Despite the challenging background of many Old Testament texts, therefore, it is his wish that such texts may be used to empower females in the future, also within a context such as the one in northern Uganda.

Magnar Kartveit makes Lavik's third point his main point: the issue of religious authority inherent in the use of Biblical passages from the Old Testament. His claim is that it is a rather dangerous task to criticize the use of certain texts without demolishing the entire religious system alltogether. Rather than challenging the entire system and questioning the authority of the Bible, he suggests an alternative approach of "authentic reading" in order to avoid abuses of the Bible. By this concept he understands "to come close to the text, learn from the text, listen to the text, and tune in to its wavelength," thus respecting the strangeness of both the reader to the texts and the texts to the reader, yet also bringing disparate texts together in a reciprocal process of communication. This is a delicate issue, and hermeneutical judgment between different texts and their topical interpretation still needs to be done.

What is special about researching formerly recruited children? On ethics and methodology

Another difficult issue regards research on and with formerly recruited children, often in a most vulnerable situation, and quite often exhausted by former research ('research fatigue'). Which methodologies should be preferred? How to plan and conduct research? For what ultimate purpose? For the reward of the interviewees, or the researcher's career? In Part IV of the book, perspectives from various disciplines help us see the perplexities and complexities, norms and possibilities in doing research on formerly recruited children.

In his ethical discussion of universal versus contextual norms, Kjetil Fretheim makes an important contribution to the research ethical dilemmas in this kind of context. Highlighting some examples of the challenges and 'ethical and methodological puzzles' implicit in qualitative and participatory research on formerly recruited children, Fretheim adresses issues such as participants' consent and freedom, their right to protection, and to have their voices heard, as well as the issue of payment for research participation. His claim is that there is need to combine ethical absolutism with ethical situationism, that there are some moral principles and standards researchers must respect and adhere to, but also a need for a considered judgement of the same principles and standards in a given context.

Ragnhild Dybdahl has co-authored an article about intervention in children's suffering and need for support with two of her former research colleagues, Nermina Kravic and Kishore Shrestha. The authors argue that the lack of strong evidence as to what kind of psychological and psychosocial intervention that is needed, poses fundamental challenges regarding the ethics of response, particularly when one takes into account the need for solid research and culturally appropriate indicators and interventions. The article is a fine contribution to 'do no harm' issues. Different approaches to, and content of, support to children affected by armed conflict are discussed.

Also Thor Strandenæs examines important aspects of research on and with formerly abducted children. His concerns are the various "whereabouts" of young children who are interviewed in the process of disarmament, demobilization, and reintegration into civil society. First, he asks, "Where, *physically,* in the process of disarmament and demobilization, in rehabilitation camps and formal and material rehabilitation in society does the interview with the informant take place?" Secondly, "Where are the ex-child soldiers in the *process* of social, physical, and psychological rehabilitation and reintegration into society when they share their stories?" In short, what are the context specific conditions of the persons you are researching? Such perspectives are very important: First, they may increase the sensitivity of the reader and the researcher to the stories and excperiences of formerly recruited children. Secondly, they may provide better and more important data. And, lastly, they may prevent the research community from stereotypes of what it means to be a 'child soldier,' let alone a 'girl soldier'.

In her article, which is written from the religious studies point of view, Gerd Marie Ådna asks herself: How can a scholar be able to professionally separate between herself and the persons she is interviewing or even only reading about? The issue she is concerned with, is the matter of reflexivity between the researcher and the non-researcher. Faced with stories of, and interviews with formerly abducted girls in northern Uganda, marked by extraordinary experiences and testimonies compared to her own safe childhood and adulthood in Norway, she ponders—betwixt and between these two worlds (Victor Turner)—the effects of research, and how it may provide hope and healing through the interaction between the interviewer and the interviewee.

References
Green, Garrett. 1989. *Imagining God: Theology and the Religious Imagination.* Grand Rapids, MI/Cambridge, UK: W.B. Eerdmans.
The Paris Principles: The Principles and guidelines on children associated with armed forces or armed conflicts. 2007. Geneva: United Nations, http://www.un.org/children/conflict/_documents/parisprinciples/ParisPrin ciples_EN.pdf (accessed 7 January 2010).

PART I

2

Where Are the Research Gaps?

Reviewing Literature on Former Girl Soldiers' Reintegration in the African Context

Milfrid Tonheim
Centre for Intercultural Communication, Stavanger, Norway

Abstract

This article draws on a literature review with a particular focus on the reintegration of former girl soldiers. Areas and topics that have attracted broad scholarly attention as well as those where more knowledge and further research are required are identified. Despite increased focus on the particularities of girl soldiers' reintegration, research on girl soldiers is still in its initial stage. The study identifies in particular self-demobilised girl soldiers and forced mothers and their children as two groups of former girl soldiers which have received very little scholarly attention.

Introduction

This article draws on a literature study focusing on the reintegration process of former girl soldiers in the Democratic Republic of Congo (DRC).[1] The study was financed by the Norwegian Ministry of Foreign Affairs as a pre-study to a larger research project on former child soldiers', particularly girl soldiers', reintegration in the DRC. The main purpose of the review was to give an overview of existing literature and research, and a second objective was to identify those areas and topics that have attracted broad scholarly attention and those where more knowledge and further research are required. The article is drawn from the full report but has abandoned the review's particular focus on the DRC, currently addressing the broader African context. It starts by providing a brief explanation of the assessment criteria and search strategies used in the literature review, and continues by giving an account of the variation of terms and concepts employed in literature on child soldiers. The following and main part of the paper addresses major findings and important discussions apparent in the literature on reintegration of child soldiers. It presents some general trends and advances, discusses main findings related to the reintegration of girl soldiers, and presents some more general issues that are important with regards to the reintegration of both girls and boys. However, the girl soldier perspective will also be apparent in the discussions of the general findings.

Assessment criteria and search strategies

The reviewed documents cover academic books and articles, research and evaluation reports, PhD dissertations, a few Master theses, as well as working papers. Literature and studies on conflict situations in Africa were prioritized based on the assumption that these would more similar to the situation in Eastern Congo than cases from Latin America and Asia. Studies focusing on the reintegration of adult ex-soldiers were in most cases excluded. However, because the literature on girl soldiers is more limited, the review contains some studies addressing adult female ex-soldiers' reintegration, as these may provide useful knowledge for the reintegration of younger girls.

The review has an exclusive focus on the reintegration process, and as there is a vast body of literature on child soldiers in general, lots of publications have not been included in this review as they do not particularly address reintegration aspects. However, since the different elements of a DDR programme; disarmament, demobilisation and reintegration, are intertwined, it was at times difficult to detach the R from the D & D. Where documents cover a wide range of topics concerning child soldiering, I have allowed myself a narrow focus, addressing only issues considered to be of particular value to the review's purpose.

The review covers only rather recent studies and literature. With a few exceptions the reviewed literature is confined to the period from 2000 till early 2009. Literature searches were conducted in various electronic databases: WorldCat, ArticleFirst, Electronic Collections Online, Bibsys, and Google Scholar. In addition, I searched web-pages of relevant organizations and research milieus.[2] Lastly, bibliographies in recent studies on child soldiers, particularly on girl soldiers, were also examined in order to trace down important research contributions in the field of reintegration.

Concepts and definitions

Child soldier

The literature on child soldiers reveals an inconsistent use and a variation of terms and concepts. Authors speak of the children as soldiers, combatants, fighters, abducted children or children associated with armed forces and groups. Former child soldiers are also addressed within the broader approach of children affected by war. In my opinion the weakness of concepts like combatant and fighter is that they may, by denoting the act of fighting, only be associated with one of the roles children have within armed groups. Soldier, on the other hand, refers to a wider variety of roles and tasks performed, as do the term children associated with armed groups. The former term, 'child soldier,' is used in the Cape Town Principles (1997), however, the more recent Paris Principles (2007) employed the term 'a child associated with an armed force and armed group.' Both concepts aim to avoid having reintegration support offered only to those who have taken a direct part in hostilities, however, the latter also helps to capture children born into armed groups.

Also with regards to girl soldiers, the literature employs a wide variety of concepts. This is particularly the case when the girl soldier has been sexually violated. Concepts such as 'forced wives,' 'bush wives,' 'sex slaves,' 'girl mothers,' and 'forced mothers' are used in the literature presented in this review. Another term introduced in Wessells' study of former girl soldiers in Angola is 'forcibly involved girls' (Wessells 2007). The girls in this particular study expressed that this term is preferable to that of 'former girl soldier' as the former underlines that their participation was not voluntary. However, research shows that some girls join armed forces voluntarily, although scholars often question the authenticity of the girls' voluntarism as there might be no other good alternative at the time of recruitment.

The two most commonly used terms with regards to girls who give birth during or after their time with an armed group are 'girl mother' and 'forced mother.' Neither one of these two terms can be used as a universally accurate term due to contextual variations relating to recruitment, tasks within the groups, abuses etc., and both terms have their shortcomings. The term 'girl mother,' used for example in the Paris Principles, does not make any reference to the girl's association with an armed group, and 'forced mother' indicates that all pregnancies within the armed groups are involuntary and unwished for. However, as the term 'forced mother' is assumed most accurate in regard to most African conflicts, this term will be employed in this article.

Moreover, the terms 'child,' 'youth,' 'minor,' 'under-aged' and 'adolescent' are often used interchangeably in existing literature, and despite some differences they often overlap (Veale 2003, 11). Some authors prefer to address these young people as youth or adolescents rather than children because when and how transition from childhood to adulthood takes place is culturally determined and variable.[3] Some of the studies underline that many of the young people that have participated in war view themselves as adults and don't want to be treated as children (cf. for example ILO 2003). Others question the very focus on age and argue that it may not be the best approach to reintegration. However, the need to draw an age limit stems from international and national legal considerations, and a focus on age is therefore both inevitable and necessary.

Without going further into the conceptual debate, the term 'child soldier' will be employed in the review's own discussions and conclusions. The concept will be employed as defined in the Cape Town Principles (1997), stating that a child soldier is:

> any person under 18 years of age who is part of any kind of regular or irregular armed force or armed group in any capacity, including but not limited to cooks, porters, messengers and anyone accompanying such groups, other than family members. The definition includes girls recruited for sexual purposes and for forced marriage.[4]

DDR programme

Also in relation to reintegration the literature reveals some conceptual diversity. Reintegration is usually one part of a larger process that most commonly is called the DDR process, signifying the disarmament, demobilisation, reintegration processes. However, some include another R which either represents 'rehabilitation' (Bragg 2006) or 'reinsertion' (Knight and Özerdem 2004), both using the acronym DDRR. Others, such as Chrobok (2005), addresses only what she calls the D&R process, indicating the process of demobilisation and reintegration. The most recent and broadly accepted principles governing DDR work with children is provided by the Paris Principles of 2007. These principles define "child reintegration" as:

> The process through which children transition into civil society and enter meaningful roles and identities as civilians who are accepted by their families and communities in a context of local and national reconciliation. Sustainable reintegration is achieved when the political, legal, economic and social conditions needed for children to maintain life, livelihood and dignity have been secured. This process aims to ensure that children can access their rights, including formal and non-formal education, family unity, dignified livelihoods and safety from harm (7).

Also the UN's Integrated DDR Standards (IDDRS) of 2006 address the particular reintegration of the child, stating that it should include:

> family reunification, mobilizing and enabling the child's existing care system, medical screening and health care, schooling and/or vocational training, psychosocial support, and social and community-based reintegration. Reintegration programmes need to be sustainable and to take into account children's aspirations (IDDRS 1.20).

Recent trends

During the last decade, there has been an increased focus on child soldiering. The review reflects the view of several authors (cf. Hart and Tyrer 2006; Wessells 2006; Honwana 2006) that the largest bulk of research on children and war deals with trauma and psychological impact of war and violence (cf. Barenbaum et al. 2004; Castelli et al. 2005; Dyregrov et al. 2002; Honwana 1998). Related to this, an ongoing debate on Western versus traditional and cultural approaches to treatment of distress and trauma is apparent in the available literature.[5] Many have stressed the inappropriateness of the Western psychological approaches by pointing to how, for example, the African understanding and treatment of trauma differs from that in the West (cf. Zack-Williams 2006 and Honwana 1998). Local traditional concepts, beliefs and practices related to healing, cleansing and social reintegration of war-affected children have gained increased attention and trust. The inappropriateness of current rehabilitation and reintegration interventions provided by aid agencies has been highlighted, particularly as it overemphasises psychological trauma treatment while neglecting the youths resilience and coping abilities (cf. Abatneh 2006; Hart and Tyrer 2006). But as noted by Wessells, the 'emphasis on deficits, which overlooked children's resilience, is now giving way to an understanding that most former child soldiers are functional and, with proper support, can transition to positive lives as civilians' (2006, x). Scholars and professionals do no longer only view the child as a victim of war but also as a survivor of war and an agent who actively seek to cope with the adversities s/he faces.

Moreover, increased attention has been given to the context in which child soldiers find themselves. A perspective which addresses the children within the wider community; their social, cultural, economic, and political contexts, is currently considered not only appropriate but necessary. Child and community alike need to be empowered to ensure successful reintegration and sustainable peace.

These are some of the important recent advances in the study of child soldiers. Nevertheless, one major weakness still remains; the lack of visibility of former girl soldiers in academic literature. No precise figures exist with regard to the total number of child soldiers neither the percentage of girls involved in war or conflict. Such figures are 'not only unknown but unknowable' due to the difficulty of gathering data in areas where child soldiers are common (Brett and McCallin 1996, 27). However, as it is almost always a significant number of girls among children involved with armed groups (cf. Paris Principles 2007; Verhey 2004; Hobson 2005), girls' war participation needs to be addressed to a much greater extent in the years to come.

Gender-specific studies on reintegration

Until relatively recently, the term child soldier meant in reality a 'boy soldier.' This is also apparent in academic work. Quite a few empirical studies do not include girls in their samples (cf. UNICEF 2003; Boothby et al. 2006), and in several others girls are only scarcely represented (cf. Betancourt et al. 2008, Taouti-Cherif 2006 and Bayer et al. 2007). However, the body of literature concerning the situation of girl soldiers during war and in post-conflict context has gradually increased in recent years, although we might agree with Wessells (2007, 3) that 'research on girl soldiers is still in its infancy.' Academic work has attempted to address different experiences of boys and girls, different perceptions of girls and boys related to stigma and victimization, and the motivation for girls and boys to demobilise and reintegrate. Such studies point unanimously to the inappropriateness of current DDR programmes to reach the girls and meet their needs and special concerns (cf. Keairns 2002; McKay and Mazurana 2004; Verhey 2004; Coulter 2006; Specht and Attree 2006). They conclude that the realities that girls face both within the armed groups and within their communities do not correspond to the reintegration programmes developed both by international and national agencies (cf. Mazurana, McKay, Carlson and Kasper 2002). Governments and agencies need to construct gender-appropriate reintegration, based upon the acknowledgment of the girls' multiple roles within the armed group, the girls' agency and initiatives, and the skills and coping strategies they have developed (cf. Mazurana and Carlson 2004).

The reviewed literature points out that more gender-specific knowledge is necessary in order to secure appropriate reintegration assistance to former girl soldiers. Studies on girl soldiers also underline that some groups of girls have been neglected more than others, both with regards to inclusion in reintegration programmes but also in research. In other words, there are currently major gaps in knowledge related to the reintegration of former girl soldiers.

Forced mothers and their children

Currently, very few studies exist on forced mothers and their children, however, several researchers stress the distinct vulnerability of these two groups (cf. MacVeigh et al. 2007; Carlson and Mazurana 2008; McKay and Mazurana 2004). Undoubtedly, the needs of forced mothers and their children have been largely neglected by researchers and reintegration programmes alike, maybe especially the needs of the children born in captivity.[6]

The particular stigmatization experienced by the former girl soldiers returning with a child and the stigmatization experienced by the child itself due to its fathers' rebel status and because it is 'illegally conceived' deserve further attention (Apio 2008). Quite a few girls forcibly married within armed groups are not accepted back into their families and communities (Carlson and Mazurana 2008). This is especially the case if their 'bush husbands' continues to be part of the girls' lives (McKay et al. 2006, 2). Hence, sometimes the girls consider the father of their children to still be their husbands while their families reject that idea. Findings in Verhey's study show that the girl may be 'physically' accepted to live with her family, but that her family would refuse to support her and the child (Verhey 2004, 16).

Another issue that needs further exploration is whether traditional cleansing rituals contribute positively to forced mothers and their children's reintegration process. Contrary to findings with regards to child soldiers in general, the SWAY study from Uganda show that forced mothers do not view cleansing ceremonies as contributing to their recovery (Annan et al. 2008). Yet other studies, such as Wessells' study in northern Sierra Leone (2006), find that girls see traditional rituals as helping to make them more acceptable to the community. Consequently, the effects of cleansing rituals seem to vary and these contextual variations should be investigated further.

As the most forgotten category of children in armed conflict (Apio 2008), the well-being of these children and their mothers need both more research and additional programming. Their particular experiences both within the armed groups and when returning to civilian life must be addressed. More knowledge and research is particularly required on the needs of the 'at-risk' children of former child soldiers, and on forced mothers' identity.

Self-demobilised girl soldiers

Studies on former girl soldiers draw attention to the huge absence of females in formal or official DDR programmes (cf. Coulter et al. 2008; Mazurana and Carlson 2004; Hobson 2005). In some demobilization programmes, for example the one following the Lusaka Protocol of 1994, girls are completely excluded or ignored (Human Rights Watch 2003). Often the girls have been excluded due to the military aspect of demobilisation where the number of weapons handed in constitutes the ultimate sign of the success of the process, or failure. Moreover, many of these women were, and still are, classified as 'dependents' or 'camp followers' and therefore excluded from benefits given to 'combatants' (cf. Mazurana and Carlson 2004; Brett and Specht 2004). The agency of both commanders and girl soldiers also help to explain the absence of girls in the DDR programmes (cf. Ollek 2007). It is, for example, unlikely that the DDR process can fully eliminate the power and authority of commanders. DDR programmes seem to rely on information from commanders and consequently the commanders mediate access to such programmes. The denial of females' inclusion in demobilisation and reintegration processes is likely an expression of commanders' vested interests. 'Military officials view girls as a form of possession and claim that girls are their "wives" rather than "child soldiers" they are obligated to demobilise' (Verhey 2004, 2). The girls' own agency is shown through their personal choice of avoiding the DDR process. The fear of stigmatization once being identified as an ex-soldier is among the main reasons why girls choose to self-demobilise and self-reintegrate (cf. Hobson 2005; Verhey 2004). Brett (2004) aptly notes that reality seems to give former girl soldiers two choices: speak out and risk stigmatization or stay silent and lead a relatively 'normal life.' It seems clear that the community's socio-cultural conceptions of girls and women constitute obstacles to their reintegration process (cf. Verhey 2004).

In order to ensure a higher degree of anonymity and consequently to reduce the risk of stigmatization and rejection, young women may choose to resettle in a new and often larger environment (cf. Barth 2002; Wessells 2007). Other scholars point to that the changes the women have gone through, both those who feel empowered and those who feel disempowered, sometimes make them reluctant to go home (cf. Barth 2002; van Gog 2008). Whatever the reason, female ex-soldiers who choose to settle outside their former communities should be assisted to find an alternative way of living (cf. Barth 2002). 'Women and girls should be free to choose where they will live, electing to return to land from which they or their partner came, or to move to semi-urban or urban areas where they may have more freedom from traditional gender roles' (UNIFEM 2004, 37). Research should seek to convey resettlement experiences of these former girl soldiers and to gain more knowledge on factors that may facilitate their reintegration process in a new environment.

As the great majority of girl soldiers exit armed groups outside the formal demobilisation process, how to discretely trace and support these young women is an urgent matter to be addressed (cf. Uvin 2007). Moreover, some studies demonstrate that former girl soldiers have been able to reintegrate on their own outside formal DDR structures, and such experiences can provide important knowledge to girls' reintegration process (cf. Verhey 2004; van Gog 2008).

Traditional gender roles

The restoration of the relationship to immediate kin and original community is argued to be central also to women's and girls' reintegration (cf. van Gog 2008). The important role of family is highlighted by many scholars (cf. Corbin 2008; Lode et al. 2007). Hill and Langholz (2003) note for example that children living with their family often show fewer psychiatric problems. A UNICEF's report (2003) on reintegration of child soldiers in Rwanda shows that the children do better when they are reintegrated with parents, particularly when reintegrated into larger households. Despite such findings, it is important to note that family reunification should not be romanticised. Studies show that some children, maybe particularly girls, join armed groups to escape from domestic violence and/or sexual abuse (cf. Keairns 2002; Coulter et al. 2008).

How families and communities receive former soldiers seems to be related to gender. Female ex-soldiers have transgressed their gender role through violence and sometimes sexual abuse and are therefore more easily rejected and stigmatized (Coulter et al. 2008) Often they are viewed as 'violent, unruly, dirty or as promiscuous troublemakers' (Hobson 2005, 2). Men, on the other hand, often seem to have strengthened their gender role through warfare. Veale's study (2003) on female ex-fighters in Ethiopia shows that the women's military identity makes it difficult to conform to traditional gendered expectations for women in civilian society. Coulter's study (2006; cf. also her contribution in the present book) on being a bush wife finds that former girl soldiers who conformed to traditional norms and expected behaviour upon returning from armed groups were more easily accepted back into their communities and families.

Brett (2004) argues that if the discrimination that drove the girls into armed groups is not changed in the aftermath of war, then the girls' prospects

are probably worse then before the war. There are obvious dangers of reproducing gender stereotypes and inequalities through DDR programmes which
do not address culturally accepted, but discriminatory, gender roles (cf.
Denov 2007b; Denov and Maclure 2007). Consequently, reintegration should
involve a reciprocal 'readjustment' by both the individual soldier and the
community (Veale and Stavrou 2003). These views are confirmed in the
Paris Principles which state that '[g]irls may join armed forces or armed
groups to escape sexual and gender-based violence, early marriage or other
harmful practices and exploitation' (2007, 23). Reintegration programmes
are encouraged to address these issues and promote 'gender equality and
freedom of choice for girls in line with international human rights norms'
(ibid.). This constitutes a challenging task which demands more knowledge
on how programmes may realise their transformational potential. How best to
support former girl soldiers' agency, how to achieve a reciprocal readjustment and promote women's rights and well-being need therefore to be
further addressed through culturally sensitive empirical studies.

Targeted versus non-targeted reintegration

Many of the current DDR programmes exclusively target former child soldiers. Taouti-Cherif's study (2006) on the 'Child Soldier Special Project
Beneficiaries' in Burundi finds that the former child soldiers participating in
the programme are in a similar or better situation than their civilian peers,
particularly economically but also socially. However, although the targeted
support has reduced vulnerability the author still notes that community support may be even better as it also will prevent resentment from community
members. Recent studies stress that singling out child soldiers contributes to
stigmatization and jealousy (Castelli et al. 2005; MacVeigh et al. 2007;
Sendabo 2004), and that they through special treatment may be viewed by
the community as rewarded for the atrocities they have committed. Even
child soldiers themselves express that programmes should include all
children affected by war as it will reduce jealousy and rejection by their
siblings and peers (cf. Chrobok and Akutu 2008).
    A non-targeted approach may be particularly appropriate for girls.
Ensuring these girls access without having to identify themselves as ex-
soldiers means that many otherwise invisible girls associated with armed
groups will receive reintegration support. Projects and programmes supporting all war affected young people are argued to reduce jealousy and stigma.
On the other hand, one may argue that targeted support may be necessary, for
example to ensure the specific, gendered support that girl soldiers both need
and are entitled to. As noted by Human Rights Watch (2003), 'the failure to

target former boy and girl soldiers specifically in a recognized program suggests that many of these children and their special needs for recovery and rehabilitation will be overlooked.' Some scholars and professionals argue that reintegration programmes should consequently be designed according to such measurable needs rather than different categories of children and youth (e.g. Annan et al. 2008). However, children's specific needs are often related to their particular experiences, for example sexual abuse and pregnancy. Whether targeted or not, reintegration programmes must be prepared to provide the help and support necessary to address these particular issues. As underlined by Santacruz and Arana (2002), the section of the population that was directly involved in the war—in particular children and young people— should not be forgotten and further marginalised but receive the assistance they need.

Non-targeted and long-term reintegration requires extensive and conti-nuous funding, but many of the studies included in this review underline that inadequate funding is one of the biggest constraints to providing child soldiers with proper reintegration support (cf. Hobson 2005; Ismail 2002; MacVeigh et al. 2007). An important question to be addressed is conse-quently how the currently preferred non-targeted approach to reintegration, where all children affected by war are included, may be implemented within evident financial constraints. More knowledge is also needed on how to couple a non-targeted and a targeted approach to reintegration, as to ensure that girl soldiers' particular needs are addressed within a framework which does not give away their status as former soldiers.

Age and reintegration

Conceptions of childhood and age are also crucial aspects to take into consideration in research on and design of appropriate reintegration assistance (cf. Boyden and de Berry 2004). The generally recognised age at which childhood officially ends and adulthood begins is 18. However, such a sharp distinction relating to age does not take into consideration cultural variations with regards to childhood and adulthood. Neither is age a good indicator of the actual stage of the child's development. Is there necessarily a great difference between the needs or capacities of a 17 year old and a 19 year old? Rehabilitation and reintegration programmes must be culturally sensitive and aware of the risk to 'infantilise' former child soldiers in their upper teens (cf. ILO 2003). Giving birth to a child will in many cultures mean that the girl has left childhood and entered into adulthood, causing forced mothers, in particular, to express that they do not want to be treated as children (cf. Apio 2008). To draw a line between and provide separate treat-

ment of women on the one hand and girls below 18 on the other may consequently be inappropriate (cf. Ollek 2007). Flexibility and cultural sensitivity
related to age should be incorporated into studies on former girl soldiers and
their reintegration process.

Cultural sensitivity and contextualization have gradually gained increased
recognition among international agencies and researchers alike. However,
reintegration programmes would most surely benefit from even more dedicated attention to local knowledge and a better understanding on how to draw
on such resources.

What is 'successful reintegration'?

Recent studies emphasise that from the point of the target group, the content
of reintegration still remains fundamentally unexamined (cf. Porto et al.
2007). More studies which explore the children's lives from their own
perspectives and address what former child soldiers and their families and
communities understand by reintegration are needed (Jareg 2005). Some
recent studies have conveyed the views of former child soldiers, particularly
on their reasons for joining or how they were recruited, their experiences
within the armed group as well as their experiences after escaping or
demobilisation (cf. Uvin 2007; Chrobok and Akutu 2008; Keairns 2002;
Boyden and de Berry 2004). However, in-depth research addressing the local
perspective on the content and the preferable outcome of the reintegration
process is still largely missing.

In Wessells' study on former girl soldiers in Angola (2007), the girls'
testimonies show an inherent problem with the term 'reintegration' as it
denotes resettling in one's community of origin. In contrast, after the war,
many of the former girl soldiers in Angola chose to settle in a new environment where no one knew them. Other studies reveal similar findings (cf.
Barth 2002; van Gog 2008). In case of settlement in a new community, the
content of current reintegration programmes might need to be reconsidered,
possibly also the concept.[7] If the purpose of research is to provide inputs for
more gender-sensitive programmes, future research must take significantly
account of former girl soldiers' experiences, views and aspirations.

Many questions remain both unasked and unanswered with regards to the
preferred outcome of a reintegration process. By which criteria or standards
may successful reintegration be defined and measured? As underlined by
many scholars, civilian identity is an important outcome (cf. Veale 2003;
Porto et al. 2007; Veale and Stavrou 2003), but what exactly does a civilian
identity entail and how can it be measured? In some studies former child

soldiers are compared to their civilian peers in how they have fared economically and socially (cf. Taouti-Cherif 2006; Annan et al. 2006 and 2008). However, whether comparison to civilian peers is the best way to assess child soldiers' reintegration success should be further explored.

The duration of a reintegration process is another aspect that needs to be further investigated. What is preferable or expected outcome after two, five, ten and 15 years? As there exist few longitudinal studies on reintegration of former child soldiers, long-term reintegration remains a rather unexplored field (Geenen 2007).

Although, definitions and assessments criteria are necessary it is important to stress that a 'one-size-fits-all' approach to reintegration will not be beneficial. The content of a successful reintegration should depend on and be flexible to the actual circumstances in which it takes place. Culture, duration of war and conflict, degree of destruction caused by war, the level of social cohesion in the communities, the level of support available, personal experiences and so on will all impact on a child soldier's reintegration process, as will the child's gender and age.

Contextual dimensions of reintegration

Knowledge about the particular conflict and context in which the DDR process takes place is necessary as this may explain both the nature and challenges of the process (cf. Borzello 2007). Each situation presents its own unique profile with specific challenges, and consequently reintegration programmes should be 'tailored to the needs of the societies in which they are implemented' (Porto et al. 2007, 110). Some important contextual realities that impact on the reintegration of former child soldiers are the country-specific conflict, whether the current situation is one of post- or ongoing conflict, whether the child soldier is reintegrating into a rural or an urban environment, and which armed group the former soldier belonged to.

Country specific research

The literature review displays that some countries and conflicts have received more scholarly attention than others. Looking at literature which focuses on country specific cases, one may conclude that war-torn West African countries have received quite extensive attention. This is particularly the case for Sierra Leone (cf. Coulter 2006; Peters 2006; Mazurana and Carlson 2004; Denov and Maclure 2006), but extensive research has also been conducted in Liberia (cf. Sendabo 2004; Utas 2005). Reintegration of child soldiers in Côte d'Ivoire, on the other hand, seems to have received relatively little attention.[8] Northern Uganda and child soldiers within the Lord's Resistance Army are clearly another area where researches in the field of child soldiers have conducted comprehensive studies (cf. Annan et al. 2006 and 2008 (SWAY); Corbin 2008; Akello et al. 2006; Apio 2007). In the southern part of Africa the conflicts of Mozambique and Angola have been the focus of several studies (cf. Honwana 2006; Boothby 2006).

   With Uganda being the exception, studies and literature on child soldiers in the Great Lakes Region conflicts are scarce. Despite a few studies on child soldiers in Rwanda (Abatneh 2006 and UNICEF 2003), Burundi (Taouti-Cherif 2006), and the Democratic Republic of Congo (Verhey 2003 and 2004: Hobson 2005; Amnesty International 2006; ILO 2003) most of the accessible literature does not concentrate on child soldiers but on the DDR process directed at adult ex-soldiers (cf. Geenen 2007; Uvin 2007; Beneduce et al. 2006).

   Sierra Leone and Uganda are the two countries that have received most scholarly attention also with respect to studies concerning girl soldiers (cf. McKay et al. 2006; Carlson and Mazurana 2008; Annan et al. 2008). More-over, certain studies have included Mozambique and Angola (McKay and Mazurana 2004 and Denov 2007a). Keairns study (2002) in Angola, Sri Lanka, the Philippines and Colombia is also worth mentioning. With regards to the Great Lakes Region, again with the exception of Uganda, studies concerning reintegration of former girl soldiers hardly exist.

Post-war setting versus ongoing conflict

Most available research on reintegration of former child soldiers concerns post-conflict situations. This is understandable due to the serious challenges related to how to conduct the collection of data in an environment of conflict and war. Lack of security, restriction of movements, lack of access, and breakdown of communications will undoubtedly complicate fieldwork, and sometimes even make it impossible. The most serious challenge is security, as research in contexts with ongoing conflict may put both former child soldiers and researcher at risk. These aspects, as well as research ethics, must be taken into consideration when planning and preparing fieldwork in a con-flict setting

   As there are reasons to avoid research in contexts with ongoing conflict there are also arguments for the opposite. The weightiest argument is probably that in situations where conflict continues, there is also a greater possible danger of re-recruitment of former child soldiers. Studies point to how successful reintegration may prevent re-recruitment, and a possible escalation of conflict (cf. UNICEF 2005). It is consequently pertinent to gain deeper insights into the particular needs of former child soldiers amidst conflict, how to best cater for their needs and how to best support them in regaining a civilian identity.

Urban versus rural reintegration

Several case studies point to dissimilarities in the reintegration into urban versus rural communities (cf. Uvin 2007; Peters 2007). One apparent difference is that former soldiers resettling in urban environments seem to keep in close contact with other ex-soldiers. At the same time the review reveals that community-based social networks are, by most scholars, viewed as essential for reintegration of former soldiers (cf. Verhey 2001; van Gog 2008).

Does this mean that ex-soldiers who resettle in urban areas, often not their community of origin, with a network consisting of fellow ex-soldiers are less likely to attain a civilian identity? More knowledge on different reintegration trajectories and outcomes depending on where former child soldiers settle down and which social networks they enter is necessary. What seems clear, however, is that research findings and programme design in rural settings cannot automatically be replicated in urban contexts and vice versa. Research should also focus on how different kinds of social networks impact on the transformation from military to civilian identity.

Group belonging

Taouti-Cherif's study (2006) on the reintegration process of former child soldiers in Burundi reveals that difficulties in the reintegration process may depend on which armed group the child belonged to. Findings show that children from one particular group seemed to have a more problematic reintegration trajectory than former child soldiers in other armed groups. With reference to the reviewed literature, it may seem like different experiences according to group belonging are especially visible related to girl soldiers. This can be illustrated through presenting some apparent dissimilarities when comparing experiences of female soldiers within liberation armies with those participating in rebel groups.[9]

Firstly, difference is obvious with regards to their recruitment. Young women in liberation wars are more likely to join voluntarily and sometimes out of ideological conviction, while women in rebel groups to a larger extent are forcibly recruited. Although some may join voluntarily, the degree of voluntarism is often questioned by scholars as these girls often do not have any good alternative.

Secondly, whether or not the girls and young women were sexually abused and which roles they performed within the armed group vary depending on the armed group and the conflict area (Kearins 2002).

Thirdly, whether or not the girls feel empowered by their military experience also seems to vary depending on which kind of armed group they belonged to and what roles they had. The assumption is that women and girl soldiers participating in liberation wars are more likely to feel empowered by their military experience (cf. Veale 2003; Coulter et al. 2008). The experience of empowerment is also linked to the cause they are fighting for and the girls' status within the armed group.

Fourthly, studies indicate that females participating in liberation wars are more likely to be viewed as heroines rather than perpetrators, particularly if the liberation army wins the war. In liberation wars, families and communities all tend to mobilise themselves as part of the struggle, and hence families may support the girls' involvement in the liberation army. In some cases there are also other family members in the armed group, and in this sense the girl is not completely separated from her family in ways that are characteristics of rebel groups. Moreover, the armed groups in liberation struggles do not normally attack the families and villages of the people whose liberation they seek. The risk of stigmatization and rejection from family and community is consequently likely to be reduced.

Fifthly, female ex-combatants in liberation wars tend to find it more difficult to readjust back into traditional gender roles than what is the case for those participating in rebel groups (cf. Coulter et al. 2008).

These aspects (how and why they joined, whether they are sexually abused, their roles within the group, whether they feel empowered or not, their status and the degree of stigmatization upon returning, and whether they readjust to traditional gender roles) are all factors which impact on the young women's reintegration process as well as their particular needs in the aftermath of war. Planning and implementation of reintegration programmes need to take these elements into consideration. The same is true for research. Research should distinguish between different armed groups and conduct comparative studies that may provide a better understanding of how group belonging impact on or determine the process of reintegration.

It is important to note that in many conflict situations girls also serve as soldiers in national military armies. Some researchers have pointed to how governments deny or attempt to cover up their own use of girl soldiers during the war (cf. McKay and Mazurana 2004). Not only in DDR programmes but also in research, child soldiers who served in governmental armed forces are often underrepresented (cf. Brett and Specht 2004). It is pertinent for future research to address the reintegration process also of these young men and women.

Concluding comments

The empirical evidence on testimonies of former child soldiers is increasing but there are still major gaps in knowledge and understanding related to the reintegration process of young persons. Research must address these gaps in knowledge and, through in-depth studies, provide information that may improve the support given to young girls and boys as they make their way back to civilian life. A failed transition from military to civilian life will most surely be fatal for the individual child but also for the community at large.

Reference list

Abatneh, Abraham Sewonet. 2006. *Disarmament, demobilization, rehabilitation and reintegration of Rwandan child soldiers.* Master thesis in sociology, University of South Africa. Available at: http://etd.unisa.ac.za/ETD-db/ETD-desc/describe?urn=etd-05212007-081452

Akello, Grace, Annemiek Richters, and Ria Reis. 2006. Reintegration of former child soldiers in northern Uganda: coming to terms with children's agency and accountability. *Intervention* 4 (3):229-243. Available at: http://www.interventionjournal.com/downloads/43pdf/akello.pdf

Amnesty International (2006) *Democratic Republic of Congo: Children at war, creating hope for their future.*

Annan, Jeannie, Chris Blattman, and Roger Horton. 2006. *The state of youth and youth protection in Northern Uganda: Findings from the survey for war-affected youth.* Survey of War-Affected Youth. Available at: http://www.sway-uganda.org/

Annan, Jeannie, Chris Blattman, Khristopher Carlson, and Dyan Mazurana. 2008. *The state of female youth in Northern Uganda: Findings from the survey of war-affected youth (SWAY), phase II.* Survey of War-Affected Youth. Available at: http://www.sway-uganda.org/

Apio, Eunice. 2007. Uganda's forgotten children of war. In *Born of war. Protecting children of sexual violence survivors in conflict zones,* ed. R.Charli Carpenter. Bloomfield: Kumarian Press.

Apio, Eunice. 2008. *Bearing the burden of blame – the children born of the Lord's resistance army, northern Uganda.* Coalition to Stop the Use of Child Soldiers. Available at: http://www.child-soldiers.org/psychosocial/english

Barenbaum, Joshua, Vladislav Ruchkin, and Mary Schwab-Stone. 2004. The psychosocial aspects of children exposed to war: practice and policy initiatives. *Journal of Child Psychology and Psychiatry* 45 (1):41-62. Reproduced and available at: http://www.child-soldiers.org/psychosocial/english

Barth, Elise Fredrikke. 2002. *Peace as disappointment. The reintegration of female soldiers in post-conflict societies – a comparative study from Africa.* International Peace Research Institute, Norway.

Bayer, Christophe Pierre, Fionna Klasen, and Hubertus Adam. 2007. Association of trauma and PTSD symptoms with openness to reconciliation and feelings of revenge among former Ugandan and Congoles child soldiers. *JAMA* 298 (5):555-559. Available at: http://jama.ama-assn.org/cgi/reprint/298/5/555

Beneduce, Roberto, Luca Jourdan, Timothy Raeymaekers and Koen Vlassenroot. 2006. Violence with a purpose: exploring the functions and meaning of violence in the Democratic Republic of Congo. *Intervention* 4 (1):32-46.

Betancourt, Theresa Stichick, Stephanie Simmons, Ivelina Ivanova Borisova, Stephanie E. Brewer, Uzo Iweala, and Marie de la Soudière. 2008. High hopes, grim reality: Reintegration and the education of former child soldiers in Sierra Leone. *Comparative Education Review* 52 (4):565-587.

Boothby, Neil. 2006. What happens when child soldiers grow up? The Mozambique case study. *Intervention* 4 (3):244-259. Available at: http://www.interventionjournal.com/downloads/43pdf/boothby.pdf

Boothby, Neil, Jennifer Crawford, and Jason Halperin. 2006. Mozambique child soldier life outcome study: Lessons learned in rehabilitation and reintegration efforts. *Global Public Health* 1 (1):87-107.

Borzello, Anna. 2007. The challenge of DDR in Northern Uganda: The Lord's resistance army. *Conflict, Security & Development* 7 (3):387-415

Boyden, Jo, and Joanna de Berry. 2004. *Children and youth in the front line.* Oxford: Berghahn Books.

Bragg, Caroline. 2006. Challenges to policy and practice in the disarmament, demobilisation, reintegration and rehabilitation of youth combatants in Liberia. *Sussex Migration Working Paper no. 29.* University of Sussex.

Brett, Rachel. 2004. Girl soldiers: Denial of rights and responsibilities. *Refugee Survey Quarterly* 23 (2):30-37

Brett, Rachel, and Margaret McCallin. 1996. *Children: The invisible soldiers.* Stockholm: Rädda Barnen (Swedish Save the Children).

Brett, Rachel, and Irma Specht. 2004. *Young soldiers: Why they choose to fight.* Boulder: Lynne Rienner Publishers.

Carlson, Khristopher, and Dyan Mazurana. 2008. *Forced marriage within the Lord's resistance army, Uganda.* Feinstein International Center. Available at: https://wikis.uit.tufts.edu/confluence/display/FIC/ Children %27s+Rights

Carpenter, C. 2007. *Born of war: Protecting children of sexual violence survivors in conflict zones.* Bloomfield: Kumarian Press.

Castelli, Lucia, Elena Locatelli, and Mark Canavera. 2005. *Psycho-social support for war affected children in northern Uganda: Lessons learned.* Coalition to Stop the Use of Child Soldiers. Available at: http:// www.child-soldiers.org/psycho-social/english

Chrobok, Vera. 2005. *Demobilizing and reintegrating Afghanistan's young soldiers: A review and assessment of program planning and implementation.* Paper 42, Bonn International Center for Conversion (BICC). Available at: http://www.bicc.de/index.php/publications/papers/paper-42

Chrobok, Vera, and Andrew S. Akutu. 2008. *Returning home. Children's perspectives on reintegration: A case study of children abducted by the Lord's resistance army in Teso, eastern Uganda,* Coalition to Stop the Use of Child Soldiers. Available at: http://www.bicc.de/index.php/ publications/papers/paper-42

Corbin, Joanne N. 2008. Returning home: resettlement of formerly abducted children in Northern Uganda. *Disaster* 32 (2):316-335.

Coulter, Chris. 2006. *Being a bush wife: Women's lives through war and peace in northern Sierra Leone.* Department of Cultural Anthropology and Ethnology, Uppsala University, Sweden.

Coulter, Chris, Mariam Persson and Mats Utas. 2008. *Young female fighters in African wars. Conflict and its consequences.* Policy Dialogue No. 3, The Nordic Africa Institute.

Denov, Myriam. 2007a. *Girls in fighting forces: Moving beyond victimhood.* CIDA's Child Protection Research Fund, Canada.

Denov, Myriam. 2007b. *Is the culture always right? The dangers of reproducing gender stereotypes and inequalities.* Coalition to Stop the Use of Child Soldiers. Available at: http://www.child-soldiers.org/psycho-social/english

Denov, Myriam and Richard Maclure. 2006. Engaging the voices of girls in the aftermath of Sierra Leone's conflict: Experiences and perspectives in a culture of violence. *Anthropologica* 48:73-85.

Denov, Myriam and Richard Maclure. 2007. Turnings and epiphanies: Militarization, life histories, and the making and unmaking of two child soldiers in Sierra Leone. *Journal of Youth Studies* 10 (2):243-261.

Dyregrov, Atle, Leila Gupta, Rolf Gjestad, and Magne Raundalen. 2002. Is the culture always right? *Traumatology* 8 (3):135-145. Reproduced and available at: http://www.child-soldiers.org/psycho-social/english

Geenen, Sara. 2007. *Former combatants at the crossing. How to assess the reintegration of former combatants in the security and development nexus? Case study: Ruyigi (Burundi) and Kinshasa (DRC),* conference paper at "Development policy and the security agenda in Africa: reassessing the relationship", 2 November 2007. Available at: http://afrika-studiecentrum.nl/Pdf/DPRNPaperGeenen.pdf

Gislesen, Kirsten. 2006. *A childhood lost? The challenges of successful disarmament, demobilisation and reintegration of child soldiers: The case of West Africa.* Norsk Utenrikspolitisk Institutt (NUPI), Paper No. 712.

Hart, Jason, and Bex Tyrer. 2006. *Research with children living in situations of armed conflict: Concepts, ethics & methods.* RSC Working Paper No. 30, Refugee Studies Centre, University of Oxford. Available at: http://www.rsc.ox.ac.uk/PDFs/workingpaper30.pdf

Hill, Kari, and Harvey Langholz. 2003. Rehabilitation programs for African child soldiers. *Peace Review: A Journal of Social Justice* 5 (3):279-285.

Hobson, Matt. 2005. *Forgotten casualties of war: Girls in armed conflict.* London: Save the Children, UK.

Honwana, Alcinda. 1998. *Okusiakala ondalo yokalye: Let us light a new fire. Local knowledge in the post-war healing in reintegration of war-affected children in Angola.* Christian Children's Fund. Reproduced and available at: http://www.child-soldiers.org/psycho-social/english

Honwana, Alcinda. 2006. *Child soldiers in Africa.* Philadelphia: University of Pennsylvania Press.

Human Rights Watch. 2003. *Forgotten fighters: Child soldiers in Angola.* Vol. 15 (10) (A).

International Labour Office (ILO). 2003. *Wounded childhood: The use of children in armed conflict in Central Africa.*

Ismail, Olawale. 2002. Liberia's child combatants: Paying the price of neglect. *Conflict, Security & Development* 2 (2):125-134.

Jareg, Elizabeth. 2005. Crossing bridges and negotiating rivers – Rehabilitation and reintegration of children associated with armed forces. Save the Children, Norway, and Coalition to Stop the Use of Child Soldiers. Available in English at: http://www.child-soldiers.org/psycho-social/english. Available in French at: http://www.child-soldiers.org/psycho-social/francais

Keairns, Yvonne E. 2002. *The voices of girl child soldiers: Summary.* Quaker United Nations Office.

Knight, Mark, and Alpaslan Özerdem. 2004. Guns, camps and cash: Disarmament, demobilization and reinsertion of former combatants in transitions from war to peace. *Journal of Peace Research* 41 (4):499-516. Available at: http://unddr.org/docs/Guns,CampsandCash,DDR.pdf

Lode, Kåre (ed.), Bitomwa Lukangyu Oneshiphore, and Adolphe Balekembaka Musafiri. 2007. *Réinsertion des enfants soldat: Un expérience du Congo,* SIK-rapport 2007:2, Centre for Intercultural Communication. Available in French at: http://www.sik.no/article 485.shtml

MacVeigh, Johanna, Sarah Maguire, and Joanna Wedge. 2007. *Stolen futures: The reintegration of children affected by armed conflict.* London: Save the Children, UK.

Mazurana, Dyan, Susan A. McKay, Khristopher Carlson and Janel C. Kasper. 2002. Girls in fighting forces and groups: Their recruitment, participation, demobilization, and reintegration. *Peace and Conflict: Journal of Peace Psychology* 8 (2):97-123.

Mazurana, Dyan, and Khristopher Carlson. 2004. *From combat to community: Women and girls of Sierra Leone.* Women Waging Peace and The Policy Commission.

McKay, Susan, and Dyan Mazurana. 2004. *Where are the girls? Girls in fighting forces in Northern Uganda, Sierra Leone and Mozambique: Their lives during and after war.* Rights & Democracy, International Centre for Human Rights and Democratic Development. Available at: http://www.essex.ac.uk/armedcon/story_id/000478.pdf

McKay, Susan, Malia Robinson, Maria Gonsalves and Miranda Worthen. 2006. *Girls formerly associated with fighting forces and their children: Returned and neglected.* Coalition to Stop the Use of Child Soldiers. Available at: http://www.child-soldiers.org/psycho-social/english

Ollek, Maya Oza. 2007. *Forgotten females: Women and girls in post-conflict disarmament, demobilisation and reintegration programs.* Master in Political Science, McGill University. Available at: http://www. peacewomen.org/resources/DDR/Forgottenfemales.pdf

The Paris Principles: The Principles and guidelines on children associated with armed forces or armed conflicts. 2007. Geneva: United Nations, http://www.un.org/children/conflict/_documents/parisprinciples/ParisPrin ciples_EN.pdf

Peters, Krijn. 2006. *Footpaths to reintegration: Armed conflict, youth and the rural crisis in Sierra Leone.* PhD thesis, Wageningen University. Available at: http://library.wur.nl/WebQuery/wda/lang/1804961

Peters, Krijn. 2007. From weapons to wheels: Young Sierra Leonean ex-combatants become motorbike taxi-riders. *Journal of Peace, Conflict & Development* 10(10). Available at: http://www.peacestudiesjournal.org.uk

Porto, João Gomes, Imogen Parsons, and Chris Alden. 2007. *From soldiers to citizens: The social, economic and political reintegration of Unita ex-combatants.* Institute for Security Studies, ISS Monograph Series No. 130. Available at: http://www.iss.co.za/index.php?link_id=3&link _type= 12&tmpl_id=3

Santacruz, Maria L. and Rubi E. Arana. 2002. Experiences and psychosocial impact of the El Salavador civil war on child soldiers. Originately published in Spanish in *Biomédica* 2002:22 (suppl. 2). Translated, reproduced and available at: http://www.child-soldiers.org/psycho-social/english

Sendabo, Teferi. 2004. *Child soldiers: Rehabilitation and social reintegration in Liberia.* Uppsala: Life & Peace Institute, Sweden.

Specht, Irma, and Larry Attree. 2006. The reintegration of teenage girls and young women. *Intervention* 4 (3):219-228.

Taouti-Cherif, Ratiba. 2006. *Beneficiary assessment of the social and economic status of the "child soldier" Special Project Beneficiaries in Burundi.* The Multi-Country Demobilization and Reintegration Program (MDRP). Available at: http://www.mdrp.org/PDFs/Burundi_ Beneficiary_Assessment_2006.pdf

UNICEF. 1997. *Cape Town Principles and Best Practices.* Available at: http://www.unicef.org/emerg/files/Cape_Town_Principles(1).pdf

UNICEF. 2003. *Analysis of the reintegration of demobilized child soldiers in Rwanda.*

UNICEF. 2005. *The disarmament, demobilisation and reintegration of children associated with the fighting forces: Lessons learned in Sierra Leone 1998–2002.*

UNIFEM. 2004. *Getting it right, doing it right: Gender and disarmament, demobilization and reintegration.*

United Nations. 2006. *Integrated disarmament, demobilization and reintegration standards.* United Nations Department of Peacekeeping Operations: New York. Available at: http://www.unddr.org/iddrs/ framework.php

Utas, Mats. 2005. Building a future? The reintegration and remarginalisation of youth in Liberia. In *No peace no war: An anthropology of contemporary armed conflicts,* ed. Paul Richards. Oxford: James Curry Ltd.

Uvin, Peter. 2007. *Ex-combatants in Burundi: Why they joined, why they left, how they fared.* Working Paper No. 3. The Multi-Country Demobilization and Reintegration Program (MDRP). Available at: http://www. mdrp.org/PDFs/MDRP_Working_Paper3.pdf

van Gog, Janneke. 2008. *Coming back from the bush. Gender, youth and reintegration in northern Sierra Leone.* Master in Cultural and Social Anthropology, Utrecht University, in African studies collection 9, African Studies Centre, Leiden. Available at: https://openaccess.leidenuniv.nl/ dspace/handle/1887/13113

Veale, Angela. 2003. *From child soldier to ex-fighter: Female fighters, demobilisation and reintegration in Ethiopia.* Institute for Security Studies, ISS Monograph Series, No. 85. Available at: http://www.iss.co.za/index.php?link_id=3&link_type=12&tmpl_id=3

Veale, Angela, and Aki Stavrou. 2003. *Violence, reconciliation and identity: The reintegration of Lord's resistance army child abductees in northern Uganda.* Institute for Security Studies, ISS Monograph Series, No. 92. Available at: http://www.iss.co.za/index.php?link_id=3&link_type=12&tmpl_id=3

Verhey, Beth. 2001. *Child soldiers: Preventing, demobilizing and reintegrating.* World Bank Working Paper Series No. 23. Available in English and French at: http://go.worldbank.org/LWKLUHCBA0

Verhey, Beth. 2003. *Going Home: Demobilising and reintegrating child soldiers in the Democratic Republic of Congo.* Save the Children,UK.

Verhey, Beth. 2004. *Reaching the girls: Study on girls associated with armed forces and groups in the Democratic Republic of Congo.* Save the Children, UK, and CARE, IFESH and IRC.

Wessells, Michael. 2006. *Child soldiers: from violence to protection.* Cambridge: Harvard University Press.

Wessells, Michael. 2007. *The recruitment and use of girls in armed forces and groups in Angola: implications for ethical research and reintegration.* Ford Institute for Human Security, "Child soldiers initiative: Building knowledge about children and armed conflict". Available at: http://www.fordinstitute.pitt.edu/pub-workingpapers.html

Zack-Williams, Tunde. 2006. Child soldiers in Sierra Leone and the problems of demobilisation, rehabilitation and reintegration into society: Some lessons for social workers in war-torn societies. *Social Work Education.*25 (2):119-128.

Notes

[1] The entire outcome of the study can be acquired at www.sik.no

[2] For example The Institute for Security Studies, Save the Children (UK, Norway) and The Coalition to Stop the Use of Child Soldiers.

[3] See for example Boyden and de Berry 2004 on social constructs of child and childhood.

4   This definition is quite similar to the definition of 'a child associated with an armed force or armed group' found in the Paris Principles (2007).

5   See for example the ongoing debate at Psycho-social Forum, www.child-soldiers.org

6   For literature on children born of war see Carpenter 2007 and Apio 2008.

7   Apio (2008) uses for example the term 'integration'

8   One exception is Gislesen 2006 where Côte d'Ivoire is one of three country cases. It should also be noted that child soldiers were only used to a limited extent during the Ivorian conflict.

9   The author recognises that the distinction between liberation army and rebel group is not clear in all war contexts.

3

Negotiated Identities

The Discourse on the Role of Child Soldiers
in the Peace Process in Northern Uganda

Tor Arne Berntsen
Royal Norwegian Air Force Academy, Trondheim
School of Mission and Theology, Stavanger, Norway

Abstract

During the course of the war in northern Uganda between the Lord's Resistance Army (LRA) and the government of Uganda, tens of thousands of children have been abducted and forced to serve as soldiers. Coming to terms with the participation and involvement of child soldiers in this context has been a key issue in the ongoing peace process. This article focuses on how disparate and contradictory notions of the child soldier have been negotiated by the various political actors that have been involved in this process. It argues that the child soldier issue serves as a discursive site of power struggle, and that the understanding of who the child soldier is has been used strategically in order to end the war and deal with the issue of justice toward former LRA soldiers.

Introduction

Rebels from the Lord's Resistance Army (LRA) have been fighting in north-ern Uganda for the past two decades in what has become Africa's longest running conflict. During the course of the conflict the LRA have abducted thousands of children, forced them to commit atrocities against their fellow children, families and other civilians. In fact, the child soldier phenomenon has been portrayed as the very defining characteristic of the war in northern Uganda. But how should a society struggling to end war and violence come to term with the involvement and participation of child soldiers? And what consequences have the child soldier phenomenon had for the overall moral and political strategies of ending the war, and promoting reconciliation within this context?

Much of the literature on child soldiers has focused on their involvement within a framework of international legal standards (Cheney 2005, 23). Although these discourses provide a crucial framework for preventing the recruitment and use of children in armed conflict, they often lack, however, a more situated analysis of how child soldiers are seen and portrayed in local circumstances.

By addressing the discourse on the role of child soldiers within the peace process in northern Uganda, this article seeks to identity and explore how the various political actors that have been involved in the peace process in northern Uganda have portrayed and dealt with the child soldier as part of the overall peace and justice discourse.[1]

It argues that the extensive use of child soldiers in the war in northern Uganda has made the question of how to deal with child soldiers one of the main issues to be addressed in the ongoing peace process. It also finds, however, that those political actors that have been involved in this process have wielded different understandings of the child soldier in order to justify and accomplish their various political and moral mandates in the peace process, thus making the child soldier phenomenon into a 'discursive site' of power struggle.[2]

In order to explore the role of child soldiers in this peace process, the article begins by outlining briefly the history of the current war in northern Uganda. It focuses on the abduction and use of child soldiers by the LRA, and explores how Joseph Kony has used child soldiers strategically to wage war against the government of Uganda and destroy the Acholi society. The article then examines how the government of Uganda and the Uganda People's Defence Forces (UPDF), the Ugandan national army, have used the child soldier issue as an argument for pursuing a military solution to the conflict. And finally, I focus on how the understanding of who the child soldier is has been interpreted and negotiated to fit local initiatives to justice and reconciliation.

Background to the war in northern Uganda

The war in northern Uganda has roots that go back to the colonial era under British rule, which furthered already existing north-south divisions in Uganda (Doom and Vlassenroot 1999, 8). Under the British, the southern

Bantu ethnic groups were favoured politically and economically and given civil servant positions, while the Nilotic and Sudanic ethnic groups of the north were treated as labour reserves. Nilotics, particularly the Acholi, were recruited in the army (Kasozi 1994, 6). Northerners continued to be economically disadvantaged and hold military jobs after independence in 1962 under the first president of Uganda, Milton Obote.

Besides north-south tensions exacerbated by the colonial state, there was a politicization of violence that took place after Uganda's independence from the British, in which violence was used to consolidate and defend political power (Doom and Vlassenroot 1999, 8). As a result of this, Acholi soldiers in the south fled north under Obote and Amin eras due to fear of ethnic extermination by the government forces. This led to a rebel rising in the north, and many Acholi soldiers joined the rebel group, the Ugandan National Liberation Army (UNLA) (ibid.).

But the origins of the war stem also from internal struggle among the Acholi. When Yoweri Museveni and his National Resistance Army (NRA) took power in 1986, he defeated the Ugandan National Liberation Army in the north. Many soldiers formerly associated with this rebel group had problems demobilizing and reintegrating and began attacking their communities. According to Heike Behrend, these young soldiers were treated as 'internal strangers' who had become impure by killing, thus bringing *cen*, the spirits of the dead, to the communities (Behrend 1999, 109).

The Acholi responded to this situation through a political uprising against the southern government of Yoweri Museveni that also had spiritual dimensions (Jackson 2009, 323). The prophet Alice Lakwena emerged and raised an army of Acholi soldiers called the Holy Spirit Movement (HSM). Doom and Vlassenroot argue that Lakwena 'offered hope for worldly as well as spiritual redemption in a dark hour of despair' (Doom and Vlassenroot 1999, 16). She combined guerrilla tactics and spiritual ritual practices, and convinced her soldiers that if they purified themselves, they would not be wounded in battle (Behrend 1998, 107). Alice Lakwena and her Holy Spirit Movement won a number of battles over Museveni's forces before she was finally defeated in 1987.

After the fall of Alice Lakwena, Joseph Kony became the new rebel leader in the north, claiming that he had inherited the spiritual powers of his predecessor. Kony established and became the leader of the Lord's Resistance Army (LRA), which consisted of many fighters formerly associated with the Holy Spirit Movement. He declared that he would overthrow Museveni's government and rule the country according to the Christian Ten Commandments.

The LRA initially enjoyed popular support among the Acholi, partly due to hostility in the region towards the southern-dominated government, led by Museveni. But as this support waned, the LRA became increasingly brutal and started attacking the civilian population and abducting children (Van Acker 2004, 350-351). These terror tactics were played out in large scale particularly after 1994 when the peace talks between the government and the LRA failed. The Sudanese government then started supporting the LRA, and contributed with safe havens and arms, presumably in retaliation for the Government of Uganda's support of the Sudan People's Liberation Movement/Army (SPLA) insurgency (Dolan 2005, 78).

The widespread scepticism among people in the north towards Museveni's government is based not only on political marginalization and ethnic tensions. The northern part of Uganda has historically also been disadvantaged in terms of social and economic development compared to other parts of the country. At the same time, the Ugandan government forces have since 1986 been guilty of a series of violations in the north that has fuelled bitterness among the Acholi. People in northern Uganda therefore have a deep mistrust in the government's objectives in relation to the north, including the various efforts to protect the civilian population against the LRA. At the same time, Kony's forces have exercised extreme violence on civilians and villages in northern Uganda to a degree that has overshadowed government violations.

The abduction and use of children by the LRA

During the course of the war in northern Uganda, thousands of children have been abducted and forced to serve as soldiers with the LRA. [3] The extensive use of child soldiers by the LRA has created an image both in media and advocacy circles of a war that ranks as horrors at the limits of our worst imaginings. However, understanding the role of child soldiers in this war implies going beyond this image of incomprehensible violence and explore the LRA and their strategy of abducting and using children as soldiers within the cultural and political context of northern Uganda. This corresponds with the view of anthropologist Kristen E. Cheney who argues that the LRA has used normative structures to indoctrinate children to serve as soldiers, 'structures within which children normally form their social and political identities in Uganda' (Cheney 2005, 33).

The LRA has often attacked and abducted children from villages and schools. After having been abducted, the children are taken to remote camps where they are trained to become soldiers. The process of training and indoctrinating these children into soldiers is often extremely brutal, and involves fear, violence and psychological manipulation. A well-used tactic is to force captured children to take part in ritualized killings of other abducted children, or the children's neighbours and families. The effect of the killings is not only to terrorize the children, but also to disconnect them from their old lives and prevent them from escaping (Amnesty International 1997, 14). Since the family traditionally is a site of children's identity formation, the LRA has been known to maintain control over children by using the idiom of family to structure the rebel group.

As part of their training, the abducted children are often given a short introduction in the most basic infantry skills, such as how to fire weapons and set an ambush. Those who disobey orders during training risk physical punishment and death, which is often set as an example to the other abductees. Once trained, most new recruits are sent out on operations. As they are usually targeting civilians or ambushing small military outposts, their effect can be devastating.[4]

When Kony took Lakwena's place the Acholi elders complained that Kony was violating culturally sanctioned justifications for and conduct in war (Finnström 2008, 208), which included the exemption of children and women from being targeted and used as soldiers. According to Finnström, Joseph Kony started attacking the civilian population and abducting children as he felt betrayed by the lack of support for the insurgency by the Acholi elders. As such, the strategy of abducting children should not only be seen as a military recruitment strategy, but also as a way of punishing the Acholi population.

At the same time, there has also been an element of protection in Kony's rhetoric on the abduction of children. Initially Joseph Kony stated that the purpose of abducting children was to protect them from an evil society (Behrend 1999, 179). In February 1991, Kony was referred saying that he started kidnapping children and young people in order to rescue them so that they could live in the New World (Behrend 1999, 182). This serves to show the ambiguousness of how children has been portrayed and used by the LRA.

The abduction and use of children as soldiers by the LRA can also be seen as a discursive strategy of undermining the government's capacity to protect its citizens. Schools are not only obvious places where children can be found and abducted, they represent also a 'material symbol of state presence in the north outside of military installations' (Cheney 2005, 34). Abducting children from schools thus challenges the government's political authority and military control. There is, from the perspective of the LRA, also an important military aspect to the use of child soldiers. By forcing the government forces to fight the very children they are set to protect, they are also made an accomplice in destroying the lives of children.

The government's displacement strategy of confining people from villages all over northern Uganda to Internally Displaced People's (IDP) camps can therefore be interpreted both as a way of protecting people from rebel attacks and also as a strategy of regaining military control over these areas. The abduction and use of child soldiers has, in other words, allowed the LRA to fight a war in which it has both exercised control over the population of the north and applied political pressure on the government (Vinci 2005, 371).

The sheer scope of abductions committed by the LRA, and the brutality of how it has been carried out, has made the issue of child abductions a direct concern for all members of society in the north. The effect that the war has had on children in northern Uganda is as complex as it is far-reaching, both for the children and for the communities at large. The abduction of children and the displacement of civilians have also led to a complete overturn in the social and generational structures of the Acholi (Cheney 2005, 32).

Traditional societies, such as the Acholi often have strong social norms regarding generational structures. As Alcinda Honwana notes from studying the use of child soldiers in Mozambique and Angola, 'Because children were abducted from their homes and schools to fight, the initiation rituals and systematic preparation of young people to become responsible adults ceased' (Honwana 2006, 32). As such, these children are not only denied their childhoods but also the possibility of becoming responsible and morally grounded citizens in their natural environment of development (ibid.).

When children escape from the rebels and return to their communities, they are often highly militarized and therefore seen as a threat to their families and communities (as discussed by Emeline Ndossi in another article in the present book). According to James Otto, secretary of Human Rights Focus, a locally based NGO in Gulu, the abduction of children has led to a breakdown of moral values among children in relation to their families and relatives, 'A life of dependency and destitution breeds lack of respect to parental authority' (ARLPI 2001, 20). Children and young people are therefore not only seen as threatened because of the war but also as threatening to the people and the communities in northern Uganda (Cheney 2005, 32).

Under the leadership of Joseph Kony, children have been abducted, indoctrinated and forced to serve as soldiers with the LRA. The understanding of the role and identity of children in this war has been strategically adapted to fit the political and military agenda of the LRA. By reshaping the lives of children and using them as instruments of war, the LRA has not only secured its own survival as a rebel group, they have also managed to put political pressure on the government of Uganda and spread fear among the people of the north. This has, in turn, placed the child soldier phenomenon at the centre of the analysis on the war in northern Uganda.

Rebels, children and the use of military force against the LRA

During the 20-year conflict in northern Uganda, the government of Uganda has pursued a number of negotiation efforts towards Joseph Kony and the LRA. However, after years of failed negotiations, the government launched on March 8, 2002, a military operation called 'Operation Iron Fist' to end the war with the rebels once and for all. A protocol was signed with the government of Sudan, allowing the Uganda People's Defence Forces (UPDF), Uganda's National Army, to attack LRA bases inside Sudan.

The UPDF deployed about 10,000 soldiers in south Sudan in order to lure out the rebels and make them surrender. The LRA, however, sent forces back into Uganda to divert attention away from Joseph Kony. As a result of the deployment of government forces to Sudan, the LRA intensified its attacks on the civilian population in several districts in northern Uganda. Abductions increased dramatically, with some estimates reaching as high as 5000 new abductees in the period from March 2002 to March 2003 (Dolan 2005, 91).

Tim Allen at the London School of Economics argues that the child phenomenon was a determining factor that led to the government's military offensive against the LRA in 2002. He argues that the extensive use of child soldiers by Joseph Kony led to a demonization of the LRA as a rebel group that is totally ignorant of their responsibility to protect children. This, in turn, created an opportunity for the government to pursue a military solution to the conflict (Allen 2006, 114).

The child soldier phenomenon can therefore be described as a key not only to understand the LRA insurgency, but also as a key to why the government has seen military force as one of the preferred means of ending the war with the LRA. Interestingly, one of the main arguments for pursuing a military solution to the conflict by the government has been to rescue the abducted children in the LRA. In an editorial article in the Kampala-based newspaper *New Vision* on March 27, 2009, the UPDF spokesperson Felix Kulayigye stated that, 'Our main objective was not killing or capturing Kony as the media likes putting it. We went to Congo to try and rescue the abductees who were still in the hands of the LRA' (Kulayigye 2009).[5]

Lt. Col. Francis Ochoka Ongom, the Civil-Military Coordination Offices and Internally Displaced Persons Monitor Officer in Gulu, explains in an interview how military force can be used to rescue child soldiers:

> In fact, it is only by engaging the LRA [with military force] that the children have the opportunity to actually escape… they await an opportunity when the UPDF launches and attacks, and that is how we have been able to rescue children (Ongom 2009).

The use of military force to rescue abducted children from the LRA has, however, been controversial. Prior to 'Operation Iron Fist' in 2002, there was a heated debate in Ugandan media between representatives of the United Nations Children's Fund (UNICEF) and the UPDF on how the Ugandan military forces should go about dealing with LRA child soldiers on the battlefield. One of the central questions was how to discriminate between abducted children and committed LRA combatants, when the rebels they would encounter could be both.

Carol Bellamy, Executive Director of UNICEF, expressed in a press release on March, 5, 2002, concern over the fate of children, since renewed fighting inevitably would bring them to the frontlines. She therefore urged the UPDF to take specific measures to secure that children were protected in combat situations. As innocent victims of adult interests, these children should be protected not only from the LRA but also from the military operations of the UPDF. 'Any strategy to resolve the broader issue must put children at its centre,' Bellamy stated (UNICEF 2002).

The UPDF, on the other hand, was trying to communicate just how difficult it is to simultaneously fight the rebels while at the same time trying to rescue the children. Shaban Bantariza, the then UPDF Director of Information and Public Relations, commented,

> We'd like UNICEF to show us how to extricate children from their hardline commanders… Children can be very hard fighters. How do you respond to a 17 year-old child who is trained and only interested in shooting? (IRIN 2002).

As the discussion between UNICEF and the UPDF demonstrates, the questions of how to deal with child soldiers in combat situations and discriminate between abducted children and committed combatants have been key issues with respect to the use of military force against the LRA.

The fact that the question of who the child soldier is has been such an important issue in this context, that it has also allowed the UPDF to strategically use different terms when speaking about the children in the LRA. The UPDF, therefore, often refers to the LRA as children whenever they surrender or are rescued. But when LRA soldiers attack military installations or are killed in army operations, they are referred to as rebels, to downplay the possibility that they have been killing innocent children (Allen 2006, 114).

By using military force to demobilize child soldiers in the LRA, the UPDF has at times been rescuing children from the LRA only to recruit them into local defence units. These local defence units have frequently been in cooperation with the Ugandan army and are expected to engage the rebels with military force. While the Ugandan authorities do not recruit minors to the national army, they have evidently been willing to recruit minors to the civilian armed defence forces (Finnström 2008, 91).

Because of the numbers of abducted children in the LRA, the Acholi civilian population has been opposed the government's military strategy in the conflict. The inter-religious civil society group, the Acholi Religious Leaders' Peace Initiative (ARLPI) has been one of the fiercest critics of the government's military strategy in northern Uganda. The Anglican Archbishop John Baptist Odama of the ARLPI declared in 2002,

> While it may be necessary to use some degree of force in preventing armed attack, we cannot forget that the LRA is made up [of] at least 70 percent abductees, mostly children, and that a direct attack against their bases would end in the destruction of many lives (Frommer 2002).

From the perspective of the local communities in the north, the use of military force against the LRA seems to undermine the responsibility of the government in this war, and the fact that many of the children have been abducted because the government has failed to protect them. It seems as a paradox that the government soldiers are killing the very children they are set out to protect.

Due to widespread scepticism among people in the north towards the government's objectives with respect to the north, the killing of children in the LRA fuels suspicion against the government among the Acholi and a feeling that the government is somehow out to get them. (Nyeko 2009; Odama 2009). Rosa Ehrenreich paraphrases this narrative thus,

> Fighting against the rebels is also designed to kill the Acholi, since the government knows full well that most of the rebels' soldiers are captive Acholi children (Ehrenreich 1998, 88). [6]

As a way of getting around the sensitive issue of child soldiers in the LRA, the UPDF has on several occasions stated that the LRA does not have any children in their ranks. On May 12, 2002, Bantariza was quoted saying that, 'Apart from the children produced by Kony and his commanders, the rest are all combatants and there are no children to rescue' (ARLPI 2002, 6). This statement can be interpreted as a way of downplaying the role that children play in the LRA altogether and thereby making the use of military force more acceptable both to the international community and to the Acholi community. But it also demonstrates how sensitive the issue of child protection has been for the government of Uganda with respect to ending the war in northern Uganda.

By having to deal with the complex social and political reality of child soldiers in the LRA, the Ugandan army has been guilty of strategically negotiating the identity of the child soldier to their own benefit. The government of Uganda and the Uganda People's Defence Forces has, in other words, been yielding different understandings of who the child soldier is to protect children from being abducted by the LRA but also to legitimate the use of military force to end the war in northern Uganda.

Children, innocence and justice towards LRA returnees

The strategic use and negotiation of the identity of children can also be identified as an integrated part in the debate on how to deal with the issue of justice towards the LRA. There is a general view among the Acholi that war in northern Uganda has taken so long because of the involvement of children (Odama 2009). The child soldier phenomenon has therefore been a central issue in the peace and reconciliation discourse in northern Uganda, and has even created some space among the Acholi communities and the authorities to negotiate a way forward.

When the Chief Prosecutor of the International Criminal Court (ICC) in 2004 announced his intentions to investigate atrocities committed by the LRA and to arrest and try those most responsible, local leaders feared that this would undermine the Amnesty Act and efforts to make peace with the rebels (Nyeko 2009). While the ICC rejects the notion of impunity for crimes such as the recruitment and use of children in armed conflicts, cultural and religious leaders argued that the Amnesty Act incorporated Acholi traditions of forgiveness and reconciliation that was the only way to finally ending the war.[7] The ARLPI, one of the main actors advocating this amnesty, stated,

Keeping in mind that the LRA, including many of its commanders is made up mostly of abductees now transformed into perpetrators, and that these thousands of abductions have been a direct result of the failure of the state to protect innocent civilians, there is no doubt that the Amnesty Law has provided a way out for thousands of persons who has been trapped in this painful situation (Khalil & Odong 2004, 10).

According to the ARLPI, amnesty and forgiveness should take precedence over the claim of bringing the rebels to justice, especially in a situation in which children have been involved and forced to serve as soldiers.

In international discourse on the peace process in northern Uganda the Amnesty Act of 2000 has generally been seen as directed towards Joseph Kony and the LRA leadership. The Gulu District Speaker, Ojara Martin Mapenduzi, seems however to confirm the statement by the ARLPI that the main argument for passing this amnesty law was the protection of child soldiers in the LRA:

> I would say the amnesty law was directed at the innocent children who had been abducted. The primary target is not Kony... We don't look at the LRA, we don't look at Joseph Kony, but we look at the innocent children, suffering in this situation (Mapenduzi 2009).

From this perspective, it appears that the main reason for passing the Amnesty Act was not primarily to protect Joseph Kony from criminal prosecutions but to secure the safe return of children from the LRA and help reintegrating them into their communities.

In national law in Uganda a child is anyone under 18 years of age. This is enshrined in the Children's Statute of 1996 that incorporates into Ugandan law aspects of the Convention of the Rights of the Child (CRC) and the African Union Charter on the Rights and Welfare of the Child. However, for rural Acholi the definition of who is a child is to a degree a process between individuals, family members and the community marked by rites of passages.

As a result of the LRA's strategy of abducting children and young people and force them to serve as soldiers in the rebel group, a majority of the child soldiers in this context are children in terms of chronological age, most are regarded as children according to Acholi traditions, and many of the rebels have been abducted. In combination, this has meant that most of the LRA returnees have been seen as child soldiers and as victims of war.

In fact, even returnees who are much older than 18 and who have had leadership positions in the LRA have been regarded as children. By labelling themselves as child abductees, adult rebels have been accepted by the community under the protecting category of being a child. The Gulu District Speaker, Ojara Martin Mapenduzi, refers to two high-profile LRA leaders, Kenneth Banya and brigadier Sam Kolo, as examples of adult LRA commanders who have come out of the bush under the protection of the Amnesty Act and who describes themselves as 'innocent children' (Mapenduzi 2009). It seems therefore that the Acholi community have come to some form of collective agreement that everyone who returns from the LRA has characteristics that enables them to be defined as a child, irrespective of their actual age. This view is explained and elaborated by Julius Orach, Dean of the Orthodox Church in the Acholi sub-region and member of the ARLPI:

> We should not only talk about separating them', he stated, 'we should treat them as one. Because even the one who is a commander has been abducted... so they are not different... they were a child here, but they grew up with the LRA... So, even if some of them were in command, they were still forced to do it (Orach 2008).

Orach argues that since it is difficult to make a clear distinction between rebel leaders and abducted children in a context of war such as in northern Uganda, they should all be granted amnesty and accepted back to their communities as victims of war. When asked if the same argument also would apply to Joseph Kony, Orach responded: 'Yes, we cannot say that the chief commanders should be treated separately' (ibid.). In contrast to this view, the Chief Prosecutor of the International Criminal Court, Luis Moreno-Ocampo, stated in an interview on July 7, 2006:

> We believe that the best way to finally stop the conflict after 19 years is to arrest the top leaders. In the end, the LRA is an involuntary army [since] the majority of fighters are abducted children. Arresting the leaders is the best way to stop those crimes... Our efforts to render justice [will] help to restore peace in Uganda (UN Office for the Coordination of Humanitarian Affairs 2006).

In an USAID and UNICEF-commissioned report from 2006, Allen and Schomerus find that the role of adults has been under-emphasised in the peace process as a result of the Amnesty Act. People refer to the LRA generally as 'our children in the bush' (Allen and Schomerus 2006, 19). The emphasis on children has contributed to an assumption that all returning LRA rebels can be treated like children irrespective of their actual age. As a result, the association between the LRA and children has contributed to the argument that those who have performed atrocities must be forgiven, and the assertion that such a view is widely accepted by the population as a whole.

Anthropologist Susan Shepler has made a similar point from studying the peace process in Sierra Leone. She argues that former child soldier's claim of innocence has been used strategically to facilitate the reintegration of children into their communities and also make it easier for community members to live with former fighters in their midst (Shepler 2005, 199).

The fact that almost everyone who returns from the LRA is seen as innocent children, allows a collective presumption of a lack of responsibility for their actions. Tim Allen finds therefore that the child soldier phenomenon in northern Uganda has led to an allocation of juvenile status to the LRA: 'It suggests that the rebels should not be thought of as normal adults. They are either children or they are young adults who have not matured properly (...)' (Allen 2006, 114).

The Amnesty Commission in Gulu admits that it might be seen as problematic that there were no distinctions made between the abducted child soldiers and the more culpable rebel leaders with respect to the Amnesty Act.[8] The flexibility on the understanding of the child soldiers meant that people who had committed or been forced to commit atrocities alike were protected from criminal prosecutions.

During the Juba peace talks that resulted in June 2007 in an Agreement on Accountability and Reconciliation there was made a formal distinction between victims and perpetrators with respect to the distribution of justice (Government of Southern Sudan 2007). The agreement introduced trial proceedings that would apply to a select few individuals, 'who are alleged to bear particular responsibility for the most serious crimes, especially crimes amounting to international crimes, during the course of the conflict' (Section 6.1). It also introduced a role for traditional, community-based justice mechanisms as a 'central part of the framework for accountability and reconciliation' (Section 3.1), which would be applied to lower-level perpetrators and those who have already received amnesty.

With the passing of the Amnesty Act with its emphasis on forgiveness towards LRA returnees, the local community has accepted the child soldier phenomenon as a site of 'moral sanctuary' from criminal prosecution. The understanding of the child soldier has, as a result of this, been adapted to fit the specific context of the peace and reconciliation process in northern Uganda in order to end the war and bring the children back home.

Conclusion

This article has explored the discourse on the role of child soldiers in the peace process in northern Uganda, and particularly how disparate and contradictory notions of the child soldier have been negotiated by the various political actors that have been involved in this process. I have argued that the abduction and use of child soldiers by the LRA in their war against the government of Uganda and the Acholi community has placed the child soldier issue at the centre of the analysis not only of the war in northern Uganda, but also in the various efforts to end the war and promote reconciliation.

Dealing with child soldiers in a context such as in northern Uganda implies dealing with the social and political complexity of children's reality in wars and armed conflicts. However, going beyond the images of incomprehensible violence and exploitation in order to explore how children have been portrayed and used in a context of conflict such as in northern Uganda can be unsettling.

At the same time, looking beyond the macabre manifestation of violence against children is not to dismiss the violence and its effect on children, nor to condone it. Rather, it enables us to acknowledge the complex moral and political reality of children in armed conflicts and thereby gain a deeper understanding of the war itself and develop a framework for effective resolution and peace building.

References

Acholi Religious Leaders' Peace Initiative (ARLPI). 2001. *Let my people go: The forgotten plight of the people in displaced camps in Acholi.* Gulu: Uganda.

Acholi Religious Leaders' Peace Initiative (ARLPI). 2002. *Seventy times seven: The implementation and impact of the Amnesty Law in Acholi.* Gulu: Uganda.

Allen, Tim. 2006. *Trial justice: The International Criminal Court and the Lord's Resistance Army.* London, New York: Zed Books.

Allen, Tim, and Mareike Schomerus. 2006. *A hard homecoming: Lessons learned from the reception center process on effective interventions for former 'abductees' in Northern Uganda.* An Independent Study commissioned by USAID and UNICEF. http://pdf.usaid.gov/pdf_docs/ PNADI241.pdf (accessed 13 August, 2009).

Amnesty International. 1997. *"Breaking God's command": The destruction of childhood by the Lord's Resistance Army.* http://www.amnesty.org/ en/library/asset/AFR59/001/1997/en/e3d1420e-ea53-11dd-965c-b55c1122d73f/ afr590011997en.pdf (accessed 29 April, 2009).

Anonymous informant. 2009. The Amnesty Commission Office in Gulu. Interview. Gulu, Uganda, 27 March.

Behrend, Heike. 1998. War in Northern Uganda. In *African guerillas*, ed. Christopher Clapham. Oxford: James Currey.

Behrend, Heike. 1999. *Alice Lakwena & the Holy Spirits. War in Northern Uganda 1985–97.* Oxford: James Currey.

Cheney, Kristen. 2005. 'Our children have only known war': Children's experiences and the uses of childhood in Northern Uganda. *Children's Geographies* 3(1):23-45.

Dolan, Chris. 2005. *Understanding war and its continuation: The case of Northern Uganda.* London: London School of Economics.

Doom, Ruddy, and Koen Vlassenroot. 1999. Kony's message: A new Koine? The Lord's Resistance Army in Northern Uganda. *African Affairs* 98 (390):5-36.

Ehrenreich, Rosa. 1998. The stories we must tell: Ugandan children and the atrocities of the Lord's Resistance Army. *Africa Today* 45 (1):79-102.

Finnström, Sverker. 2008. *Living with bad surroundings: War, history, and everyday moments in Northern Uganda.* Durham, London: Duke University Press.

Frommer, Linda. 2002. Uganda and Sudan join hands to fight LRA. *News from Africa,* 21 April. http://africa.peacelink.org/tools/print.php?id=908 (accessed 21 April, 2009).

Government of Southern Sudan. 2007. *Agreement on accountability and reconciliation between the Government of the Republic of Uganda and the Lord's Resistance Army/Movement.* Juba: Sudan. http://www.beyond juba.org/peace_agreements/Agreement_on_Accountability_And_Reconci liation.pdf (accessed 24 August, 2009).

Government of Uganda-UNICEF. 2001. Abductions in Northern and South-Western Uganda 1986–2001, *Country Programme 2001–2005.* http://www.internal-displacement.org/8025708F004CE90B/(httpDocume nts)/2F68FFB88812387C802570B7005A54EF/$file/UNICEF+Abducted +Children+Database+(November+2001).pdf (accessed 26 August, 2009).

Honwana, Alcinda. 2006. *Child soldiers in Africa.* Philadelphia: University of Pennsylvania Press.

Integrated Regional Information Network (IRIN). 2002. Uganda: UNICEF repeats call for release of LRA abductees. *United Nations Office for the*

Coordination of Humanitarian Affairs, 6 March 6. http://www. irinnews. org/PrintReport.aspx?ReportId=30611 (accessed 24 August, 2009).

Jackson, Paul. 2009. 'Negotiating with ghosts': Religion, conflict and peace in Northern Uganda. *The Round Table* 98 (402):319-331.

Jørgensen, Marianne W., and Louise J. Phillips. 2002. *Discourse analysis as theory and method.* London: Sage.

Kasozi, Abdu Basajabaka Kawalya. 1994. *The social origins of violence in Uganda, 1964–1985.* Montreal & Kingston, London, Buffalo: McGill-Queen's University Press.

Khalil, Sheik Musa, and Matthew Odong. 2004. Position paper on Amnesty Law. *Fighting History in Uganda: Mennonite Central Committee (MCC) Peace Office Publication* 34 (2):8-10 http://www.mcc.org/peace/pon/ PON_2004-02.pdf (accessed 15 April, 2009).

Kulayigye, Felix. 2009. We gave the peace talks our best. *The New Vision,* 27 March.

Mapenduzi, Ojara Martin. 2009. Gulu District Speaker. Interview (taped), Gulu, Uganda, 30 March.

Noll, Christian. 2009. The betrayed: An exploration on the Acholi opinion of the International Criminal Court. *Journal of Third World Studies* XXVI (1):99-119.

Nyeko, James. 2009. Programme Coordinator for the Acholi Religious Leaders' Peace Initiative. Interview (taped), Gulu, Uganda, 30 March.

Odama, John Baptist. 2009. Archbishop of Gulu Archdiocese, and member of the ARLPI. Interview (taped), Gulu, Uganda, 31 March.

Ongom, Francis Ochoka. 2009. Civil Military Coordination Officer and Internally Displaced Persons Monitor Officer, UPDF. Interview (taped) Gulu, Uganda, 27 March.

Orach, Julius. 2008. Dean of the Orthodox Church in the Acholi sub-region and member of the ARLPI. Interview (taped), Gulu, Uganda, 11 August.

The Paris Principles: The Principles and guidelines on children associated with armed forces or armed conflicts. 2007. Geneva: United Nations, http://www.un.org/children/conflict/_documents/parisprinciples/ParisPrin ciples_EN.pdf (accessed 14 December, 2009).

Pham, Phuong., Patrick Vinck, and Eric Stover. 2007. *Abduction: The Lord's Resistance Army and forced conscription in Northern Uganda.* University of California, Berkeley Human Rights Center and Tulane University Center for International Development.

Shepler, Susan. 2005. The rites of the child: Global discourses of youth and reintegrating child Soldiers in Sierra Leone. *Journal of Human Rights* 4:197-211.

UNICEF. 2002. *Press release: UNICEF calls for release of child soldiers by LRA.* http://www.unicef.org/newline/02pr061ra.htm (accessed 24 August, 2009).

United Nations Office for the Coordination of Humanitarian Affairs. 2006. Kony will eventually face trial, says ICC prosecutor. http://www.globalsecurity.org/military/library/news/2006/07/mil-060707-irin01.htm (accessed 16 September, 2008).

Van Acker, Frank. 2004. Uganda and the Lord's Resistance Army: The new order no one ordered. *African Affairs* 103 (412):335-357.

Vinci, Anthony. 2005. The strategic use of fear by the Lord's Resistance Army. *Small Wars and Insurgencies* 16 (3):360-381.

Notes

[1] While the term 'child soldier' is commonly used, this is not a precise term. A definition is provided in the Paris Principles and Guidelines on Children Associated with Armed Forces or Armed Groups. It states, "'A child associated with an armed force or armed group" refers to any person below 18 years of age who is or who has been recruited or used by an armed force or armed group in any capacity, including but not limited to children, boys and girls, used as fighters, cooks, porters, messengers, spies or for sexual purposes. It does not only refer to a child who is taking or has taken a direct part in hostilities' (Paris Principles 2007, 7). Although I acknowledge that the term 'child soldier' is not a precise legal term, it has, however, been commonly used in the peace and reconciliation discourse in Northern Uganda. The purpose of this article is also to demonstrate that the term is contested, and that the child soldier phenomenon within the context of the peace process in Northern Uganda carries a range of meanings and implications.

[2] The term discourse can be defined as 'a particular way of talking about and understanding the world (or an aspect of the world)' (Jørgensen and Phillips 2002, 1). A basic epistemological notion for understanding discourse is that our ways of talking does not neutrally reflect our world, identities and social relation but that it rather plays an active role in creating and changing them. The term discourse thus directs attention to the ways in which language frames the way we understand the world, specific phenomena, moral and political terms, etc. By exploring the discourse on the role of child soldiers in the peace

process in northern Uganda, I am particularly interested in how the child soldier phenomenon has been understood and portrayed by the various actors that have been involved in this peace process, and the discursive strategies and mechanisms that have been applied in dealing with the child soldier issue as part of the overall peace and reconciliation discourse.

3   A study carried out by UNICEF covering the period 1990–2001, found that 28,902 people had been taken from Gulu, Kitgum and Pader, Apac and Lira; about 10,000 of these were children (Government of Uganda-UNICEF 2001). By 2001, 16,000 had returned, 5555 of those who remained were children. Another 10,000 children are believed to have been taken in 2002–2004, during the 'Iron Fist' operations, but there are no accurate records from this time. A study from 2007 estimated that 72,000 people had been abducted by the LRA since the start of the conflict, of which 38,000 were children. (Pham et al. 2007). The LRA has also abducted children from Sudan and the Democratic Republic of Congo, who are not counted for in abduction statistics.

4   Although most abducted children are used as soldiers, many are given other tasks in the rebel group, such as porters or cooks. Girl abductees are often given away as "wives" to senior LRA commanders (Mapenduzi 2009).

5   Although this statement refers to the joint military operation 'Operation Lightning Thunder' which was initiated in December 2008 against LRA bases in the Central African Republic, the Democratic Republic of Congo and Southern Sudan, I think it is a relevant statement in this context as it shows how UPDF representatives have argued for the use of military force to rescue abducted children in the LRA.

6   Christian Noll makes the argument that the Acholi experience of the war is defined by a narrative of betrayal. The Acholi look at external interventions to end the conflict in northern Uganda through a lens that is formed by past and present betrayals, and this is a meta-narrative that, according to Noll, 'shapes the perceived, experienced, and expected reality for the Acholi (Noll 2009, 117).

7   For a discussion on the importance of the Acholi worldview in the reintegration of child soldiers, see the article by Christine Mbabazi in the present book.

8   Interview with an anonymous informant at the Amnesty Commission Office in Gulu. 27 March 2009.

4

Constrained but Not Choiceless

On Moral Agency among Child Soldiers

Bård Mæland
School of Mission and Theology, Stavanger, Norway

Abstract

An ongoing ethical discussion, also with a legal counterpart, regards whether children who have taken part in armed groups, often forcibly recruited and deliberately indoctrinated, and otherwise heavily constrained, can be said to exercise moral agency. This discussion, which has both descriptive and normative dimensions, is pursued based on a theory of decision-making as well as examples drawn from various conflicts on the African continent.

Introduction

The world's estimated 300,000 child soldiers[1] are regarded a global phenomenon in two-thirds of the world's ongoing or recently settled conflicts (Singer 2005, 28), often with grave human suffering as an immediate consequence. In some of these, underage soldiers make up almost the entire force, as is the case with the Lord's Resistance Army of Northern Uganda. An ongoing ethical discussion, also with a strong legal counterpart, regards whether children who have taken part in armed groups, often forcibly recruited and deliberately indoctrinated, and otherwise heavily constrained, can be said to have exercised moral agency. If this *somehow* can be demonstrated, one may be able to move beyond monolithic images of either drug-addicted children with an AK-47 hanging around their necks, or abducted girls who have been forced into sex slavery or atrocities that stretch our imagination beyond what is conceivable.

One way to pursue this discussion is to emphasise the *normative* questions whether child soldiers are morally responsible and culpable for war crimes they have committed. Such questions have been raised by the philosopher Jeff McMahan:

> Do conditions of ignorance and duress in which child soldiers normally act ever make their action morally permissible, even if the war in which they are fighting is unjust and even if they commit war crimes? Even if their initial action in fighting is wrong, is it permissible for them to kill in individual self-defense when they are threatened? Or is their action somehow exempt from moral evaluation altogether? Might it be that even though they act wrongly, they are fully exculpated by their nature as children, in conjunction with the conditions in which they act? Can they be seen as morally responsible agents at all? Can they deserve punishment, or blame? (McMahan 2007, 1)

One sees that many of these questions combine the perspectives of moral philosophy and legal justice, with the perspective of child psychology. A more explicit focus on the status of a child from a psychological perspective, may approach the issue of moral agency with a focus on the moral *development* of children who have been recruited into armed groups and who have taken part in armed conflicts. One may here not only ask the questions about responsibility and culpability, but examine whether the children have been morally sensitive and deliberate in carrying out their actions.

In his book *Child Soldiers: From Violence to Protection*, the psychologist Michael Wessells (2006) draws the attention to these aspects of children's military agencies. He states that, 'how children who are born into groups like the LRA, living all their formative years with them, will learn positive, life-affirming values and morals strains one's imagination' (ibid., 142). Moreover, as a more general statement about the wider group of children who have been members of armed groups, he maintains that, 'The suggestion that child soldiers are morally lacking sits poorly with evidence that many child soldiers show moral sensitivity before, during and after their time in armed groups (...)' (ibid., 143).

Furthermore, based on an examination of extant literature and research from the last decade on how children and youths within armed groups can be said to exercise moral agency, I will suggest that, although moral agency is often heavily constrained, it can still be found a limited, yet important way among child soldiers. However, due to the nature of their constraints under which they are exercising such agency, the main agency, and hence the major accountability for e.g. atrocities committed by underage soldiers, should be carried by their leaders.

My methodology in this article will be to present first an analytical framework based on a philosophical analysis of responsibility and culpability through the notion of decision-making. Next, I present and discuss selected examples from various African contexts in order to identify important aspects of moral agency among young soldiers.

What does it take to be a moral decision-maker?

In an article about the debate around moral responsibility and culpability for war crimes, the Norwegian philosophers Helene Ingierd and Henrik Syse discuss the notion of decision-making in war, maintaining that this notion is central to whether or not a person can be pleaded guilty for something (Ingierd and Syse 2005). '*To be morally responsible for a given action*', they suggest as a criterion for judging whether one should be regarded as morally responsible or not, '*one must somehow have the character of a decision-maker*' (ibid. 95, emphases original). Since there is an obvious potential for application to other groups than adult soldiers, their philosophical analysis of decision-making as a prerequisite for responsibility may be worthwhile to have a look at. Hence, what does it actually take to be a decision-maker?

First, they assert, to be a decision-maker assumes that one *could have acted differently* (ibid. 86). If a soldier is coerced to do something, where no choice existed, he or she should not be regarded as guilty. In legal terms, forced action and otherwise deprivation of free choice or volition, so-called 'duress,' exempts from legal responsibility, and may result in partial or full exculpation.[2] Hence, choice is vital for the exercise of moral (and legal) agency. We see here an example of an extreme on the scale between what Ingierd and Syse calls 'obedience to authority and the demands of conscience' (ibid., 85). For example, if a soldier is threatened by immediate execution of not carrying out the orders of a commander, one should not blame the soldier but his commander (ibid., 94). Based on an examination of prominent philosophers of the ethics of war, such as Augustine, Francisco de Vitoria, and Michael Walzer, Ingierd and Syse find that all three agree that to be held responsible for war crimes requires that one 'has any real involvement in making the fatal decision(s), and/or acts wilfully and knowingly as a result of those decisions' (ibid., 95).

Regarding the last item in this quote, the issue of knowledge is a rather tricky one. In the initial set of questions by McMahan, *ignorance,* in addition to duress, was mentioned as a possible argument for moral permission, despite acts of war crime. In the Rome Statue of the International Criminal Court (Rome Statute of the International Criminal Court 1998), the legal framework of the International Criminal Court, knowledge is defined as 'awareness that a circumstance exists or a consequence will occur in the ordinary course of events' (Art. 30.3).[3] Based on this understanding, can a child really know about his/her behaviour? And: what does it actually take to be fully aware of what one is doing in combat?

In the Rome Statute, in addition to the fact that to conscript and enlist 'children under the age of 15 years into the national armed forces or using them to participate actively in hostilities' is regarded a war crime (Art. 8.2.b.xxvi), the Court has no jurisdiction over persons who were below the age of 18 when the alleged crime took place (Art. 27).[4] This parallels the Optional Protocol to the Convention on the Rights of the Child on the involvement of children in armed conflict (2002).[5] Children are thus exempted from indictment, which may be understood as an expression of what McMahan denoted 'the nature of the child.' Another expression of a similar point is found in Article 53 (2.c) of the Rome Statute, which mentions that, even when it is apparent that genocide, crimes against humanity or war crimes have taken place, the Prosecutor may decide not to prosecute if 'a prosecution is not in the interests of justice, taking into account all the circumstances, including the gravity of the crime, the interests of victims and *the age or infirmity of the alleged perpetrator,* and his or her role in the alleged crime.'

It should be noted at this point that it seems that the Special Court of Sierra Leone, the ad-hoc tribunal set up for judging the war crimes after the end of hostilities in Sierra Leone is slightly more strict in that it expected *some* children, i.e. the ones aged 15-18 years, to be sufficiently responsible for their action to be indicted for trial, even though none have been prosecuted (Allen 2006, 92). One is here also reminded about the fact that the age at which children make a transition into adulthood varies indeed from culture to culture. For purposes of participation in rituals, the age of 13 may apply somewhere, whereas for legal purposes, such as eligibility for marriage, may be somewhat higher (Cohn and Goodwin-Gill 1994, 7). Since particular ages (15 and 18) mentioned in the international conventions do not necessarily correlate with puberty, adult rites-de-passages or the voting age, one should for developmental reasons (moral and psychological) not make the age absolute.

Secondly, the *level of responsibility* should also be considered as important for the judgment of the deeds and misdeeds of, for example, a single lower-ranking soldier. Ingierd and Syse gives the example of the Iraqi prison scandal of Abu Ghraib, where prison guards in one sense were the concrete decision-makers, but where such disgusting actions may have been encouraged by the higher-ranking leadership, including permission for torture provided by State Secretary Donald Rumsfeld. Ingierd and Syse maintains that, though such higher officers and political leaders may not have committed the actual war crimes, 'they can still be held responsible for creating an atmosphere or giving general orders that have made it appear morally defensible or possible, even desirable to commit such acts' (ibid., 86). This, however, does not exempt the soldier from responsibility as long as there was a choice. As long as there is a real moral choice, 'reference to superior orders is no general exempting condition,' reminding us of the verdicts of the Nuremberg trials (ibid., 94).

Based on this presentation of the analysis of 'decision-making' as a way of establishing a meaningful content to moral agency, I will in the remainder of this article explore whether selected literature on child soldiery in an African context show traces of moral agency among children who have voluntarily or coercively been recruited as members of armed forces or armed groups. To put it simply, can there be identified a space for *some kind* of moral choices among child soldiers? And, if so: how is this space exploited by underage children? My exploration will cover cases taken from various phases of the life of a child soldier, i.e. recruitment; the time with the group; and the return to ones local community of origin.

Why they choose to fight? Sources of motivation

One of the issues pertaining to child soldiery that has been researched in diverse context, is what kind of motivation and reason they had for joining the armed group voluntarily, if this was the case, which of course was often not the case. So, why do children participate in armed conflicts if they can choose not to?

In *Child Soldiers: The Role of Children in Armed Conflicts* by Ilene Cohn and Guy S. Goodwin-Gill (1994), such different motives and reasons are explored, based on findings from El Salvador, Guatemala, Israeli occupied territories, Liberia, and Sri Lanka.

Departing from their assumptions 'that most young participants are neither physically forced nor coerced into joining an armed force of group,' which is substantiatied in their study, they found that the root-causes of the conflicts in which the children participated, 'go far towards explaining their participation' (ibid., 10). The question pertaining to the interest of this article therefore arises: can root-causes such as poverty and repression, which remove children and youths from their parents and relatives, schools, fields, etc., be fully operative and still leave room for the agency of young soldiers on their way to becoming members of armed groups? In other words: are they destined to become soldiers as long as these causes prevail, or can their actions be viewed as matters of individual choice, partially or wholly, and with moral qualities? One option is to affirm the former part of the question, and explain seemingly voluntary recruitment as partly determined by causes such as desperation, indoctrination, militarisation, experiences of physical violence, and manipulation by people in their 'ecologies' (ibid., 30). On the other hand, the root causes of the conflict may also cause the children to choose to join forces in order to combat those root causes. Cohn & Goodwill-Gill mention for example how children in Liberia were the first to join armed groups (ibid., 23). Nevertheless, the line between voluntary or not is a fine, and very fuzzy one as 'no one makes a decision in a vacuum' (ibid., 24).

Among the young soldiers who chose to fight, some motivations may be highlighted in order to show how choice and moral qualities may describe the constrained agencies of these girls and boys. Firstly, to many young people joining armed forces may appear the better of bad alternatives (ibid. 33). Living in a refugee camp without envisaging any improvement of one's situation, perhaps orphaned, various roles in a rebel group may seem attractive in many respects. This may be interpreted as pure desperation, but it is mentioned in Cohn & Goodwill-Gill[6] how children at an early age also may create imaginations of political life that challenge for example their parents' views. Thus, political agency may intermix with moral agency. In Michael Wessells' broad study of child soldiers, a number of motivations, highly esteemed in most societies where child soldiering is prevalent, are mentioned as illustrations of the ethos and ethical sensitivity of children who participate in armed forces:

> Often, children's decisions to engage in political violence reflect their ethical sensitivity to injustice, and many are willing to die in a struggle to end oppression. Some children decide to join an armed group out of an ethos of wanting to protect or support their family. Although popular images have suggested that the children who became soldiers are bad seed or enjoy random violence, this view conflates the excesses of a few with the more moderate behaviour of the majority. Of the children who join an armed group by choice, many do so to achieve higher goals such as political independence, protection for their villages, or family well-being (Wessells 2006, 143)

Children's desire to improve their situation may also include fantastic imaginations, such as the promise of future rewards and adventures for their military contribution, which may not materialise in the end. The latter example may show how what appears to be a child's opting for the bettering of one's situation, may eventually display a lack of mental capacity to reason and decide (cf. the legal criterion of *mens rea*), and hence another version of a constrained agency, despite all good intentions and moral sensitivity. I do not say this in order to weaken the conclusion of Wessells above, which I think is right. But I want to emphasise the matter of constraints, which are the shadows in which most children's agencies operate.

Children's manipulation of images of agency

One's understanding of young soldiers' agencies depends largely on one's imagination of what a child or young person is. In an article based on ethnographic studies of former youth soldiers in Sierra Leone in the period of 1999 to 2001, towards the end of the civil war in this country (1991–2002), Susan Shepler has shown how two different discourses about children compete (Shepler 2005). One of the discourses emphasises that children are 'innocent' and 'apolitical,' informed by Western constructions of childhood, hence with an 'abdicated responsibility' ('I didn't choose to fight, I was forced, I was drugged, I was too young to know any better') (ibid., 199), despite reports about rape, murder, looting, and amputations by machete committed by the same children. The other, which is the traditional one, understands children as 'hardworking and humble,' hence attached with choice, responsibility and the possibility of culpability.

Interestingly, at this intersection between the local everyday practice (hardworking and responsible) and the global norm (innocent and with rights) for the protection of children, the issue about the agency of children immediately comes to the forefront. The irony of the passivity of gaining and preserving immunity and impunity based on the Convention of the Rights of the Child (CRC) of 1989 is well illustrated by Shepler's ethnographic field-work, where young ex-combatants display an attitude of exploiting the situation to their advantage, often at the cost of other people in the area. Not only they, but also other actors in the community use the discourse of child soldiers for their own purposes, in varying contexts. Hence, should child soldiers be regarded as merely passive, representatives of wartime non-agency, or are they better viewed as having agency (ibid., 200)?

It may be useful for the process of reintegration of youth ex-combatants not to be held responsible for what they did whilst carrying arms. 'Juvenile justice' brought by the international community, however, is not unambiguously understood at once by the local community, into which one seeks to reintegrate young men and women. Shepler asserts that to equip this group with *rights,* may invert the social hierarchy in similar ways as to how the society was turned upside down during the time of conflict (ibid., 205). Put bluntly: whereas the local perception of the problem of youths, based on the core value of humility, is that they are disrespectful and 'uppity,' and thus should be brought back to their proper position at the lower end of the social hierarchy, the rights given them from the Convention of the Rights of the Child, on the other hand, encourages them to 'stand up for themselves and make their voices heard' (ibid.). One may interpret this as an outright clash of agencies and understandings of autonomy. Along this line, Shepler concludes thus:

> So, by accepting the Western model of youth, Sierra Leonean youth gain something—ease of reintegration and forgiveness—but they lose something as well, namely a kind of political agency that is absent from Western youth (ibid., 206).

Hence, what may ease reintegration may not necessarily increase their role as political agents within a society. To illustrate this, Shepler includes an example about how a school for 100 ex-combatants became a heated issue in a local neighbourhood (ibid., 201f). Eventually, the tension broke out in violence between the local population and the 'rebel children,' whom they feared, but whom they also accused for being disrespectful and treated too well after all the bad things they had committed.

The dilemma remains: should children, whose recruitment is regarded a war crime, according to international law, and who have committed the worst kinds of war crimes and atrocities, just be forgiven in order to smooth the process of reintegration? Are they not accountable for what they did during the conflict? Are they merely victims, not perpetrators, not even to some degree? These are the kinds of impasses that are not addressed effectively by international criminal law and its current practice of prosecution.

Initiatives have been taken, however, to find a way out of this dilemma and impasse. Through approaches such as transitional justice and restorative justice (cf. Drumbl 2007), attempts have been made to find ways of children and youths to contribute to their own reintegation (cf. International Center for Transitional Justice 2009). A range of possible means may be possible for this aim, e.g. truth commissions to the creation of memorials, enabling formerly recruited children to tell their stories and at the same time raising the awareness of the communities and society of the experiences of this group of persons. Other means have been to make amends and compensations if age, ability and time permit. In Sierra Leone, e.g., former child soldiers even formed a 'community development organisation' to help repairing schools and roads. This may be a very direct way of strengthening the process of reintegration through a combination of holding such person responsible and still aiming at inclusion and mutual restoration. Through this option, which can be seens as located between mere forgiveness and brute punishment, young people may contribute creatively and decisively to their own reintegration. In my opinion, this appears to be a powerful way of expressing the gist of this article: that such young persons are moral agents. If they are not merely regarded as victims, they should therefore be expected to rebuild what they destroyed. A similar conclusion from a legal point of view, yet based on several anthropological studies on child soldiering, is drawn by Mark Drumbl (2009, 9):

> Moreover, when child soldiers are constructed as completely lacking in agency during conflict, the need for accountability mechanisms to actively engage with them postconflict correspondingly diminishes and, what is more, perceptions regarding their ability to play a vigorous or independent role in postconflict reconstruction dim, relegating them to the perimeter of the transformative project.

Compartmentalisation and disengagement: Coping with moral tension

The above mentioned complexity and dilemmas of young soldiers' agency, may create a moral tension not only in relation to the society into which they are reintegrating, but also within themselves. It seems that various strategies have been employed by children who developed a discrepancy between the ideal world and the actual reality they became part of. This is the point of departure for some consideration by Michael Wessells about how children deal with the ambiguity of colliding moral standards of the armed group and the local community. This is a field, however, that has been examined very little.

Some children, Wessells maintains, may *redefine* themselves completely, becoming one with the new group. Seen from the perspective of indoctrination, one may see that their identity has been subjected to that of the group. That it is also a voluntary individual choice, may be harder to grasp. Yet, this may take place when, for example, young people seek transformation through a group of like-minded political activists. Secondly, some employ a *compartmentalization* strategy. During the time of war, the civilian compartment is downplayed and minimalised, which in next turn bodes well for reintegration, since there is still something left after all, which makes up a base on which further moral development may take place. Thirdly, Wessells mentions a *flip-flop* strategy, i.e. 'hopping forth and back between two moral worlds' (Wessells 2006, 146). Often one sees how soldiers employ alternative personas through their use of 'jungle names,' a kind of 'doubling' that may neutralise the effect of antisocial action and thus dissociate them from culpability (Singer 2005, 73). One sees here an extreme form of what the psychologist Albert Bandura has coined 'moral disengagement' (Bandura

2002; Singer 2005, 32, n11). In this, not only a dehumanisation of and contempt for the enemy takes place, but also ones self-respect breaks down. This double mechanism is tellingly expressed by one of Peter Singer's informants in *Children at War:*

> I can never forget being in the battlefield for the first [time]. At first, I couldn't pull the trigger. I was lying almost numb in ambush watching kids my age being shot at and killed. That sight of blood and crying of people in pain, triggered something inside me that I didn't understand, but it made me past the point of compassion for others. I lost my sense of self (ibid., 84).

According to Michael Wessells, one may discern between the moral discourse of the group, and the moral discourse of the child within the group (Wessells 2006, 143). Another way to put this is to discern between the code and agency of the group on the one hand, and the individual reasoning and agency on the other. All groups have standards, explicit or merely implicit. One example of this is how the Lord's Resistance Army of Northern Uganda employs a strict code of purity and compliance with the Ten Commandments, manifesting itself in, for example, the fact that your hand will be cut off if you try to steal. Moreover, in most groups there will be a perceived the Good Us versus the Evil/Bad Others. The moral universe thus shrinks fundamentally.

Yet, even within such a heavily restricted and constrained social structure one may find a notion of individual moral agency. One such example is found in an interview with the LRA 'colonel' Thomas Kwoyelo, captured by the joint forces of Uganda, DR Congo and Southern Sudan 3 February 2009, two months before the interview took place.[7] The interview covers Kwoyelo's experience from the abduction into the forces in 1987 at the age of 15, his initiation and formation as soldier, experience with Joseph Kony's leadership, through to the capture. At the end of the interview, he is asked the following question by the journalist (who happened to be Els De Temmerman, the author of the *Aboke Girls*, about the 139 girls who were abducted by LRA from St. Mary's boarding school in Aboke, Northern Uganda in 1996):

> Q: How do you feel about the atrocities committed by the LRA?
>
> A: I feel bad. My own uncle and his three children were killed by the LRA. My situation in the bush was like that of a dog and his master. When you tell a dog to do something, it will act as instructed. All orders came from Kony. He was the chairman. He ordered attacks, abductions, ambushes. It was upon the individual commander to show restraint or exaggerate. When you were ordered to ambush a vehicle and return with money and goods, it was up to the commander to kill all the passengers or to keep

some alive. But it was impossible to question any of Kony's orders. He would believe
you were against him and kill you.

Empowerment, escape, compliance and silence: Ambiguous female agencies

Perhaps the most decisive moral choice youths can make during their time in
an armed group, is to venture to run away, despite all threats of punishment if
one is detected.[8] The very fact that children manage to escape must, in my
opinion, be regarded as one major element in their moral agencies and an
evidence for a moral choice: they wanted to flee and opt out of the group,
which demonstrates a space for some kind of choice, notwithstanding the
difficulties to do so, and under the immense threats of being captured and
brought back to the commanders of the group. For many, however, to leave
was not regarded a choice at all. According to Beth Verhey this fact is rather
complex, especially for girls and youth mothers:

> Girls themselves often do not see leaving the armed group or their 'military husband'
> as a choice. This is due to the real threat of violence and recrimination as well as
> socio-cultural upbringing where girls are expected to be submissive and accepting of
> men. Further, once a girl becomes associated with an armed group and is used
> sexually, she becomes identified socially as a 'military wife'. If a girl has a sexual
> contact with a man—whether voluntarily, by rape or by assumption due to being taken
> by an armed group—outside of marriage and the dowry, she is considered to 'no
> longer have any value' in society. Knowing these social views, girls may not seek to
> be released or demobilised in the same way as boys because they are more fearful of
> the social stigmas they will face upon returning to their family and community.
> Certainly this is complicated even further if the girl becomes pregnant and bears
> children by these relations (Verhey 2004, 2).

Even though there were no real choices for fleeing from the group, the
girls and young women may still have exercised some kind of agency. In this
the issue of 'autonomy' is brought on the table. The issue of autonomy is
discussed in Honwana (2006, 96) in relation to women and girl soldiers she
interviewed in the late 90s at Josina Machel Island, an island outside southern Mozambique, affected by the war in Mozambique, which ended in
1992. She asks whether females in war have a possibility at all to exercise
personal agency in a heavily constrained environment, or whether they have
agency in every situation and exercise it through deliberate strategies. This is
a version of the 'victim versus agent (viz. perpetrator)' alternatives.
Certainly, according to Honwana, forcible recruitment, captivity, indoctrination, and sexual abuse points in direction of victimisation. However,

collective language such as 'we attacked,' 'we killed,' and 'I participated,' voiced by women whom as girls participated in the effective but brutal RENAMO militia groups, indicate that they were also agents, not to say perpetrators (ibid.).

What kind of agency, though, were they conducting, asks Honwana. Based on a distinction between strategies and tactics found in the study of 'the practice of everyday life' by Michel De Certeau (De Certeau 1988), Honwana suggests that the way in which these youths managed to make the best out of their situation, having lost the hope of any future at all (ibid. 91), should be called *tactical agency* (ibid. 96). This kind of agency is characterised by the fact that it may not change the immediate life conditions, and may be ignorant of the ultimate consequences and aims of their actions, but has had—in the case of the Mozambican girls—the capacity to 'to make modest gains and avoid further injury and harms' (ibid.). In short: child soldiers are not devoid of agency, but retain an agency of the weak, yet indeed a very limited one.

One example of this, is how friendship and solidarity with other girls in the same situation emerged. Friendship can evolve through activities such as girls doing their hair together, and even choosing to go to the front together (Wessells 2007, 15). Thus, despite grave humiliation and abuse, these girls made choices that helped them develop social relationships and making the best out of their situation. Another example is how girls opted for becoming a commander's wife, rather than serving as a sexual object of soldiers in the group, sometimes raped by a new boy every day. Although necessity may drive girls to seek more permanent relationships with one single commander, and consequently more protection and a less heavy duty, this may also be seen as a conscious agency of the girls. Some of them even managed to live with their husband from the military past after the peace had come, despite severe challenges to return to their home village, not least if their husband had been involved in atrocities in that particular village (Honwana 2006, 85-86).

A similar finding found from the Liberian War experiences of young women is reported by the Swedish researcher Mats Utas: 'Women who failed to team up with any of the local 'big men' became the worst victims of war' (Utas 2005, 59). Moreover, they also become involved in the armed groups in order to protect their families (ibid., 74). In order to 're-operationalize the inimical opposition of victim/perpetrator, civilian/soldier' he takes issue with 'prevailing views on agency and gender stereotypes in war,' arguing for a 'sliding scale between abundant agency and *victimcy* [i.e. minimal amount of "war agency"].' He concludes that, 'Whatever choiceless decisions intro-duced to these young girls into the war system, they all had in common that they soon got used to the system and thus created different ways to master it. (...) The wrong choice might end one's life' (ibid., 54f, emphasis original, and 75).

One constraint that marked the limited agency told about in Honwana's study is that the young soldiers were powerless in avoiding suffering and witnessing atrocities (ibid., 97). This, together with the sexual abuse they went through, turned out as very difficult to articulate. Hence, silence prevailed among the interviewees when such issues were touched upon. However, Honwana did not interpret silence as nothing or void, but as important, indeed powerful language. As she interviewed these former girl soldiers, she noticed how girls were uncomfortable talking about their experiences in the armed groups. Similarly, families and other people surrounding the girls also rarely disclosed much about the girls' past lives in war. Honwana, relying on Veena Das and her examination of the role of women during the Indian Partition (Das 1987), also describes this as an act of conscious agency, i.e. 'their refusal to put words to the experience, in the ability to hold it inside and be silent about it' (quoted in Honwana 2006, 80).

Hence, girls who conduct this kind of agency should not be regarded 'super-victims', but recognised and esteemed for their potential significance for the post-conflict retrieval of the society (Park 2006, 316).

Socio-cultural honour and ancestral spirits: The greater frameworks of moral agency

The aforementioned strategy of silence should, moreover, not only be understood as a sign of deliberation and moral agency; it is also an expression of a complex social reality surrounding the acts and pasts of former child soldiers, as seen in the quote of girl mothers who chose to remain with their 'husbands'. This complex issue belongs also to a wider reality than that of moral versus immoral agency. In many communities where child soldiery prevails, not least in Africa, matters of honour and shame make up a fundamental interpretive framework for behaviour. In her study from Mozambique, Honwana describes for example how dishonour does not depend entirely upon whether the young woman consented or not to 'immoral' sexual relations. More important is how her acts impact on her family at large (Honwana 2006, 80). Thus, moral agency across these tabooed issues is not merely connected to sexual (im)morality, but rather to the social stigma that is attached by a social system where honour and shame matter the more. One may denote this an ethic of honour-compliance.

An even wider context includes the universe of ancestral spirits. How war crimes and the relation to these spirits affect the homecoming of child soldiers can be illustrated by an example from Uganda. Olara Otunnu, Special Representative of the UN Secretary-General for Children and Armed Conflict, explains the phenomenon of a norm called *lapir* within the Acholi culture of Northern Uganda:

> Before declaring war the elders would carefully consider their *lapir*—to be sure that their community had a deep and well founded grievance against the other side. If this was established to be the case, war might be declared, but never lightly. And in order to preserve one's *lapir*, strict injunctions would be issued to regulate the actual conduct of war. You did not attack children, women or the elderly; you did not destroy crops, granary stores or livestock. For to commit such taboos would be to soil your *lapir* with the consequence that you would forfeit the blessing of the ancestors, and thereby risk losing the war itself (quoted in Singer 2005, 10).

Thus, we see how warfare is restrained and backed with a combined moral-ancestral argument. Or better: observance of the ancestors implies constraints in warfare, and is thus intimately morally bound. We see here a clear coincidence between the conventional *jus in bello* (the constraints of warfare), both in its moral and legal forms, and African traditional religion. Hence, the moral agency of individuals in this context cannot be separated from the rules that apply for the dynamic relationship between humans and their ancestors, within a communal framework. It is within this perspective, according to Tim Allen, that rituals may be experienced as most effective in confirming ex-soldiers as social and moral persons (Allen 2006, 164), though Allen himself still argues that the overall role of rituals has been somewhat overstated.

Conclusive remarks: The collective moral responsibility of protection

The mother of the first groundbreaking study of the effects of war on children as a global problem, the Mozambican Graça Machel, interprets the unimaginable figures as to how children are affected by war, including the widespread use of children in armed groups, thus:

> These statistics are shocking enough, but more chilling is the conclusion to be drawn from them: more and more of the world is being sucked into a desolate moral vacuum. This is a space devoid of the most basic human values; a space in which children are slaughtered, raped, and maimed; a space in which children are exploited as soldiers; a space in which children are starved and exposed to extreme brutality. Such unregulated terror and violence speak of deliberate victimization. There are few further depths to which humanity can sink (Machel 1996, 5).

The combat against child soldiery is therefore a deeply moral struggle, and it is a global one. As such, the strategies should be those of the societies; globally, regionally, nationally and locally. On the tactical level, however, children—despite forced recruitment and harsh indoctrination—may do their best to preserve their humanity, and should be valued for this.

It is indeed straining one's imagination to ask how children, who have been abducted, indoctrinated, forced to kill a brother or mother, for whom violence has been normalised, can become firm and sound moral agents? (Wessells 2006, 142). On the other hand, it is the more important to pay this issue due attention in order to avoid stereotypes of extreme personalities and morally lacking behaviour. Child soldiers comprise a complex phenomenon (ibid., 142f).

Lastly, there is a higher responsibility that belongs to the collective sphere, surrounding the young persons of concern. For the local community, the national authorities, and, at the last: the international community, the moral agency that is requested is that of protection. This aspect of the entire issue of child soldiery is reflected by Alcinda Honwana, who sees this as a matter, eventually, of reinforcement of contextual perceptions of childhood and norms for child protection:

> International humanitarian law and local notions of childhood determine the way we understand these phenomena today. The recognition that international law is unable to protect children from war and prevent their recruitment into armed forces calls for a re-examination of the notions of childhood behind such agreements and the real capacity to enforce them, given their different socioeconomic and cultural contexts in which laws are drawn up and conflict takes place. The way forward lies in reinforcing norms and value systems for child protection based on indigenous local world views and meaning system (Honwana 2006, 47).

A variety of factors explain the complexity of the use of child soldiers. Often the 'supply' side of the issue has been focused (e.g., level of poverty, orphan rates, and availability of small arms), at the cost of the 'demand' or 'market' side (e.g., organisational structure and resource endowment) (Andvig and Gates 2007). In a discussion about what counts as the most influential variable for the increase of recruitment of children for participation in armed groups, what is highlighted as very important, is the access to and degree of protection of children in IDP and refugee camps (Achvarina and Reich 2006). In a situation where it remains a demand for recruitment of children and young persons, for various reasons, it is imperative to reinforce the protection of them. This is the duty of national authorities as well as the international community. This is not the responsibility of the children and youths. But it may well be that gaining a nuanced understanding of their different agencies, even where international crimes have been committed, may also contribute to protection and the promotion of their interests, (Drumbl 2009, 16).

References

Achvarina, Vera, and Simon F. Reich. 2006. No place to hide: Refugees, displaced persons, and the recruitment of child soldiers. *International Security* 31 (1):127-164.

Allen, Tim. 2006. *Trial justice: The International Criminal Court and the Lord's Resistance Army*. London: Zed Books.

Andvig, Jens Christopher, and Scott Gates. 2007. Recruiting children for armed conflict. http://www.fordinstitute.pitt.edu/papers/Gates-Andvig07. pdf (accessed 23 April 2009).

Bandura, Albert. 2002. Selective moral disengagement in the exercise of moral agency. *Journal of Moral Education* 31 (2):101-119.

Cohn, Ilene, and Guy S. Goodwin-Gill. 1994. *Child soldiers: The role of children in armed conflicts*. Oxford: Oxford University Press.

Das, Veena. 1987. The anthropology of violence and the speech of victims. *Anthropology Today* 3 (4):11-13.

De Certeau, Michel. 1988. *The practice of everyday life*. Berkely: California University Press.

Drumbl, Mark A. 2007. Atrocity, punishment, and international law. Cambridge: Cambridge University Press.

Drumbl, Mark A. 2009. Child soldiers: Agency, enlistment, and the collectivization of Innocence. Working paper. *Washington & Lee Legal Studies Paper No. 2009-07.* Available at: http://ssrn.com/abstract= 1424110 (accessed 26 January 2010).

Honwana, Alcinda. 2006. *Child soldiers in Africa*. Philadelphia, Penn.: University of Pennsylvania Press.

Ingierd, Helene, and Henrik Syse. 2005. Responsibility and culpability in war. *Journal of Military Ethics* 4 (2):85-99.

International Center for Transitional Justice. 2009. Children and transitional justice. Available at: http://ictj.org/static/Factsheets/ICTJ_Children-TJ_ fs2008.pdf (accessed 26 January 2010).

Machel, Graça. 1996. Impact of armed conflict on children: Expert report for the United Nations: United Nations. Available at http://www.unicef.org/graca/a51-306_en.pdf (accessed 12 January 2010), 1-78.

McMahan, Jeff. 2007. Child soldiers: The ethical perspective. Available at http://www.isn.ethz.ch/isn/Digital-Library/Publications/Detail/?ots591= 0C54E3B3-1E9C-BE1E-2C24-A6A8C7060233&lng=en&id=45682 (last accessed 6 March 2010), 1-16.

Park, Augustine S.J. 2006. 'Other inhumane acts': Forced marriage, girl soldiers and the Special Court for Sierra Leone. *Social & Legal Studies* 15 (3):315-337.

Rome Statute of the International Criminal Court. 1998. Available at: http://untreaty.un.org/cod/icc/statute/romefra.htm (accessed 25 April 2009). United Nations.

Shepler, Susan. 2005. The rites of the child: Global discourses of youth and reintegrating child soldiers. *Journal of Human Rights* 4:197-211.

Singer, Peter Warren. 2005. *Children at war.* New York: Pantheon Books.

Utas, Mats. 2005. Agency of victims: Young women in the Liberian Civil War. In *Makers & breakers: Children & youth in postcolonial Africa,* edited by A. Honwana and F. De Boeck. Oxford: James Currey.

Verhey, Beth. 2004. Reaching the girls: Study on girls associated with armed forces and groups in the Democratic Republic of Congo. Save the Children UK and the NGO Group: CARE, IFESH and IRC, 1-35.

Wessells, Michael. 2006. *Child soldiers: From violence to protection.* Cambridge, Mass. and London: Harvard University Press.

Wessells, Michael G. 2007. The recruitment and use of girls in armed forces and groups in Angola: Implications for ethical research and reintegration. Available at http://www.isn.ethz.ch/isn/Digital-Library/Publications/ Detail/?ots591=0C54E3B3-1E9C-BE1E-2C24-A6A8C7060233&lng=en &id=45789 (last accessed 23 April 2009).

Notes

[1] The very notion of child soldier is problematic. It is in particular problematic for the children and youths who have taken part in armed conflicts for several reasons: the label 'child soldier' awakens painful memories from their past lives, it fuels stigmatization among people into whose society they should reenter and build a future, and, lastly, it

reflects only a minor aspect of their overall life experience (Wessells 2006, 8). It may also exclude those who were not taking part in combats within the armed group (Verhey 2004, 6, n1). So, what are the reasons for still using it? First, according to the Optional Protocol of the UN Convention on the Rights of the Child (called the 'child soldiers treaty,' ratified by nations such as the DR Congo and Uganda, but not by the U.S.), a child is defined as 'every human being below the age of 18 years unless, under the law applicable to the child, majority is attained earlier' (Art. 1). Thus, there is a legal reason for using this notion. Secondly, these children have participated in various ways, often in non-combatant ways, in armed groups, and should therefore be regarded as soldiers in an inclusive sense.

[2]   See 'duress', Wikipedia (accessed 13 October 2008).

[3]   http://untreaty.un.org/cod/icc/statute/romefra.htm (accessed 13 October 2008).

[4]   Tim Allen, the author of *Trial justice: The International Criminal Court and the Lord's Resistance Army* (2006), himself an anthropologist, doubts whether formerly abducted children, though above 18 at the time when alleged crimes were committed, a category that will fit many, will be dealt with by the International Criminal Court (Allen 2006, 93).

[5]   http://www2.ohchr.org/english/law/crc-conflict.htm (accessed 15 October 2008).

[6]   A reference is made to Neil Boothby and John Humphrey, 'Under the Gun – Children in Exile,' V. Hamilton, ed., U.S. Committee for Refugees, Washington, D.C., 1988.

[7]   Sunday Vision online, http://www.sundayvision.co.ug/detail.php?mainNewsCategoryId=7 &newsCategoryId=130&newsId=679194, published 25 April 2009 (accessed 2 October 2009).

[8]   The opposite may also be case, e.g., when someone chooses to remain with a group in order to continue struggling for liberation, in the face of personal costs and against all odds of 'victory.'

5

The Dynamics of Children Associated with Armed Forces and Challenges of Building Peace in Uganda

Deusdedit R.K. Nkurunziza

Makerere University, Kampala

Abstract

The article discusses the phenomena of children associated with armed forces in Uganda; highlights the causes and factors which bring about active involvement of children in war. The article further argues that building peace and reconstruction in northern Uganda should take into account effective integration of formerly abducted children. The article proposes democratic governance and active participation of civil society organizations as indispensable strategies to prevent abduction and recruitment of children. As a whole, the article calls for a paradigm shift from economies of war to economies of peace as a possible global strategy to prevent child soldiering in the emerging global world order.

Introduction

Uganda's post independence history is characterized by political instability and armed conflicts which have had a profound impact on the social-moral fabric of the country, on the civilian populations including children. The impact of Uganda's armed conflicts on children is a significant area of research and currently there are enormous information gaps regarding the scale of Uganda's conflicts on children.

The phenomenon of formerly abducted children is an issue which should be at the center of building peace and reconstruction in northern Uganda.

This is a critical issue which the Government of Uganda, local authorities in the country and development partners has to squarely face so as to develop a society free from fear and free from war.

This article has three objectives: first it makes analysis of the factors precipitating the involvement of children in war; secondly it advocates for proactive policies at local, national, regional and international levels that focus on proactively preventing child soldiering by enhancing peace for integral human development; finally it calls for a paradigm shift from economies of war to economies of peace.

To achieve these objectives, the article briefly discusses Uganda's background to the phenomenon of children getting actively involved in war; highlights the causes of armed conflict in Uganda which precipitate the emergency of children associated with armed forces; analyses challenges and complexities for integration and rehabilitation of formerly abducted children; finally the article proposes democratic governance and active involvement of civil society organizations as a strategy for preventing abduction of children and recruitment of children by armed forces.

Root causes of armed conflict in Uganda

The phenomenon of children associated with armed forces in Uganda is a byproduct of armed conflicts. On one hand it is a result of an effort by the armed forces to protect children caught up in the middle of war and on the other hand it is a result of a strategic military option to abduct and inscript children as combats. In order, therefore, to address the phenomena of children associated with armed groups in Uganda, one has to tackle the root causes of armed conflict (Cohn and Goodwin-Gill 2003).

While a number of causes for armed conflict in Uganda have been identified as colonial legacy, poverty, religion, ethnicity; one can realistically point to politics and system of governance as the trigger of armed conflict in Uganda. This is further aggravated by absence of justice system that is reliable and trusted to build confidence and to hold together the social fabric of the people. Once people feel rejected, marginalized, threatened and pushed to the wall, they tend to take up arms struggle as a weapon of self-protection and recognition. This process necessarily triggers armed conflict which in turn breeds a fertile ground for child soldiers (Singer 2005). In such circumstances the children are victims of war and in the process they are trained by the armed forces to become active soldiers, hence the concept of child soldiers. Uganda's armed conflicts provide another story of how war negatively impacts on children and youth (Machel 2001) and particularly girls

(McKay 2004). The impact of armed conflict on children is multifaceted, far-reaching and profound (Williamson 2007). Uganda's experience of armed conflict demonstrates how war violates all rights of children. During armed conflict, children are displaced, separated from their families, denied basic need, unlawful recruitment in armed forces and armed groups, sexual violence, killing and maiming, and trafficking are some of the direct consequences of Uganda's armed conflicts on children (Apio 2008).

The phenomenon of children associated with armed forces in Uganda

Uganda is one of those countries, which has had a host of children who have been associated with armed forces. The gravity of the problem of children associated with armed forces in Uganda came to light as a result of the insurgency in northern Uganda and the children's abductions by the Lord's Resistance Army to serve in combatant positions.

Uganda's phenomenon of children getting actively involved in war can be traced back to the war in the Luwero triangle in the early 1980s, when the National Resistance Army (NRA) was fighting to take over political power (Dodge 1991). In 1986, when the National Resistance Army took over the government in Uganda, one of the concerns of the international community was the use and presence of children in the National Resistance Army.

The presence of children in the National Resistance Army reveals the complex and far-reaching problem of the effect and impact of armed conflict on children and society as a whole. It is reported that the National Resistance Army picked and looked after children who had been abandoned as a result of the war. They had to pick and protect these children but in turn they trained them as combatants who came to be commonly known as "Kadogos"; some of whom have grown to become influential actors in the current government system.

According to the NRA, abandoned children were cared for in small numbers in the beginning, but by 1983 more and more school-aged children were absorbed into the NRA. As UNLA operations intensified and threatened to remote NRA camps where these children were kept, a decision was taken to disperse the children and give them basic self-defence training to reduce risks. NRA officers "adopted" these children and looked after their food, clothing and shelter. After receiving basic self-defence training, the children soon accompanied the officers, carried weapons, ran errands, cleaned and cooked, and in this way became royal contributors to individual officers and the NRA as a whole. They were highly motivated, reliable and dedicated, often instilled with a strong sense of revenge triggered by the UNLA atrocities against their families, friends or village which had driven them to the NRA in the first place (Dodge 1991, 51-52).

There is no empirical evidence yet to establish whether the use of children during Uganda's protracted struggle by NRA as described by Dodge in the above quotation was a coincidence to protect and to take care of abandoned children, or intentional and strategic to recruit them. Whatever the answer will be to this question, there seems to be no doubt that after 1986, in northern Uganda, the option to abduct and recruit children as combatants both by the Lord's Resistance Army and by Uganda People's Defence Forces (UPDF) was both intentional and strategic. In northern Uganda, the children became a target, abducted and recruited as combatants (Apio 2008). The experiences of the girl child soldier are particularly disheartening and complex; they did not only serve as combatants, they were also raped and given to military commanders as wives.

Children during the insurgency in northern Uganda became victims of child soldiering. They were abducted and used as combatants by the Lord Resistance Army (McKay and Mazurana 2004). They were also used by Uganda People's Defence Forces (UPDF) to protect the people from LRA. As a result, children were involved militarily at three levels: first, they were abducted by LRA to build and boast their army; secondly, the UPDF used the children to protect people from LRA; then, the formerly abducted children returnees from the LRA were strategically given a safe landing by the UPDF.

The children that returned from LRA seem to have found it difficult to adapt to the normal environment. They were used to carrying guns, living in bushes and taking or giving orders. They easily found a safe haven with UPDF, who were also ready to take them on because they knew the enemy better. The formerly abducted children returning from the bush prefer to stay in the armed ranks other than returning to civilian life.

Another aspect of children getting actively involved in the insurgency in northern Uganda was at the level of home guards. Children seem to have been recruited as "home guards." For example in Unyma IDP camp, children were trained to guard their local IDP camp in case of any LRA attacks. Children, below 18 years of age were trained in military tactics and equipped with arms to protect themselves and their camps.

The children were targeted by the Lord's Resistance Army because they are easy to manipulate. They listen and learn quickly, they take instructions and are obedient. They are readily controlled, easily brainwashed and they ask minimum of questions. Children, because of their docility and age, do not easily form rebellious groups in an armed camp to orchestrate a rebellion. They also eat less compared to adults, consequently it is cheaper to engage in and deploy an army of children rather than an army of adults. Furthermore, they are not paid but manipulated and controlled. This might explain why over 90% of LRA combatants are abducted children (Veale and Stavrou 2002).

This reveals an ethical dimension to the whole question of child soldiering; it is a new form of military slavery. Child soldiering is a new form of slavery that targets the exploitation of humanity starting with the child. It is a problem that needs to be tackled by focusing on the root causes of war.

Understanding the root causes of child soldiering

Speaking with one of the elders in northern Uganda he had a sad story to tell concerning the situation of the children during the insurgency period. "Our children, because of the hopelessness of the situation in our region, have preferred to go to the bush than to wait and die here of hunger."

A situation of war and poverty brings about fear, insecurity and hopelessness, which in turn make children leave their families and take up arms as a means of attaining livelihood. In other situations the children are abducted and forced to join in the fighting. Children having lived in poverty, violence and insecurity easily flock to the military as the only hope for their security by wielding the gun themselves. In the military they are trained to kill the aggressor before he kills them. Consequently, children in war zones and areas of insurgency, looking for protection and survival, easily take up child soldiering as an indispensable alternative.

In order to tackle the issue of child soldiering, there is need for both the international community and national governments to avail resources for the strategic implementations of the human security paradigm to ensure sustainable peace and economic welfare of the people, especially children and youth in countries that are vulnerable to armed conflict.

Child soldiering: a fundamental breach of children's rights

The involvement of children in armed conflict constitutes an attack on the most ethical foundations of society (Fisher 1998). The presence of child soldiers contravenes the international, regional and national legal instruments on children rights. The 1989 Convention on the rights of the child (CRC) provides the normative and legal framework of the rights of children; it spells out the basic rights of children in all contexts: the right to survival; to develop to the fullest; to protection from harmful influences, abuse and exploitation; and to participate fully in family, cultural and social life. In addition to its provision and guiding principles which apply to all children in all countries, the convention contains articles specific to the protection and care of children in armed conflict (CRC, Article 22, 38 and 39).

According to the Convention on the rights of the children, armed conflict violates children's rights; it violates their rights to life, to health, to education, to adequate standard of living, to protection from abuse, exploitation, neglect, discrimination and recruitment into the military.

The Optional Protocol to the Convention on the Rights of the Child clearly stipulates on the involvement of children in armed conflict and asks State parties to take all feasible measures to ensure that persons who have not attained the age of 18 years do not take a direct part in hostilities. The African Charter of the Rights and Welfare of the Child also articulates the rights of children. In light of these legal frameworks, the reality of child soldiers is a fundamental violation of international law. These legal instruments have been strengthened by the proceedings of the Special International Court of Sierra Leone, which has recognized the use of child soldiers as a crime. This means that anyone or a state using children in the form of soldiers can now be prosecuted and charged.

Effective integration of formerly abducted children

Northern Uganda currently presents both to the state in Uganda and to the international community real challenge of peace building. The challenges of peacebuilding include creating a conducive environment for the integration and rehabilitation of formerly abducted children (Heeren 2006). There is also the need to voluntarily resettle people who have lived in internally displaced camps for over twenty years. This peacebuilding process also includes the reconstruction of the broken down social, cultural and physical infrastructure; the need to consolidate social cohesion among the communities; curbing and managing the influence of warlords and developing values of non-violence and national unity.

Building peace in northern Uganda has to take into account reintegration of formerly abducted children; empowering them with skills to become productive rather than being seduced back to taking up of arms as a means of livelihood, hence transiting from insurgency to a new environment of violent crime. A situation where the formerly abducted children, now youth and grown-up adults, can resort to violent crime as a means of livelihood has to be proactively prevented. Effective integration of formerly abducted children, therefore, has to take into account social development and poverty eradication (Honwana 2006).

The study conducted by Chrobok and Akutu (2008) underlines that children and youths formerly abducted by the LRA need counseling, emotional and physical support, education, vocational training, income generation, recreation, play and earn a living. Effective integration empowers the formerly abducted children to contribute positively to their families and communities (Jareg 2005). Community-based reintegration programme which includes other conflict-affected children is the most effective manner to organize reintegration (MacVeigh, Maguire and Wedge 2007). Integration programmes should also be gender sensitive and give special attention to girls who have been involved in and affected by war (Hobson 2005; Jareg 2005).

Need for democratic governance

Prevention of child soldiering in Uganda will also strongly depend on the establishment of democratic constitutional governance, rule of law with promotion and respect of human rights and children's rights in particular and sustainable development geared towards eradication of poverty and enhancing quality of life for all.

There is need to be proactive both at local, national, regional and international levels by designing and implementing policies of peace for development and development to enhance peace; promoting equality, justice, nondiscrimination and non-marginalization. In other words, there is need of systems and institutions of governance at all levels that are democratic, transparent, promoting equity and equality of all. In this regard, local governments are important stakeholders and key agents in the process of rehabilitating and integrating child soldiers. They provide a structure for popular participation, which should proactively focus on the integral welfare of children in the communities.

Civil society organizations, particularly community-based organizations at the grassroot levels have also a critical role to play in protecting children and preventing armed conflict. They, however, need sensitization on children's rights and principles of nonviolence so as to become agents of socio-economic transformation and development by putting pressure on the political leaders and governments and hold them accountable.

Civil society organizations are key actors in disseminating and developing new shared social structures, perceptions, values and beliefs that will protect children and serve to prevent recurrence of protracted armed conflict organized at grass root levels. In the case of Uganda, for example, the West Nile and Eastern Uganda did not register such high numbers of child soldiers as was the case in northern Uganda. Community structures at grassroot levels that enhance the protection of children and are resilient against armed conflict are a sign of hope for the future without armed conflict and for preventing child soldiering.

Civil society organizations have a critical role to play to avert the possibility of the resurgence of war and play an indispensable task of building mutual trust and tolerance between the belligerent and contending parties; they consequently constitute the best partners in the process of reintegrating and rehabilitating children associated with armed forces.

Conclusion

This article has democratic governance and peace for development as a strategy of preventing child soldiering in Uganda. For this to happen there is need of policies and action focusing on peace for development and development to enhance peace. There is urgent need to create conditions conducive to peace and opportunities for development bringing about quality of life for the people and children in particular.

There is no magic formula and no singular strategy or set of tactics that will create peace and end the phenomenon of child soldiers unless the different actors at all levels become genuinely committed to peace for development and development to enhance peace. Developing and implementing proactive policies which enhance the reciprocal relationship between peace and development seems to be the best alternative to preventing child soldiering in Uganda. This has to include effective integration and empowering the formerly abducted children and developing opportunities for their employment.

References

Apio, Eunice. 2008. Bearing the burden of blame – the outcome of children born of the Lord's Resistance Army, northern Uganda. http://www.child-soldiers.org\psycho-social\english (accessed 16 January 2010).

Chrobok, Vera, and Andrew S. Akutu. 2008. Returning home – Children's perspectives on integration: A case study of Children abducted by the Lord's resistance Army in Teso, Eastern Uganda. http.//www.child-soldiers.org/psycho-social/English(accessed 16 January 2010).

Cohn, Ilene, and Guy S.Goodwin-Gill. 2003. *Child soldiers: The role of children in armed conflict.* Oxford: Clarendon Press.

Dodge, Cole. P. 1991. Child soldiers of Uganda and Mozambique. In *Reaching children in war: Sudan, Uganda and Mozambique*, ed. Cole P. Dodge and Magne Raundalen. Bergen: Sigma Forlag.

Fisher, Nigel. 1998. *Children in armed conflict: Policy framework and priorities*. Ottawa : UNICEF Canada.

Heeren, Nick. 2006. Sierra Leone and Civil War: Neglected trauma and forgotten children. http://www.child-soldiers.org/psycho-social/English (accessed 16 January 2010).

Hobson, M. 2005. *Forgotten casualties of war: Girls in armed conflict.* Save the Children. UK.

Honwana, Alcinda. 2006. *Child soldiers in Africa*. Philadelphia: University of Pennsylvania Press.

Jareg, Elizabeth. 2005. Crossing bridges and negotiating rivers: Rehabilitation and reintegration of children associated with armed forces. http://www.child-soldiers.org/psycho-social/english (accessed 16 January 2010).

Keitetsi, C. 2004. *Child soldier*. London: Souvenir Press.

Machel, Graca. 2001. *The impact of war on children*. London: Hurst &Company

MacVeigh, Johanna, Sarah Maguire and Joanna Wedge. 2007. *Stolen futures: The reintegration of children affected by armed conflict.* Save the Children UK. Also available at http://www.savethechildren.org.uk/en/docs/stolen_futures.pdf (accessed 16 January 2010).

McKay, Susan. 2004. Reconstructing fragile lives: girls' social reintegration in northern Uganda and Sierra Leone. http://www.publications.oxfam.org.uk (accessed 16 January 2010).

McKay, Susan and Dyan Mazurana. 2004. *Where are the child mothers? Child mothers in fighting forces in northern Uganda, Sierra Leone and Mozambique: Their lives during and after the war.* Canadian International development Agency.

Singer, Peter Warren. 2005. *Children at war*. New York: Pantheon Books.

Veale, Angela and Aki Stavrou. 2002. *Reintegration of former Lord's Resistance Army child soldier abductees into Acholi society*. Pretoria, South Africa: Institute for Security Studies.

Williamson, Roger.2007. Children and armed Conflict: Toward a policy consensus and future agenda – Ten years after the Machel Study. http://www.wiltonpark.org.uk/documents/conferences/WP840/pdfs/WP84 0.pdf (accessed 23 January 2010).

PART II

6

Domesticating the Bush[1]

Chris Coulter
Uppsala University

Abstract

During the course of the Sierra Leonean war thousands of girls and women were abducted from their homes during rebels attacks. An overwhelming majority of these girls and women suffered physical abuse, frequent rapes, and pregnancy as a result. Many were also subjected to forced marriage, becoming so-called bush wives, but some also became rebel fighters. There is no easy way to generalize the position of abducted women in postwar society, experiences and strategies are very personal and diverse, but it became evident that many families and local communities were not very eager to forgive girls and women who had been with the rebels, and sometimes they saw little difference between the abductees and the fighters who abducted them. The purpose of this article is not only to account for both the personal and structural dimensions of these diversities, but also to trace some commonalities in the reintegration strategies of young women formerly associated with the rebel forces in postwar Sierra Leone.

Introduction

The Sierra Leonean war began on 23 March 1991, when a small rebel group, the Revolutionary United Front (RUF), entered southeastern Sierra Leone from Liberia. The war went on in varying intensity throughout the 1990s, and peace was officially declared on 18 January 2002. The war has been described as one of the more brutal in the late twentieth century, its level of brutality compared to that of Rwanda or even Cambodia in the 1970s. The RUF rebels have been accused of committing widespread atrocities such as cutting off people's limbs, rape, and creating mass destruction, but all fighting factions targeted civilians. Today, after three elections, six governments, four peace accords, four coups d'état, and the deployment of one of the largest peacekeeping operations ever mounted by the United Nations, the country enjoys a fragile stability.

During the course of the war, many thousands of girls and women were abducted from their home areas when rebels or other fighters attacked and looted. An overwhelming majority of these girls and women also suffered physical abuse, frequent rapes, and pregnancy as a result. Some were used as forced labor, and some were forced to witness or to participate in the killing of relatives. A majority of abducted girls and women were also subjected to forced marriage, becoming so-called bush wives, and some also became rebel fighters. During the decade-long war, most of them had also fallen in love, some had married, others had divorced, and most had had children. Whatever their personal circumstances, they grew from girls to young women during a period of intense and sometimes extreme social change. Some girls and women managed to escape within days or months after their capture, but others stayed with their captors for up to ten years, and some still live today with their bush husbands. Some fled from war zones, but many also took the opportunity to loot and fight in the destructive trail of rebels or other fighters. These young women also have varied experiences of postwar society; some had been welcomed back to their families and communities while others were ostracized and expelled. The way they communicated their war and postwar experiences also varied, according to factors such as context, arena, personality, and position in household.

Toward the end of the war many abducted girls and women were released, some escaped, and many were abandoned by their bush husbands. But there were also those who stayed with their bush husbands and commanders, some out of fear, others by choice, and those who had nowhere else to go. There were those who lived in informal conjugal relationships with their bush husbands, had children or were pregnant, and were reluctant to leave for an uncertain future with their natal families. They were also concerned for their 'rebel children,' fearing that the children would not be well treated. Others were hesitant about returning and being forced to marry men who had paid their bridewealth when they were young. A few women told me that they loved their bush husbands, or that they felt loyal to them for saving their lives, and for those reasons did not want to leave. A former human rights advisor to the UN Mission in Sierra Leone also speculated that the reason some bush wives did not return home was because they 'knew of no other life' (O'Flaherty 2004, 58). Whatever their reasons, many were uncertain of what would happen to them in postwar society.

Postwar positions

There is no easy way to generalize the position of abducted women in postwar society. Experiences and strategies were very personal and diverse. The purpose of this article is to account for both personal and structural dimensions of these diversities, but also to trace commonalities. A couple of years after the declaration of peace, many abducted women and female ex-combatants had eventually returned to their families. Most of my informants said that people had been very hostile toward them when they first returned. In postwar Sierra Leone it was not uncommon for 'rebel women' to be stigmatized and verbally and physically abused by their families, husbands, and communities. Most of my informants feared that people would find out about their rebel past and tried hard to keep the full extent of their war experiences secret. That which was not 'known' should not be socially articulated. By staying with the rebels for so many years, from the perspective of their families and communities, abducted girls and women had become rebels too, whatever the circumstances of their participation. The war the rebels waged in Sierra Leone, albeit not alone, had wreaked havoc on the country and its population. Many people had lost everything they owned, and everyone knew someone who had been killed or mutilated, raped or abducted. These were things that were not easily forgotten.

Many informants expressed feelings of being excluded and marginalized in their households and in the larger communities. Eighteen-year-old Mameh had been abducted and spent two years with the rebels. Mameh described her life as very difficult when she returned to her village, and she told me that people in her village had said that she 'had come with rebel blood,' and despite her efforts to behave well, they had said that she could 'change at any time.' People feared that rebel women could become violent and wreak havoc in the community. I interpreted this fear of rebel women and the unwillingness to forgive and reintegrate them into society as a social inability to cope with women's deviant wartime and postwar behavior. It became clear that many families and local communities were not very eager to forgive girls and women who had been with the rebels, and sometimes they saw little difference between the abductees and the fighters who abducted them. This meant that for the majority of my informants, and many women like them, their fears about returning were realized. One young woman I met frankly stated that she had been anxious about going home 'for them to maltreat me – and so it happened.' Paul Richards tells of a woman who had escaped after more than two years with the rebels. This woman, Rose, 'was unable to return home, since people vowed vengeance upon her, believing that in surviving she had somehow become a committed member of the RUF, rather than treating her as *a survivor of an experience they could not comprehend*' (Richards 2005, 135, my emphasis). Returning bush wives also divided families; whereas some family members were happy about their return, others were more skeptical.

Notions of shame and shameful behavior played an important part in the reintegration of girls and women who had been abducted by rebels, whether they had been fighters or not. Women who had spent many years with the rebels were worse off and seemed more severely tainted by being associated with the rebels. My informants said that they were not free to talk about their experiences of war in the context of postwar society. This meant in many cases that the presumptions their families and communities had of their experiences were based on rumors and notions of rebel brutality, not on conversations with them. These notions of 'wicked' rebels were further reinforced if the girls and women behaved in a manner unacceptable to their families and communities, and if they had problems adapting to the more 'traditional' feminine ideal of subservience and acquiescence, hard work and self-restraint.

After the war, many of my informants were regarded by their families and communities as having engaged in socially deviant behavior. This type of nonconformity to local social norms in some cases led to social disapproval, which was manifested in an experience of social exclusion, stigma, and shame. Many of my informants said that due to their war experiences they were excluded from participating fully in the life of the community; for example, some found it very difficult to get married. In a society where the opportunities for women are few beyond the role of wife and mother, these girls and women became a social dilemma. Parents did not want to exclude their daughters, they wanted them to become moral women, but the price of this morality was sometimes very high (cf. Bunting 2005, 26). Like many young women in her situation, one of my informants, Aminata, was made to understand that she had 'disgraced' her father and 'shamed' her family, (*I don shame*). Although Aminata's shame emanated from behavior associated with events outside the confines of her own moral community, when she returned home the relationships the war had severed could not be realigned in any conceivable way. The shaming of the family caused by Aminata's war experience and postwar behavior dishonored her father. However, Aminata's father's honor did not rest on the protection of her body in the same way as has been described, for example, by Maria Olujic (1998) for Bosnia. But, as the father of a rebel, her father's dignity and social standing had been violated. One might speculate that since her father had few material resources and depended on the income of his son, his social status was restricted, and his daughter's history with the rebels and her current behavior became a problem to him in upholding his status and reputation in society.

The village and the bush

In Kabala and the surrounding villages, for people who had not participated actively in the war, the relationships between bush husbands and bush wives were seen, just as the people who had stayed with the rebels for a long time were seen, as 'wild' and belonging to 'the bush.' The process of rehabilitation and reintegration was thus often framed in terms of taming or domesticating their bushlike behavior. Only those who managed to change their behavior, or people's impression of their behavior, were successfully reintegrated; for the rest, there was stigmatization or, at worst, social death. For people in Koinadugu District, 'the bush' is a serious matter. The bush is in a dialectical relationship with the town and the village; they are opposed yet define each other. Formerly abducted women had no prestige or position of status in postwar society, and of course, stigma is the negative reciprocal of prestige.

The same mechanisms and behavior that enabled girls to survive the war, that made them independent and strong, often became a problem when they returned home, and therefore also often hindered their reintegration. Susan McKay, a psychologist with extensive experience in working with girls in war-torn societies, writes that abducted girls in Sierra Leone 'learned how to survive during the conflict' but states that this same survival mechanism often interfered with their reintegration (2004, 25). 'Girls who were in a fighting force for a long time may deviate seriously from the norm in terms of their behavior: they may be aggressive and quarrelsome, use offensive language, abuse drugs, smoke, and kill and eat other people's animals (ibid.), and in her work with female ex-combatants, Mariam Persson (2005, 38) found that many were suffering from behavioral problems, they would become aggressive and were often accused of 'behaving like men.'

In the area where I did most of my fieldwork, ideal female behavior included subservience to elders, being humble, refraining from shouting or using foul language, and showing restraint in the display of emotion, whether it be pain or anger. All these examples were key elements in the socialization of women in this setting. 'Rebel behavior' contrasted with these 'traditional' ideals, and female ex-combatants and abductees were made to understand that through their *abnormal*, bushlike, and antisocial behavior they shamed their families. This was communicated through physical and social isolation. My informants described situations that demonstrate how they were severed from the flows of social reciprocity, from information, and from participation in communal activities. One woman described how her mother got up and left as soon as she sat down next to her, how her younger siblings refused to do errands for her, and how she was refused food. Other women described how they were treated like the children they had been when they left, not like the grown up women they had become. For some female ex-fighters, it seemed that it did not matter what they did, they were always reminded by others of their rebel past. As one of Persson's informants expressed it, 'In their eyes we will always be rebels' (2005, 33).

There was little doubt that these women's involvement with the rebels in general and as fighters in particular, constituted a break with the way they had been brought up, and with the values of their society and culture. A prevalent attitude among people I met, whether in towns or in villages, was that 'rebel women' were maltreated because they did not *behave* in a morally accepted manner. People would say that these women and girls were 'not used to village life' but to 'that free life with the rebels,' and that 'they don't know how to talk to people,' or that 'they don't know how to behave.' There was also that lingering threat or suspicion that they, especially those who had been fighters, might do something rash or uncontrolled. Whenever there was an argument involving one of my informants, I noticed that everyone was quick to condemn them for their 'rebel behavior,' whatever the nature of the argument.

The unacceptable wildness of women

Whereas humanitarians saw the abducted women as innocent victims, their families perceived them as potentially dangerous. The notion of 'the innocent victim,' then, in many ways challenged local idioms of shameful behavior. Many people associated the rebels with the bush, they were wild and sometimes seen as nonhuman. The people they abducted became, by association, wild and nonhuman too. This concerned not only their social behavior but also to some extent, at least implicitly, their having been sexually active; both were seen as a direct result of their having spent a long time in the bush. It was believed that this experience had changed them radically in ways not acceptable to families and communities.

Women being seen as wild, uncontrolled, and unpredictable, however, has precedence in prewar society (cf. Ferme 2001, 62) and was one of the reasons why women have to be 'domesticated.' Older women actually told me that the purpose of female circumcision was to calm and control women's wildness. There are few models against which to measure the status and position of female ex-fighters. Most of the women I met did not conform to the cultural notion of 'big women'. Still there are other variables that are comparable. Because just as big women have been described as morally ambivalent, uncontrollable, and as making difficult wives, so too are female ex-fighters and bush wives viewed as confounding norms of ideal feminine or wifely behavior. Although bush wives were not supposed to possess secret knowledge and practice as did traditional big women, one might assume that the experiences of the bush might in equal terms have elicited 'an excess of respect and fear in others' (Ferme 2001, 160, on big women).

Although I have focused almost exclusively on women, it was apparent that there were differences in how female and male ex-combatants were received and reintegrated into postwar society. In Kabala where I lived, I did observe that although most people knew who had been a male combatant or not, such men were not ostracized in the same way as women. People might be frightened of them, and might talk about them when they were not present, but in general they were tolerated. One reason could be that, as opposed to most female fighters, most male fighters had demobilized and had been given vocational training, supplies, and money, and thereby respect and legitimacy. After the war, while returning boys and men seemed to be considered a valuable addition to the native household economy, women were perceived as unproductive and were not, like men, regarded as potential contributors. Male ex-combatants were also high on the priority lists of both government and aid agencies, as they were perceived to be a real threat to peace and stability, and therefore their containment and reintegration became a prime concern.

However, another reason was definitely the issue of morality. To quote Susan Shepler, 'Girls face an explicitly *moral* discourse about their participation in war' (2002, 1; see also Persson 2005, 16) in ways much different from boys. As in prewar Sierra Leone, men's sexuality was never a sensitive issue in postwar society; on the contrary, it was to be expected, and it reinforced their masculinity. The moral discourse surrounding women's participation in the war was very different from that surrounding men's. In a study on child ex-combatants in Sierra Leone, it was noted that whereas almost all boys expected to be welcomed back by their families, only half of the girls thought that their families would be happy to have them back (Bennett 2002, 46).

Former bush wives were generally looked on with suspicion and distrust. Some women were nonetheless able to reverse their initial position of social uncertainty and ambiguity, and there were ways women could maneuver around these sentiments of suspicion. The most obvious was that many women (and their families) never openly admitted that they had been abducted, saying that they had been displaced or had become refugees, or downplayed the length of abduction. It seemed that people were generally more distrustful of a woman who had spent many years with the rebels. Many of my informants thus tried to keep their wartime experiences secret for fear of people's finding out about the full extent of their rebel past (see also Persson 2005, 21). By completely conforming to social rules and obligations, former bush wives and female ex-combatants could be accepted as full members of their communities. However, this did not apply to all women. Some informants said that even if they tried to conform to social and cultural norms, they were still socially excluded. In Kabala there were also a few women who could not or would not conform. According to informants, these women had been normal before the war but after they returned home behaved as if they were crazy (*dem craze*); they wore disheveled and unkempt clothes, had dirty and nappy hair, they drank alcohol, were aggressive, and cursed and insulted people. Women like this were not believed to be possessed, a condition which it was believed could be locally cured, but they had been 'damaged' by the war in a way that people could not understand or explain. NGOs would say that they were traumatized, but this word meant little to the people I talked to.

In the early postwar period in Kabala, the hospital was run by Médecins Sans Frontièrs (MSF), and it distributed legal drugs that were sometimes used to control deviant behavior. In another work I have described how one woman told how she had been helped during her vocational training with her behavioral problems (Coulter 2009). She said, 'I was only idle, they were giving me medicines, I was very aggressive, but now I know how to be humble. They have removed wickedness from me.' And a local NGO worker told me that in their project for war-affected women, some girls would suddenly start shouting in class, and 'they will become crazy, so we will take them to hospital, where they sedate them.' This excessive display of uncontrolled behavior was often seen as unnatural and something that was discouraged and, if necessary, controlled by medical substances.

There were those in the communities who were more tolerant, however, who saw this type of 'wild' behavior among abducted girls as a result of the drug abuse they had been subjected to and of their experiences while with the rebels, and saw these emotional outbursts as something to be expected initially. But for those girls and women who, a couple of years after the end of the war, would still become aggressive and 'quarrelsome,' little tolerance was shown. Some women who had returned home eventually decided to leave, as life had become too difficult for them. Many lacked viable livelihood opportunities and many others found that they had changed so profoundly that they could not or would not adapt to their communities (cf. McKay and Mazurana 2004, 37).

In some cases, it seemed that the past experiences of my informants could be, if not forgiven, then simply and conveniently 'forgotten.' It was not only the actual events and experiences of war per se that members of families and communities reacted against, it was their permutation into postwar life—their intrusion in the present—which was problematic. To some extent, then, as long as an abducted girl or woman, fighter or not, behaved well and complied with 'traditional' norms, and the effects of her wartime experiences were not too obvious, people were more inclined to accept her. This is not uncommon in war-torn societies, and Schroven noted that 'many people wish to return to 'traditional' notions of social interaction, opposing the war's chaos and instead seeking stability and a familiar order' (2005, 87). Getting married was often seen as a solution to many of the problems surrounding abducted young women and female ex-combatants in postwar society. For girls, marriage was seen as solving the problem of reintegration in a way that was unavailable to boys (Shepler 2002, 13). It was assumed that through marriage they would become more honorable and would be kept busy with the chores of domestic life. In other words, marriage was seen for many abducted girls and women as the only viable option and the only way to reintegrate, yet this proved to be difficult, as few families wanted 'rebel women.'[2] This may be related to the fact that men and their families knew that abducted women had been sexually active during the war; rebel women were 'damaged goods.' That marriage, and not other means, was the preferred solution to a social problem can most likely be related to the fact that marriage, not education or work, has been the dominant trajectory in the lives of girls and women. Shepler noted that some NGOs even 'encouraged girls to marry their former commanders and captors' (2002, 14).

Of victims and wives

Many women were so unhappy with their postwar lives that they often spoke of returning to their bush husbands. One young woman I met, Finda, continued to meet her bush husband in secret, as her parents had told him not to come to their house. When I asked her why she was still seeing him, she replied, 'Because no one loves me again, and for the children.' Like many others in similar situations, many of my informants found that their parents and community did not accept their bush husbands and therefore they could not formalize these relationships. Although these women were called 'wives' and their relationships with their men were called 'marriages,' these were prefixed by 'bush' and as such were not culturally valid, since they had not been negotiated or sanctioned by family or community. The 'transfer' of these girls and women to their so-called husbands had not been legitimate: they had been abducted, and remunerations to the girls' and women's families had been made neither for the emotional loss of a family member nor for their reproductive and productive labor, as is customary in 'traditional' society. Schroven notes that the terms *bush wives* and *bush marriages*, 'related the origin of the marriage to the bush, and were therefore "uncivilized," "unregulated" and also implied rebel associations. As such they had not been sanctioned and were therefore often considered "un-approvable"' (2005, 76). Bush marriages were not proper marriages, as Mariatu so emphatically pointed out, somewhat upset by my question about it:

> Is that marriage? That type of marriage was to pass time. If it should have been me, as the country is cool [at peace], I should have said, 'I don't love you any longer.' This is because one day, as you were in the bush, one day he will treat you that way. In the bush, as I was with him, it was to save my life, [for him] not to kill me. But now, I know that when he kills me, they will kill him. So I will say, 'I don't want you.' But some [abducted women] are with them, giving birth to children for them. Some, up to now, they are not thinking of their relatives.

Despite the obvious brutalities of and suffering in war, some of my informants felt that life in the bush had not been that bad, especially favored wives of rebel commanders, who had lives of relative wealth during the war (cf. McKay and Mazurana 2004, 93). Looting also seemed to be a reason 'why some women stayed in the movement: in a society which had so depri-ved them, they knew that they would never get the opportunity to earn legally a fraction of their gain from raiding and looting towns and villages' (Mansaray 2000, 146). These women often did not like the prospect of a return to impoverished communities. Their elevated status during the war did not translate into prestige in postwar society, and many were very disappoin-ted with their situation. Not only did they not or could they not disarm, they were frequently abandoned by their bush husbands and ostracized in the communities they returned to. One of Persson's informants told her, 'In a way life was easier in the bush, I was the wife of a commander and people respected me for that. Now I have to live with people calling me bad names and mistrusting me, I have to bear the shame of having been a rebel' (2005, 42). Considering the hardships many women experienced in postwar society, it is not surprising that some of them became nostalgic for, or idealized, the past. These feelings were also infused with ambiguity, as they were just as ashamed to admit having enjoyed the war as they were of having been in it. But there were also those like Musu who were happy that the war was over but still did not want to return to a 'traditional' way of life.

Given the hardship many of my informants encountered when they returned home after the war, it is not surprising that some of them decided to leave. There were those who thought that it had not even been worth coming back. There were many instances where girls went back to their bush husbands after they had been reunited with their families.[3] For some it seems that leaving their village was less a choice than a necessity, and the return to a bush husband sometimes had less to do with love and loyalty to him, than that village life had been unbearable due to harassment and provocation, or sometimes just poverty. In Persson's words, 'To stay meant to every day have to face those who knew their past and that blamed them for their losses and suffering. It meant constant stigmatization and rejection' (2005, 33). I have also mentioned Kadi, she who at the age of nine was abducted by the rebels and had stayed with them for six years. Kadi was her mother's youngest child, around 16 years at the time of my fieldwork. She had a baby daughter with her bush husband, and she was waiting for him to send a message for her to join him in the soldiers' barracks in the town where he was stationed after being recruited by the new army. Kadi said she still loved her bush husband, although he had first deserted her when she became pregnant. Kadi's father had died, her brothers had all left Kabala to look for work in Freetown, and she lived with her mother, sisters, and other female in-laws. Kadi's mother had been dead set against the marriage between Kadi and her bush husband and made it clear that she had not accepted the marriage, but being poor and unable to provide for Kadi and her young child, she realized that she had little to bargain with, and silently, but still reproachfully, let Kadi leave for her husband when he finally sent for her. I drove Kadi myself to Makeni, where she was to take transport to the town where her bush husband lived. She wore her nicest clothes and seemed happy but also a little subdued; she talked little during the trip. Some time before her departure, I had arranged for her to go to school and had also given her a school uniform and some books. She had tried for a couple of months, and I believe she also really wanted to please me, but she found it hard to return to school and told me with some difficulty that she wanted to quit. In the circumstances she was facing, returning to her bush husband was one of the few options she could envisage, and she took it.

To sum up, some of the women I interviewed said that they loved their bush husbands and felt grateful to them for saving their lives during the war. Others said that they had few prospects of getting another husband and that at least the bush husband, if he had disarmed, had received some sort of vocational training with some hope of getting work and money. However, what in the case of the women who wanted to formalize their marriages with their bush husbands but had families that would not sanction this relationship? There are still many girls and young women who feel that these relationships should be formalized and accepted by their families because, the alternative, leaving parents and family to live with a man who has been rejected, has great social ramifications, especially if they live in the same community. Girls and women risk facing a complete break in social relations with their kin in such situations, thereby severely limiting their ability to negotiate their position in relation to a husband or, alternatively, his kin. They have nowhere to turn if the marriage fails, and the relationship for future generations is permanently severed. As I have mentioned, after marriage most women have frequent contact with their families. In most cases, the young women, their families, and also their former bush husbands would try to settle disputes by all possible means, through religious leaders, chiefs, and so-called 'mamy queens,' or through mediation by other relatives or family members, before resorting to actions that would, at worst, mean social exclusion. My research shows that it was not only the rebel abduction itself that defined the status of abducted women and female ex-combatants in postwar society but also *how* they behaved after returning to their communities. It was clear that in assuming traditional female behavior like subservience and humbleness, and in some cases religiosity, many formerly abducted women improved their status in postwar society and were less discriminated against in everyday social life. However, for some this came at a high cost and was far from easy.

Concluding remarks

In this article I have focused on issues concerning the relationships between abducted girls and the families and communities they returned to. In Sierra Leone, peace did not entail a return to normalcy, and although many had suffered throughout the war, peace did not necessarily mean the end of violence and abuse for many rebel women. Many were afraid to return home, fearing rejection by their families and communities. With good reason, they were afraid of being punished for returning with rebel children, for not being virgins, and for being called rebels. The women they had become were very different from the girls they had been when they were abducted. In postwar society many people were very suspicious of ex-rebels and distrusted them, and abducted women were not exempted.

Although many women were later stigmatized for having been raped, some were not, and although many women were viewed with suspicion for having fought with the rebels, again, others were not. Many people were disturbed by the fact that female fighters had killed and engaged in other brutal acts, and this characterized the way they viewed these women in postwar society, but others just shrugged and explained that a lot of bad things happened during the war, this was nothing exceptional. The postwar consequences of war rapes in Sierra Leone differed immensely from Bosnia, for example, where most families would shun their raped daughters because of permanent damage to the family honor (Olujic 1998). Even so, because rape was still seen in Sierra Leone as shameful for the victim, especially if she had been a virgin, most abducted women who tried to fit into society kept experiences of sexual abuse a secret. The way people in the communities interpreted war rapes, was grounded in preexisting notions of rape and sexual morality. As I have argued consistently, Sierra Leone is a country full of diversity and contradiction, and some of my informants who had been abducted, virginated, and had been fighters still managed to acclimatize well into postwar society, if they managed to conform to cultural conventions of feminine behavior, and if their social circumstances and the composition of their household were such as to make this change possible.

References

Bennett, Allison. 2002. The reintegration of child ex-combatants in Sierra Leone with a particular focus on the needs of females. Unpublished MA dissertation, University of East London.

Bunting, Annie. 2005. Stages of development: Marriage of girls and teens as an international human rights issue. *Social & Legal Studies* 14 (1):17-38.

Coulter, Chris. 2009. *Bush wives and girls soldiers: Women's lives through war and peace in Sierra Leone.* Ithaca: Cornell University Press.

Ferme, Mariane C. 2001. *The underneath of things: Violence, history, and the everyday in Sierra Leone.* Berkeley: University of California Press.

Mansaray, Binta. 2000. Women against weapons: A leading role for women in disarmament. In *Bound to cooperate: Conflict, peace and people in Sierra Leone*, edited by A. Ayissi and R.-E. Poulton, 139-162. Geneva: United Nations Institute for Disarmament Research.

McKay, Susan. 2004. Reconstructing fragile lives: Girls' Social Reintegration in Northern Uganda and Sierra Leone. *Gender and Development* 12(3):19-30.

McKay, Susan, and Dyan Mazurana. 2004. *Where are the girls? Girls in fighting forces in Northern Uganda, Sierra Leone and Mozambique: Their lives during and after war.* Quebec: Rights & Democracy.

Olujic, Maria B. 1998. Embodiment of terror: Gendered violence in peacetime and wartime in Croatia and Bosnia-Herzegovina. *Medical Anthropology Quarterly* 12 (1):31-50.

Persson, Mariam. 2005. *'In their eyes we'll always be rebels' – A minor field study of female ex-combatants in Sierra Leone.* Uppsala: Uppsala University, Developments Studies.

Richards, Paul. 2005. Green book millenarians? The Sierra Leone War within the perspective of an anthropology of religion. In *Religion and African civil wars*, edited by N. Kastfelt. London: Hurst & Company.

Shepler, Susan. 2002. Post-war trajectories for firls associated with the fighting forces in Sierra Leone. (English language version of Les Filles-Soldats: Trajectoires d'apres-guerre en Sierra Leone, originally published in *Politique Africaine* 88: 49-62).

Schroven, Anita. 2005. Choosing between different realities: Gender mainstreaming and self-images of women after armed conflict in Sierra Leone. M.A. thesis, Georg-August-Universität.

Notes

[1] This article is based on the chapter 'Coming Home—Domesticating the Bush' in my book *Bush Wives and Girl Soldiers* published by Cornell University Press 2009.

[2] A Sierra Leonean friend of Shepler's told her that he definitely did not want such a girl married into his family and suggested instead that 'rebel boys and girls should be married to each other, then there would be no stigma' (as quoted by Shepler 2002, 14).

[3] In a reunification program in the district of Kono, the organization International Rescue Committee (IRC) reported that it had reunited 196 girls and young women with their families. They had been provided with a 'reunification package' consisting of blankets, buckets, and other household utensils, and the families and the returning girls had been 'sensitized' to ameliorate the process. Despite this, after a few months, as many as 157 girls had left their families and either returned to a bush husband or gone to live with friends in urban areas. According to IRC social workers, many of these girls and young women 'just couldn't cope with the family situation or village life' (Interview with IRC Child Protection Unit, Kono, 11 August 2004).

7

The Acholi Worldview

Why Rituals Are Important for the Reintegration
of Formerly Recruited Girls in Northern Uganda

Christine Mbabazi Mpyangu
School of Mission and Theology, Stavanger, Norway
Makerere University, Kampala, Uganda

Abstract
This article explores the Acholi worldview and social structure as a framework for rituals used in the process of reintegration of formerly recruited girls in northern Uganda by the Lord's Resistance Army. It focuses in particular on the Acholi beliefs and practices, the Acholi social structure and lays emphasis on the role of the clan leader as well as the family. It contributes by elucidating them and revealing how they relate to the practical tasks of reintegration. This article makes a contribution by offering an ethnographic analysis showing how beliefs and practices influence the reintegration process. It further identifies key actors who ought to be consulted and included in any work on reintegration. Any effort towards reintegration should heed the Acholi worldview.

Introduction

Northern Uganda is in the process of reintegrating people back to their communities having been scattered in different places during the insurgency in the last two decades. This article is concerned with the female children that were abducted by the Lord's Resistance Army (LRA) and used as soldiers. My focus is on formerly recruited girls who have either been rescued or have escaped and are now trying to settle down in the community. To be able to reunite with families and the community, these girls have to go through certain rituals. What is it that convinces the girls, their families and the communities that rituals are so important that they must be performed? My thesis is that there must be elements that form part and parcel of the Acholi worldview which impel them to perform such rituals. The question to be dealt with here is why do the Acholi of northern Uganda deem it necessary to conduct rituals especially with regard to the reintegration of formerly abducted female children?

The article follows an anthropological analysis. The interconnectedness between the Acholi beliefs, practices, social structure and the necessity for the performance of rituals points to the idea that rituals performed in the process of reintegration are founded in a nexus of relations which form part and parcel of the Acholi worldview. In other words, the rituals used do not just emerge, they are well known to the performers and they serve to maintain both social and cosmological order of the community.

The purpose of this article, therefore, is to contribute to the understanding of the significance of Acholi cultural beliefs and practices in the process of reintegration of formerly recruited girls in northern Uganda. In the article, I will briefly mention who the Acholi are, some important Acholi beliefs and practices and the Acholi social structure.

Under social structure, I will underscore the role of the clan leader as well as the family in the process of reintegration with special regard to the performance of rituals. The family plays a vital social, cultural and economic role in the returning and reintegration of the female former child combatants.

This will then be followed by some conclusive remarks which point to the fact that designers of reintegration programmes ought to take into account the Acholi cultural practices, in order to be appropriate, effective and relevant. The article reveals that cultural beliefs and practices are widely used by Acholi people and they see them as key for re-entry into the community. Unfortunately, these beliefs and practices have often been marginalised in official reintegration programmes, which is inappropriate because a people's culture influences their perception of various issues of their lives profoundly. It is upon that backdrop that I deemed it necessary to analyse some of these cultural beliefs and practices.

This article is based on an ethnographic fieldwork that took place in 2008 and 2009 respectively. In the first field study, I spent two weeks in Gulu collecting data concerning the place and role of rituals in the process of reintegration. I conducted in-depth interviews with fourteen formerly recruited girls, six community elders, eight social workers and one religious leader. Insight was gained through participatory observation, when I went and witnessed the 'stepping of the egg ritual' of one boy who had spent twelve years in the bush. This was particularly important for me because ten out of the fourteen girls that I interviewed had told me that they had stepped on the egg, which is a re-entry ritual to the community. These interviews were held in different places such as homes of formerly recruited girls. This enabled me to see for myself the living environment of some of the girls, which would aid my analysis of the reintegration process. The Acholi community elders were interviewed either from home or in an office; most social workers however were interviewed from their offices.

In the second field work, I followed up two female formerly recruited children; Loretta and Rosette. Both of them went through rituals when they returned to their families. The purpose of following them up was to capture their perceptions on the efficacy of rituals in the process of reintegration. This was to be a good starting point in the analysis of rituals and their bearing towards reintegration. Again I participated in observing two more rituals which included the burial of bones of one found dead in a given area in Amuru district. (I understood that the burial of bones was widely being done since people were returning to their villages from the IDP camps and so they would not be settled because of *cen*, an angry spirit haunting the living for not having given the deceased a decent burial). The other ritual had to do with the cleansing of the land (*moyo cer*) in order to appease and petition the ancestors for blessings of peace and fecundity upon their land.

Who are the Acholi?

The Acholi are an ethno-linguistic group of the upper Nile Valley which dwells on the East Bank of the Bahrel-Gazel about a hundred miles North of Lake Albert. The Acholi in Uganda live predominantly in the districts of Gulu, Kitgum, Pader and Amuru, a region commonly known as, Acholi-land. The Acholi are kin to the Shilluks of the White Nile, the Alur of West Nile, and the Jopadhola of eastern Uganda as well as the Luo of Kenya.

One elder interviewed in Gulu district described the origin of the Acholi in the following way: "The Acholi people came from Sudan and our grandfather was Shilluk during their migration, they went to Bunyoro, and the others, the Luo of Kenya and the rest remained here, hence the Acholi land" (Interview 2008). There seems to be agreement that the Acholi came from Sudan and that they belong to the Luo group. The Acholi community currently could be faced with several questions regarding their identity as Thomas Harlacher (Harlacher et al. 2006, 24) noted, "In times of war and social disruption, the identity of a people is often both questioned and emphasized by themselves and the people around them." Collective identity is very important yet paradoxical because it can create resilience as well as collective fatalism or a sense of resignation. Nonetheless, it is important to know who the Acholi are as we attempt to discuss the environment in which rituals are performed in relation to the reintegration of the female ex-child soldiers. The best way of identifying the Acholi is to investigate their world-view, including their beliefs, practices and rituals as well as their social structure and clan system. I will start by exploring the former, then turning to the latter.

Why the Acholi worldview is important

Worldview is a term coined from "the German word *Weltanschauung. Welt* is the German word for 'world' and *Anschauung* is the German word for 'view' or 'outlook' (…). Additionally it refers to the framework of ideas and beliefs through which an individual interprets the world and interacts with it" (http://en.wikipedia.org/wiki/World_view; accessed 25 February, 2009). The Acholi have a worldview that influences the way they interact with what surrounds them, and even shapes their views of war and conflict. They have cherished beliefs, practices and a social structure which greatly impacts their interpretation of what is good or bad, clean or dirty, and consequently leads them to create order as required, as is the case with the necessity to perform rituals.

It is important to consider the Acholi worldview in order to understand how Acholi communities receive and take steps to support the reintegration of formerly recruited girls. The Acholi for instance have a clear perception regarding rituals since they know why it is so important for one to perform them. If one thinks of a worldview as an explanation and interpretation of the world as well as an application of this view to life, then it becomes important to examine the explanation and interpretation of the Acholi regarding their rituals and moreover what they think will be the most succinct and understandable explanation. This therefore, implies that what the Acholi think or perceive of rituals in the process of reintegration will have a great impact on the process of reintegration of formerly recruited girls, in Northern Uganda.

Worldviews form a component of our lives that we see and hear them daily. What the Acholi, say, perceive and do everyday shape their view of life. According to Lisa Schirch of Eastern Mennonite University, "Worldviews are shaped by five interacting elements; perception, emotional sensual cognition, culture, values and identity" (2005, 39). Perception has to do with how people make sense of their experiences and ascribe them meaning.

During my field research in northern Uganda, I was concerned with how people perceived the use of rituals in the process of reintegration because this perception has great implication for the extent to which they think rituals can aid the female ex-child combatants to settle down in the community. For instance formerly recruited girl children interpret their experiences in captivity and attribute meaning to them. Such experiences as forced marriage, sexual violence, killing, giving birth from the bush, hunger etc have left everlasting marks on their lives and may have profound effects on the way they view life. This will in turn have consequences for the interpretation they have of the role of rituals performed as they return to the community. Perception is dialectical because in Acholi land, the elders, the female ex-child combatants and the rest of the people may have different perceptions of rituals. By dialectical I mean the different levels of perception by the different parties in the Acholi community. Where as the various elements that shape worldviews are important I deem perception central because it is at the core of any worldview as people search for meaning and that is why in this article I have chosen to further reflect upon it.

Beliefs and practices of the Acholi

If Acholi rituals are an enactment of their beliefs, what then are these beliefs? The Acholi believe in *Jok*, and Heike Behrend in her work *Alice Lakwena and the Holy Spirits* notes that "*Jok* can be translated as spirit, force or power" (1999, 106). Stephen Arthur Lamony (n.d.) in a working paper observed that "The Acholi belief is concrete, local and powerfully existential." The Supreme Being in whom they believe is *Jok-kene* or *Rubanga*. *Jok-kene* is not some deity who lives up there and has nothing to do with the lives of people. This implies that *Jok-kene* is close to the Acholi, lives among them and is involved in their daily lives.

However Jok can do both good and evil. There are many different *Jogi* ('spirits-'plural of *Jok*) who reside in specific abodes such as rivers, rocky outcrops, mountains, forests etc. For instance each clan has its own *Jok* or *Jogi* which it depended upon for success in agriculture, hunting and in times of war. Many Acholi still believe in the power and presence of *Jok*, even if their understanding of *Jok* has been transformed through the adoption of external religious beliefs. Thus Jacan Ngomlokojo Jalobo says that "the pendulum of beliefs among the Acholi (…) keep swinging from traditional African to either Christianity, Islam and vice-versa, depending on how natural calamities visit an individual in a society" (1999, 1-2).

In the current context in northern Uganda, the concept of *cen* is being discussed because it seems to impact negatively on the Acholi community in light of the war. Usually in conflict and post conflict zones people complain about hunger, mortality rate, diseases, poverty, homelessness and much more, but northern Uganda is concerned about the angry spirits of those who were killed during the insurgency and were never buried. The *cen* is believed to have harmful effects, if not appeased. Liu Institute in their report "Roco wat I Acholi; Restoring Relationships in Acholi-Land: Traditional Approaches to Justice and Reintegration" noted that *Cen* is understood as the "entrance of an angry spirit into the physical body of a person or persons that seeks appeasement, usually in form of a sacrifice in case of a wrongful death, compensation and reconciliation between the clan of the offended and offender" (2005, 12).

The spirit manifests itself as *cen* and haunts people who have done wrong by entering their mind or body in form of visions and nightmares that may result in mental illness and sickness until the wrong is put right. According to Tim Allen, "many Acholi believe in *cen* (a polluting spiritual force), which afflicts those exposed to violent death with nightmares and illnesses" (2006, 55). It is this belief in an angry or polluting spiritual force which urges families to perform rituals to cleanse the girls when they return home, so that they and the rest of the family will not be disturbed. The SWAY Report (2006, 17) found out that "the collective understanding of cen is that it can spread from one person to another polluting a family or community." This finding further elucidates the centrality of cleansing the girls when they return to the community.

In Alero Sub County for example bones of the dead were buried and the person who saw them first had sleepless nights because he believed that *cen* was responsible for that situation. This is in line with what the study by Liu Institute reveals, namely that "*cen* can gather in places where a person's death occurred, and enter one who moves through this place" (2005, 12). They go on to explain that

> treatment of the dead and dying are central processes and practices in Acholi for example if one dies in a bad way (…) the spirit of the dead will not rest or will actually seek to correct the wrong committed in the form of *cen*. As a result elaborate burial and funeral rituals and ceremonies have evolved to show respect to the dead, and are considered vital to maintain the well being of the clan.

This explains why the Acholi of northern Uganda are currently carrying out *moyo ce*r (cleansing a vast land) which is an ancient ritual intended to cleanse the land of evil spirits or bad omen. For example on the 23 January 2009, I witnessed burial of bones of one found dead in the Pabwo area, who was buried by the *Bwobo* clan.

This is done to ensure the well-being of the people because they believe that when *cen* disturbs them, they scream, they become violent and cannot rest. For example if a young girl returns to the community having stayed in the bush for years and finds that the community has got an interpretation of death and killing she will be asked to perform certain rituals because the people believe in their power to cleanse her. My field findings reveal that, most of the female ex-child soldiers have killed, witnessed many being killed, or stumbled over dead bodies and are therefore susceptible to *cen*, which can only be dealt with by the performance of certain rituals.

An Acholi informant who worked with Gulu Support the Children Organisation for seven years contended in an interview that "among the Acholi the spirit world is a reality" (Interview 2009). In the traditional Acholi belief system, things do not just happen, there is an explanation for every occurrence, and there are spiritual means of redress. The female ex-child soldiers will be told for example how the culture of the Acholi deals with killing and this will occasion the performance of a given ritual.

It is on this background that the girls formerly associated with the armed group have to be aware of the fact that if they have killed, or touched dead bodies, they are unclean and ought to be cleansed. Not only have they offended others but the spirits of the dead will haunt them, because they believe that the spirits of the dead, if not appeased, will harm their families and the communities. For purification and in order to escape the haunting spirits they must go through special rituals to enable them to reintegrate in family and society. A key part of the belief system (as I understand it) is also that there is a system of dual obligation. The living are obligated to practice the rituals when spiritual harmony has been destroyed (as occurs when living people touch the dead), and in turn the ancestors in the spirit world are obligated to protect those who practice the rituals and demonstrate appropriate respect. To not conduct a ritual when one is needed leads the ancestors to withdraw their protection, allowing *cen* to cause harm.

For the Acholi, then, the notion of social and cosmological order is the main factor behind whatever they consider good or bad, right or wrong, sacred or, profane, pointing to the fact that their well-being is connected to nature, spirits as well as human relations. These relations do influence social interaction and therefore if someone has killed another, then a ritual has to be performed to restore relations not only between the killer and the bereaved family but also between the clan of the killer and the spirits who may get angry and strike hard at the family or the *cen* which may inflict serious pain on the family and clan at large. Even Jalobo maintained that "The Acholi also had the notion of what was profane and sacrilegious and from time to time, sought the appropriate advice of the diviner *ajwaka* in cases of misfortune, miseries and all sorts of evils (…)" (1999, 3). Thus, Acholi people have a complex spirituality which leads them to see rituals as a necessary part of the reintegration process.

The use of rituals in the reintegration of female formerly abducted children is paramount. This view is shared by Fiona Shanahan and Angela Veale in this book, in their article "The Girl is the Core of Life': Social Reintegration, Communal Violence and the Sacred in Northern Uganda," under the theme "Cultural Resources in mediating reintegration." They see rituals as cultural tools in enhancing the reintegration of female formerly recruited children. I have in this article, also argued that rituals are a valuable practice of the Acholi, well embedded in their worldview and unquestionably significant in the process of reintegration.

The Acholi social structure and the clan system

This section seeks to address the social structure of the Acholi community, the importance of which is to establish the way the Acholi people interact and whether that interaction has any impact on how rituals are performed and why they are performed.

The existence of a social structure is a fundamental and necessary feature of any given human society. "It is evolved not only to impact on certain conceptions of human nature but, also to provide a framework for both the realisation of the potential, goals, and hopes of the individual members of society and the continuous existence and survival of society" (Gyekye 1998, 45). Communities in the world are organised differently, some are hierarchical and others are egalitarian. It is through understanding the structure of the Acholi community that we can get to know who the actors and agents are and who exactly influence social action in this very society. It is my contention that the actors in this society, particularly, the clan elders, chiefs, family heads have an important role to play in the return and settling down of all formerly abducted persons especially the female ex-child soldiers.

The Acholi community has got a strong clan system where every individual finds belonging, for instance the Lamogi and the Bwobo clans. All these clans have got chiefs commonly referred to as *rwodi*. All the clans together have an overall leader known as the paramount chief of the Acholi. He is the overseer of all the clans and the other elders report to him. The family is an important component in the social structure because it plays a significant role in reintegration of former child combatants. If the family is receptive and helpful, the returning child will feel secure and accepted and this will generate confidence for that child to live with others in the society.

In the category of elders it is the clan leader who is most important when it comes to the discussion on rituals and under the Acholi social structure I have treated him as a social actor and an authority in matters pertaining to rituals.

The clan leader as a social actor and an authority on ritual phenomena

A clan elder is referred to by the Acholi as *ladit kaka* and a clan is called *kaka*. The clan system including its leader is important to understand if we are to grasp its social impact on the Acholi identity. One's clan was significant even in pre-colonial times when "there was no real Acholi ethnic identity, but only various clan identities, which determined one's belonging to a territory and political unit, the chiefdom" (Behrend 1999, 16).

An important role of the clan leader is to organize people for rituals and sometimes even preside at their performance. Normally, however, it is the clan elder who presides. Most Acholi are interested in their traditional rituals and they understand them as communal practices than as individual events. This is evidenced by the large numbers of people that turn up to witness any kind of ritual taking place. For example many informants during my field study in Gulu district in February 2008, stated that they had gathered to the *rwot* palace to witness the rituals that were being performed for the returning former combatants. Most informants stated that they have never heard of any disputes arising from the issue of whether rituals should be performed or not, one even added that "you see everyone knows the importance of our rituals, so they go for them" (Interview 2009).

With this in mind it is naturally easy for the clan elder to organize the people for the rituals. The process of organizing for ritual may vary from one ritual to another depending on what is involved in the ritual itself. It is therefore the role of the clan elder to inform the clan members that a given ritual will take place, its purpose, venue and the parties involved, as well as what is required for the ceremony. It is again the clan elder that gives the instructions which will be followed during the ceremony.

On 23 January 2009, I witnessed the role of a clan leader in organizing for rituals. In Pubwo village in Alero Sub county, Amuru district, two ceremonies took place among Acholi belonging to the Bwobo clan. One ritual involved the burying of bones of one person found dead. The second rite involved the cleansing of the land occupied by that clan (*moyo cer*). In both ceremonies, there was evidence of prior preparation and organization. Both ceremonies involved a goat, a cock and two sheep which were used differently at the two rituals. Secondly, both rituals were presided over by the clan elder who said certain words before the ritual. For instance during the burial of bones, he said, "You, you died in a painful way, you were fighting, we do not know how it all happened and we do not know who killed you. But we as *Bwobo* clan, today, we choose to give you a decent burial, whoever killed you follow him or her but leave our clan free."

In his book *The Acholi my souvenir,* Jalobo notes that "one of the most important roles of an Acholi clan elder was officiating at and presiding over all functions and rituals pertaining to Ancestral worship" (1999, 66). This I noticed also during the field study in Gulu. Many informants, when asked who was responsible for the performance of rituals would answer that it is the elders and especially the clan leader (*ladit kaka*). Allen, in his work *Trial Justice*, made a similar point when he interviewed an individual on who ought to perform a certain ritual *"Can the Rwot of Payira perform mato oput and other healing ceremonies? No, that has to be done by the elders of each clan [kaka]"* (2006, 154).

Here the response implied that ritual activities are largely the work of the clan elder. For example, in the *moyo cer* rite, *ladit kaka* slaughtered the sheep to cleanse the clan and their entire area. And before slaughtering the animal he said. "You sheep, I give you to our elders (*ludito*), so that they may be happy with us at this moment. Let us not be disturbed by the spirits of the dead *(cen)*. Also let our women walk free, let them be fertile and produce children and let us live in peace."

It should be mentioned that in the context of reintegration a clan elder will be found extremely important to guide the clan members on what rituals to do and how they ought to be done. For instance, if one member of a clan killed a person from another clan deliberately or with malice aforethought, then an Acholi ritual of reconciliation will be organized and performed.

A clan elder is a prestigious social actor in Acholi community, especially with regard to the performance of rituals. Rituals are not mere routines; they are done with a purpose. Thus the report from the Liu Institute notes that *"ladit kaka* (elder) would conduct a series of rituals within village settings and household compounds in order to appease the ancestors and ensure that the moral order was upheld" (2005, 11).

A clan leader is an important personality in the life of all those returning to their homes because all people desire to belong to a family, and for the Acholi, a clan is a very important superstructure of the families. This is maintained again by the Liu Institute: "Historically, the good health and happiness of the Acholi individual was always situated in the context of the harmony and well-being of the clan" (2005, 10). It should be mentioned therefore that a clan *kaka* is an important environment for reintegration of the female ex-child soldier. Given the backdrop that most Acholi understand *kaka* as their point of belonging, in the performance of rituals to receive the female ex-child soldiers back and help them settle down in the community, it is vital to remember that they settle in a clan which spells out their identity.

Rituals were found to discernibly help in the reintegration of formerly recruited girls. In Gulu, for example, Rosette was formerly recruited by the LRA and returned home, then went through rituals. She told me in two different interviews that rituals had greatly enabled her to reintegrate in the community because the people related with her and her son well and that she felt forgiven and accepted. In Mozambique where child soldiers were reintegrated back to the community Alcinda Honwana noted that rituals had played a vital role in enabling the children reintegrate (Honwana 2006).

The role of the family in ritual performance in the process of reintegration

A family is the basic unit of the society and it is a vital environment for growth and development. For example among the Acholi they had what they call *Wang Oo* where all members of a family sat around the fire in the evening and the elders taught the young ones. It was during such moments that the family and clan core values were passed on from one generation to another. A family in Acholi is made up of the father, commonly referred to as *won-ot* and the mother who is called *min-ot,* as the children and other relatives such as grandparents, cousins. It is not strange among the Acholi to find a child growing up in an uncle's family.

If the family is such an important place to belong, then it is important to highlight the role it plays in the performance of rituals that are meant for reintegration. During the field study some of the female ex-child combatants said that their families were very supportive when they returned from the bush. Some girls said that they were received by their parents, especially the mothers and they "brought egg, *opobo* [a slippery twig used in the stepping of egg ritual] and *Layibi,* [a long stick used by the Acholi to open the granary where dry food crops especially grains such as beans, groundnuts sorghum, and millet are stored] stepped on them and then I entered the house" (Interview 2008) some said "my mother welcomed me, and bought me many clothes" (Interview 2008). Others prayed for their daughters, having received them back from captivity. A family is a very important component of the Acholi social structure; we cannot speak of reintegration proper if we do not look at the role of the family as it is an integrated part of the clan.

To begin with, the family welcomes the children back to the community and in most cases the welcome ceremony involves the performance of some rituals such as *nyono tongweno* (stepping on the egg) and this will usually involve the family members that the child finds at home as well as any other members of the community. The family members organize everything required for the ritual to be performed. Hence, it is vital to mention that the family is a fundamental environment for ritual action. Not only that but also the beliefs held by a given family will greatly influence the kind of rituals that will be done. For example some families only do the traditional rituals whereas other families mix what is Christian, such as prayer, with the traditional rituals.

Through the family the female ex-child soldiers receive forgiveness from their family members and the community at large, particularly after performing certain rituals. For instance, it is the family members that take the initiative to ask what the girls could have done while in the bush. One important question that is asked is, whether one killed. Then the rituals that cleanse those who have killed will be arranged and the perpetrator will ask for forgiveness. Subsequently they will try to settle down and find a place as civilians in the community.

The administrator at Gulu Support the Children Organisation said that one of the greatest tasks of the social workers was to look for or 'trace' the families of the children, identifying any family member surviving and establishing the exact relationship. Subsequently, they inform them that "your child is coming home." Thereafter a family reunion would be organized and it is the family that informs the clan members who in turn arrange for the ceremonies that have to do with the reintegration of a given female formerly recruited child.

The ability to conduct the rituals clearly depends on the families' financial capacity. Yet the wider reintegration process depends on many factors. Concerning rituals, it should be noted that money will be required to buy all that is needed for a given rite or ceremony. Moreover, most rituals conclude with a meal and that will involve buying what is enough for all those who will have gathered to witness the rituals. Many families are faced with very low incomes because of the aftermath of the war and so they face a great challenge when it comes to such ceremonies.

Conclusive remarks

Reintegration has typically been defined by outsiders who have not taken into account local cosmology and practices. Put bluntly, most reintegration planners and programmers do not think much about employing spiritually grounded methods of the kind that this article describes. This article shows how important it is to put at the centre local understandings, beliefs and practices.

The Acholi beliefs and practices, their social structure and particularly the position of the clan elder and the family do provide the bedrock for ritual performance in the process of reintegrating female ex-child soldiers in northern Uganda. Among the Acholi, the spirit world is a reality and so the notion of *cen* is critical because it directly relates with the current context of reintegration in which people are returning home after the prevalence of relative peace in the northern part of the country. The fear that surrounds the Acholi with regard to those who have killed, those who have died and have not been buried, and the consequences that follow, are responsible to a great extent for the performance of rituals that are believed to aid the process of reintegration in northern Uganda.

In this article I have underscored the position of the clan leader as a social actor and an authority in ritual matters and that he is charged with the duty of organising and presiding over all ritual activity and therefore fulfils an important condition of ensuring that the rituals do take place during this process.

The article also has highlighted the role of the family as an important one pointing out that it is the family that welcomes the children when they return and all the rituals whether traditional or Christian have their basis in a family. Besides, it is the family that has to find the money to buy all that is required for the rituals to take place. I noted also that it is the family that paves the way for forgiveness and consequently reconciliation with the community, by listening to the girls' stories such as the killing experiences. Then the relevant rituals are arranged and then performed which sets off the whole process of reintegration. It was noted also that the economic capacity of the family is an important issue when it comes to reintegration, given that money is required to be able to carry out most of the rituals.

References

Allen, Tim. 2006. *Trial justice: The International Criminal Court and the Lord's Resistance Army*. London: Zed Books.

Allen, Tim, and Mareike Schomerus. 2005. *A hard homecoming: Lessons learned from the reception centre process on effective interventions for former 'abductees' in northern Uganda*. Unpublished manuscript of study commissioned by UNICEF and USAID, Kampala.

Annan, Jeannie, Christopher, Blattman, and Roger Horton. 2006. The state of youth and youth protection in northern Uganda: Findings from the Survey for War Affected Youth (SWAY). UNICEF Uganda. Available at http://chrisblattman.com/documents/policy/sway/SWAY.Phase1.FinalRep ort.pdf, accessed 7 March 2010.

Behrend, Heike. 1999. *Alice Lakwena and the Holy Spirits. War in Northern Uganda 1986-97.* Oxford: James Currey.

Gyekye, Kwame. 1998. Person and community in African thought. In Coetzee, P. H and A.P.J. Roux, *African philosophy reader.* Routledge, London and New York.

Honwana, Alcinda. 2006. *Child soldiers in Africa.* Philadelphia, Pa.: University of Pennsylvania.

Jalobo, Jacan Ngomlokojo. 1999. *The Acholi my souvenir.* Kampala. Fountain Publishers.

Lamony, Stephen Arthur. n.d. *Approaching national reconciliation in Uganda: Perspectives on justice systems.* Kampala.

Liu Institute for Global Issues and Gulu District NGO Forum. 2005. Roco Wat I Acholi: Restoring relationships in Acholi-land: Traditional approaches to justice and reintegration. Vancouver, Canada, Liu Institute for Global issues. Available at: http://www.ligi.ubc.ca/?p2=modules/liu/publications/view.jsp&id=16.

Harlacher, Thomas, Francis Xavier Okot, Caroline Aloya Obonyo, Mychelle Balthazard, and Ronald Atkinson. 2006. *Traditional ways of coping in Acholi: Cultural provisions of reconciliation and healing from war.* Kampala: Intersoft Business Services Ltd.

McKay, Susan, and Dyan Mazurana. 2004. *Where are the girls? Girls in the fighting forces in Northern Uganda, Sierra Leone and Mozambique: Their Lives During and After the War,* Montreal: Rights and Democracy.

Schirch, Lisa. 2005. *Ritual and symbol in peacebuilding.* Bloomfield, Kumarian Press.

8

'The Girl Is the Core of Life'
Social Reintegration, Communal Violence and the Sacred in Northern Uganda

Fiona Shanahan and Angela Veale
University College Cork, Ireland

Abstract

This chapter explores diverse community perspectives related to girls and young women formerly associated with the Lord's Resistance Army, some of whom returned with children, in particular focusing on the use of cultural resources in social reintegration. The methodology consisted of in-depth interviews and focus group discussions with fifty participants—including Acholi Elders, Ajwakis (spiritual healers), local leaders and displaced never-abducted girls, women and men. A Grounded Theory analysis identified the following three categories; (1) Things Fall Apart—examining cultural constructions of 'girlhood' and the communal meanings of violence against girls, (2) Identity tensions presented by young mothers and their babies to the community of return, contributing to stigma enacted within specific social contexts and (3) The use of cultural resources in social reintegration. Culturally rooted community routines and practices are often overlooked but are central to a full understanding of social reintegration.

Introduction

Young women formerly associated with armed groups, in particular those who have returned with children born in captivity as a result of forced marriage have been identified as an extremely vulnerable group with regard to psychosocial reintegration (McKay and Mazurana 2004). Globally demobilization, disarmament and reintegration programming has traditionally underserved girls and young women (Keairns 2002; Verhey 2001) and young mothers have been found to have significant difficulties returning to education and training when compared to childless formerly-associated peers (Annan et al, 2008). Academic discourses concerned with this population have examined explanations for girl soldiering (Shepler 2004; Brett and Specht 2004; Annan and Blattman, 2008, Carlson and Mazurana, 2008), recruitment patterns (Verhey 2001; Paez 2001; Keairns 2002; Coalition to stop the use of child soldiers 2008), experiences and roles within the fighting forces (Nordstrom 1997; Mazurana et al. 2002; Keairns 2002;) and reintegration processes (Veale 2003; McKay and Mazurana 2004; Jareg 2005; Honwana 2006; Wessells 2006; Veale and Stavrou 2007; Chrobok and Akutu 2008). Extensive regional survey data from northern Uganda (Survey of War Affected Youth, 2008) has indicated that female youth formerly-associated with the LRA have gone on to live relatively successful lives and are no more violent than their peers (Annan, Blattman, Carlson and Mazurana 2008). Studies focusing on formerly associated males found they vote in higher numbers and are twice as likely to become community leaders (Blattman 2008). Serious emotional distress and estrangement were found to be the exception rather than the norm among formerly associated girls and women, including long term abductees, forced wives, and forced mothers, prompting the authors to note that 'returned young women are strong and resilient, not traumatized pariahs' and that abduction experiences were poor predictors of need (Annan et al, 2008).

These positive outcomes should not contribute to assumptions that support is not required. Rather they are an indication of the social and developmental changes and transitions that can occur in the lives of young mothers and their children, and stimulate further questions about their agency, relationships and use of symbolic and cultural resources in mediating their own reintegration and that of their children. There are still concerns on the ground that a small number of girls and young women are experiencing sustained difficulties with reintegration. Recent surveys have found that a minority of formerly-associated females exhibit serious psychosocial reintegration difficulties, whether psychological distress or persistent community and family rejection (Annan et al. 2009). Ethnographic work emanating from these studies has explored how abduction experiences may exacerbate problems such as intimate partner violence, which emanate from wider structural issues (Annan and Brier 2010). It is clear that the dynamics of reintegration are far more complex than dichotomizing formerly abducted females as either 'traumatised' or 'resilient.' The authors of Survey of War Affected Youth (SWAY) point out that the majority of formerly-associated females report serious family and community problems upon return, but are mostly accepted by their families, and relations improve further over time. We explore reintegration as an ongoing relational process, whereby changes occur between people in specific social contexts.

Recent developments in cultural psychology avoid dichotomizing the individual from cultural and communal aspects of experience. If we see reintegration as a relational process, we also need to cast light on community perspectives. In this chapter, we explore the contribution of a socio-cultural perspective on how reintegration is done informally—how young women's families and communities respond within their own systems of knowledge and practice. Thus this research attempts to address the following question; how do members of formerly abducted girls' communities of origin make meaning of reintegration, experience challenges and actively respond to returned girls and young women and their children?

This paper employs a socio-cultural lens (Vygotsky 1962; Rogoff 1990; Wertsch 1998; Valsiner 2000) to explore community representations and narratives surrounding formerly abducted girls and their children in communities of return in Gulu and Kitgum. There have been recent calls within the literature for in-depth, culturally grounded research on reintegration as a social practice, informed by ethnographic and social psychological perspectives, particularly in Sierra Leone (Shepler 2004) and northern Uganda (Finnström 2008). We employ an analytical focus on cultural resources, a concept which draws on Vygotsky's notion of a cultural tool (Vygotsky 1978) and consists of material tools (cameras, soap) and symbolic tools (songs, stories, rituals), which mediate how we interpret the world and act in it. How do community members use cultural resources—stories, representations, images, rituals—to make meaning of and respond to returning girls and young women? The concept of mediation is central here, as our relationship to the world is mediated by cultural tools, both material and symbolic, which become, consequently, the forms through which experience takes shape. As Wertsch writes "to be human is to use cultural tools, or mediational means that are provided by a particular cultural setting." (2001).

Methodology

Participants

Participants were identified through local contacts, and asked if they would be interested in participating in the research. There were fifty participants in total, thirty-nine female and eleven male. The age range of participants was 18 to 65. Interviews were conducted in Gulu and Kitgum districts and all participants self-identified as Acholi. Interviews were conducted by appointment and usually took place in participants' homes in the villages or Internally Displaced Person's camps, while focus group discussions were carried out in a central outdoor meeting area in the IDP camps with one focus group with elders at the Paramount Chief's palace.

Procedure

Selective sampling was used in order to explore a variety of community positions. Categories of respondents (e.g. Acholi elders, ajwakas, local leaders, groups of young women) were outlined with research assistants who were from the local area who then approached people fitting these descriptions and invited them to be involved in the research. In-depth interviews were employed with cultural informants such as Acholi Elders, Ajwakas (traditional healers), and the Camp Commandant of an Internally Displaced Persons camp and displaced young women. Focus group discussions were held with displaced young women, parents, Acholi Elders, local leaders and Ajwakis. Interviews and focus groups generally lasted 1.5 hours although there was an amount of variation in this dependant on the wishes of interviewees for example two interviews with Acholi Elders lasted over three hours. Interviews were structured around community-based social, spiritual and justice responses to social reintegration of girls and young women formerly associated with the LRA. A semi-structured interview schedule was used structured along thematic lines, as it allowed participants a great deal of flexibility in exploring and elaborating on divergent themes and ideas. In the interviews, the discussion often broadened to reflect on the endemic experiences of sexual violence and consider the experiences of never-abducted girls and young women. The interviews and focus groups were informed from a 'ground-up' approach and, in common with research within the grounded theory tradition, did not impose particular specific hypotheses on the interview situation from the outset.

Interviews were conducted by the first author through a local interpreter. All interviews were recorded and transcribed in English. Two research assistants were involved in this research, one male and one female, both of whom were trained by the first author and prior to any interviews were involved in in-depth discussions about topics of the study, research ethics and participated in role play interviews in order to identify any potential concerns and agree on culturally appropriate translations of key terms. The method of analysis was grounded theorizing (Glaser & Strauss, 1967).

Ethics

This project was informed at all stages by the primary guiding principle to 'do no harm.' All participants volunteered to be involved in the study, and were fully aware of their right to cease their participation at any time, withdraw their data or refuse to answer certain questions. A detailed informed consent process was undergone in Luo (the local language). Also, verbal consent procedures were in place whereby participants had the option to mark the form once it had been read and explained to them and have the signature witnessed by a third party. Participants were members of a war-affected population and as such present specific ethical concerns. This research was focused on cultural and community-based responses to the social reintegration of formerly-associated young women and their children, and thus did not focus on interviewees' personal experiences of the conflict. This stage of the research was concerned with local community responses to reintegration and no formerly abducted young women were interviewed. In some cases, individuals offered personal experiences or experiences of others in order to illustrate a point (as is common in Acholi oral histories and the tradition of the *wang oo*), space was given to do this without intrusive follow up questions.

Analysis

Exploring people's uses of cultural tools in reintegration offers a new way of investigating socio-relational processes of change.

Things Fall Apart—the role of community narratives, images and rumours in mediating reintegration processes.

What are the narratives of reintegration? How do local people understand and make sense of returning girls and their children? Are these different from NGO narratives?

In an interview conducted between the first author and Acholi Elders in the Paramount Chief's Palace in Gulu in 2007, a Musee named Otim referred to the novel to evoke his sense of the *meaning* of the collective experiences of the Acholi. In discussing the reintegration of children born in the bush he referred to the Acholi customary law, which holds that children born outside of marriage belong to their maternal family and are treated the same as any other child in that family. He went on to say, "In a traditional Acholi setting no child is without a base. There is nothing like street child in Acholi, today I hope you have come across the book of Professor Chinua Achebe?" 'Things fall apart' I replied, 'Things fall apart,' he repeated softly, 'that is the real situation of Acholi today.' In this moment, Otim used Chinua Achebe's narrative to make meaning of his own. He situates the stories and the suffering of the Acholi within a wider context of communal violence. The difficulties faced by returning young women and their children are thus understood as part of a wider story of oppression. Otim, like many other Acholi Elders I came to know well during my fieldwork, expressed a deep sense of loss and anxiety at the conditions of life during war, conditions he often perceived as chaotic and meaningless.

The meaning of these events, the violence and oppression enacted against the Acholi, is constructed through the appropriation and use of symbolic tools such as narratives (Vygotsky 1978). As Achebe himself writes "People create stories create people; or rather stories create people create stories." Bits and pieces of the stories of others can be appropriated and used to create our own individual and collective life narratives, and help us to make meaning of ourselves, suffering and being in the world. This is reminiscent of Claude Levi-Strauss' concept of *bricolage* to describe the way in which people use bits and pieces of the symbolic and the material they have available to them to confer meaning to events (Levi-Strauss, 1962). Thus people become authors of their own stories and fates. Community members likened the experiences of formerly abducted girls to those of other girls in the community—both groups experienced rape, poverty, displacement, hunger and the deaths of loved ones, One of the most common phrases used about abduction in northern Uganda was 'It could happen to you' indicating the universality of the experience.

One common image in participants' narratives was the archetype of the 'Acholi girl' or 'traditional girl' and her safe, protected space at the centre of social and familial systems. This idea is elaborated by Okello, an Acholi Elder:

> You see the girl is the core of life. Life is centred on the girl that is why they were treated special. One they bring in wealth, they are the people on which the whole life of the family is centred on the girl. You see much actually happened, as I was telling you these girls were removed sometimes in front of the family... They were taken away to the bush and a lot of things happened there, things that should never be happening.

The young girl seems to be a central figure in this collectively imagined community of 'the life that should be living' or *'piny maber,'* a good life in an environment without extreme conflict. The representations of innocence and purity afforded to the image of the young girl may be equated with ideas of the purity or viability of the Acholi community itself. Nordstrom (1997) discusses how attacks upon girls may act as attacks upon the nation state. Thus an attack on the body of the girl becomes an attack on the 'body politic.' The LRA have articulated the aim of destroying the Acholi tribe and replacing with a new Christian Acholi (LRA/M, n.d., cited in Finnström 2008). The rape of girls may be seen at once a pragmatic act—to create through forced pregnancy a 'new Acholi,' and to raise the necessary military capacity needed to fight the war, and also to create profound destruction, done with an aim of exerting control over the civilian population.

The rape of girls and women in the Internally Displaced Person's camps by the UPDF was also represented as a method of exerting power over the civilian population. As a young man in a displacement camp in Kitgum said "The army men rape the young girls because they have power over us. To show the men we are weak and cannot protect them." Thus attacks on girls may be also locally represented as attacks on the identity and self-determination of the clan or indeed the Acholi as a group. These ideas were illuminated by Otim, an Acholi Elder in Gulu, when discussing LRA violence:

> Traditionally an Acholi man would be the last person who would be happy seeing his wife being abused or his daughter being abused. The way the women were raped, the way the daughters were raped in the presence of their parents, the men were very very hurt. In fact it is just a reflection, an indication or a confirmation by the perpetrator that the man was useless, because the impossible could happen in his presence. So the man, women should not take it that men didn't suffer, psychologically men suffered worst.

It is important to note here that there is significant disagreement as to the extent to which the rape of girls in the presence of family members has actually happened in northern Uganda, and this was in fact disputed within this interview. These kinds of war stories and rumours, particularly related to young girls or pregnant women (see for example Nordstrom 1997) exist within many cultures affected by armed conflict and contribute to collective and divergent narratives of terror, suffering and resistance.

What does this mean for reintegration? These participants framed girls' experiences of abduction and forced marriage within wider collective experiences of oppression. Girls are situated within family and community contexts rather than solely addressed as individual 'victims.' The 'victimhood' of formerly associate girls is likened to the experiences of never-abducted girls who have been raped or forced into marriage with UPDF soldiers. This questions dominant government and NGO narratives, which focus on children abducted by the LRA as the principal victims of the conflict. This focus of many interventions on a specific small group of victims/survivors, while politically prudent, does not address the victimisation experiences of the wider community. Understanding the experiences of girls and young women as communal events impacts local reintegration processes; interviews and discussions with community members evoked narratives of shared suffering that fostered group cohesion to resist violence but also acknowledged that widespread victimization impacts on existing support structures.

Examining these narratives leads to a deeper understanding of the complex identity challenges presented by returning females. Community members are confronted with their inability to protect girls, initially from abduction and now from challenges upon return particularly displacement, extreme poverty and sexual violence. Community-based narratives consider government rapes and the effects of displacement on girls and women, in addition to LRA atrocities. The narratives reflect the place of returned girls within interdependent systems and evoke a broader conception of victimization than approaches solely focused on individual formerly abducted girls and young women.

Identity tension—a situated exploration of stigma

From a socio-cultural perspective, the concept of stigma may be understood as existing in the relational context between individuals participating in social practices rather than either in the social environment or in the individual. In order to understand and respond to stigma it is necessary to explore the immediate social contexts, cultural activities and social interactions within which it is used. Stigma may be more likely to occur within social interactions and contexts within which there is a fear of 'contamination', a high degree of uncertainty regarding the actor who is stigmatized and visibility or knowledge of the attribute that is stigmatized.

'Stigma' in the case of children returning with their mothers was not perceived by respondents to operate as a permanent mark—a scarlet letter or constant state of shame or rejection. Rather the dynamics of 'stigma' surrounding children seems to be context specific and originate from a combination of fear and attempts to regulate behaviour. In many interviews respondents stressed the positive aspects of such children. As Levi an Elder in Gulu described:

> Many of these girls have children and they are coming home. A girl with a baby is more comforting to the parents. At least you know she has a baby, ok the father is not known so long as the boy or the child is healthy, quite a lot of them are taken care of by the parents. I have one here and I am looking after the child very well, she is already part of me.

Women participating in a focus group in Layibi also illustrated this point;

R. They are always kept in the same way. A typical Acholi do not segregate against children, whatever the case. People are more sensitive with them.

R. Maybe that girl has brought a child from a brilliant family to their family.

The collective identity of the Acholi as welcoming and caring for children is stressed here. This aspect of cultural identity was often invoked in discussions surrounding children born in captivity. Here this narrative serves a protective function in the lives of returned girls and their children as it reinforces relational systems of protection. Mothers participating in this focus group elaborated on this theme;

R. As a parent, being like that your daughter came back with a child so you have to praise God given that your child has come back. So you will not treat that child in any bad way because that child came from the bush or his father is still in the bush, you only take charge because that is a part of you. The only unfortunate thing is if by any chance the father is mad and lie madness can be inherited from father to child, then you will have to battle with the child. The girls did not go there because they wanted to but they were forced by circumstances. So you have to take these children like they were not born from the bush but were just born from home just like your own children. If you treat them well the child will grow up to be a responsible person who will take up responsibility of the home.

I. (interpreter) How about other community members?

R. Outside people like neighbours normally stigmatize these children and it is always common with children that are stubborn and when they have gone and done something wrong these children will be abused and references will normally be made of where they are born or where they came from.

R. So if a child goes to the neighbours' place and is playing with their child and then suddenly hits that child from nowhere, the mother of that child will come out and start saying 'I am tired of these sort of children, who were born from the bush, go back to your home.' So this depends normally on the child. If the child can listen the stigmatisation of the child is not normally there. But if the child is stubborn the stigmatisation of the child is a must.

I. If that child is stubborn in the family, would people ever refer to the way he was born?

R. Yes if the child is being stubborn, people will become annoyed and they will mention the way he was born, they will tell him even to go to the father.

Group discussion with Megos in Gulu district.

This rich narrative illustrates communal perceptions surrounding returning children and indicates a number of divergent positions. The narrative of the child as part of the family is counter-pointed with fears related to the 'stranger' father. The potential of the child to 'take up responsibility in the home' indicates an acknowledgement of the child's place as part of the family and their right to engage fully in familial life and practices—the 'possible self' of the child born in captivity as a committed family member is invoked. Conversely, fears of inherited dangers, as demonstrated through unsanctioned or non- normative behaviours such as madness, aggression and stubbornness, create shaming responses within the community. Stigmatisation here is linked to the breaking of norms or misbehaviour, in terms of teaching the child, and is described as an active, malleable force—with a regulatory or 'taming' function—rather than a static 'mark' permanently affecting a child born in captivity.

Changing relational contexts were linked to altered identities of children. In cases of girls returning with children and then remarrying the relationship between the child and the new husband was considered by community members as problematic. Displaced young women in Gulu discussed a number of cases whereby a new husband would become threatened by the presence of another man's child in the family. In families of some young mothers, both formerly associated and not, the husband would see the child as a stranger to him, which in these participants' experience could lead to abuse of these children.

> He won't want to see the eyes of the child there. Only you and maybe the child he is going to have with you.
>
> Rebecca, displaced girl, Gulu district

Acholi customary law would indicate that a child born outside of marriage would become part of the mother's family. However, within changing family structures and new relationships the child's place becomes less secure. This was said to result in the separation of mother and child although there were cases cited where the new husband would accept and care for the child. Within interviews and discussions local leaders, mothers and displaced young women cited numerous cases where mother and child were separated, due to remarriage.

> No man wants to take care of another man's kids. Because they are also poor they can not afford so much and also he will look at those kids as strangers to him not his own.
>
> Tandi, displaced girl, Gulu district.

What may be distinctive here are the shades of difference between acceptance and belonging. If the child 'misbehaves' or displays non-normative behaviour such as aggression or commits minor infractions their possible identity as a 'child from the bush', a 'rebel child' or a 'stranger' may be invoked. In the years to come, issues over land rights, or interpersonal issues such as relationships or conflicts may result in these alternative identities being brought into the open and belonging contested.

You know in Acholi, in all clans of Acholi, sometimes you get people from other clans. Maybe they have problems there, like murder...and then you run, you come and join another clan and so forth. Now one can stay very comfortably in that clan but maybe after some time someone will say ah no he does not belong to that you know... He came from oh somewhere... and out of anger someone can say a lot of abusive words, isolating you. But in general Acholi are very very good, at harbouring differences and seeing some way...
...
L. Maybe the two girls will be loving the same boy you know? And one will say 'oh you don't belong to this clan (laughs)'. These things will then come out.

I. If the child is with his mother's family, would he inherit in the normal way although his father was from the bush?

L. If he has been living there and is part of that family he has that right to inherit property. He is already a part of that family.

I. If the child ever did something wrong would the circumstances of his birth ever be brought up

R. That will also come out, if the child misbehaves, that will also come out. Yeah in case that child wants to take over everything from his family. That child wants to take over everything, everything in that family, leaving other children in that family that is where the past will come out. Because those other children will even do it saying 'You have just come to this family, you are not really part of this family,' that is when it will come out.

I. So family disputes over land and things like that...

R. Yeah

Levi, Acholi Elder, Gulu district

The idea of 'stigma' is explored here as context bound and used in specific social relational contexts through the words and actions utilized by other community members to temporarily exclude returned children. Lawrence describes how in times of interpersonal difficulty, such as a conflict over romantic relationships or land, rivals would invoke the child's identity as 'other' in order to attack their social status and right to claim resources within the clan. Thus stigma is a tool at the disposal of other community members should they need to compete as to birthright—full belonging within the clan—which the child does not fully possess. This is likened to the experience of those who come to the Acholi from different tribes, indicating that 'stigma' here is more about belonging and social status within clan structures than about the specific circumstances of a child's birth. With regard to the legal rights of these children, particularly land rights and inheritance, ideas of belonging or entitlement are tied closely with tribal or kinship structures.

In a focus group with never abducted girls in Amuru, girls described the specific difficulties facing their peers who had been formerly associated with the LRA. A recurring theme throughout these participants' narratives was a lack of control in sexual relationships, and this was discussed with regard to formerly abducted and never abducted girls and young women alike. The key issue of sexual relationships requires detailed exploration, as if the experiences of young women within the LRA, particularly forced marriage and sexual violence, are to be addressed within healing or justice fora, it is essential to also address the continuing victimisation of female youth upon return and the shared experiences of never abducted girls. This is necessary in order to avoid privileging one group of survivors (or rather one period of victimization—as formerly-associated girls and young women often contend with abuse upon return) and rather to address ongoing collective experiences of sexual violence. Displaced young women, young men, parents, elders and local leaders all spoke of endemic sexual violence in the IDP camps and perpetrated by UPDF soldiers. In discussions surrounding abducted girls specifically, never abducted peers stressed the continuing victimization upon return 'home' particularly surrounding factors constraining the agency of young women, and young mothers in particular.

So the parents will be there, the parents are giving her some assistance they are giving her shelter and her kids, giving her feeding, clothing maybe a little of education, because we can put that the majority are poor so the parents cannot afford education for these kids at a higher level, and her she cannot do anything, say even if she is taken to a tailoring course, she will see in a day tailoring she earns 500s she will see that there is no future for her sending her kids to school. So with that she can easily be tempted to become a prostitute to just be going walking from a man to a man, from a man to a man.

Tandi, displaced girl, Gulu district

In social contexts of extreme poverty the necessity of an independent income is stressed, particularly if the girl or young woman has children to support. The lack of options available to young mothers with regard to income generation and the extremely low returns on activities such as tailoring were understood to lead to a reliance on transactional sex for material needs, with abuse in sexual relationships a significant theme. The economic realities of young mothers' lives are central to their ability to assume positive social roles in the community. Participants stressed the lack of opportunities available to low income young mothers, whose marginal place in the community is both a cause and a consequence of their inability to provide for their children financially. These issues apply not only to formerly-associated young women, but also to the many other young girls and women who were raising children alone. These new family units were said to be particularly vulnerable, as they did not fit within local practices governing the division of labour, as Alice, an ajwaka in Gulu outlined, in relation to young women formerly associated with the LRA.

> As a result life becomes very difficult for them, even basic things become a problem, like if children and men take those responsibilities it would be ok.

In contexts where traditional support structures are under extreme stress, the economic vulnerability of young mothers may create a sense of tension within the community. Stigma may be enacted in these relationships as a result of daily frustrations and pressures, rather than as necessarily a consequence of abduction experiences themselves. These issues are central to effective reintegration programming, whereby stigma may be dealt with more effectively through income generation activities and by drawing on local resources for change rather than standard NGO 'sensitization' models.

This theme explores the dynamics and mechanisms of stigma; a key distinction here is that stigma is enacted within a particular social context, cultural activities and social relationships, rather than existing within the individual. The mechanisms of stigma are malleable and are closely connected with fears and anxieties within the community which stem from spiritual issues and fears of contamination, changes in social norms surrounding gender roles and ideas of the unknown surrounding violence witnessed or perpetrated and the affect of this on the peace of mind of girls and children.

Cultural Resources in mediating reintegration

Participants drew on a wide repertoire of cultural tools in formulating responses to formerly abducted girls and their children. These included counseling and storytelling, herbal medicine, rituals such as *nnyono tonngweno*, *moyo piny* and *tumu*, engaging formerly-associated girls and young women in communal practices such as cooking or cultivation, meetings between families in cases of forced marriage and putting protections in place against victimization. For the purposes of this paper we reflect on some discussions with groups of formerly-associated young women's never-abducted peers in Internally Displaced Person's Camps. These participants identified multiple strategies for social change and transformation.

Participants explored mechanisms of protection of formerly-associated girls and young women and the need for community based local support for vicitms of rape and sexual violence upon return. A discussion of the corruption and inadequacy of police services highlighted the need for grassroots contacts and links for girls. This was seen as a vital resource in reintegration, improving the formerly associated girl's well being and emotional security, as a displaced young woman explains.

> Because when they see that they cannot be abused sexually, emotionally, they will see that the world is also accepting them. You see? So in spite of what happened to me, the world also recognises me as someone important because the world is there to protect my right, you see? the world is there to protect my feelings, my interests. So whoever comes and abuses me I still have a refuge, if you come and abuse me I will always have somewhere to turn to.

Participants stressed the importance of engaging formerly-associated girls and young women in communal practices. The participation of returned girls in shared activity with other girls their own age and particularly with women elders such as megos and aunties was described as a vital resource in social reintegration.

> Because elders will also be very important particularly women, mothers, these mothers will be very important in teaching them cooking, to make their home, that is very important because we know that in Acholi a nice girl, a good girl will always be loved to be married by anyone, she will always know how to cook. So they will teach them how to cook, how to be cooking this traditional food, they will teach them how to behave in the home as a mother.. I believe that will also have an impact on them, as a mother you have to be clean, weed your garden if it's there, do things at the right time, don't bark at kids, you see?

Linking formerly-associated girls and young women to female support systems is done here through shared practice. The formerly-associated young mother is engaged in a relational process whereby the elder as an expert guides her through the acquisition of locally valued skills and behaviours. This role of elders and family members was also stressed in providing relationship advice and counseling. This was seen to be particularly important in cases where formerly-associated girls were in relationships with boys who had also been abducted, and participants stated that discussions with formerly abducted boys and men were needed to deal with the problems of continuing sexual or domestic violence upon return to civilian life.

> Because to me personally [author's name] I say that these people need to be re-educated as to how to handle a human being, how to handle a wife, how to handle a child, how to handle my children, how to handle my sisters and the entire community I live in, how to handle human beings generally. Much as I do agree that we as human beings have weaknesses, but should be at a normal level, not abnormal the one that they have been doing in the bush.

Community responses to formerly abducted girls acknowledge the complexity of social reintegration and the many intersecting issues that further complicate it. A relational approach allows for an exploration of these issues in greater depth as they are enacted within the specific social contexts of northern Uganda.

Conclusion

While recent contributions to the literature have illuminated the resilience and strength of formerly abducted girls and young women, there remains a gap in our understanding of how reintegration processes work in families and communities. The socio-cultural approach explored here allows for the complexity and contestation within reintegration as a relational process. In this paper we focused on the identity challenges presented by returning girls and their children to the communities of return, resulting in enacted stigma within specific social contexts. There are concerns raised on the ground that while children born in captivity are accepted by families and communities, there do exist moments of tension, that may reoccur in the years to come. We also explored community members' responses to mediating stigma through facilitating participation of young women and their children in valued social practices. Culturally rooted community routines and practices are often overlooked but they are central to a full understanding of social reintegration.

References

Achebe, Chinua. 1954. *Things fall apart*. Nairobi: African Writers Series.

Annan, Jeannie, Chris Blattman, Kristopher Carlson and Dyan Mazurana. 2009. *Women and girls at war: Wives, mothers and fighters in Uganda's Lord's Resistance Army.* unpublished working paper.

Annan, Jeannie, Chris Blattman, Kristopher Carlson and Dyan Mazurana. 2008. *A way forward for assisting women and girls in northern Uganda,* Survery of War-Affected Youth (SWAY).

Annan, Jeannie, and Chris Blattman. 2008. On the nature and causes of LRA abduction: What the abductees say. Forthcoming in *The Lord's Resistance Army: War, peace and reconciliation in northern Uganda.*

Annan, Jeannie, and Moriah Brier. 2010. The risk of return: Intimate partner violence in Northern Uganda's armed conflict. *Social Science and Medicine* 70 (1):152-159.

Blattman, Chris. 2009. From violence to voting: War and political participation in Uganda. *The American Political Science Review* 103(2):231-247. Also available from http://chrisblattman.com/documents/research/2009.V2V.APSR.pdf.

Brett, Rachel. 2002. *Girl soldiers: Challenging the assumptions.* New York: Quaker United Nations Office.

Brett, Rachel, and Irma Specht. 2004. *Young soldiers: Why they choose to fight.* Lynne Rienner Publishers Inc: Colorado.

Carlson, Kristopher, and Dyan Mazurana. 2008. *Forced marriage in the Lord's Resistance Army, Uganda.* Feinstein International Center: USA.

Chrobok, Vera, and Andrew Akutu. 2008. *Returning home: Children's perspectives on reintegration. A case study of children abducted by the Lord's Resistant Army in Teso, eastern Uganda.* London: Coalition to stop the Use of Child Soldiers.

Finnström, Sverker. 2008. *Living with bad surroundings: War, history, and everyday moments in northern Uganda.* Duke University Press.

Glaser, Barney and Anselm Strauss. 1967. The Discovery of Grounded Theory. Strategies for Qualitative Research. Sociology Press.

Honwana, Alcinda. 2006. *Child soldiers in Africa.* Philadelphia: University of Pennsylvania Press.

Jareg, Elizabeth. 2005. Crossing bridges and negotiating rivers: The rehabilitation and reintegration of children associated with armed forces. Save the

Children, Norway. www.childsoldiers.org/resources/psychosocial, last accessed 10 April, 2008.

Keairns, Yvonne. 2002. The voices of girl child soldiers: Summary. Quaker UN Office: Geneva.

Levi-Strauss, Claude. 1966. The Savage Mind. The Nature of human society series. Chicago. University of Chicago Press.

Mazurana, Dyan, and Susan McKay. 2001. Child soldiers: What about the girls? *Bulletin of Atomic Scientists* 57 (5):30-35.

Mazurana, Dyan, Susan McKay, Kristopher Carlson and Janel Kasper. 2002. Girls in fighting forces and groups: Their recruitment, participation, demobilization, and reintegration. *Peace and Conflict: Journal of Peace Psychology* 8 (2):97-123.

McKay, Susan and Dyan Mazurana. 2004. *Where are the girls? Girls in fighting forces in Northern Uganda, Sierra Leone, and Mozambique: Their lives during and after war.* Montreal: InternationalCentre for Human Rights and Democratic Development. Available from www. ichrdd.ca, last accessed 4 July 2009.

Nordstrom, Carolyn. 1997. Girls and warzones: Troubling questions. Uppsala, Sweden: Life and Peace Institute.

Paez, Erica. 2001. *Girls in the Colombian Armed Forces: A diagnosis.* Terre des Hommes: Osnabruck.

Rogoff, Barbara.1990. *Apprenticeship in thinking: Cognitive development in social context.* New York: Oxford University Press.

Shepler, Susan. 2004. The social and cultural context of child soldiering in Sierra Leone. Presented at a Workshop on Techniques of Violence in Civil War, Centre for the Study of Civil War, International Peace Research Institute in Oslo, Norway, 20 August, 2004.

Valsiner, Jan. 2000. Culture and human development, Sage, London (2000).

Veale, Angela. 2003. From child soldier to ex-fighter: Female fighters, demobilization and reintegration in Ethiopia. Monograph No. 85. Pretoria: Institute for Security Studies.

Veale, Angela, and Aki Stavrou. 2003. The reintegration of the Lord's Resistance Army child abductees in Northern Uganda. Pretoria: Institute for Security Studies.

Veale, Angela, and Aki Stavrou. 2007. Former Lord's Resistance Army child soldiers abductees: Explorations of identity in reintegration and reconciliation. *Peace and Conflict: Journal of Peace Psychology* 13:273-292.

Verhey, Beth. 2001. *The demobilization and reintegration of child soldiers: El Salvador case study*. The World Bank. Available from www.world bank.org (accessed 1 March 2007).

Vygotsky, Lev. 1962. *Thought and language*. Cambridge, MA: The MIT Press.

Vygotsky, Lev. 1978. *Mind in society*. (Trans. M. Cole). Cambridge, MA: Harvard University.

Wertsch, James. 1998. *Mind as action*. NewYork NY: Oxford University Press.

Wertsch, James. 2001. Narratives as cultural tools in socio-cultural analysis: Official history in Soviet and post-Soviet Russia. *Ethos* 28 (4):511-533.

Wessells, Michael. 2006. *Child soldiers: From violence to protection*. Cambridge, MA: Harvard.

9

Stigma as Encountered by Female Returnees and the Role of the Church in Northern Uganda

Emeline Ndossi
School of Mission and Theology, Norway
Makumira University College, Tumaini University, Tanzania

Abstract

Stigmatization is one of the major challenges encountered by female returnees from the Lord's Resistance Army (LRA) in northern Uganda. This article explores the phenomenon of stigmatization as it is experienced by female returnees. Factors leading to stigmatization are such as atrocities these women committed while they were in the bush, violations of Acholi cultural values, and traumas leading to behavioral problems. Working against the stigmatization, Christian communities played several important roles, such as contributing to the formation of the amnesty law, caring for returnees, conducting sensitization programs, education and counseling programs. The empirical data for this article are mainly from Catholic, Anglican, Orthodox churches of the interfaith organization known as the Acholi Religious Leaders Peace Initiative (ARLPI), which also includes Muslims. Religious leaders, rehabilitation centre workers, female returnees and other lay people have been consulted.

Introduction

One of the greatest problems that female returnees from LRA face during reintegration is stigmatization. According to Joanne Corbin, "harassment of [LRA returnees] by community members was a major challenge of reintegration" (Corbin 2008, 329). Susan McKay, Dyan Mazurana and

Sverker Finnström[1] say that formerly recruited young mothers face more stigmatization than boys face (McKay and Mazurana 2004, 37; Finnström 2008, 193). During my field research 2008 and 2009 in Gulu District, northern Uganda, several interviewees said stigmatization is one of the major challenges encountered by female returnees from the LRA. One of the lawyers working with them said that, "the fact that they are ex-child soldiers and they are women makes them double vulnerable."[2] These women sometimes experience gender-based stigmatization. Several of the female formerly recruited young mothers who shared their experiences of stigmatization through the translator.[3] One of them said, "when she came back, life was not that easy because of stigmatization."[4] When further questioned whether the practice is over due to the fact that several institutions in northern Uganda are working against the practice, this mother said, "Stigmatization is still there, only that they are the ones who just give up. They [i.e. the female returnees] don't care. It used to be very intense. It hurts them. As time passed by, eventually they got used to it."[5]

For the female returnees to survive against stigmatization some of them have developed coping mechanism of ignoring this situation which they cannot avoid. Another one said, "It is hard for them because there is stigmatization. To men who want to marry them, they say, 'How can you bring a girl who is from the bush?'" [6] Unfortunately, the experience of being stigmatized affects not only themselves but also their children. As one of them complained, "There is still stigmatization at the community levels because she remembers one time when there were young kids from the camp who stoned her children, saying, that they are rebels."[7] Another returnee also complained that her family was harassed by some of the community members. She said, "Usually people are saying her mother is keeping a returnee child who may seek revenge."[8] In other cases their presence puts themselves, their children and those who host them at risk.

Several church leaders admitted that stigmatization is a problem to the female returnees from the LRA. One of the church leader was of the opinion that, "The greatest challenge is that some people don't cooperate with them. They feel rejected."[9] Another church leader supported this view when he said that, "Some communities have not been good to these people, and they have been pointing fingers."[10] This problem of stigmatization, which formerly abducted young mothers encounter, has been highlighted in some media publications in Uganda. In a Ugandan newspaper article ("Ex LRA chiefs harass former wives") in the *New Vision* 19 September 2008 it was reported that female ex-child soldiers in northern Uganda were pictured protesting while holding banners against some community members that are harassing them. The author, Lydia Namubiru, is cited saying, "The end of Lord's

Resistance Army (LRA) insurgence in northern Uganda and their escape from captivity promised a new life. But, alas for them, the reality outside the bush proves harder than they had expected" (Namubiru 2008). She also said that the girls are "facing big problems. They get a negative reception from some people" (ibid.).

Stigmatization for formerly abducted young mothers is there even though not all the community members do so. One of the rehabilitation centre workers I interviewed was of the opinion that they had "not had cases where children have been rejected by the whole community; we have individuals who stigmatize the child."[11] In the following section the concept of stigmatization will be illustrated as it is understood in the northern Ugandan context.

The concept of stigmatization as it is understood in northern Uganda

The concept of stigmatization has a broader meaning depending on the context in which it is used. In *The Concise Oxford Dictionary* the term is defined as a "mark of disgrace associated with particular circumstances, quality, or person". According to the findings in the northern Uganda situation, it seems that stigmatization results from an attitude of regarding a person or an act of that person as shameful and unacceptable in the community. The response of the community members towards such a shameful and unacceptable act has been expressed in various manners. As one of the young mothers said "If someone gets drunk, the person can utter anything against us."[12] A rehabilitation centre workers said, "We had cases when the community calls them names."[13] One of the lay people said, "Sometimes the community members discriminate against them."[14] Life seems insecure due to such acts against them.

In another case, one of the church leaders, illustrating further some of the experiences that these female returnees encountered due to stigmatization, said:

> I will give you an example of a girl whom we did not know how to help. She went through the rehabilitation centre and went home. The World Vision (WV) built a house for her. She was trained in tailoring and was given a sewing machine and the capital to start a business. When she went home, her brother and other people rejected her. They ordered her to leave and take the evil child with her as that will not be accepted in the community. So, she was chased out of the house built by WV and her brother took the sewing machine and the capital away. She went back to rehabilitation centre and this is where our parish priest got the information and helped to solve it out.[15]

From the above comments it is evident that stigmatization is sometimes accompanied by acts of verbal and physical violence against the female returnees. This is part of a global pattern in which some of the returnees say that they are sometimes ridiculed, called names, and even assaulted (Wessells 2006, 195). From the data collected during the field work and from other published sources, different reasons were given as the cause behind such acts of stigmatization towards the formerly abducted young mothers as explained below.

Causes for the stigmatization of the female LRA returnees

There are several reasons leading to the stigmatization of the female returnees from the LRA when they return to their communities in northern Uganda. Partly, it is historical and has to do with the way the LRA has conducted the war and the atrocities they have committed on the community. But also there are psychological, social, and moral reasons related to life experiences they had while in the bush and the consequences associated with it. The section below states the reasons given for the practice of stigmatization on these women.

Stigmatization as a reaction against the LRA atrocities to the community

When these female returnees from LRA were in the bush, they were sent back to their communities to commit atrocities on their own relatives and other community members. They killed, tortured, and looted things from their own community members including in some cases their own relatives or people they had known well before they were abducted. When they came back from the LRA, some of the community members are still hurt because of the atrocities committed on them. A church leader, elaborating on the experiences of these young mothers, said:

> It is just because of the nature of the conflict. Because it has been like when the rebel comes they abduct me from this village. When I am recruited, they force me to carry out abductions in my own village. So, maybe I come and abduct your own son and your own daughter and I am known in the village so next time I come back, and your daughter is not back what feeling will you have. You will always have that feeling? 'Where did you put my daughter?'[16]

As a result, some of them want to seek revenge on the returnees. In one case the congregation had to intervene because a case broke out in a family. The family members were chasing away a young mother saying "You have come home again? You killed us here. You burned our houses. We don't want you."[17] According to McKay and Mazurana citing Women's Commission for Refugee Women and Children (2001) they say that "UNICEF estimates that 80 percent of the LRA is comprised of abducted adolescents who [were] forced to attack their own families, neighbours, and villages." (McKay and Mazurana 2004, 28). The consequence when they come back is that some community members put them in trouble. Also the violation of cultural values because of their lifestyle in the bush puts them in trouble.

Violation of cultural values as a reason for stigmatization

While in the bush the female returnees were required to fight and engage into sexual relationship with men in a manner that is contrary to the Acholi cultural values. According to Archbishop John Baptist Odama:

> Making the women fight a war is against Acholi cultural values. A woman was seen as peace-maker so much that it was women who were giving blessings…The women never fought and they were not to be attacked even if there was fierce fighting. Women and children were never touched…but this time this is something strange which has happened where women or girls are being forced to fight. So now the peace-maker is made the author of violence. This is completely against the culture; the peace-maker is made the author of violence.[18]

This view was also supported by other informants, e.g., one of the rehabilitation centre workers said, "In fact women never fight, even in Acholi culture. It is a taboo to kill a girl child or a woman. Even in older days, if you killed a woman, it would be difficult for you to be cleansed."[19] Another rehabilitation centre worker further added that making these women fight was contrary to Acholi culture. She said, Acholi women didn't go to the war. But what used to happen if they are attacked or overpower the men, they would take their wives and children as captives. We used what we have as (opiri) if they overpower your men, you become slave.[20]

According to the above informants, involving these women in war and violent acts is contrary to the roles that women hold in Acholi culture. The community looks at such acts as exceptional and in inappropriate. In addition, the female returnees while in the bush were involved in sexual relationship with men in a manner that is contrary to the culture. As one of the church leader said:

> In the tradition of Acholi, in older times when a girl is growing she just stays virgin during her childhood stage. What the rebels have been doing is against the Acholi tradition. You cannot sleep with her in the bush that is against the Acholi. Many girls who have gone in the hands of rebels are really against the culture of Acholi.[21]

Another rehabilitation centre worker supported this view by saying "It was a taboo to have sex with a woman in the bush."[22] Due to the violation of cultural taboos they are stigmatized by some of the community members. In support of the sexual abuse that these women experienced while in the bush, it was reported in the aforementioned *New Vision* article that "Men shun these girls. You hear men say amongst themselves: Do you know how many people used this one?" (Namubiru 2008). Stigma associated with being raped makes the life of the formerly abducted young mothers much harder after returning to their communities. McKay and Mazurana citing a paper by Joy Angulo[23] say that "Reintegration was harder for girls because they faced negative attitudes and perceptions due to their forced loss of virginity (the term used in northern Uganda is 'defilement')" (McKay and Mazurana 2004, 37).

For women with children, stigma may spill over to them since the children will be severely stigmatized for being illegitimate and also a 'rebel child.' As one of the church leader said:

> Some girls when they come back they have children already. The girl and the children have to stay at the mother's place. This has been a problem to other people. They look at the child as a different person. Like this one they met in the bush and the girl got pregnant. The parents don't know which clan the child belongs to.[24]

Further illustration by Finnström indicates that, "in the perspective of most Acholi, a woman is married into her husband's patrilineage and its wider social group (Kaka)" (Finnström 2008, 185). The children are expected to belong to the clan of the husband. Single motherhood causes a lot of problems for these women; they suffer lack of a sense of identity and belonging. He further added, "Because when they were abducted, they were married and as a wife is the ex-wife of so and so."[25] Since identity is socially constructed, these women are victimized by social values of a patriarchal society in which the identity of married women is valued and recognized only in relation to their husband (Goodhart 2007, 190). There were concerns from some of informants that those oppressive cultural values play a role towards the stigmatization of the formerly abducted young mothers. Supporting this view one of the church leaders said that, "Our African culture also is a bit biased against women especially for these girls when they come."[26] Some of the oppressive cultural values cause stigmatization for the female returnees and makes their lives much harder. Another community worker was of similar view when he said that "culture is oppressive to women on other issues."[27] Religious communities' counteracting stigmatizations on formerly abducted young mothers have to be transformative agents against oppressive cultural values in Acholi land causing stigmatization of formerly abducted young mothers.

Personal behaviour as a challenge during the reintegration

Due to their experiences in the bush, some returnees face significant challenges in the community. Some mothers exhibit behavioural problems as indicted by one of the community members. One of the rehabilitation centre workers commented as follows:

> There are kind of things and if you're not careful they harm each other like the story of the returnee who was sent to the garden to harvest sweet potatoes. So she went with the young brother. But she just turned and chopped her brother to pieces. Then she came back home. So she was asked where your brother is. She said I left him in the garden. So when they went, they found him…So when you live with them in community you have to be careful.[28]

Some of them don't behave well said the rehabilitation centre worker, "Some of them when they return, they like fighting so much. Now it is a problem. For them any exchange of words means fighting." She added "You may accept her but you never know what they might do."[29] Some don't fit in easily due to their lifestyles." He further added "sometimes these girls do not behave well, they feel the same way they were living in the bush they should live at home now."[30] As stated by McKay and Mazurana reasons for such behavior may be caused by the fact that they "themselves have changed so profoundly as a result of their association with fighting forces that they no longer fit into the community." (McKay and Mazurana 2004, 37).

Having explained some factors leading to the stigmatization of returnees from LRA, I will explain in the following section some of the measures taken by the Christian Communities in northern Uganda against the practice of stigmatization.

The role of the Christian communities against stigmatization

The Christian community in northern Uganda is among the most active institutions involved in the reintegration of the LRA of formerly abducted young mothers. Over 90 percent of the populations of northern Ugandan people are Christians, (McDonnell and Akallo 2007, 37). The empirical data related to the Christian communities cited for this article was mostly obtained from the Catholic, Anglican and Orthodox churches united to form the interfaith organization known as the Acholi Religious Leaders' Peace Initiative (ARLPI), which also includes Muslims. The Christian members in the ARLPI body are the largest in northern Uganda and active in the reintegration of LRA returnees. Members from Muslims, World Vision (WV) and GUSCO (Gulu Support for the Children Organization) were consulted as they also collaborate with Christians to support the female returnees to work against stigmatization. The empirical data was obtained from fieldwork research done in the Gulu District in 2008 and 2009.

A greater percentage of the Christian community in northern Uganda has either been abducted in the bush or lives as displaced persons in camps. The term used by some of the church leaders was 'life in captivity' to express the experience of being driven away from their homes as a result of the LRA war.[31] This is a biblical term related to the story of the sons of Israel while in captivity.

According to the words of the Roman Catholic Archbishop John Baptist Odama, churches in northern Uganda consider it part of their mission and nature to help the needy:

> If you talk in a religious language [the church] is a Good Samaritan. Does not mind about what sex, what language, what color, what religions; all these are secondary. He goes for the good of the needy provided there is somebody in need the church is meant to address it, as part of her nature.[32]

Commenting further as to why the church is involved in helping the returnees Bishop Benjamin Ojwang of northern Uganda is cited as saying "The church role (...) is a prophetic role to speak on behalf of the voiceless" cited (Taylor 2005, 564). The Mothers' Union website further cites Bishop Benjamin Ojwang saying "We cannot give up because that means throwing the Bible away...We have to struggle even up to the end" (Taylor 2005, 565). The church is thus there to fulfill its mission of helping these children and the community expects her to provide leadership when the church is in crisis. According to Kevin Ward:

> The importance of Christian leaders as a voice for Acholi people and churches as channel for local expression has grown over years... The churches have means of access to people that [is different from other institutions]. Church leaders and traditional leaders in the community overlap. The church not so much 'represent' local opinion as provides a channel by which local opinion can express itself (Ward 2001, 201).

Christian communities have as well been very active in addressing the problem of stigmatization of the formerly abducted young mothers as analyzed below.

The formation of an amnesty law

The church played an important role in the formation of the amnesty law in collaboration with other local leaders and the government. The formation of the amnesty law in northern Uganda played a key role in encouraging the formerly abducted children to come back from the bush to their communities and have the right of protection. As one of the religious leaders said:

> Our role as religious leaders as far as reintegration is concerned, we have done a lot in that area, because the Amnesty Law that you hear about was really a making of All Religious Leaders Peace Initiative (ARLPI). I must say ARLPI stood up side by side with other leaders in place especially like the local leaders and members of parliament.[33]

He further added, "The objective was really reintegration because however much we try to alienate, putting away our children who are abducted, it will really be a loss to the community."[34] Kevin reported from New Vision, 23 March 1999 saying that:

> The idea of amnesty was being mooted strongly in early 1999 whereas previously the government had been adamant that only a hard line make sense (...). When Archbishop-elect John Baptist Odama was appointed he stated that his great aim was to bring peace to the north, an unexceptional thing to say in itself. But he went on to talk about Kony and LRA rebels as 'prodigal sons who can be forgiven and received back into the society' (quoted in Ward 2001, 207).

In 1999 the Government introduced an Amnesty bill into Parliament (Ward 2001, 208). The Amnesty law was helpful in motivating some of these returnees to come back to their communities and it promised protection.

Christian communities as receptive and caring centres for the formerly abducted mothers

When the female returnees came back from the bush, the Christian communities received them and encouraged the rest of the community to do so. In fact, churches played the key role in receiving these children either straight from the bush or rehabilitation centers and getting them back to their relatives. Since the churches in northern Uganda are with the people, they have been helpful to support these young mothers when they arrive from the bush, to trace and reunite them with their relatives.[35]

Some of the returnees are Christians and when they come back they join their churches. Archbishop John Baptist Odama said, churches receive the returnees " ...in the chapel or in the place of prayer and then they pray with them. They also encourage the people, by preaching the word of God to them, administer sacraments, even baptizing and also preparing people for confirmation, for marriage, and so on."[36] Also churches cooperate with other institutions, for example rehabilitation centers, to make sure that the formerly abducted mothers are received and taken care of within their communities. One rehabilitation worker said:

> Rehabilitation centres cooperate with the churches to reinsert these children into the community. The church doesn't have a specific role but with these children we encourage them to go to the church, and you know the teaching in the church is all about having love to one another, and at least is encouraging people in their lives, so we also tell them maybe if you have a child of this kind in your area or in your church as a religious leader you need to pay attention.[37]

Churches are invited by rehabilitation centers, e.g., in GUSCO and WV to lead prayers, teach and counsel the returnees. Upon their completion of the rehabilitation centre period, during the reinsertion period, there are those who prefer the Christian rituals rather than the traditional ritual. Church leaders vary in their opinion on the practice of the two rituals. As one of them commented, "the Church as well as cultural leaders we are saving human beings. We don't go there to mix things because we know our limits."[38] The comment indicates that some of the church leaders are positive towards traditional ritual even though they do not participate in them. The Christian community is there when Christian rituals are needed. One intention of the Christian ritual is to make it possible for these children to be received within their communities. Churches also provide follow up programs such as home visitation programs to comfort and reconcile them and their families in case there is a crisis. As reported by one of the church leaders:

> So the church goes to such people. We have Christians who work on our behalf, the Christians who voluntarily work on our behalf they bring us the information from different sources so when they bring that to us then we can support, sometimes we make an appeal ...Today we support this one the next time we support another one.[39]

The complaint of several church leaders was that the war has devastated the church economically and this makes it hard for the Christian community to meet all the challenges encountered by female returnees. With little resources they have, they give reception and care to all the returnees. This is helpful in making them feel welcomed, accepted and valued.

Sensitization programs against stigmatization

Churches are involved in programs known as "sensitization programs" which are mainly focused against stigmatization. In these programs, churches cooperate with NGOs such as GUSCO and WV and also community leaders to educate the families of the returnees and the rest of the community against the practice of stigmatization. According to one worker in the rehabilitation center, the stigmatization programs aims at the following:

> To educate the community on how they should live with those children. Tell them that these children need special attention, they need love, they need care from the community as any other person in the community, and then because of that the community will come to understand truly we need to give these children special attention and live with them. They will one time get to normal life. They should not feel that these children cannot do something good for the community.[40]

The NGOs have expertise in sensitizing community and works with the churches and other community leaders at the grassroots. One of the religious leaders elaborating on the role of the ARLPI leaders, said:

> Since we formed our organization we have been working very close with the community and sensitizing them at the grassroots for the forgiveness and reconciliation several times right from 1998. The ARLPI they have what they call 'peace animators' right from the subcounty to county, we coordinate with them and this is through our program officers who go and meet with them and they mobilize the communities for us. The workshops are held whereby they are sensitized. [41]

The leader from the Catholic Church said sensitization programs are done at different levels and the intention is also to empower the community so that they can work out the solution by themselves. He said,

> Sensitization goes to the smaller unit in the community and can be the family or the parish level whereby if in a following up we realize there are difficulties of a returnee getting reintegrated into the community, and then we organize community discussion sometimes. In that small village setting whereby we moderate the discussion they tell us what are like the challenges that are affecting the reintegration and how best they think it can be solved. They work it out within themselves and come up with a solution at times comes up with bylaws for the community.[42]

According to an interview with Kenneth Gong done in Kitgum 23 September 1999, Ward reports that "One message that the churches inculcate, and that seems to be in line with the general expectations of the community, is that there should be no victimization of the returnees, they should not be called *Olum (rebel) or LRA*" (Ward 2001, 207). When questioned by me (I) about the impact of sensitization, some of the formerly abducted young mothers (FR) had the following opinion:

> **FR:** When they say you are from the bush, they said many men might have slept with you.
>
> **I:** But they say sensitization program is working.
>
> **FR:** Yeah, it is working.[43]

Another one said through the translator:

> **FR:** As compared to the first time she came life was hard because she was not used to the community and people here were arrogant, but these days they can talk, share and help.[44]

There seems to be positive results even though stigmatization is still there.

The churches educate the returnees for good moral values and self-reliance

The church educates the community and the children for good moral values so that they can live peacefully together in their communities. The church leader said the "church teaches forgiveness and reconciliation so that these children are accepted in the community." He further added, when these children "come to the church, they learn about forgiveness and love. Just to forget what has happened."[45] The theme of forgiveness according to Christian teachings has played an important role in the process of accepting the LRA returnees back into their communities. Archbishop John Baptist Odama describes the needed reconciliation as follows.

> Reconciliation between the one who has done wrong (so he agrees he has done wrong) and the one whom this wrong has been done (accepts the pain of having suffered from the hands of the other one). But what makes a change is that the one injured does not want to be overcome by the spirit of attack, the spirit of aggression towards the other one. 'You say that was a wrong way. I am not going to follow that way with you. Instead I put the good side of me, and my good side is I accept you. Despite the mistake you have done to me I accept you; I forgive you so therefore I am not going to be overcome by that to do revenge. No. No.' [46]

Besides the teachings related to forgiveness and reconciliation, the Christian communities also educate the community on other good moral values. These values are helpful in enabling the returnees and the community to take responsibility for their lives and for others and live in harmony with each other. Education for good moral values and self- reliant has been helpful in changing the attitude of people and counteracting the acts of stigmatization towards the LRA returnees. Counselling is another program which has been important for the traumatized returnees.

Counselling programs for the traumatized returnees

Due to traumatic experiences in the bush, some of the female returnees have psychological problems which cause some of the community members to stigmatize them. The churches have counselling programs for the returnees. Counselling programs have been established in collaboration with other institutions like the NGOs such as WV and GUSCO. The WV rehabilitation workers said:

> We have a very strong community structure. We have what we called as counselling Aid. Our staffs are in pay roll at every subcounty. We have community volunteers, care givers. The counseling aids are on the payroll, volunteers are motivated. Actually we want to avoid children coming to the centre. They are the link.[47]

Beside such programs some churches have home visitation programs to counsel these children. Counselling is helpful in healing the traumatic problems for these children. This program is extended not only to returnees but to their families as well.

Conclusion

This article reports that stigmatization is a major challenge that the female returnees encounter during their reintegration in northern Uganda.

The impact is not only on female returnees but also on their children and relatives who host them. The expressions related to stigmatization towards formally female returnees vary. There are several reasons stated for the stigmatization of the female returnees in northern Uganda. As indicated, the different programs done by the Christian communities have been helpful to minimize the impact of stigmatization on the formerly abducted young mothers but have not eradicated it. The findings indicate that some factors leading to stigmatization of female returnees are unique and need special attention, e.g., cultural values which are oppressive to formerly abducted young mothers. To counteract stigmatization to formerly abducted young mothers, Christian communities have several important roles to play.

References

The concise Oxford dictionary of current English, ed. Robert E. Allen, and F.G. Fowler 1990: Caren Press.

Corbin, Joanne. 2008. Returning home: Resettlement of formerly abducted children in northern Uganda. *Disasters* 32 (2):316-335.

Finnström, Sverker. 2008. *Living with bad surroundings: War, history and everyday moments in northern Uganda.* Durham and London: Duke University Press.

Goodhart, Michael. 2007. Children born of war and human rights: Philosophical reflections. In *Born of war: Protecting children of sexual violence survivors in conflict zones,* ed. R. C. Carpenter. Bloomfield: Kumarian Press.

McDonnell, Faith, and Grace Akallo. 2007. *Girl soldier: A story of hope for Northern Uganda's children.* Michigan: Chosen.

McKay, Susan, and Dyan Mazurana. 2004. *Where are the girls? Girls fighting forces in northern Uganda, Sierra Leone and Mozambique: Their lives during and after war.* Canada: Rights and Democracy: International Centre for Human Rights and Democratic Development.

Namubiru, Lydia. 2008. Ex LRA chiefs harrass former wives. Newspaper article, *New Vision,* Kampala, Uganda, 19 September.

Taylor, Jenny. 2005. Taking spirituality seriously: Northern Uganda and Britain's 'Break the Silence' Campaign. *The Round Table* 94 (382):559-574.

Ward, Kevin. 2001. The armies of the Lord: Christianity, rebels and the state in northern Uganda, 1986-1999. *Journal of Religion in Africa* 31 (2):187-221.

Wessells, Michael 2006. *Child soldiers from violence to protection.* London: Harvard University Press.

Notes

[1] Susan McKay and Dyan Mazurana have done extensive studies on the reintegration of female ex-child soldiers in several parts of Africa. In this citation they quote from a report from the Great Lakes Strategy Workshop, School of Monetary Studies, Nairobi,

November 7-9, 2002. Sverker Finnström has written several publications related to the conflict in northern Uganda.

2   Interview with a lay person, 13 February 2008, at her residence in Gulu District.

3   All the interviews with female returnees were done using a translator from Acholi to English.

4   Interview with a female returnee, 14 February 2008, at a church office, Tailoring School, Gulu District.

5   Ibid.,

6   Interview with a female returnee, 14 February 2008, at a church office, Tailoring school in Gulu District.

7   Interview with a female returnee, 8 February 2008, at GUSCO rehabilitation centre, Gulu District.

8   Interview with a female returnee, 8 February 2008, at GUSCO rehabilitation centre, Gulu District.

9   Interview with a church leader, 8 February 2008, at Acholi Religious Leaders' Peace Initiative (ARLPI) Office, Gulu District.

10   Interview with a church leader, 10 February 2008, at a parish office, Gulu District.

11   Interview with a rehabilitation centre worker, 13 February 2008, at GUSCO rehabilitation centre, Gulu District.

12   Interview with a female returnee, 14 February 2008, at a church office, Gulu District.

13   Interview with a rehabilitation centre worker, 13 February 2008, at GUSCO Rehabilitation Centre, Gulu District.

14   Interview with a social worker, 9 February 2008, at a hotel, Gulu District.

15   Interview with a church leader, 12 February 2008, at a church office, Gulu District.

16   Interview with a church leader, 14 February 2008, at a church office, Gulu District.

17   Interview with a church leader, 7 February 2008, at a church office, Gulu District.

18   Interview with the Archbishop John Baptist Odama, 13 February 2008, at the Roman Catholic Cathedral, Gulu District.

19   Interview with a rehabilitation centre worker, 13 February 2008, at GUSCO rehabilitation centre, Gulu District.

20   Interview with rehabilitation centre worker, 11 February 2008, at World Vision rehabilitation centre, Gulu District.

21   Interview with a church leader, 8 February 2008, at ARLPI, Gulu District.

22   Interview with a rehabilitation centre worker, 13 February 2008, at GUSCO rehabilitation centre, Gulu District.

23   "Gender, abduction and reintegration in northern Uganda" (Occasional Paper No.6), Kampala, Uganda: Makerere University, Department of Women's Studies, 2010.

24   Interview with a church leader, 7 February 2008, at church office, Gulu District.

25   Interview with a rehabilitation centre worker, 11 February 2008, at World Vision rehabilitation centre, Gulu District.

[26] Interview with a church leader, 14 February 2008, at church office, Gulu District.

[27] Interview with a community worker, 9 February 2008, at a Hotel, Gulu District.

[28] Interview with a rehabilitation centre worker, 11 February 2008, at World Vision Rehabilitation Centre, Gulu District.

[29] Interview with a social worker, 9 February 2008, at a Hotel, Gulu District.

[30] Interview with the rehabilitation centre worker, 11 February 2008, at World Vision Centre, Gulu District.

[31] Interview with a church leader, 10 February 2008, at a church office, Gulu District.

[32] Interview with Archbishop John Baptist Odama, 13 February 2008, at office, Gulu District.

[33] Interview with a Muslim leader, 6 February 2008, at a mosque office, Gulu District.

[34] Ibid.

[35] Interview with a church leader, 7 February 2008, at a church office, Gulu District.

[36] Interview with the Archbishop John Baptist Odama, 13 February 2008, at a church office, Gulu District.

[37] Interview with a rehabilitation centre workers, 14 February 2008, GUSCO rehabilitation Centre, Gulu District.

[38] Interview with a church leader, 10 February 2008, at a church office, Gulu District.

[39] Interview with a church leader, 7 February 2008, at a church office, Gulu District.

[40] Interview a rehabilitation centre worker, 14 February 2008, at GUSCO rehabilitation centre, Gulu District.

[41] Interview with a Muslim leader, 6 February 2008, at mosque office, Gulu District.

[42] Interview with a church leader, 14 February 2008, at church office, Gulu District.

[43] Interview with a female returnee, 22 January 2009, GYDA, Gulu District.

[44] Interview with a female returnee, 23 January 2009, at World Vision rehabilitation centre, Gulu District.

[45] Interview with a church leader, 7 February 2008, at a church office, Gulu District.

[46] Interview with the Archbishop John Baptist Odama, 13 February 2008, at a church office, Gulu District.

[47] Interview with a rehabilitation centre worker, 11 February 2008, World Vision Rehabilitation Centre, Gulu District.

10

'I Had No Idea You Cared About Me'

Empowerment of Vulnerable Mothers
in the Context of Reintegration

Miranda Worthen
University of California, Berkeley

Susan McKay
University of Wyoming

Angela Veale
University College Cork, Ireland

Michael Wessells
Columbia University

Abstract

This article reviews the literature on empowerment and situates empowerment within the context of a multi-year participatory action research study with young women and girls who were formerly associated with fighting forces and armed groups in Sierra Leone, Liberia, and northern Uganda and had children of their own during the conflict and with young mothers considered by their community to be especially vulnerable.[1] The authors put forward suggestions about how empowerment of this particularly vulnerable population can happen.

Introduction

Girl Mothers in Armed Groups

As has been described in this volume by Tonheim, young women and girls have been recruited into armed groups in conflicts throughout the world. Girls and women have played a particularly large role in the context of civil wars in sub-Saharan Africa. McKay and Mazurana (2004, 14) documented the presence of girls in government or rebel groups in 38 countries where civil wars occurred between 1990 and 2003 (Mazurana et al. 2002, 103). While many girls have been forcibly recruited, like boy children, others join voluntarily, often in response to violence perpetrated against their family or community (Machel 1996; McKay and Mazurana 2004). Girls play a variety of roles in armed conflict, ranging from fighters to porters and from cooks to captive wives (McKay and Mazurana 2004, 14).

Many girls and young women become pregnant and have children during the conflict as a result of rape or in the context of partnerships formed with 'bush husbands' (McKay and Mazurana 2004; Coulter 2006). As one young woman who had been associated with an armed group in Sierra Leone reported to us, 'everyone was having babies all the time!' McKay et al. (2006) point out, these young mothers typically have not benefited from formal disarmament, demobilization, and reintegration (DDR) programs.

Instead of going through formal processes of DDR, girls and young women with children often return to their communities or settle in new communities on their own or with a peer group (McKay et al. 2006). Some women maintain their partnerships with bush husbands, while other women use the opportunity provided by the end of the conflict to leave these relationships. While some young mothers actively choose to avoid DDR, hoping to blend back into communities on their own, others do not know that they are able to benefit. Evidence from several conflicts suggests that stigma against girls and women is so great that some choose not to go through formal or even informal DDR (e.g. NGO arranged support), hoping to avoid further marginalization.

Often the design of DDR itself is not conducive to the participation of young mothers. DDR efforts have been adult driven and out of touch with young people's perspectives, goals, and capacities. This is even more markedly so in the case of girl mothers. Formal DDR processes are designed to remove weapons from circulation, ensure force restructuring and create a durable end to hostilities, but girls and young women often do not carry arms and, despite playing a role in the conflict, are not perceived as threatening to peace or stability. Formal DDR processes have discriminated against girls and women and have taken into account neither the gendered nature of recruited children's war experience or the unique, gendered situation of young women and mothers after exiting the armed forces or groups. 'Armed, adult male fighters,' Mazurana et al. (2002, 116) write, 'are the near exclusive priority for most disarmament, demobilization, and reintegration (DDR) programs, significantly marginalizing all children, but girls in particular.' Even in cases where DDR policies have explicitly encouraged participation of children, such as in Liberia, where those under the age of 18 were not required to turn in guns in order to receive services, young women between the ages of 18 and 25 reported that one barrier to their participation in DDR was that they did not have weapons (Specht 2006).

When young mothers do join formal DDR processes, they often find that they are unable to participate in aspects of reintegration programs like skills training because there are no provisions for childcare (McKay et al. 2004). Young mothers also report that promises made during DDR have not been fulfilled. For example, one young mother in Monrovia, Liberia asked us: 'Will this project be like DDR, where you promise to pay our school fees and then leave after one month?'

Young women and girls who return from armed groups with children face stigmatization and marginalization from communities,[2] whether they go through formal DDR or return independently (Burman and McKay 2007). Young mothers are often viewed by the community as having violated community norms by having children outside the recognized societal marriage norms (McKay et al. 2004; McKay et al. 2006). They are frequently labeled as sexually promiscuous and can be regarded as 'spiritually polluted' (Denov 2007; Green and Wessells 1997; Wessells 2006). In addition, these young mothers have often developed attitudes or habits during their time in the armed groups that are considered culturally inappropriate, for example getting into fights or cursing.

Community members themselves are also recovering from the devastating effects of war, and individuals find it challenging to imagine how they can help young mothers recover, preferring to render the young mothers and their children invisible so they can focus on rebuilding their own lives. One community leader in Freetown, Sierra Leone, for example, told us: 'It is not that the parents were wicked, but they do not have enough to feed themselves much less a girl when they don't even know who impregnated her. To feed someone when they don't know who impregnated her is very hard.' In other communities, the fear of 'spiritual pollution' from girl mothers and their children also contributes to their isolation by community members (Betancourt et al. 2008).

The Participatory Action Research Study with Girl Mothers and their Children

The Participatory Action Research Study with Girl Mothers and their Children (PAR) was initiated in October 2006. The research began in response to a growing awareness that the needs of girls and young women who had children of their own while they were associated with armed groups were not being met (Robinson and McKay 2005; McKay and Mazurana 2004). The study seeks to learn what successful reintegration means to young mothers and what can be done to support them in achieving reintegration, as they understand it.[3] While a full description of the PAR is beyond the scope of this article, some background to the project will be helpful.

The study is jointly coordinated by the authors and operates through a partnership with ten child protection agencies (NGOs) working in Liberia, Sierra Leone, and Uganda.[4] Three country-based African academics also work with the study. Each partner agency operates in two locations, forming groups of approximately thirty girls and young women who had children while they were associated with armed groups or who are considered by the community to be especially vulnerable.[5] Communities themselves defined vulnerability and often included young age, orphanhood, or disability. In all, over 650 girls and young women and over 1200 of their children have been a part of the study in twenty communities in the three countries.

As may be inferred from its title, the methodology and philosophy of the PAR is participatory action research. Participatory action research has been defined as 'an approach to research that aims at promoting change; that occurs through a cyclic process of planning, data collection, and analysis; and in which members of the group being studied participate as partners in all phases of the research, including design, data collection, analysis, and dissemination' (Brown et al. 2008). In the context of this study, the girls were located at the center, with important decisions being made by them while the agencies and organizers provided monitoring and support.

PAR emerged from Paulo Freire's *Pedagogy of the Oppressed* (1968) and has been adapted to the field of development, most richly by Robert Chambers (Freire 1970; Chambers 1994). PAR privileges 'local knowledge' and situates the participant as the expert with respect to his or her own situation. Other core principles of PAR are respect for the local community and inclusivity. PAR is not a singular methodology, but rather a set of prin-ciples with a basket of techniques and approaches that can be adapted to particular contexts.

The structure of this PAR is different in each field site and in each country because of distinct approaches to organizing. In Sierra Leone and

Liberia, organizations collaborate but do not attempt to create a universal approach. In Uganda, the four agencies created an integrated budget and hired a research coordinator to facilitate the study in the field sites. Therefore, there is no unified history that perfectly captures the nuances of how the study developed in each site. However, a general framework for how each unfolded can be outlined.

Each country team began by identifying communities where there were likely to be a large number of formerly associated girl mothers. Once these potential field sites were identified, agency personnel began outreach to local leaders and stakeholders, specifically reaching out to elder women and midwives. The study was explained to these local community members and there were a series of engagements to assess whether collaboration between the community and the PAR would be possible. If community members were supportive of the PAR, then they helped to identify a small number of girl mothers who were formerly associated or identified as particularly vulnerable. Agency staff members then contacted these girls and young women and, over a period of days or weeks, explained the PAR. In some sites, elders recruited the full cohort of thirty girl mothers, while in other sites the initial group of girl mothers recruited other girl mothers that they knew to join the project. All participants who agreed to join the PAR went through an informed consent process according to a protocol accepted by the University of Wyoming Institutional Review Board.

After recruitment, participants were provided training on how to do research and supported in conducting research using a wide array of modalities to learn from each other, their children, other girl mothers, and community members about the problems girl mothers face in their community. They then shared what they had learned and decided upon social actions to address some of the problems they identified. While at this point all sites diverged, there was a remarkable similarity to the obstacles identified in each community, which were in the critical areas of livelihood, health, and education.

Theories of Empowerment

Empowerment has taken an increasingly central role in development and humanitarian organizations since the 1980s (Luttrell et al. 2007). Empowerment theory was brought to development practice through the work of Freire and through the feminist critique of Women in Development. The 1995 Beijing Platform for Action further encouraged the focus on empowerment, and specifically included the perspectives of youth and girls, identifying that they often experienced even lower status than women or boys (Worthen

1994). Within the development context, empowerment has been conceptualized as a process, an outcome, or some combination of the two. Although there remains little consensus about what empowerment means, development agencies, governments, inter-governmental organizations like the World Bank, and others now agree that empowerment is good. Empowerment, as Parpart, Rai and Staudt (2002, 3) have argued, has 'become a "motherhood" term, comfortable and unquestionable, something very different institutions and practices seem to be able to agree on.'

Many definitions of empowerment focus on participation in decision-making. For example, Bystydzienski (1992) describes empowerment as a process through which a person who is oppressed gains control over her life. The World Bank defines empowerment as 'increasing the capacity of individuals and groups to make choices and to transform these choices into desired actions and outcomes' (Alsop and Norton 2005, 4). The UK Department for International Development defines empowerment as '"individual's acquiring the power to think and act freely, exercise choice, and to fulfill their potential as full and equal members of society"' (Smyth 2007, 584).

Rowlands argues that empowerment goes beyond this, writing that:

> Empowerment is thus more than participation in decision-making; *it must also include* *processes that lead people to perceive themselves as able and entitled to make* *decisions* (...) Empowerment must involve un-doing negative social constructions, so that people come to see themselves as having the capacity and the right to act and influence decisions (1997, 14).

Rowlands agrees with Kabeer who said that 'such power cannot be given; it has to be self-generated' (Kabeer 1994, 229). For Rowlands, at the core of the process of empowerment is a psychological process of change, including the 'development of self-confidence and self-esteem, and a sense of agency, of being an individual who can interact with her surroundings and cause things to happen' (1997, 111, 113). 'Dignity,' meaning 'self-respect, self-esteem, and a sense of being not only worthy of respect from others, but of having a right to that respect' is also essential to Rowlands' notion of empowerment (1997, 113, 129-130).

While some people view empowerment as an aim in and of itself, others view empowerment as of instrumental value for increasing the effectiveness of development aid, improving governance, and contributing towards economic growth (Alsop 2005, vii). Those who write about the instrumental use of empowerment recognize its 'intrinsic' value. While acknowledging the importance of empowerment for individuals, Yuval-Davis also argues that 'empowerment of the oppressed, whether one fights it for one's own—individual or group—sake, or that of others, cannot by itself be the goal for feminist and other anti-oppression politics' (Yuval-Davis 1994, 193). For Yuval-Davis, social change that is the product of empowerment is essential. Many who write about empowerment write of the kind of power that is enacted in empowerment as 'power within.' While Kabeer argues that empowerment is 'self-generated,' we believe that empowerment, like power, is interpersonal and inter-relational. If, as Foucault (1980) argues, power is expressed in interactions, empowerment, as well, happens in interactions. It does not emerge from within a person without context. Empowerment can emerge as a property of a conversation or an interaction. Thus while empowerment shapes an experience from 'within,' it is still deeply relational.

Weingarten and Cobb (1995) propose that 'discursive practices' can be empowering. Their notion of empowerment hinges on recognition: a sense of empowerment can be generated through 'one person experiencing another person as accepting and elaborating what she has to say' (1995, 259). The act of accepting and amplifying another person's meaning can occur through conversation, or, as will be described later, through collective actions, such as putting on a drama.

In this manner, experiencing empowerment as an individual cannot be considered in isolation from the experience of being part of a collective. Rowlands identifies this aspect of empowerment as 'collective empowerment,' which she asserts is intertwined with personal empowerment in a circular manner: 'participation in the group may feed the process of personal empowerment, and vice versa' (1997, 115). The examples given later in this article illustrate the importance of this sense of oneself within a community allowing participants to, as Rowlands writes, 'achieve a more extensive impact than each could have had alone' (1997, 15).

In the context of the PAR, this process of recognition and empowerment occurs between the young women participants themselves and between the organizers or agency staff and the young women participants. In the examples we give below, we will explore how interpersonal interaction, which amplifies a person's experience and then allows for self-recognition, lays the foundation for further actions that empower and for the emergence of a psychosocial state where a woman is able to see herself as a rights-holder, and thus situate herself within a human rights framework. This position of entitlement then enables the participant to take part in further actions that empower through giving voice, agency, and achieving the fulfillment of rights claims.

Empowerment in the Context of the PAR

Examples from the PAR study allow for an exploration of how empowerment can happen when working with girls and young women considered the 'most vulnerable' in their communities (Robinson and McKay 2005). The first, lengthier story provides a window into how empowerment happens. After this story, we share several quotes from different participants that help focus on particular aspects of the processes at play.

The first author met Sarah[6] on the first visit by one of the organizers to her community in northern Uganda. The study was just beginning and the young women and girls gathered by our partner agency and community elders were not fully clear on what the study was about or how it would work. As in other communities, Miranda explained the goals of the project through an interpreter and answered many questions.

Sarah did not stand out during the meeting. She did not participate more or help explain the idea to those seated closest to her, as some of the other young women did. But at the end of the meeting, she came up to Miranda with a serious look on her face and took Miranda's hand. Speaking in halting English, Sarah said, 'I had no idea that you cared about me. You live so far away, and your life has not been touched by this conflict. Why do *you* care about *me*?' Moved, Miranda told her that she thought her life was as important as anyone else's life, and that she had a right to a better experience. It was clear that Sarah was not just speaking about herself and Miranda concretely, but also in an existential manner—someone like her and someone like Miranda. Miranda told Sarah that every person in the world deserved an opportunity to thrive, that we all have a right to a decent life. Sarah looked at Miranda as though she had said something profound and said, 'Thank you.'

Four months later, we all had a chance to meet Sarah, this time in Kampala, where we were holding an annual meeting for people who work on the study in all three countries. Eight young mothers who were participants in the study were selected by their peers in Sierra Leone, Liberia, and northern Uganda to represent them at the meeting. Sarah was one of those selected. In the first day of the meeting, Sarah shared her story with the conference participants. She explained how her uncle had been caring for her, but kicked her out and told her to seek support from her father. Her father told her that it would be a waste to educate her. She was doing agriculture work in exchange for food for herself and her child when the PAR started in her community. She described how working in a group with the other girl mothers and interacting with the staff of the child protection agency running the PAR in her community impacted her life:

This study came and in the group discussions [with other girl mothers] we shared ideas, learned the stories of one another, learned how to care for our children. We have never seen a project which cares for girl mothers because they have wasted their time, they want them to get married, you are supposed to care for the child, care for the husband—ah what is this? So [the child protection agency] came and the [research assistants who work with us] came and we were very much encouraged, now we know that people are caring for us. The other ones they say you are expired—they use that language 'expired,' 'expired.'[7]

On the third day of the meeting, Sarah and the other girl mother representatives addressed the conference and asked for more attention and support for their communities. They lacked funds to educate their children; they sought assurance that if they attained a high school degree they would be supported at university; they wanted better medical care, gardening tools, and costumes to enhance their cultural performances. These young women asked a room full of child protection staff, UNICEF personnel, donors, and academics for the tools to help them achieve access to education, health, and livelihood.

Sarah's story illustrates the transformative impact of feeling supported and treated with respect. For Sarah, her growing understanding of herself as someone worthy of respect and her sense of dignity emerged through interactions with her peers and with those outside her community who were involved in daily operations of the PAR and in coordinating the study. The sense of recognition that she felt in sharing her story with other girl mothers and hearing their stories in return fits with Weingarten and Cobb's notion of empowerment as a discursive practice wherein a person experiences another as accepting and amplifying of her own story. In this case, peer support was validated externally by those associated with the study—Miranda and child protection personnel—who expressed caring and concern for Sarah and the other girl mothers in her community. Sarah was able to resist internalizing the pejorative labels that others used to describe her because she felt recognized as deserving of care by others. The support from those like her and the support from those outside of her community mutually reinforced one another and laid the groundwork for her participation at the conference.

Now feeling empowered, seeing herself as one worthy of respect and dignity, Sarah was able to envision herself as a rights bearer. With this new sense of identity, she was able to advocate for her rights and the rights of others in her situation to be fulfilled. In this manner, Sarah was not able to advocate for herself until she had undergone a transformation brought about through interactions with insiders and outsiders that enabled her to see herself as someone worthy of respect and dignity. Sarah had to feel empowered first before she could engage with outsiders in a way that might produce further support for her empowerment.

Several other short examples from the PAR will help us explore additional aspects of the process of empowerment. Miranda Worthen and Susan McKay collected the quotes below on visits to field sites in Sierra Leone and Liberia during the second year of the study. They were offered in response to open-ended queries in focus group discussions with participants about what they were doing in the study and whether they had experienced any changes as a result of their participation.

The first two quotes highlight the transformative impact of mutual sharing between girl mothers. The first refers to a drama that the young mothers improvised together about what it was like for them when they returned to their community after the war.

> I thought that I was the only one that was hated. When I saw in the drama that others were also treated like that I no longer felt alone.

> Our meetings have created a sense of one-ness among each other and now we share our burdens. We are each other's sisters.

Both these young mothers experienced a transformation through sharing their stories with others who had similar experiences of stigmatization and marginalization. Through working together on a drama, the first young woman had the experience of seeing her own story reflected back to her. The second young woman experienced this same 'amplification' and 'elaboration' of her story through sharing that emerged in the meetings that the young mothers held with each other. Both young mothers no longer felt isolated or alone, but understood their own experiences within the context of a broader social group.

Several participants expressed how confidence placed in them by the organizers, the agencies, and the other girl mothers involved in the PAR altered their sense of self and gave them an incentive to try to lead better lifestyles. In one community where the young mothers had decided to start a micro-credit project to support their livelihood development, one young mother put it this way:

> So little ended up helping so much. The little you gave me made me want to take better care of myself. I now try to get good clothes and wash my skin and brush my hair and eat good food. The little bit you gave me made me try harder.

Another woman reported that she no longer spent her money on 'drinking and smoking' because 'from within I feel a change.' Prior to the PAR, these two young women had internalized the disrespect they felt from others in their community. Through the PAR, they experienced what it was like to be cared for, treated with dignity, and to be relied upon, which motivated this change from within. These young women were now beginning to think of themselves as worthy of respect, dignity, and the trust placed in them.

As Rowlands describes, this emergent sense of personal empowerment and sense of connection with others in similar circumstances helps facilitate expressions of collective empowerment. This is well illustrated by another young mother who told us about a drama that her group had performed publicly for the community:

> We did a drama about what it was like when we came back from the bush and people shied away from us. The drama also reflected the alienation that we felt when we came back.... We did our play to the community and they said that they wanted to join us and join in our activities. Before, others were shy of us, and now, they talk upright to us. We used the drama to bring those who were shy of us closer again.

This young woman told her story using only 'we' statements. She understood that she was not alone—others, too, had been stigmatized. Because those in her group had shared their stories and gained a sense of validation from learning that their stories were similar, the group was able to seek collective recognition for their experience from their community. The group of girl mothers as a collective enacted the story of what it had felt like to come back to the community and be isolated before the very people who had made them feel alienated. In this instance, the community *did* recognize them: community members altered their treatment of the girl mothers and now talk 'upright' to them. Ending this isolation and alienation by community members was the first step towards the young mothers gaining a full position in their community.

While some young women experience support from their families before gaining respect from their communities, for others the reverse is true. In either direction, however, feeling empowered and respected with regards to one group facilitates empowerment in other domains, as can be seen in the following quote:

> My mother used to abuse me and blame me for my children, but now I make soap that the community buys, my mom sees me better.

In this instance, the young woman had experienced a shift in her relationship to her community and attributed to that shift a transformation in her relationship with her mother. Where she had once been viewed as worthless in the community, now the community recognized her soap-making skill and people engaged with her as a saleswoman, purchasing her products. Her mother, who had previously abused and blamed her, shifted her perception after observing how community members saw her daughter and, presumably, noting that her daughter was engaged productively in supporting herself and her children. The young woman does not speak about her own sense of self worth changing. Rather, she focuses on her experience of recognition by others: when the community saw her as valuable, her mother learned to see her as valuable, too.

The final two quotes illustrate how this sense of empowerment (with respect to self, other girl mothers, community, and family), can enable young mothers to take actions that will further empower them, particularly with respect to structures to protect human rights. The young women focus on how prior to the PAR, they would not have availed themselves of the supportive structures within the community. With their new self-respect and their shifted role within the community, however, they are able to use these structures, which led them to feel further empowered.

> Before the PAR came, I was not considered worthy in the community. If there was fighting and I was walking nearby, someone would automatically blame me even if I was not at fault. Now if the community sees me in conflict or if something is stolen, they do not blame me. They see me taking care of myself and they see my business is going well and so when I complain of something, they listen to me and believe my side of the story.

> My boyfriend beat me when I wouldn't loan him money. But we went to the chief. Before he wouldn't support me and now he wants my money. We decided to separate. He took one of our children and I kept the other one. I am not happy that we're separated, but I was not going to give him my money and I was not going to tolerate him beating me. Before I wouldn't have gone to the chief because I didn't have confidence because I was provoking people in the community. But now I know my rights, I stand like a woman so I can go to the chief.

Both of these women report that they would not have previously had their perspectives believed by the community or the chief, or even availed themselves of these resources for judgment and arbitration. However, now that they believed themselves worthy of respect and experienced respect from the community, they were able to protect themselves from continued violations in the form of theft and domestic violence. Although the same structures for addressing conflict in the marketplace or in the home were in place prior to the PAR, the young women were effectively excluded from using these structures because of their marginalized status. Feeling entitled to respect, dignity, and rights, and believing that others validate their entitlement, allowed them to engage with the structures that protect them.

Conclusion

Practitioners should be cognizant of the level of (dis)empowerment among the people they are working with, be they formerly associated young women or any other vulnerable population. Programs should be designed to meet the particular capacities and needs of the population, understanding that in some instances, targeted work to facilitate empowerment will be necessary before further work on development or human rights will be able to take root and reach its potential.

In our experience, when the population that is being engaged with has repeatedly had their rights violated, empowerment is a necessary starting point. The examples above demonstrate some of the ways that participants experience empowerment through interactions and establishing relationships that foster awareness within a person that she is worthy of respect and dignity. These empowering interactions occur within groups of girl mothers, and between girl mothers and outsiders, including study organizers, agency staff, community members, and family.

This new sense of self worth has been an essential starting point for participants in the PAR to envision themselves as deserving of human rights like access to education, livelihood, and healthcare, and as entitled to protection against rights violations like sexual violence. Once the young mothers in the PAR feel entitled to their rights, then they create opportunities to feel empowered through their personal and collective struggle to attain fulfillment of their rights, whether these actions happened at the intimate level of a woman and her boyfriend or at an international conference.

References

Alsop, Ruth. 2005. *Power, rights and poverty: Concepts and connections.* Washington, DC: World Bank Publications.

Alsop, Ruth, and Andrew Norton. 2005. Power, rights, and poverty reduction. In *Power, rights and poverty: Concepts and connections*, ed. R. Alsop. Washington, DC: World Bank Publications.

Betancourt, Teresa S. et al. 2008. High hopes, grim reality: Reintegration and the education of former child soldiers in Sierra Leone. *Comparative Education Review* 52 (4):565-87.

Brown, David R. et al. 2008. A participatory action research pilot study of urban health disparities using rapid assessment response and evaluation. *American Journal of Public Health* 98 (1):28-38.

Burman, Mary, and Susan McKay. 2007. Marginalization of girl mothers during reintegration from armed groups in Sierra Leone. *International Nursing Review* 54 (4):316-23.

Bystydzienski, Jill. 1992. *Women transforming politics: Worldwide strategies for empowerment.* Bloomington: Indiana University Press.

Chambers, Robert. 1994. The origins and practice of participatory rural appraisal. *World Development* 22 (7):953-69.

Coulter, Chris. 2006. *Being a bush wife: Women's lives through war and peace in northern Sierra Leone.* Uppsala: Uppsala University.

Denov, Miriam. 2007. Girl soldiers and human rights: Lessons from Angola, Mozambique, Sierra Leone and Northern Uganda. *International Journal of Human Rights* 12 (5):813 - 36.

Foucault, Michel and Colin Gordon. 1980. *Power/knowledge: selected interviews and other writings, 1972–1977.* New York: Pantheon Books.

Freire, Paulo. 1970. *Pedagogy of the oppressed.* New York: Continuum.

Green, Edward C. and Michael G. Wessells. 1997. Mid-term evaluation of the province-based war trauma team project: Meeting the psychosocial needs of children in Angola. Richmond, VA: Christian Children's Fund. http://pdf.dec.org/pdf_docs/PDABP857.pdf (accessed 25 November, 2009).

Kabeer, Naila. 1994. *Reversed realities: Gender hierarchies in development thought.* London: Verso.

Luttrell, Cecilia et al. 2007. Understanding and operationalising empowerment. Swiss Agency for Development and Cooperation. http://www.poverty-wellbeing.net/en/Home/ Empowerment/More_on_Empowerment (accessed 25 November, 2009).

Machel, Graça. 1996. *The impact of armed conflict on children.* New York: UNICEF.

Mazurana, Dyan E. et al. 2002. Girls in fighting forces and groups: Their recruitment, participation, demobilization, and reintegration. *Peace & Conflict: Journal* of Peace Psychology 8 (2):97-123.

McKay, Susan et al. 2004. Known but invisible: Girl mothers returning from fighting forces. *Child Soldiers Newsletter* 6:10-1.

McKay, Susan and Dyan Mazurana. 2004. *Where are the girls? Girls in fighting forces in Northern Uganda, Sierra Leone, and Mozambique: Their lives during and after war.* Montreal: Rights and Democracy.

McKay, Susan et al. 2006. Girls formerly associated with fighting forces and their children: Returned and neglected. Coalition to Stop the Use of Child Soldiers. http://uwacadweb.uwyo.edu/MCKAY/Documents/girls%20ang%20v5.pdf (accessed 25 November, 2009)

Parpart, Jane L., Shirin M. Rai, and Kathleen Staudt. 2002. *Rethinking empowerment: Gender and development in a global/local world.* London: Routledge/Warwick Studies in Globalisation.

Robinson, Malia and Susan McKay. 2005. A conference on girl mothers in fighting forces and their post-war reintegration in southern and western Africa, at The Rockefeller Foundation Bellagio Center, Bellagio, Italy. http://www.child-soldiers.org/psycho-social/Bellagio_Conference_Report_(2005)_-_Girl_Mothers_in_Southern_and_Western_Africa.pdf (accessed 25 November, 2009)

Rowlands, Jo. 1997. *Questioning empowerment: Working with women in Honduras.* Oxford: Oxfam.

Smyth, Ines. 2007. Talking of gender: Words and meanings in development organisations. *Development in Practice* 17 (4-5):582-588.

Specht, Irma. 2006. Red shoes: Experiences of girl-combatants in Liberia. ILO, UNICEF, and UNDP.

Weingarten, Kaethe, and Sarah Cobb. 1995. Timing disclosure sessions: Adding a narrative perspective to clinical work with adult survivors of childhood sexual abuse. *Family Process* 34:257-269.

Wessells, Michael. 2006. *Child soldiers: From violence to protection.* Cambridge: Harvard University Press.

Worthen, Miranda. 1994. What Beijing means to me. *Advance* (UNICEF newsletter) October.

Yuval-Davis, Nira. 1994. Women, ethnicity, and empowerment. *Feminism and Psychology* 9 (3):179-97.

Notes

[1] Throughout this article, we refer to 'girl mothers' and 'young mothers.' We use the term 'girl mother' to refer to individuals who either became pregnant or had a child before the age of 18. At the point of joining the PAR, some of these 'girl mothers' were over the age of 18, and thus are also referred to as 'young mothers,' meaning individuals between the ages of 15-30.

[2] See also the contributions by Emeline Ndossi and Fiona Shanahan and Angela Veale in this book.

[3] The PAR with Girl Mothers has been funded by The Oak Foundation, ProVictimis Foundation, Compton Foundation, UNICEF West Africa, and the Rockefeller Bellagio Study Center.

[4] In Liberia partners are Save the Children, UK, Touching Humanity in Need of Kindness, and Debey Sayndee at the University of Liberia; in Sierra Leone partners are Christian Brothers, Christian Children's Fund, Council of Churches in Sierra Leone, National Network for Psychosocial Care, and Samuel Beresford Weekes at Fourah Bay College; in Uganda partners are Caritas, Concerned Parents Association, Transcultural Psychosocial Organization, World Vision, and Stella Nema at Makerere University. Without the dedication of these partners, the study would have been impossible. We also wish to acknowledge the remarkable girl mothers who participated in this study, who are too numerous to be thanked individually.

[5] The decision was made to not exclusively recruit formerly associated girl mothers because of concerns that focusing on this population could further stigmatize them (Robinson and McKay 2005).

[6] Not her real name.

[7] Verbatim transcripts from day one of Kampala meeting, October 2007.

11

Women and War
in Northern Uganda

A Theological Reflection on the Dignity of
Women in the Reintegration Process

Sr. Therese Tinkasiimire
Makerere University

Abstract

This article discusses how women in northern Uganda have been facing challenges of conflict and how their dignity has not been respected in the process. Even though women in northern Uganda have suffered and endured physical, mental and psychological torture while in the bush and in IDP camps for more than twenty years, many of them have also emerged out of this with new knowledge and tactics on how to live a new life. These women because of their involvement in the war have discovered hidden talents, which they would never have known under normal circumstances and which now in some instances may give them the freedom and independence to live in society without interference. In reflecting upon the women's experience in northern Uganda, the author makes use of "women defined theology" as put forward by Laurenti Magesa. Its primary purpose is to remove women from the situation of being marginalized socially, politically, and religiously. The goal of this theology is to ultimately accord the rightful dignity not only to women but to all human beings as well as all God's creation.

Introduction

This article discusses how women in northern Uganda have been facing challenges of conflict and how their dignity has not been respected in the process. There is hope that the reintegration efforts may restore the dignity of both men and women because all people living in the northern part of Uganda have experienced this bitter conflict.

We know that conflict is an inevitable aspect of human interaction, an unavoidable concomitant of choices and decisions. The problem, then, is not to count the frustrations of seeking to remove the inevitability but rather of trying to keep conflicts in bounds. This is what is needed in the case of northern Uganda. The people of Uganda must find ways of ending this conflict because it has taken a big toll on the population, especially women and children. In traditional African society such people would have been spared of such suffering, because at that time women and children were viewed and treated differently from modern times. They were more respected and protected during wartime.

The role of women in war: Past and present

In most African societies and cultures women are viewed as polite, soft-spoken, dignified, receptive, gentle and weak, yet today many are involved in bitter conflicts, voluntarily or forcefully against their will. Many people still hold the traditional ideas about women and their assigned roles. For example women are not supposed to go to war or get involved in intertribal conflicts. They are supposed to be protected at all costs. In traditional African societies some people were exempted from participation in wars or even being killed such people included: women, children and the elderly. To harm such people was considered as taboo. One representative example of how culture has protected women from the ravages of war is given by Miriam Agatha Nwoye who says that:

> Traditional Somali customary principles which state that the under listed crowned heads cannot be killed in war: women and children. And, among the Somali, according to Mohamed there is a saying, 'whoever commits this sin is considered to be a coward and is ostracized. Killing women and children breeds perpetual conflicts.' The next group of crowned heads is refugees. Other groups are the elderly and the sick (Nwoye 2006, 93).

This means that some people were well protected during war time, this means at that time customs were respected and war was orderly and organized. However, today many women are involved in conflict situations all over Africa because the ways of waging war has drastically changed.

Although it is good for culture to advocate for the protection of women against the ravages of war, yet it denies women their God-given freedom in many ways. Many women in Uganda due to ignorance accept their inferior status as assigned by culture. Miria Matembe a woman activist in Uganda says that, "Women the world over have been and continue to be marginalized, down-trodden and exploited. They have been treated as second class citizens and in some societies, less than human beings. They are abused and dehumanized. Why? Because of ignorance. Society lacks knowledge of who women really are. Sadly, women too do not know they are in the eyes of God. Hence they have accepted this society-given inferior status. This must change!" (Matembe 2009, 19). This shows us why women after the war, especially those who have been on the battle field are reluctant to go back to their former society-assigned roles, such as being a gentle, humble house wife, or a woman who can be buttered, abused and keep quiet, they fight back and defend themselves.

In many traditional African societies it was a taboo for women to engage actively in war, but today this has changed drastically. A few examples will demonstrate this. For example, Meredeth Turshen and Clotilde Twagira-mariya say that, "In modern forms of war, especially civil wars and wars of liberation, women are also combatants; women resist and fight back; they take sides, spy, and fight among themselves; and even when they don't see active service, they often support war efforts in multiple ways, willingly or unwillingly," (Turshen and Twagiramariya 1988, 1). They give the example of the civil war of 1980s in Uganda where some women were soldiers, integrated into the National Resistance Army. Some women like Gertrude Njuba supported the army with material requirements. She also mobilized funds and recruited soldiers. She was a key person in that war. She was not a victim but an active participant. This shows us that the traditional view of women and war has changed and that women either choose or are forced to fight actively alongside men.

It is said that there was a woman among Kony's people named Poline Angom who was possessed by twelve spirits. These spirits assisted Kony's army in fighting: "The spirit General Steven worked as commander in chief and operated in the frontline. He darkened the foe's vision in battle" (Behrend 2004, 186). This woman was trusted by Kony and his group, other-wise they would not have let her use her magic to predict what was going to happen. She was actively involved in the war. The examples of women being actively involved, in war negates the idea which portrays men in armed conflict as perpetrators of war and women as benign bystanders or victims. This is further confirmed by Caroline N.O. Moser and Fiona C. Clark who say that although military armed forces have been male-dominated institu-tions, in recent years women have increasingly joined both formal and infor-mal armed groups (Moser & Clark 2001, 9).

Despite active participation in war, women's efforts are not recognized. People still look at women as victims of war. Maybe this is because the number of women who are active actors in war is still small. Or perhaps, people are still stuck in their old ways of thinking that women are supposed to be protected during wartime when times have changed, in that the mode of fighting is different, and women have also been exposed to new ideas and ways of looking at themselves. Many women are eager to use their God-given talents whenever an opportunity arises. Despite all this, when war breaks out most people who suffer most are women and children. This can be illustrated by the Kony's war in northern Uganda.

Victimcy and suffering

Many women in northern Uganda have been victims of war in different ways. For example many young girls have been abducted by Kony and taken into the bush to become rebels against their will. One of the obvious examples is that of the Aboke girls. On 9 October 1996, 139 girls were abducted by the rebels from St. Mary's College. This is a Girls' Senior Secondary School in northern Uganda. The Deputy Headmistress Sr. Rachele followed the rebels and was able to rescue 109 girls, but the other thirty girls were left behind with the rebels. Those who remained with the rebels suffered a lot and some of them were killed, others got pregnant and became the rebel commanders' wives. Some of these girls, like Ellen and Esther, escaped because they did not want to become Kony's commanders' wives as others were forced to be wives of rebels. Ellen tells of how she and Esther escaped:

> It was nearly nine o'clock: time for the radio contact. As the commander got busy installing the solar panel, a helicopter suddenly appeared on the skyline. To Ellen it was like a sign from God. As everybody ran for cover, she grabbed Esther's hand and pulled her to a small circle of grass under a tree... they started running as in the direction where they had heard a mamba pass the night before... As they entered the barracks, Ellen thought she was dreaming. We have made it, we are free (Temmerman 2002, 78-79).

Some of the girls were not so lucky, so they were turned into rebel fighters and suffered a great deal. These girls had not planned on early marriages, they had high hopes for their future, but all was shattered on that fateful night. They found themselves living in the bush and participating fully in rebel activities. Their education and future plans went down the drain. Some of these girls hoped to become important people in the country like being government ministers, doctors, or even Church ministers. These girls' human dignity was not respected, they were abused and downtrodden. These were not the only girls or women who suffered at the hands of the rebels and even the National Army. For example a report in the blog by STGINU (Stop the Genocide in Northern Uganda), a human rights activists group concerned about the genocide that has been taking place in northern Uganda for the last 19 years, reports the story of Stella, a resident of Pabbo camp, who sits in front of her hut to narrate her ordeal saying that:

> Stella was awakened by heavy footsteps treading outside her makeshift shack. She realized very soon she may breathe her last. It was about 11:00p.m. The moon brightly shone over Pabbo internally displaced people's camp, Gulu. Her heart missed several beats, then began pounding in her ears. (...) Anguish seized her. She tried to calm herself, but could hardly stop the violent shiver that shook her from head to toe. (...)

Stella narrates:

> As I leaned on the mud wattle wall, my heart sank when I heard someone banging on the tin door (...). "Funguwa mulango (open the door)," a man shouted. (...) They were flashing torches, so glimpses of light fell on them. I recognized one of them (...). He was a popular soldier in the camp. They were six men. They ordered me and my 10 year-old daughter to go out. I knew they were UPDF soldiers not rebels. (...) After a distance, they ordered us to lie with our faces on the ground. As they raped me in turns, they were doing the same with my daughter. She stopped struggling at some point. I think I also blacked out. (...) I woke up with a start. The pain was like I had been sliced between the legs. My daughter was bleeding profusely. For four days she refused to come out of the hut. My bright girl has since dropped out of school, other children laugh at her (STGINU 2005).

On 27 February, 2005, the *Monitor,* the Ugandan popular newspaper, reported that "A gang of marauding rebels mutilated eight women in Ngomo-romo, Kitgum district recently" (Wasike 2005, 2). The reporter said that one of the Government Officials condemned this as a heinous crime against humanity perpetuated by elements opposed to the peaceful resolution of the conflict in northern Uganda. In Apach, another district in the North, the rebels battered to death eleven people the same year (27 July) and most of these were women. The Uganda Army's spokesperson said that they had deployed special troops to track down the rebels and make sure that they pay for the pain they have inflicted on women.

Another incident occurred in Adjumani, in 2005, one of the districts in the northern part of the country. It was said that, on the Women's day 8 March, the government officials had assured the people in the north that there were enough forces to ensure security in that part of Uganda, but on 11 March at midnight the rebels attached Dzaipi, one of the villages. The rebels hacked six people to death, burnt 76 houses, and left the whole village in disarray. The attack left 490 people displaced from their homes with no food or property (Nandutu and Goli 2005, 2). The government brought in food but many people feel that this is not enough; the government ought to do more to bring peace to this part of the country. Some people say that if the international community could get involved, the war would end within a short time. However, the psychological consequences of the conflict will continue existing for a very long time even after the war. For example the children born and raised in the camps will live with this experience for the rest of their lives. The psychological and physical torture that goes on in the camps, experienced by these people, especially women and girls leave unhealed wounds which, if not properly handled, could take a lifetime to heal or may remain forever. In addition, all those infected by HIV and AIDS virus while at the camps might end in death. The government of Uganda needs to put in place ways of dealing with these traumatized people after the war and for many years to come. Some people in Uganda especially those in the northern part of the country say that the government does not have the will to end the Kony war or even assist victims of this war.

As Uganda 10 August 2005 declared a public holiday to mourn the former Vice President John Garang and other seven Ugandans who died in a plane crash in Southern Sudan, Maggie Alerotek, in her article "Will Uganda get a day to condemn massacre?" (Alerotek 2005), expressed her "wish that the same could be done for the thousands of people of northern Uganda who have perished in cold blood in the on-going war between LRA and UPDF." She longed for the day when "different leaders, Ugandans and some members of the international community would come together to condemn the different forms of atrocities taking place, as well as having all the different religious leaders to pray for the return of peace in the region." I think that, this would be the only way our country Uganda would show the world that she cares about her people. In fact every Ugandan should identify with the bereaved families of the deceased because each individual soul is of infinite worth and infinite dignity.

The people who lived in the internally displaced people's camps (IDP) lived under very appalling conditions characterized by lack of food, overcrowding, poor sanitation, poor shelter, they lacked proper medical care, and their children could not access educational facilities and services. All these affected women more than other people because, women in that situation became the breadwinner and if there was little food, they would go hungry as they feed their husbands and children first before thinking about themselves. In Uganda women are supposed to train their children in good behavior but in the IDP situation this was impossible, so the mothers suffered greatly in seeing their children's bad behavior. The IDP camps became breeding grounds for misconduct for many young people, and this makes it difficult for parents to engage in their children's moral formation.

IRIN, a branch of STGINU, has been working in northern Uganda since 2008 seeking to provide humanitarian information in support of the peace process to local communities and at the same time to enable the voices of local people to be heard by as wide an audience as possible. This enables the women's experiences to be known by many people. This is confirmed by Hilda Twongyeirwe, the IRIN Coordinator, who says that "Sharing and publishing these stories is one way of raising awareness about the atrocities of war and making the world reflect more closely on what happened in armed conflict" (IRIN 2008, 4). IRIN is doing a good job by bringing these stories and experiences of the people, especially women and children to a large audience. Otherwise many people would not know the truth of what really has happened. It is also hoped that the international community will get to know and perhaps intervene. It would help people to realize that suffering, wherever it is found, is evil and people need one another to alleviate it.

We may want to ask ourselves whenever a war breaks out, who suffers the most? The stories and experiences of women in northern Uganda where conflict has been raging on for more than twenty years give us a clue. Women and children have been affected the most, make up the most vulnerable affected population. It is estimated that in northern Uganda about 1-2 million people have been displaced and live in camps, among which women and children make up a vast majority. Here, they live in congested camps with very little space for families to function properly. These displaced women and children cannot meet their demands for food, safe drinking water and sanitation, plus health care. The food distributed by World Food Program (WFP) is limited to pulses, cereals and vegetable oil. Most of the time people go hungry for many hours and sometimes days, especially the women who are the care-providers. A woman always gives food to her husband and children and, if there is nothing left, she stays hungry and waits for the next distribution. Food is brought in from Kampala, the capital city, which is about 200 miles away, and at times it is snatched by the rebels before reaching the camps. People in these camps live in extreme poverty and are also vulnerable to HIV/AIDS because of moral breakdown. Some young women resort to prostitution for survival and hence the rapid spread of HIV/AIDS.

Women as peacemakers

Many women have been involved in counseling war victims. Let me mention but some.

One religious sister by the name of Sr. Mary came to Kampala in the last week of April in the year 2009 and stayed with us at our house (this is a sisters' convent) in Kampala for a week. She had come to look for relief for the young girls who have been living with her sisters at their convent, for three years now. She narrated a story of one young woman who had run away from her village of Ngomoromo. She told Sr. Mary her sad story of how she was raped by three soldiers one after another and she got pregnant and was afraid to tell her parents, so she ran away. Sr. Mary counseled her and then talked to her parents and convinced them to accept her back. She gave birth to a beautiful baby girl late last year. The unfortunate thing is that she does not know the real father of her baby. This has implications because in northern Uganda, and in Uganda as a whole, children belong to the husband's clan. Children without fathers are not accepted in the community. There is a young man who wants to marry this young woman. Sr. Mary is trying to convince him to adopt this little girl as his own so that she can have a clan where she belongs. Sr. Mary is acting as a peacemaker. I think that this sister is trying to restore the dignity of that young woman.

Another woman who acted as a peacemaker in northern Uganda was Betty Bigombe. She tried to broker peace between the LRA and the government of Uganda. After holding some peace talks with rebels she came to the conclusion that the Government's policy of 'talk and fight' was proving to be a stumbling block to her efforts. For example, the LRA had a satellite phone which they used to talk to the peace brokers but this was destroyed by the UPDF, so the option left was to use a mobile phone and this could only be possible when they moved into the MTN zone. In this way Bigombe's efforts were hampered by mistrust between the two rivals. Bigombe said that there was need for confidence building on both sides before the peace process could move forward and have a meaningful solution.

Some of this confidence building seemed to come from the Association formed by parents whose children had been abducted by the rebels. The Association is known as Concerned Parents Association. It is based in Lira under the leadership of Mrs. Angelina Acheng Atyam. Angelina's daughter, Charlotte was one of the Aboke girls who were abducted in 1996. When I had a telephone conversation with Angelina in July 2008, she told me that inside her the spirit was always urging her not to keep quiet like many other parents had done but to have her voice heard loud and clear, he knew that was the only way her daughter and many others would be saved. At first she used to pray a lot but she realized that this alone was not enough. So she along with Sr. Rachele and other parents whose daughters had been kidnapped at the same time formed the Association. The reason for this was that they could meet regularly and support each other in their pain and at the same time pray together. This made more sense to them, in addition it would help them to advocate for the release of their daughters. At first they thought that advocacy would yield good results but this did not happen. They appealed to the national and international leaders, for example they made arrangements and met the President of Uganda but nothing happened. Angelina was invited to the United Nations to tell their story. In addition to this the First Lady, Hillary Clinton invited her to the White House but this effort was in vain. This showed that perhaps advocacy had failed to yield the desired fruits for these parents.

Angelina said that she was helped by the Mennonite Central from the U.S.A. who sent representatives to the Association. These representatives when they came they had a meeting with the members of the Association and asked them the type of help the members needed. The parents said that they wanted to be trained to become peace-builders and trauma healers. Mennonite Central responded by sending professionals who worked with the parents in forming local small support groups and training them. Currently there are more than seventy small groups at village level who are busy working with formerly abducted children, most of them girls. These parents help the returnees to become committed to non-violence because military solutions as has been demonstrated by the northern Uganda war never solves problems instead they make them worse. The rejection of the military violence must be accompanied by sincere forgiveness and commitment to work for peace.

This shows us the power of grass-root organization by the parents of the abducted children in northern Uganda. They started in Lira, spread to Apach, Kitgum, Pader and Gulu districts. Parents, especially women have done a good job in this area. It is said that some of the returnees who have undergone the training are also trying to help others. It is possible that peace that is springing from the grass-root members will be lasting.

Theological reflection

In reflecting upon the women's experience in northern Uganda I will use the theology known as "Woman-defined theology," informed by liberation theology. Its primary purpose is to remove women from the situation of being marginalized socially, politically, economically and religiously, which they have suffered almost universally (Ndung'u and Mwaura 2005, 88). We may ask: What is women's rightful dignity as children of God? When we look at the situation of women in northern Uganda and Africa as a whole, especially in irregular warfare, we find that their dignity is trumped upon physically, mentally and spiritually. They are deprived of their freedom by being forced into war where they are sexually abused and made to bear unwanted children. Yet we find that in such wars both men and women suffer, though differently. The women in northern Uganda can only rebuild their lives and have their dignity restored if the reintegration process, that is in place right now, can make this a priority. I believe that these women were created in the image and likeness of God but this image has been disfigured in many ways during the war. This image needs restoration through counseling, education, sensitization and prayer. There is also need for forgiveness and reconciliation. I think that Mrs. Angelina Atyam's Association is doing a good job in trying to bring together the grass root people to try and reconcile and rebuild their lives anew.

Many women who came back from the bush were not accepted in their communities. They were discriminated against and nicknamed rebels, killers and so on. The communities need to be sensitized and educated that God still loves these women despite their mistakes. They are still God's children. We have to remember that some of these women were forced into war against their will, some of the children they bore were as result of rape. It is not entirely their fault. The woman-defined theology would help us understand the situation of these women and hence society would treat them differently. In fact the woman-defined theology would insist on restoring to these women their due human dignity and respect. These women need to have their voice heard by finding space and avenue where they can tell their stories.

The woman-defined theology advocates for serving God in happiness and joy. But how can the women in northern Uganda possibly do this when some of them live in abject poverty? These women can only serve and praise God in happiness if they are assisted to get jobs and earn a living. This would be one of the liberating elements that can bring them near God. Jesus was not a rich person but he did not live in abject poverty, he lived a modest life. Some of these women would like to follow his example. It is true that happiness is not found only in material things, but the Lord always wants us to have enough so that we may not be too poor, which may lead us to steal, or too rich, which might lead us to forget God.

The goal of woman-defined theology goes further than just looking at women alone. It is ultimately concerned with the rightful dignity of all human beings as God's children, and even beyond human, the dignity of all creation. In this latter concern, woman-defined theology is attentive to Paul's insight in Romans 8:19-23 and 2 Corinthians 5:19, that true liberation is universal and it involves humanity and the rest of creation together. In war situation not only women suffer but men as well plus the rest of creation. Therefore, in woman-defined theology, there are no exclusive "women's issues" in theology. All issues affect women, men and creation inclusively. Inclusiveness thus becomes a central point in this way of doing theology. All are creatures of God.

According to this theology, woman-defined theology is properly a joint effort of women and men to interpret the scriptures as they relate to women in a common search for new inclusive meanings. For African woman-defined theology, inclusiveness is central to the content itself as well as its quality. Both men and women need to bring their God-given talents together to rebuild what has been damaged in the war in northern Uganda. Women have been left behind in the African context. There is great need to include them in different activities, such as education, and training for different jobs, including military. Theology is genuine and liberating only when it includes all, that is, scholars and non-scholars, the rich and the poor. Any effort by feminism to marginalize men is reverse discrimination, and undercuts the whole liberation objective. Both the marginalization of women and men is sin against God's plan for universal solidarity. Both deny the dignity of the human person and diminish him or her. Paul says that, all creation is diminished in situations where oppression distorts divine presence in the universe. This is because creation represents the presence of God on earth. God is everywhere, omnipresent. Since the universe is permeated by divine presence and orderliness, hence discrimination, marginalization, physical, mental and psychological torture and abuse constitute a destruction of this order and is not acceptable. It can be seen clearly that any oppression or mistreatment and abuse of human beings, especially women and children and other creatures, as it has happened in northern Uganda and other parts of Africa, perverts God's design in order of creation and tears it apart.

The killing, raping of women in northern Uganda, and burning of property and other forms of destruction in armed conflicts go against God's design for humanity. Therefore, human beings have sinned and fallen short of God's glory and are in need of a savior, to bring about reconciliation and wholeness amongst themselves and with God. God is always ready to forgive if only human beings can turn to God with a repentant heart. It is the responsibility of everyone in Uganda and Africa as a whole to see to it that the bitter conflicts are resolved peacefully by putting in place structures of democracy and good governance by the government perhaps assisted by the international powers, if Uganda fails to do it alone.

Conclusion

In this article it is evident that in the modern warfare both women and men are active participants. The idea of looking at men as perpetrators of war and women as victims is somehow a thing of the past where people used to wage conventional wars. For example in Kony's war in northern Uganda, women engaged in active combat. However, in the northern Uganda war, many women were also victims of war for example some women were raped, shot at, killed and sexually abused in different ways. For some of the women who returned from the war, their contribution was not recognized properly. Instead they were rejected by their family members as killers and prostitutes. Some of the children born in the bush were not accepted by the community. And some of the women who came back from the bush now live in abject poverty.

Some women tried to act as peace-makers. For example, Betty Bigombe tried to initiate peace talks between the NRA rebels and the Government of Uganda but did not succeed because the government used the policy of "talk and fight," which made peace negotiations impossible. Another person who worked for peace was Sr. Rachele, the deputy headmistress of St. Mary's Aboke. She pursued the rebels who had abducted 139 students from the school. She negotiated for their release, and managed to have 109 girls released. Other women wrote about the war situation in northern Uganda trying to bring to the fore the horrible atrocities that were taking place in that area. This helped to get the attention of the local and international communities. Many NGOs came in to save the situation by providing the people with food relief, medical care and even shelter.

In addition to this, women like Angelina and her group of Concerned Parents Association have become a voice of the voiceless both at the national and international level. They have formed groups to sensitize people to get committed to non-violence, forgiveness and learning to live in peace. They are convinced that military violence cannot solve problems as the war in northern Uganda has demonstrated. The power of grass-root organization proves that this can help people achieve their goals.

The woman-defined theology seeks to find out the place of women in the world as children of God. The women in northern Uganda have been deprived of their human dignity. Men also have been oppressed though in a different way. The woman-defined theology advocated for liberation of both women and men because they are all children of God. Oppression wherever it is found is evil and goes against God's will. War, especially irregular warfare, like the one in northern Uganda, dehumanizes people both men and women. There is need for reconciliation and to restore wholeness, both for human beings and creation. When God created the world God saw that it was good (Genesis 1:31). It is therefore the responsibility of human beings to keep it as it supposed to be.

References

Alerotek, Maggie. 2005. Will Uganda get day to condemn massacres? Blog at STGINU, http://stginu.blogspot.com/2005_08_01_archive.html (accessed 20 January, 2010).

Behrend, Heike. 2004. *Alice Lakwena and the Holy Spirits: War in northern Uganda 1985–97.* Kampala: Fountain Publishers.

IRIN. 2008. Today you will understand: Women's war stories from northern Uganda. Available at: http://www.irinnews.org/Report.aspx? ReportId= 79306 (accessed 15 January, 2010).

Matembe, Miria. 2009. *Woman in the eyes of God: Reclaiming a lost identity.* Kampala: New Life Publishers.

Moser Caroline N.O., and Fiona C. Clark. 2001. *Victims, perpetrators or actors? Gender armed conflict and political violence.* London & New York: Zed Books.

Nandutu, Agnes, and Amacha Goli. 2005. Newspaper article. *Daily Monitor,* 11 March. Kampala: The Monitor Company.

Ndung'u, Nahashon, W., and Philomena N. Mwaura. 2005. *Challenges and prospects of the Church in Africa: Theological reflections of the 21st Century.* Nairobi: Paulines Publications, Africa.

Nwoye, Miriam Agatha Chinwe. 2006. Role of women in peace building and conflict resolution in African traditional societies: A selective review. Available at: http://www.afrikaworld.net/afrel/chinwenwoye.htm (accessed 15 January, 2010).

STGINU. 2005. I was raped by men who should have guarded me. Blog at Stop the Genocide in Northern Uganda, 27 June, 2005. Available at: http://stginu.blogspot.com/2005_06_01_archive.html (accessed 11 January 2010).

Temmerman, Els De. 2002. *Aboke girls: Children abducted in northern Uganda.* Kampala: Fountain Publishers.

Turshen, Meredeth, and Clotilde Twagiramariya. 1988. *What women do in wartime: Gender and conflict in Africa.* London and New York: Zed Books.

Wasike, Alfred. 2005. Newspaper article. *The Monitor.* 27 February. Kampala: The Monitor Company.

PART III

12

"The Lord Destroyed the Cities and Everyone Who Lived in Them"

The Lord's Resistance Army's Use of the Old Testament Sodom/Gomorrah Narrative

Helen Nkabala Nambalirwa
School of Mission and Theology, Stavanger, Norway,
Makerere University, Kampala, Uganda

Abstract

This article is based on a field study carried out by the author in February 2008 and January 2009. It is demonstrated how members of the Lords' Resistance Army (LRA) are using the Old Testament to spearhead their rebellion in the Acholi sub-region. The main focus is on how the biblical Sodom/Gomorrah narrative is being used to justify the different actions carried by the LRA members against the people of Northern Uganda.

Introduction

This article is about the use of the Old Testament by the Lord's Resistance Army (LRA), the rebel group in northern Uganda, which has been fighting the government of Uganda for over 20 years now. Their major claim is the desire to establish a government based on the Ten Commandments. It is clear from my research findings that the Old Testament plays an important role in the ideology of the LRA. The research findings show in particular a continuous use of the Sodom/Gomorrah narrative by the LRA ex-combatants. Therefore, in this article my question of concern is to find out the purpose of their use of the Sodom/Gomorrah narrative.

I will start the article by presenting how ex-LRA soldiers are using the Sodom/Gomorrah narrative in relation to their actions in the northern sub-region of Uganda. This will be followed by an analysis of their use of this narrative, after which I will conclude by attempting to give an answer to the question pointed out above, thus: What is the purpose of the ex-LRA's use of the Sodom/Gomorrah narrative?

The Sodom and Gomorrah narratives as used by the LRA members

The Lord's Resistance Army (LRA) was formed in the late 1987 by Joseph Kony, a self-proclaimed messianic prophet, with a mission to free the Acholi people of northern Uganda by overthrowing the government and installing a system based on the biblical Ten Commandments. Joseph Kony is from Odek in Southern Gulu and he is said to be a cousin of Auma Alice *Lakwena* (*Lakwena* means messenger), but he had never been a member of Alice's group, the Holy Spirit Movement. It is sometimes reported that Kony is a former Catholic catechist. However, Robert Gersony (1997, 30) says this is inaccurate. On the contrary, it is Kony's father who was a Catholic catechist and his mother is Anglican while his brother was believed to be a witch doctor. Upon his brother's death, Kony believed he inherited his brother's powers, and at the age of 26 he started his LRA group.

In the early years, Kony was reported to be guided by a "spirit general staff" of about 14 spirits, which included: the spirit of *Silly Slindi Mackay,* a Sudanese female chief of operations commander who worked together with *Kamki,* a Chinese, also in charge of operation; *Owora* an Alur (Ugandan), a commander; the spirit of *Juma Oris* (the leader of the West Nile Bank Front); a Chinese Deputy Chief (*Ing Chu/Insu*) commanding the imaginary jeep battalion and in charge of gifts like speaking in tongues; and a Briton (*King Bruce*) commanding the stones to turn into grenades. In addition, there was (*Jim Brickley*), an American spirit who was believed to be fighting with Kony's troops as long as they obeyed his commands but would turn against them if they disobeyed; *Byianka* an American war planner; *Sinaska,* a Chinese intelligence spirit; Dr. *Salen,* an Italian working with herbs and western drugs; *Oriska the Bore,* an American who was the chairman of all other spirits; *Soly Yakobo* from Europe, who was a great teacher responsible for teaching LRA members; *Karlo Lwanga* a Uganda Muganda spirit in charge of Peace talks; and lastly *Ali Salongo,* a Tanzanian chief controller.

During my field studies carried out in February 2008 and Jan 2009, I interviewed some formerly abducted children, ex-LRA high ranking commanders, religious leaders, politicians and some other members of the Acholi community. Ex-LRA members who stayed in the bush for three months to those who stayed for over 14 years were interviewed.

I discovered that, as they struggle to fulfil their claim of wanting to establish a government based on the biblical Ten Commandments, the LRA members use many Old Testament narratives in relation to their actions which according to them are all aimed at ensuring that the Ten Commandments are respected. Notable here is the fact that, while the LRA claim that they are fighting to restore the Ten Commandments, they seem to be breaking some of them (cf. Temmerman 2001, 154). For example, even when one of the commandments says that one should not kill, the LRA have been torturing and killing people. As a military force claiming to be fighting to restore the biblical Ten Commandments, their actions seem contradictory to what their actual practice appear to be. No wonder, therefore, the LRA has been branded as a force which breaks the commandments it seeks to restore.

However, this is not the view of the ex-combatants I interviewed. These ex-LRA members believe that they did not kill, they only executed duties on behalf of God. Talking about the restoration of the Ten Commandments, Arnold (all names of interviewees quoted in this article are fictional), an ex-LRA commander in charge of women and girls, and chief advisor to Kony, says: "For him [Kony], you have to destroy the people who do not believe."

The obvious tension in my view between theory and practice as far as the LRA in relation to the Ten Commandments is concerned, was a central topic in many of my interviews. To my surprise, many of my informants did not share the view that the LRA is breaking some of the commandments they are seeking to restore. On the contrary, they argue that all actions carried out by the LRA are sanctioned by God. This can be seen in some of Kony's teachings to his followers. As Arnold explains: "We also asked him [Kony] that this is the Ten Commandments, one of them says thou shall not kill. He said that one does not stop people who have sinned to be killed. That is why God also sent the angel to destroy Gomorrah."

In the same voice, Christopher, an ex-LRA member in charge of operation, recalls:

> I heard the history and the teaching that there were a lot of problems in Sodom and Gomorrah. And [...] Satan had become too much that he had overpowered God. Then God sent fire to go and burn Gomorrah and Sodom. So you must know that God could come and say that "today you people are sinners and I have come to punish you!" God uses people to punish people so they can reform. The LRA is using ammunition, and

you know very well ammunition plus ammunition fires human beings. That is why they say we are killing, but we are not. We are just fighting to protect the commandment.

The use of the Sodom and Gomorrah narrative in relation to the killings and other many atrocities committed by the LRA is supported by other informants. For example, in an interview with Gregory, also an ex-LRA soldier, he says: "LRA is just defending the Ten Commandments. You will see that what they are doing is even written in the Bible. Just like in Sodom and Gomorrah, God used someone to destroy the sinners."

John, an ex-commander and catechist in the LRA for 18 years, also uses the same argument when he argues that some killing is bad, but not all killing is. This prompted me to seek an explanation as to when killing is justified and when it is not. In response to my question, John explains that when someone breaks the Ten Commandments, such a person should be killed because that is disobedience. But the act of killing innocent people is what is bad. To me it seemed as though John was contradicting himself, but not to John. To affirm his views, John argues:

> You know this thing is very difficult to understand because Kony refers us to the Bible. He says "God does what … he wants to do." If he wants to kill, he sends a person on earth as he sent in the past. In the past, God sent rain to clear and finish people and it rained for 40 days. Many were killed. Also God sent the angel of death to finish the people in Sodom and Gomorrah. That was the anger of God.

On the issue of God using someone to do what he wants, Gregory confirms John's views when he asserts:

> Just like in Sodom and Gomorrah, God used someone to destroy the sinners. Even now, they use human beings to go and fight and you hear people saying God has punished the clan of these people, but you find it is not God fighting but the fellow people.

No wonder, the LRA also believes they are God's chosen generation whose task is to get rid of the sinners in Acholiland so as to give way for a new generation, which is pure. In support of this, Daniel an intelligence officer working with the president's office, explains:

> They also like to bring this story of Sodom and Gomorrah especially when he [Kony] is preaching to his people. He says this is already a lost lot like Sodom and Gomorrah who did not follow God's word and had to perish in fire. So he uses these stories to instil and verify to them that they are a chosen race and the rest are bad.

The case is not different for Dona, a female ex- soldier in charge of the sick bay. When asked about the various atrocities committed by the LRA, she responds:

> Killing? At first God himself killed the people by sending the flood during Noah and Gomorrah. But at Kony's time, according to Kony, he has sent the Holy Spirit and it is now the Holy Spirit sent by God which is doing the work.

In a follow-up interview with Dona, she affirms: "God is punishing Uganda as Sodom and Gomorrah. People are not following the teaching from the Bible, they have gone astray."

Steve, a former controller in the LRA, is of the same view with Dona when he observes:

> You see, when you look at the situation in Uganda now, it is similar and coming to what happened in Sodom and Gomorrah because people are not even respecting their fellow people, and [there are many] prostitutes. I think that is why God destroyed Sodom and Gomorrah. And when you see the wife of that man Lot, his woman did not obey the commandment and this you can compare with what Kony does also. Those who do not obey are killed and destroyed.

In relation to Steve's observation, Duncan, an ex-LRA member and former bodyguard of Kony, recalls:

> The only thing he was telling us is that God is going to punish this world because people have left the Ten Commandments. They don't follow. So times will come when such kind of things which were happening in Sodom and Gomorrah will be happening in this world.

This view is seconded by Arnold when he narrates:

> When Bishop Odama [the Roman-Catholic Archbishop of Gulu] came there, he [Kony] said, "I ask you Odama, who killed people in Gomorrah and Sodom? Was it God or Satan?" They said "God." And he [Kony] asked him, "Why do you teach people that it is Satan who kills? God is a man who does anything he wants even if you have not done anything bad. He can choose to kill as many as possible." He [Kony] said Acholi deserved punishment from God because they have turned away from God. He wanted to justify and tell people that it is God who kills. And it is better to blame God but not the spirit on him because he [Kony] knows the spirit is doing the command of God.

Summing up, according to the ex-LRA members whose testimonies we find above, what is happening in Uganda today and Northern Uganda in particular is being equated to what was happening in the Old Testament narrative of Sodom and Gomorrah. In the sense that, just as people in Sodom/ Gomorrah cities had sinned and were punished by God through total destruction, so have the people in Northern Uganda. Thus, the people in Northern Uganda equally deserve to be destroyed so as to pave way for a new generation. According to the ex-LRA combatants, they have been chosen by God to accomplish this mission.

Analysis of the LRA testimonies in light of the Sodom/Gomorrah narrative

I will start this section with an analysis of the sample of my informants, and this will be followed by an analysis of the testimonies of the ex-LRA members in relation to the biblical text from where I will proceed to conclude.

From the above testimonies it is evident that the narratives about Sodom and Gomorrah play some role in the LRA rhetoric as far as the restoration of the Ten Commandments is concerned. What is worth mentioning, though, is the fact that, looking at the sample of informants whose testimonies we see above reveals that only one (Dona) is female. It was quite a struggle finding females who were in high ranking positions no wonder, Dona was among the few female ex-combatants I managed to interview during my field research. She was one of the very few with good knowledge about the use of the Bible by the LRA and the only one who talked about the Sodom/Gomorrah narrative and how it was used by the LRA members. This could imply that in the LRA there is a patriarchal kind of system where most influential positions are for men.

Secondly, just like Dona, it was discovered that all the interviewees who referred to the narrative of Sodom/ Gomorrah as a way of justifying the LRA actions in Northern Uganda served in the LRA for over 10 years and they were in high ranking positions in LRA position as opposed to the formerly abducted children who had no rank at all or had stayed in the bush for shorter periods who admitted to having heard about the narrative but were not aware of the reason why it was used during the teachings. For example, Christopher an ex-LRA commander in charge of operation, stayed in the bush for almost 20 years. Arnold had been in charge of girls and women and was a chief advisor to Kony and had served in the LRA for a period of 18 years. The same is true for John, an ex-LRA catechist, and Steve, an ex-LRA controller. Duncan, also an ex-LRA member and former bodyguard of Kony stayed in the bush for 16 years. Dona, the female ex-LRA commander in charge of the sick bay stayed in the LRA for 14 years. And, Gregory served as an LRA soldier for 12 years. The reasons as to why this is so could be many, but in my view, as already mentioned, it seems that the longer one stayed as an LRA fighter in the bush, the more they understood the teachings of the group and thus they were converted into believing in their actions as being biblically grounded. But what is the Sodom/Gomorra narrative all about?

In Genesis 18 and 19 we are presented with the narratives about two cities, Sodom and Gomorrah. As Mulder (1992, 100.VI) points out, "an analysis of chapters 18 and 19 shows that the role played by the people of Sodom (and Gomorrah) originates in an independent tradition that was only secondarily linked to the Abraham stories." According to the narrative, God reveals his intention to destroy Sodom and Gomorrah because of its sins. There was a lot of immorality going on in the cities (Genesis 18:20) and the outcry of the people had reached God (Genesis 18:21). According to Mulder, the nature of the transgressions of Sodom was mainly immorality consisting of sexual debauchery, human hubris and violation of the law of hospitality (cf. Mulder 1992, 100.VI). After God's revelation, what follows here is a negotiation between God and Abraham whereby Abraham pleads with God to have mercy upon the cities should a certain number of faithful people be found there. A major theological point we see in this conversation is God's willingness to forgive the cities if even 10 faithful men are found there (Genesis 18:32). The climax comes when God sends his angels to confirm the cries that had reached him.

When the two men (strangers) come into the city, they are invited by Lot for a meal in his house. But before they go to bed, the people of Sodom surround Lot's house and demand that Lot hands over the strangers so that they may know them (Genesis 19:4). Lot pleads with them not to do such a thing to his guests and he even gives them an alternative: to take his daughters. This is rejected by the people and they even remind him that he is a stranger in their land after all. Seeing that he has been overpowered, the angels pull him back into the house and strike the men with a blinding light. It is at this stage that the angels tell Lot of the impending doom that is to befall the cities and they instruct him to go and get all his relatives so that they can go out of the city. Lot goes to tell the message to the men who were engaged to his daughters but they do not believe him, so they refuse to come with him. In the same way Lot delays his exit, but as time is running out he is hastily taken out of the city with the help of the angels (Genesis 19:16). As soon as he is out, God immediately rains down fire and brimstone out of heaven to destroy the cities (Genesis 19:24). But God remembered Abraham and saved his nephew together with his family (Genesis 19:29).

My first observation on this is that, in some cases it is clear that the narrative was just a part of Kony's teachings to his soldiers, although my informants seem not to be in position to explain why Kony the LRA leader chose to teach this particular narrative to them. However, one probable reason could be that as a Roman-Catholic, Kony could have learnt about this narrative in church before the start of the fighting. Therefore, with such a narrative at hand, Kony could easily find it suitable to convince his followers that they were an army of God. So, with this, one can say that he wanted to legitimize his orders and thus give an assurance to the LRA members that whatever actions they are carrying out are according to the divine will.

This assumption is based on Arnold's testimony who narrates that they asked Kony why they were killing, though one of the commandments was against it. As Arnold explains, Kony told them that this did not exclude the sinners and he referred to the Sodom/Gomorrah case where the sinners were destroyed by God himself. The same idea is reflected in the conversation between Bishop Odama and Kony as told by Arnold. The same idea is also seen in a statement by Dona at one point when she says that according to Kony, God has sent the spirit upon him to destroy all the sinners. J. Carter Johnson (2006, 1) seems of the same view when he writes that Kony uses passages from the Pentateuch to justify mutilation and murder.

On the other hand, it seems that those ex-LRA members who stayed in the bush longer are only finding a firm excuse for their actions, so they decide to use this Sodom/Gomorrah narrative as a justification for their actions, which among others include the Atiak massacre of 17 April 1995, where almost a whole village was destroyed (Briggs 2005, 116). This idea is also based on some statements made by ex-LRA members such as Dona who asserts that God is punishing Uganda now like Sodom and Gomorrah. Similar views are raised by Christopher and John among others. So in such cases as these the ex-LRA members seem to make the statements which justify their actions in relation to the Sodom/Gomorrah narrative by themselves. This could probably be because of the fact that these members had stayed in the bush as LRA combatants for a long period of over 10 years. Therefore, they could have already been assimilated into believing the biblical based ideologies of the LRA especially that they are fighting to protect the Ten Commandments. As a result, they find a reason in the Bible to justify their actions and in this case it is the Sodom/Gomorrah narrative.

In relation to the text of the narrative, the ex-LRA members seem to equate their role to that of the angels in the Sodom/Gomorrah narrative. As a group with a self-understanding that they are a chosen people commanded by God to fight for the commandments, the LRA members seem to suggest that they are messengers of God who are acting on his behalf to execute the divine duties. This is vividly seen when Christopher concludes one of his testimonies above by saying that while people say that the LRA is killing, he believes that they are not. What they are doing, is to fight so as to protect the Commandments. Also, as pointed out by Arnold, according to Kony fighting to restore the Ten Commandments means destroying all the people who do not believe. It is this self-understanding which probably compels the LRA members to use the Bible in order to legitimize their actions.

Furthermore, the claim by the LRA members that they are being used by God to destroy the sinful Acholi, like God used the angel to destroy Sodom and Gomorrah, seems to be based on Genesis 19:13 where the angels tell Lot about their intention to destroy Sodom for its sins.

This verse seems to suggest that God used the angels to destroy the cities. However, on further reading one finds that it is God himself who rained down sulphurous fire upon Sodom and Gomorrah, not angels. In Genesis 19:24 it is clearly indicated that the destruction upon Sodom and Gomorrah came ultimately without any intermediary or human agent (cf. Fields 1997, 160). Gerhard von Rad (1961, 212) seems to be of the same view when he writes, "At the climax of the event Yahweh appears speaking and acting directly without any mediator." This could imply that the ex-LRA members' continuous claim that God uses someone to kill or to destroy others, like he sent the angels in Sodom and Gomorrah, finds no proper basis in the Sodom/Gomorrah narrative. The justification, therefore, breaks down at this point.

In addition to that, in Genesis 18 we find that Abraham pleads with God not to destroy the cities if a certain number of faithful people are found in the cities, and surely God is willing to reverse this intended calamity should a specific number of faithful people be found in the cities. This explains why no sentence is passed before the visit of the angels. But as it says in Genesis 19:4, before the guests had gone to bed all the men from Sodom, both young and old, surrounded the house. This verse seems to suggest that the entire population of Sodom was involved in the sin (cf. Fields 1997, 77). Mulder (1992, 100.VI) further affirms this when he writes: "No one in Sodom was exempt from the sin." However, for the case of Acholiland, even when many of these ex-LRA members continuously talk of the need to destroy Acholi land because of the people's sins, many of them do not mention the actual sin which the Acholi people have committed. Yet, Steve attempts to mention the actual sins in northern Uganda, such as prostitution and lack of respect for fellow people. But other than the mentioning, there is no substantive evidence he provides to prove whether it was in order to punish these sins that the ex-LRA soldiers were carrying out all sorts of atrocities against the Acholi. It becomes even harder to believe that those were the sins in Acholiland when Els De Temmerman writes that during an interview with George, a highly placed commander in LRA, he was asked a question concerning the reason why Kony was killing the Acholi people who belong to his ethnic group, to which George responded (2001, 156):

> The Acholi people had become disloyal to him [Kony].They had turned away from him like Israel had turned away from God in the Old Testament. They had served foreign gods in their country as teachers, civil servants or refugees. They had entered the government system and sided with the great enemy Museveni. They ought to be punished for that.

Therefore, from the above statement, it seems that the LRA are only equating what is happening in Acholiland to what happened in the Old Testament and the reason for doing this is none other than finding a way of justifying their actions.

In relation to the above, in chapter 18 of Genesis we find that before God destroys the cities, he contemplates whether he should reveal to Abraham what he is about to do. Indeed in verse 20 of the same chapter God does reveal to Abraham and gives him reasons as to why he will destroy these cities. But in the case of the testimonies we have presented above, other than the claim made by Kony to his followers, we are not presented with any other information to show that God revealed to any one other than those involved in the act what he was about to do. This leaves one wondering whether what these ex-LRA members are claiming is something that was actually revealed to them by God or something that they choose to pick up and use for purposes of justifying their actions.

Besides, before God passes judgment and sentence against Sodom and Gomorrah, he sends his angels to prove the cries that had reached him (cf. Genesis 18:20). After the attack on Lot's guests, a sentence is passed. As Fields (1997, 77) writes, "all this suggests that the vile actions of the Sodomites were taken by the messengers to be a confirmation of the accusations against Sodom with the result that the planned punishment was allowed to go forward." However, we do not see this happening in Acholiland before the LRA members start their so-called "divine mission" to punish the people in Acholi land. Yet also, in Genesis 19:29, before destruction befalls Sodom and Gomorrah, care is taken for saving Lot and his family because he was good. So the Angels hastily took him and his family out of the city before the calamity. But when it comes to the LRA claims, they do not tell us of anyone who is saved by God before destruction other than the LRA members themselves. Arguably, therefore, what the ex-LRA members are doing is finding a way of legitimizing their actions by referring to the narrative.

Another observation is the aspect of duration of the destruction of the cities. In the Sodom and Gomorrah narrative, the destruction took place within a particular time frame. When one reads from Genesis 19:28, it is shown that the next morning Abraham got up and looked down and he saw dense smoke rising up. The biblical narrative seems to suggest that the destruction had already taken place the previous evening and it was a destruction which was complete and sudden. Fields (1997, 159) seems to be of the same view when he suggests: "It is logical to infer from the presentation in the Genesis version of the Sodom and Gomorrah tradition that the destruction of the cities was sudden: God rained fire and brimstone upon them, Gen. 19.24." But getting back to the LRA, it is undoubtedly clear that the insurgency has lingered on for over 20 years now. The ex-LRA members I interviewed do not even have a clue as to when this so-called "punishment" upon Acholiland will come to an end. This makes it hard for one to find reconciliation between the beliefs and claims of the LRA members that they are chosen by God to carry out his mission since their actions seem to have no time limit.

Lastly, one finds that the LRA members are meeting a lot of resistance from various political groups around the world such as the UPDF at a regional level and the International Criminal Court in a broader perspective. While resistance may have been present in the Sodom and Gomorrah narrative, say for example the resistance the angels had received when all the members in Sodom surrounded Lot's house with a desire to know them (verses 4 -5, at the house of Lot), it is very clearly indicated in Verse 10 that the angels overpowered the people. However, this happens not to be the case for the LRA where there is a lot of resistance from other external forces. Consider also that there are many reports of LRA-members dying while in combat. So, if these LRA members are really a pure people sent by God to fight the sinners, why is it that in some cases they seem to be overpowered? How can one explain the deaths and injuries on the LRA side? Such shortfalls only seem to affirm the assumption that most probably when these ex-LRA members refer to the Sodom/Gomorrah narrative, they are only doing it so as to legitimize their actions.

Conclusion

In conclusion, just as Fields suggests regarding the continuous use of the narrative that it seems as though Sodom is an idea of epitomization which serves as a useful example of wickedness and judgment which transcends historical reality and provides the prophets with the tool to illustrate the depths of sin into which the people's they address had sunk and severity of the punishment they would receive (cf. 1997, 184). It is therefore possible that, in the same way, these ex-LRA members have found that this Sodom/Gomorrah narrative presents them with similar incidents of Yahweh's action of destruction as those they have committed in northern Uganda. Therefore, this coupled with teachings from their leader, Joseph Kony, like we observed in the interviews with my informants, probably these ex-combatants prefer to use the Sodom/Gomorrah narrative as a reason to explain their actions in northern Uganda. It is upon this, therefore, that I conclude by arguing that the main purpose for as to why the ex-LRA members refer to the Sodom Gomorrah narratives is to legitimize their actions.

References

Briggs, Jimmie. 2005. *Innocents lost: When child soldiers go to war*. New York: Basic Books.

Fields, Weston W. 1997. *Sodom and Gomorrah: History and motif in Biblical narrative*. Sheffield: Sheffield Academic Press Ltd.

Gersony, Robert. 1997. *The anguish of northern Uganda: Results of a field-based assessment of the civil conflicts in northern Uganda*. USAID and United States Embassy, Kampala, Uganda. http://www.internal-displacement.org/8025708F004CE90B/(httpDocuments)/3FF99DEEED86A1D38 02570B7005A5558/$file/The+anguish+of+northern+Uganda.pdf (accessed 6 January 2010).

Johnson, J. Carter. 2006. Deliver us from Kony. *Christianity today* Vol. 50, No. 1. Available at http://www.christianitytoday.com/ct/2006/january/18.30.html (accessed 6 January 2010).

Mulder. M.J. 1992. Sodom and Gomorrah. In Freedman, David Noel (ed.) *The Anchor Bible Dictionary*. New York: Doubleday, 99-103.

Rad, Gerhard von. 1961. *Genesis: A commentary*. Transl. By John H.Marks, Philadelphia: Westminster Press (The Old Testament Library).

Temmerman, Els De. 2001. *Aboke girls: Children abducted in northern Uganda*. Kampala: Fountain publishers.

13

Killing Children with God's Permission?

The Rhetoric of Retaliation in Psalm 137

Marta Høyland Lavik
School of Mission and Theology, Norway

Abstract

Through an examination of the rhetoric of retaliation in Psalm 137, this article explains how hurt religious feelings culminate in a wish for retaliation over the enemy (v. 9): "Blessed is the one who seizes and smashes your babies to the rock!" Does Psalm 137 then give God's permission to kill children? The Psalm neither addresses, nor answers this, but interpreters are nevertheless puzzled with the question. The key to understand this prayer for revenge lies in the underlying hurt religious feelings of the characters portrayed in the Psalm. In ancient as well as in modern times, acts of hatred are sometimes justified referring to resources of religious traditions and sacred texts, and Psalm 137 is relevant in the context of children and war. If not read with an ethical consciousness, it is possible to take Psalm 137 as an encouragement to kill children in the name of God.

Introduction

Like many armed groups in the world, The Lord's Resistance Army (LRA) in northern Uganda uses children as soldiers. Joseph Kony, leader of the LRA, is by his soldiers looked up to as a Moses figure who leads his people towards the promised land—a land which in turn is intended to be governed by the ten commandments. This mosaic authority of Kony can be traced back to Old Testament texts where Moses appears as a liberator, a lawgiver and a prophet.[1]

It is understandable that armed groups such as the LRA do violent acts with the gun in one hand, and the Bible in the other. When the Bible has authority in a society, biblical texts play a role in life—also in military circles (see Kartveit in the present anthology, and Temmerman 2001). It should not be a secret that some biblical texts describe violence and killing without questioning these acts (see Barton 1998, 1-2, and Nambalirwa's and Holter's articles in the present anthology). This article will therefore add to the discussion by analysing one representative Old Testament text that opens up for acting violently against children: "Blessed is the one who seizes and smashes your babies to the rock!" (Psalm 137:9). This prayer of retaliation can be taken as an encouragement to do acts of hatred and revenge—in ancient as well as in modern times. Psalm 137 is therefore relevant when it comes to the question of children and war.

For many interpreters—myself included—it is difficult to agree with the psalmist in this rage. Still, a key to understand the hatred at the end of Psalm 137 lies in the rhetorical shape of the psalm. In recent years, several literary interpretations of Psalm 137 have appeared, and these studies have inspired me to examine the rhetoric of retaliation in Psalm 137 (cf. Bar-Efrat 1997, 3-11, Savran 2000, 43-58, and Berlin 2005, 65-86).

v. 1
Beside the rivers in Babylon
there we sat and wept
when we remembered Zion.
v. 2
On the poplars in the midst of her,
we hung up our lyres.
v. 3
For there our captors asked us words of a song,
our abductors,[2] joy:
"Sing for us a song of Zion!"
v. 4
How shall we sing[3] the song of YHWH
on foreign soil?
v. 5
If I forget you, Jerusalem,
may my right hand forget (me)!
v. 6
May my tongue stick to my palate,
if I not remember you!

If I will not ascend to Jerusalem
with joy upon my head![4]
v. 7
Remember, YHWH, Jerusalem's day,
against the sons of Edom
those who said: 'Lay bare, lay bare,
until her foundation!'
v. 8
Daughter of Babylon, the devastated,
blessed is the one who rewards you
the recompense you gave us!
v. 9
Blessed is the one who seizes and smashes
your babies to the rock!

Date, composition and genre

Scholars debate whether Psalm 137 is composed during or after the exile.[5] Although this is an interesting discussion, the question of dating is of no consequence in this article as my aim is to describe the rhetorical shape of the text. Regardless a dating during or after the exile, it is evident that the text portrays the situation for the exiled as difficult (cf. Berlin 2005, 65): "'Exile' does not necessarily mean living outside of the former Kingdom of Judah. (…) Exile is not only a geographic place, it is a religious state of mind."

Most scholars argue for a composition of three stanzas in Psalm 137 – although there are proposals to divide the psalm into two, four or five parts (cf. Becking 2009, 191). The two most common ways of delimiting Psalm 137 are the following: (i) vv. 1-3, 4-6, 7-9, or (ii) vv. 1-4, 5-6, 7-9. In this article, the delimitation in point (i) is followed.

Classifying this psalm has proved to be difficult as it moves between at least three genres. The psalm has thus been proposed to be a communal lament for Jerusalem, a modified Zion psalm, and a malediction against Edom and Babylon, due to the contents of the three stanzas: vv. 1-3(4) have elements of a communal lament, vv. 4(5)-6 of a Zion psalm, and vv. 7-9 of an anathema (cf. Ahn 2008, 267, 271-274). This Psalm transforms the song of Zion into a lament for the lost Jerusalem, it is (cf. Berlin 2005, 69 and 71): "(...) a song about cultic singing in the absence of the Temple."

The rhetoric of retaliation in Psalm 137

Psalm 137 starts with weeping (v. 1) and ends with a wish for retaliation over the babies of the enemy (v. 9). Let us examine the psalm stanza by stanza in order to understand this shift from crying to cruelty.

Psalm 137:1-3 Lament over the lost Jerusalem

The first stanza of the psalm opens with the rivers of Babylon and ends with Zion, and the contrast between these two entities sets the theme not only for this stanza, but for the psalm as a whole. A well known Old Testament motif is the Babylonian conquest of Jerusalem with the destruction of the first temple, and the deportation of the leaders and some of the people. What associations of exile does this first stanza of Psalm 137 create? It can be debated whether or not Babylon here refers to the geographical place of the historical Babylon of Nebuchadnezzar or not. As a literary motif, however, Babylon functions in Psalm 137:1 to underline all that is negative, in contrast to the positive images of Zion and Jerusalem (Watson 1997, 566). Traditionally, scholars have assumed that life in exile in itself is a cause of sorrow, and suffering and exile have been connected. More recently, however, it has been argued that life in Babylon as such was not that bad (cf. Scott 1997 and Becking 2009, 190): "(...) the actual fate of the exiled Judaeans was not as harsh and bitter as often has been assumed." Whether or not this perspective on the life conditions for the exiled can be verified, it does not change the fact that many Old Testament texts portray the period of the Babylonian exile as something negative, and our text belongs to this negative tradition.

Psalm 137 opens by letting the speakers of the psalm express what it feels like being "beside the rivers in Babylon" (v. 1). In Hebrew, it is rare that a verse begins with an adverb of place, but when it does, it gives the place mentioned emphasis. Also verse 2 begins with an adverbial phrase of place: "On the poplars in the midst of her, we hung up our lyres." Whether or not the speakers are in Babylon or Jerusalem is debated among commentators, but is of no consequence for the present study. From a literary perspective, the condition of being removed and remote is the point when Babylon is set up against Zion and Jerusalem (cf. Berlin 2005, 67). The contrast between Babylon on the one side, and Zion and Jerusalem on the other side is underlined by the word *šm*, "there," twice in this stanza (v. 1 and v. 3) as well as by the expression '*dmt nkr*, "foreign soil," in v. 4. Another contrasting element in v. 1 is the mentioning of the rivers in Babylon. The dry land of the exiles is here indirectly compared with the more fertile area in which they now dwell. When Zion is thought of, the people feel sorrow (cf. Becking 2009, 196). The Hebrew verb *bkh*, "to weep," or "to utter a sad sound or cry," is mostly used in contexts of grief and humiliation (cf. Deut 34:8; 2 Sam 1:24; Ezra 10:1), and more rarely in contexts of joy (cf. the Jacob narrative, Gen 29:11; 33:4; 46:29). Here, it is used in the context of grief over the lost Jerusalem in contrast to the joy the people would have felt if they were present in the temple. Another contrasting element in this first stanza is that between quietness and singing. The poplars in the midst of Babylon where the lyres are hung (v. 2), portray in a concrete and visible way the state the exiles find themselves in: the lyres are out of reach where they hang useless in the trees (cf. Kugel 1994, 209-210). Unlike the song of joy, this cry of sorrow has no musical accompaniment.

What does the mourning imply? Even before the temple was destroyed, a mourner was not permitted to engage in acts of public joy. After the destruction of Jerusalem, all Judeans are in this sense mourners—as they are cut off from the cultic worship of God, and of Zion (cf. Körting 2006, 83). They are forbidden to sing praise to God, and in this context, the request from the captors to sing songs of Zion is provocative, and cannot be fulfilled (cf. Anderson 1991, 43). As Adele Berlin puts it (cf. Berlin 2005, 8): "'Joy' has the cultic meaning of being in God's presence, worshipping in the Temple (...)." This kind of joy, this kind of Zion/Lord-songs is impossible to perform in a foreign land, removed from the Temple." Then, while sitting in sorrow by the rivers of Babylon, the people are requested to be glad and sing a song of Zion (v. 3):

> For there our captors asked us words of a song,
> our abductors, joy:
> "Sing for us a song of Zion!"

Why is the request to sing the songs of Zion so provocative? (Cf. Brenner 2003, 87): "Clearly, the singing does embody religious identity (...). It does so for the captors as well as for the victims." Far away from a destroyed temple, the request to sing the songs of Zion is taken as an insult. (For another view, see Kugel 1994, 185 and Brenner 2003, 78). The tension is created when the captors and abductors—those responsible for the fate of the Judeans—ask the people in exile to sing as if they were at home in the temple. This request makes bigger the contrast between the actual life in exile and the remembrance of the home with the destroyed temple that had to be left behind. From the way the rest of the text is shaped, it is clear that this insult is what accelerates the negative emotions that end with the harsh wish for retaliation.

Psalm 137: 4-6 Mourning in the absence of the temple

The memory of Zion determines the way of thinking and behaving for the mourners of vv. 1-3. In this second stanza of the psalm, vital parts of the body are included in the mourning. The request to sing a song of Zion (v. 3) is answered by a rhetorical question (v. 4): "How shall we sing the song of YHWH on foreign soil?" The word *ỳk*, "how", is characteristic for songs of lament. The explanation (vv. 4-6) is ironically formed as a song (cf. Brenner 2003, 77 and Berlin 2005, 68). If the song asked for by the captors ever was performed, the captors would have had no idea about what was being sung as they did not know Hebrew, and could believe that they heard a song of Zion (cf. Renfroe 1988, 526-527). It is however not a song of Zion that is sung. Verses 5-6 are formed as an oath in first person singular (if *x*, then *y*): If Jerusalem is forgotten for the speaker in the psalm, then the body will wither. Vital parts of the body do not function: If the psalmist is to forget Jerusalem, he will rather forget his right hand—which normally would play the lyre (v. 2). And he will rather have his tongue—which would normally sing (v. 3)— fastened to his palate (cf. Rendsburg and Rendsburg 1993, 388). Not only is the right hand used when one plays the lyre. It is the right hand that is raised when one gives an oath. Likewise, the tongue is not only used for singing. The tongue that utters the oath will not be able to speak if the punishment for not keeping the oath is fulfilled (cf. Bar-Efrat 1997, 7). As is often pointed at by commentators, most of verses 5-6 are formed as a chiasm. This fine chiasm of vv. 5-6 together with the first person singular creates a striking closeness between what is said, and how it is said:

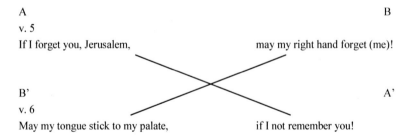

A   B
v. 5
If I forget you, Jerusalem,   may my right hand forget (me)!

B'   A'
v. 6
May my tongue stick to my palate,   if I not remember you!

Expressing the punishment for not keeping the oath through physical terms gives the message an existential meaning as "I" is not only the one who utters the oath verbally, "I" will be physically affected if the oath is not fulfilled. Also the shift from third person plural (in vv. 1-4) to first person singular (vv. 5-6) diminishes the distance between the speaker of the psalm and the message he utters, and underlines the existential meaning of what is described. Verses 4-6 are put in a way that (cf. Becking 2009, 198): "(...) the singers want to protect themselves from giving up their religious traditions." The end of verse 6 is difficult to translate properly into English. What does it mean to "ascend to Jerusalem with joy upon my head"? Both v. 3 and v. 6 uses the same word for "joy," *śmḥh*, and I think Bar-Efrat is right when he says about the last part of v. 6 (cf. Bar-Efrat 1997, 8): "This verse, which began with parts of the head (tongue and palate), ends with the whole head (in the sense of highest point)." There are various ways of translating this part of the verse, but the essence seems to be more or less the same, namely that Jerusalem is to be the highest joy for the speaker of the psalm.

Psalm 137:7-9 Retaliation over the enemy

The unpleasant contents of the last stanza of Psalm 137 have caused much uneasiness for readers of this text.[6] One way out of the problem is to regard vv. 7-9 not original to the psalm (cf. Gunkel 1968, xxx). Another way is to see whether the psalm itself gives any clue to why a wish for retaliation is uttered. This article argues that the way the psalm is shaped rhetorically, shows that the call for retaliation starts at the beginning of the psalm. This does however not get us away from the cruel words of retaliation, and for the ancient Israelite (cf. Bar-Efrat 1997, 8): "[t]he intention is of course that God draw practical conclusions with respect to the Edomites." The day of Jerusalem is the fatal day, and the people can not forget it. The therapeutic aspect of Psalm 137:7-9 is pointed at by several interpreters (cf. Renfroe 1988, 525 and the following quote from Brenner 2003, 87):

> However, and without minimizing this: (...) how else can the powerless be rid of the poison of anger and hate, the frustrated wish for revenge, if not by giving verbal expression to it?

A psychological key to the issue of violent texts can also be seen in biblical texts such as Jer 10:25 and Psalm 79:6-7. However, although our text does not describe the actual act of killing, the accepted rule in ancient societies was execution when a wish for retaliation was expressed (cf. Mowinckel 2004, 44).

The first four verses of Psalm 137 are held in first person plural, whereas the next two verses are in first person singular. The three last verses use an imperative or exclamation. The shift from plural (vv. 1-4) to singular (vv. 5-6), together with the exclamation to YHWH in the end, function to emphasise the emotional stress. In verse 7 YHWH is addressed in direct speech, and is called upon to remember the day of Jerusalem: "Remember, YHWH, Jerusalem's day, against the sons of Edom, those who said: 'Lay bare, lay bare, until her foundation!'" The first words of verse 8 also function as an address: "Daughter of Babylon, the devastated …" After this opening, verses 8 and 9 continue with two sentences that both start with the formula *'šrê*, "blessed is the one who…":

v. 8
…blessed is the one who rewards you
the recompense you gave us!
v. 9
Blessed is the one who seizes and smashes
your babies to the rock!

To be noticed on a structural level is the balanced gender language of this last stanza: "Sons of Edom" (v. 7) and "daughter of Babylon" (v. 8) are addressed, and "your babies" to be smashed to the rock (v. 9) belong to both of them. The wish to kill babies is cried out to YHWH and as such, this wish for retaliation (cf. Becking 2009, 201): "(…) is not a god-less cry for cruelty." YHWH is asked to take revenge on behalf of the people. This curse-like plead for retaliation is held in the language of beatification. Twice, in vv. 8 and 9, the word *'šrê*, "blessed is the one who…" is uttered in the context of a curse (cf. Mowinckel 2004, 52):

Among the cursing Psalms, attention must be drawn to Ps. 137 (…). The prayer finally passes into a direct curse in a particularly refined form, namely as a word of blessing on the person who shall inflict the most cruel revenge on Edom.

This contrast between vocabulary and contents makes the wish for retaliation strong and harsh. Why this hatred? The feeling of being mocked and humiliated for one's religious identity ("Sing us one of the songs of Zion!", v. 3), adds new feelings: anger and hatred, and these negative emotions are underneath the wish for retaliation that is uttered in vv. 7-9. The captors who ask for a song of joy (v. 3), receive the opposite—a song of judgement. This verbal revenge is first stated in general terms—a wish that Edom's sons and the daughter of Babylon will receive the same as they have given to others (v. 7-8), and then as a specific wish for retaliation over a certain group of people by the enemy (v. 9): "Blessed is the one who seizes and smashes your babies to the rock!"

The contrast is sharp: The one who brings misfortune over the enemy is *'šrê*, "blessed." YHWH is asked to not forget the cruelty of Edom and Babylon toward the Judeans (cf. Berlin 2005, 69): "If the poet must remember Jerusalem, then God must remember Jerusalem's enemies." The psalmist formulates the hatred and wish for retaliation through attacking the enemy at its weakest point—by attacking the most vulnerable members of the community, the defenceless babies. We know from several Old Testament texts that warfare in ancient Near East (as elsewhere) is not described as humane (cf. Kraus 1978, 1086): "Die Aussage in 9 ist (...) ein Hinweis auf die Grausamkeit der antiken Kriegshandlungen überhaupt. Vgl. Hos 10,14; 14,1; Nah 3:10; Jes 13:16; 2Kö 8,12 (Luk 19,44)." The idea of smashing little children is present in several texts in the Old Testament, see for instance Isa 13:16; 14:21; Nah 3:10, Hos 14:1. There is however no evidence in biblical texts that the enemies of Israel and Judah did throw infants against the rock—as is implicit in Psalm 137:8-9 (cf. Brenner 2003, 85): "(...) where have we found in the Hebrew bible that the 'enemies', or Babylonians, or Edomites for that matter, did throw infants against the rock, as is claimed in vv. 8-9?". Although Old Testament texts do not prove it, scholars claim that killing small children this way was (cf. Allen 1983, 237): "(...) a feature of ancient Near Eastern warfare."[7]

Summing up

The three stanzas show a negative development: from sorrow (v. 1) to revenge and retaliation (v. 9). The stanzas are tied together by common elements. The words "remember" and "forget" occur together with Zion and Jerusalem five times, and in all three stanzas, and the following words give associations to the musician: lyre, song, right hand, tongue. Of contrasting elements are the following central: Weeping and joy, singing and quietness, rivers and dry land, Babylon and Zion/Jerusalem. Babylon is mentioned in the beginning (vv. 1-2) and at the end of the psalm (v. 8), and envelopes the psalm.

From the rhetorical shape of Psalm 137:1, it is clear that what provokes the mourning is not the state of being situated in Babylon, but remembering Zion and all Zion means when one is far away. In Psalm 137:1, Zion stands for all that shapes the identity—both culturally and religiously—for the people in exile. In vv. 1-4, the speaker of the psalm speaks in third person plural, as a representative for the community. In verses 5-6, the verbs change to singular in number, and the speaker forms a curse at himself. The shape of the psalm can be summarised as follows: (i) The rhetoric of Psalm 137 is built up around hurt religious feelings. (ii) The request to sing the songs of Zion from those described as the captors and abductors is perceived as an act of mockery. (iii) By giving words to negative emotions, the ground is laid for the hatred that culminates in the wish for retaliation over the weakest part of the enemy—the babies (v. 9).

Does Psalm 137 give God's permission to kill children?

Why is Psalm 137 relevant in an anthology about formerly recruited children in northern Uganda? As we know that the LRA bases some of its ideology on Old Testament texts, the present article addresses the biblical aspect of LRA's rhetoric. Psalm 137 stands here as a representative example of biblical texts that can be interpreted to legitimise violence.

Has an examination of the rhetorical shape of Psalm 137 then enabled us to understand the words of retaliation in this text? The psalm does not explicitly express feelings like: "I am hurt, I feel sorrow, I am angry" etc. Still, from the rhetorical shape the psalm is given, it is clear that Psalm 137 shows how mocking and humiliation can hurt religious feelings, and how such feelings can result in a prayer of retaliation. For the ancient Israelite, such words of retaliation functioned not merely therapeutic—as a way of getting rid of negative feelings. The uttered words had power to fulfill what they said. Does the text then give God's permission to kill children? Psalm 137 does not answer this question, neither does it question that the prayer of retaliation stands against the Old Testament commandment "You shall not kill" (Exod 20:13). What the present analysis shows, though, is that the way Psalm 137 is shaped opens up for an interpretation that would answer yes to the question of whether or not it is legitimated to kill children in the name of God.

Why, then, is it not acceptable for me to do as the psalmist here wishes? First, although there is a gap of several thousand years between the ancient Israelites and the readers in the twenty-first century, the texts are the same. When texts containing a violent message are read, there is need for an ethical consciousness (cf. Barton 1998, 2): "(…) to accept (…) the ethical implications of the unappealing passages (…) seems implausible at best and ridiculous or even immoral at worst." In ancient as well as in modern times, rules are set up by societies for people to follow (Barton 1994, 12), and there are norms and laws in my society that protect children against violence and crimes. Second, as an Old Testament scholar in the twenty-first century, I cannot jump over the long history of interpretation in Old Testament studies in particular, and in theological studies in general. This implies that I am not the first one to interpret the text, neither am I an innocent reader. Thus, the history of interpretation helps me to place my own reading into an interpretative context, and helps me to judge between periphery and center in biblical texts. Third, I need to reflect upon the complex questions concerning the authority of the Bible, and how to deal with texts with a violent message in societies where the authority of the Bible is strong (see Magnar Kartveit in the present anthology). These three points mean that although an ancient holy text opens up for killing babies in the name of God, this does not automatically mean that it is an act that should be pursued (cf. Barton 1998, 1-3). However, if read straight forward and without taking into consideration the three points just mentioned, this text can easily be taken as an encouragement to kill—even babies—in God's name. This is so because the text itself does not question the violent message it contains.

We do not know if Psalm 137 is part of the ideological framework of the LRA. What we know, however, is that in ancient as well as in modern societies, acts of hatred and revenge are sometimes justified referring to resources of religious traditions and sacred texts. This psalm has shown itself to be relevant when it comes to the question of children and war as it reminds us that in some cases, love for one's own people and religion is accompanied with negative wishes over the others—and these wishes are (cf. Bar-Efrat 1997, 11): "(…) sometimes understandable, but never laudable (…)."

References

Ahn, John. 2008. Psalm 137: Complex communal lament. *Journal of Biblical Literature* 127 (2):267-289.

Allen, Leslie C. 1983. *Psalms 101-150.* Waco: Word Books (Word Biblical Commentary; 21).

Anderson, Gary A. 1991. *A time to mourn, a time to dance: The expression of grief and joy in Israelite religion.* University Park: Pennsylvania State University Press.

Bar-Efrat, Shimon. 1997. Love of Zion: A literary interpretation of Psalm 137. In *Tehilla le-Moshe. Biblical and Judaic studies in honor of Moshe Greenberg*, ed. M. Cogan et al., 3-11. Winona Lake: Eisenbrauns.

Barton, John. 1994. The basis of ethics in the Hebrew Bible. *Semeia* 66:11-22.

Barton, John. 1998. *Ethics and the Old Testament. The 1997 diocese of British Columbia John Albert Hall lectures at the Centre for studies in religion and society in the University of Victoria.* London: SCM Press.

Becking, Bob. 2009. Does exile equal suffering? A fresh look at Psalm 137. In *Exile and suffering. A selection of papers read at the 50th anniversary meeting of the Old Testament Society of South Africa OTWSA/OTSSA,*

Pretoria August 2007, ed. Bob Becking and D. Human, 183-202. Leiden: Brill (Oudtestamentische Studiën; 50).

Berlin, Adele. 2005. Psalms and the literature of exile: Psalms 137, 44, 69, and 78. In *The book of Psalms. Composition and reception*, ed. Peter W. Flint and Patrick D. Miller, 65-86. Leiden: Brill (Supplements to Vetus Testamentum; 99. Formation and Interpretation of Old Testament Literature; 4).

Brenner, Athalya. 2003. 'On the Rivers of Babylon' (Psalm 137), or between victor and perpetrator. In *Sanctified aggression. Legacies of biblical and post biblical vocabularies of violence*, ed. Jonneke Bekkenkamp and Yvonne Sherwood, 76-91. London: T&T Clark International.

Doom, Ruddy, and Koen Vlassenroot. 1999. Kony's Message: A New *Koine*? The Lord's Resistance Army in northern Uganda, *African Affairs* 98:5-36.

Freedman, David Noel. 1971. The structure of Psalm 137. In *Near eastern studies in honour of William Foxwell Albright*, ed. Hans Goedicke, 187-205. Baltimore: John Hopkins.

Goulder, Michael. 1998. *The Psalms of the return. (Book five, Psalms 107-150): Studies in the Psalter, IV*. Sheffield: University of Sheffield 1998 (Journal for the study of the Old Testament. Supplement series; 258).

Gunkel, Herman. 1968. *Die Psalmen*. Göttinger Handkommentar zum Alten Testament, 2, Die poetischen Bücher, 2, Göttingen: Vandenhoeck & Ruprecht, 5th edition 1968.

Hartberger, Birgit. 1986. *"An den Wassern von Babylon...": Psalm 137 auf den Hintergrund von Jeremia 51, der biblischen Edom-Traditionen und babylonischer Originalquellen*, Frankfurt am Main: Peter Hanstein (Bonner biblische Beiträge; 63).

Hoffman, Yair. 2003. The fasts in the book of Zechariah and the fashioning of national remembrance. In *Judah and the Judaeans in the Neo-Babylonian Period*, ed. Obed Lipschits and Joseph Blenkinsopp, 169-218. Winona Lake: Eisenbrauns.

Kellermann, Ulrich. 1978. Psalm 137. *Zeitschrift für die Alttestamentliche Wissenschaft* 90:43-58.

Kraus, Hans-Joachim. 1978. *Psalmen 60-150*. Neukirchen-Vluyn: Neukirchener Verlag.

Kugel, James L. 1994. *In Potiphar's house: The interpretive life of biblical texts.* Cambridge: Harvard University Press.

Körting, Corinna. 2006. *Zion in den Psalmen.* Tübingen: Mohr Siebeck.

Mowinckel, Sigmund. 2004. *The Psalms in Israel's worship. Vol II.* Tr. by D.R. Ap-Thomas. Grand Rapids: Eerdmans.

Mwebe, Charles Muwunga. 2003. The genesis and nature of the LRA in northern Uganda. *African Ecclesial Review* 45 (4):349-372.

Nambalirwa, Helen Nkabala. Ongoing PhD-project. "There is no difference between Moses and Kony": Old Testament motifs in the rhetoric of the Lord's Resistance Army.

Oduyoye, Mercy Amba. 1997. *The Psalms of Satan.* Ibadan: Sefer Books.

Rendsburg, Gary A. and Susan L. Rendsburg. 1993. Psychological and philological notes to Psalm 137. *The Jewish Quarterly Review* 83 (3-4):385-399.

Renfroe, Fred. 1988. Perisflage in Psalm 137. In *Ascribe to the Lord. Biblical and other studies in memory of Peter C. Craigie*, ed. Lyle M. Eslinger and Glen Taylor, 509-527. Sheffield: Sheffield Academic Press (Journal for the Study of the Old Testament; 67).

Risse, Siegfried. 2006. Wohl dem, der deine kleinen Kinder packt und sie am Felsen zerschmettert: Zur Auslegungsgeschichte von PS 137, 9. *Biblical Interpretation* (14/4):364-384.

Savran, George. 2000. "How can we sing a song of the Lord?" The strategy of lament in Psalm 137. *Zeitschrift für die Alttestamentliche Wissenschaft* 112 (1):43-58.

Scott, James M. 1997. *Exile: Old Testament, Jewish, and Christian conceptions.* Leiden: Brill.

Spieckermann, Hermann. 1989. *Heilsgegenwart: Eine Theologie der Psalmen.* Göttingen: Vandenhoeck & Ruprecht (Forschungen zur Religion und Literatur des Alten und Neuen Testaments; 148).

Temmerman, Els de. 2001. *Aboke Girls: Children abducted in northern Uganda.* Kampala: Fountain Publishers.

Watson, Duane F. 1997. Babylon in the NT. *The Anchor Bible Dictionary*, ed. David Noel Freedman, 565-566. New York: Doubleday.

Weinfeld, Moshe. 1979. Burning babies in ancient Israel: A rejoinder to Morton Smith's article in *JAOS* 95 (1975), 477-479. *Ugarit-Forschungen* 10:411-413.

Notes

[1] Kony rarely gives interviews, and the LRA does not distribute pamphlets or booklets that show the ideology of the armed group. Information about the religious aspect of the rhetoric of the LRA is therefore mainly traced from formerly recruited children, cf. an ongoing PhD-project by Helen Nkabala Nambalirwa: "'There is no difference between Moses and Kony': Old Testament Motifs in the Rhetoric of the Lord's Resistance Army." The key words liberator, lawgiver and prophet are applied to Kony in her work. For a brief background to the religious aspect in LRA's rhetoric, see Doom and Vlassenroot 1999, Mwebe 2003, and an interview with Kony and leaders of the LRA by Sam Farmar, "I will use the ten commandments to liberate Uganda," *The Times*, June 28, 2006, http://www.timesonline.co.uk/tol/news/world/article680339.ece?print=yes&randnum= 1151003209000 (accessed 28 October, 2009).

[2] For the translation of this *hapax legomenon*, see Kellermann 1978, 45.

[3] For this translation, see Renfroe, 1988, 524, footnote 34.

[4] For this translation, see Freedman 1971, 197-198.

[5] For a recent overview of the discussion, see Ahn 2008, 270-271. See also Kellermann 1978, 51-52; Allen 1983, 238-239; Hartberger 1986, 4-7; Spieckermann 1989, 117-118; Goulder 1998, 226-227 and Hoffman 2003, 180.

[6] For a recent overviews of solutions to the interpretation of v. 9, see Risse 2006, 364-384. Cf. also the more extensive history of interpretation provided by Hartberger 1986. Due to the curse in vv. 7-9, Psalm 137 is by Mercy Amba Oduyoye classified as a Psalm of Satan, see Oduyoye 1997, 27: "The most satanic beatitudes will be found in Psalm 137:8 & 9."

In Jewish liturgical prayer books, vv. 7-9 of Psalm 137 are usually not recited, for references see Brenner 2003, 85-86: "(...) *whenever it* [Psalm 137] *is recited only the first six verses are recited. The offending vv. 7-9 are removed from the relevant prayers and services*" (her italics).

[7] For a similar view, cf. Becking 2009, 200: "Warfare in ancient Near East cannot be labelled as very human towards the enemies. Brutal acts against humanity and especially against the life of young children is evidenced in the Hebrew Bible." See also Ahn 2008, 268: "The issue accosting the 587 group (vv.7-9) were the collective experiences of the destruction of Jerusalem and the more personal and particular pathos of the atrocious dashing, decapitation, mutilation, or burning of little children—the loss of an entire generation." For a related discussion, see Weinfeld 1975, 477-479.

14

Women and War in Northern Uganda and Ancient Israel

The Interpretative Role of Academia

Knut Holter
School of Mission and Theology, Stavanger, Norway

Abstract

As part of a research program on reintegration of female, former child soldiers in northern Uganda, the essay focuses on academia's interpretative role vis-à-vis women's experiences of war and religion. Proceeding from some biblical narratives on women's experiences of war in ancient Israel, it is asked how academia may enable women exposed to similar warlike situations in contemporary northern Uganda to develop interpretations that allow religion to play liberating rather than oppressing roles.

Introduction

Academia is often, and sometimes rightly so, accused of hiding in ivory towers, rather than joining ordinary people's struggle for better lives. The conference in which this essay was presented—and indeed the research project the conference was circling around, a project on reintegration into society of female, former child soldiers in northern Uganda—is an example of the opposite. Here, the tools of academia are not used for constructing architecturally sophisticated ivory towers, rather for participating in oppressed women's struggle for better lives here and now.

The reintegration project acknowledges that religion plays important roles—for better and worse—in the processes the female, former child soldiers have been and still are exposed to. For better, in the sense that religion, with its ethical values, behavioral patterns, canonical texts and sacred rituals, may be used positively to build up society, individuals and in our case female, former child soldiers. But unfortunately also for worse, in the sense that religion may be used, and has indeed been used negatively as well, to destroy society, individuals, and in our case female child soldiers.

This double role of religion places a heavy responsibility on its official interpreters, being the inside interpreters, speaking normatively and constructively on behalf of the religious community itself, or the outside interpreter, such as those speaking descriptively and critically on behalf of academia. Acknowledging this double role of religion, the reintegration project has identified the northern Ugandan Lord's Resistance Army's (LRA) use of the Old Testament as one of its research cases. According to the LRA, their aim is to establish a society built on the Ten Commandments, the main ethical code of the Old Testament. The internal justice and ethos of the LRA—including what most external observers would call unjust and unethical oppression of child soldiers, female as well as male—are therefore to a great extent legitimized by reference to Old Testament texts and motifs.

In response to LRA's general focus on the Old Testament, one of the Ph.D.-students in the reintegration project, Helen Nkabala Nambalirwa, analyzes LRA's particular use of Old Testament texts and motifs, which seem to have a legitimizing function with regard to their oppression of female child soldiers. In an essay included in the present anthology, Nambalirwa offers some glimpses into her material, with particular attention to LRA's use of the Old Testament narratives about Sodom and Gomorrah. According to Nambalirwa, LRA's use of Old Testament texts and motifs in relation to their oppression of female child soldiers is of a rather accidental nature. In many cases, the texts and motifs that are used have little or nothing to do neither with war nor women. Still, the canonical authority of the Old Testament, it seems, makes it possible for the LRA to let more or less any text or motif serve their interpretative and legitimizing concerns.

However, I would argue that the canonical authority of the Old Testament might be used in the very opposite direction, too. Rather than letting more or less accidentally selected Old Testament texts or motifs be used to legitimize oppression of female child soldiers, one could turn the whole thing around and ask how Old Testament texts and motifs that describe oppression of women in war and warlike situations, can be used in today's reintegration and healing processes vis-à-vis women with corresponding experiences, such as in northern Uganda. I believe that socially engaged biblical scholars may have something to contribute to such reintegration and healing processes, as we engage in dialogue with female, former child soldiers over biblical texts and motifs. First and foremost female—and in our case Ugandan—biblical scholars like Nambalirwa, whose cultural background and gender allow them to interact directly with the northern Ugandan women. Nevertheless, I dare also to include people like myself—a European and male biblical scholar—in the acting 'we,' as we, too, may be able to contribute to this dialogue with our textual and hermeneutical skills, although not necessarily in direct interaction with the former child soldiers. The contribution of socially engaged biblical scholars would be to suggest Old Testament texts about oppression of women in war, texts that—when read together with young women in northern Uganda—might serve to mirror and help to verbalize their experiences. But then, as biblical scholars we would also be able to counter these texts with other Old Testament texts, promoting freedom from oppression and hope for the future. This would create rooms for the former child soldiers to counter their humiliating experiences with new sets of biblical texts, carrying the same canonical authority as those used to oppress.

Such an approach would textually speaking be in line with the Old Testament tendency of juxtaposing seemingly contradictory texts, thereby inviting its readers to reflect on the plurality of Old Testament voices (Brueggemann 1997). Further, such an approach would methodologically and hermeneutically speaking be in line with the comparative paradigm, so influential in African biblical scholarship (Anum 2000), and particularly with the paradigm's attention to how biblical texts and motifs may be used to interpret contemporary African experiences and concerns (Holter 2002, 88-100; Holter 2008, 14-52). Therefore, in an attempt to draw some attention to academia's double role as far as interpretation of classical religious texts is concerned—not only asking what the texts meant historically, but also asking how they may be used today—I will in the following discuss how biblical scholarship may contribute to the reintegration and healing processes some female, former child soldiers in northern Uganda just now are exposed to. I will enter the topic in three steps; first I will point out some relevant Old Testament texts, corresponding to what I think are the experiences of the female child soldiers, then I will relate these texts to a couple of central hermeneutical positions in contemporary biblical scholarship, and finally I will discuss these texts and hermeneutical positions in relation to some practical perspectives.

Some relevant Old Testament texts

War and warlike situations are a central motif in the Old Testament, to be found throughout the entire textual corpus. In our pragmatic search for women's experiences thereof, the Book of Lamentations may serve as a suitable entry, for two reasons. First, because Lamentations reflects the major Old Testament experience of war and warlike situations, that is the sixth century B.C. Babylonian conquest of Jerusalem. This experience had suffering for civilians in general and women and children in particular as a consequence. Second, Lamentations is a suitable entry for us also because of its extensive use of female metaphors. Occupied and destroyed Jerusalem and Judah are here depicted as a woman; previously a queen, now a slave; previously with many lovers, now lonely with none to comfort her; previously with many children, now with these children being exiled (Lamentations 1:1-2, 5).

As part of Lamentations' general portrayal of Jerusalem and Judah as a lonely and suffer-ing woman, two textual examples may serve to illustrate her particular vulnerability as a woman, in relation to the situation of war and warlike situations. The first example depicts the Babylonian occupants as raping women and girls in the occupied city and villages. According to Lamentations 5:11,

> They raped the women in Zion,
> and the virgins in the villages of Judah.

Rape is discussed by both narratives (cf. Genesis 34; Judges 19; 2 Samuel 13) and legal texts (cf. Deuteronomy 22:25-27) in the Old Testament. What is echoed in Lamentations 5:11, however, is different from the more general discussion of singular occurrences of rape in these texts. Here, it seems to be a question of rape as part of a military strategy. This becomes clear when we read Lamentations 5:11 together with the following v. 12 (and vv. 13-14):

> Princes were hanged up by their hand,
> the faces of elders were not honored.

The two verses form a parallelism (in the Hebrew text with regard to structure as well as sound), where the same acting subject—'they,' that is the Babylonian occupants (explicitly in v. 11, implicitly in v. 12)—humiliate the women and virgins as well as the princes and elders. Together the two verses depict a situation where rape is part of the occupant's more general oppression. In order to weaken the moral of the occupied population, societal structures (the roles of 'princes' and 'elders') as well as cultural conventions (the roles of 'women' and 'virgins') are attacked (Berges 2002, 289-290; Renkema 1998, 608-611).

A similar experience of rape as part of an occupant's 'policy' versus the occupied population may lie behind Isaiah 51:23-52:1:

> (...) your tormentors, who said to you: 'Fall prostrate that we may walk over you.'
> And you made your back like the ground, like a street to be walked over.
> Awake, awake, O Zion, clothe yourself with strength.
> Put on your garments of splendor, O Jerusalem, the holy city.
> The uncircumcised and defiled will not enter you again.

This text, too, depicts Jerusalem in a female imagery and, as pointed out by Bebb Wheeler Stone (1992, 85-86), the language reflects women's experiences of sexual assaults as part of the sixth century B.C. Babylonian conquest.

What we see in Lamentations 5:11, therefore, is an example of an occupant's use of rape as a strategic weapon against the occupied population, a weapon that takes advantage of the particular vulnerability of women (Thistlethwaite 1993; Keefe 1993).

Another example that may serve to illustrate the situation of the lonely and suffering woman in Lamentations—and again her particular vulnerability as a woman—depicts a situation where the Babylonian occupation has caused starvation. According to Lamentations 4:10 (cf. also Lamentations 2:20), the starvation had disastrous consequences in the form of cannibalism (Berges 2002, 249-250; Renkema 1998, 518-520):

> With their own hands compassionate women
> have cooked their own children,
> who became their food
> when my people were destroyed.

The motif of starvation, resulting from the Babylonian King Nebuchadnezzar's siege of Jerusalem, is also expressed in 2 Kings 25:1-3. Still, closer to Lamentations 4:10 is a narrative related to another siege, the Aramean King Ben-Hadad's siege of Samaria, as narrated in 2 Kings 6:25-29:

> There was a great famine in the city; the siege lasted so long that a donkey's head sold for eighty shekels of silver, and a quarter of a cab of seed pods for five shekels. As the king of Israel was passing by on the wall, a woman cried to him, 'Help me, my lord the king!' The king replied, 'If the Lord does not help you, where can I get help for you? From the threshing floor? From the winepress?' Then he asked her, 'What's the matter?' She answered, 'This woman said to me, "Give up your son so we may eat him today, and tomorrow we'll eat my son." So we cooked my son and ate him. The next day I said to her, "Give up your son so we may eat him," but she had hidden him.'

2 Kings 6:25-29 depicts an extreme situation; a starvation so severe that a donkey's head is sold at a price corresponding to the price of two or three

slaves (cf. Exodus 21:32). This is then the context of the motif of a mother eating her own child. As a literary motif, it causes a wide range of emotions in the reader, from pity to disgust. Basically, though, it is a motif that expresses a perversion of the concept of motherhood. Rather than the mother giving life to the child, the child is killed to give life to its mother (Berlin 2002, 75).

Let these texts and motifs from Lamentations suffice to illustrate a couple of aspects of women's experiences of war and warlike situations, according to the Old Testament. What these texts and motifs have in common is that they touch the particular vulnerability of women in such situations. The motif of rape as a strategic weapon differs from other examples of violence, in the sense that it may result in a shameful and unwanted pregnancy, and eventually a child that the mother in spite of the circumstances will struggle to rescue from other consequences of war and oppression. Likewise, the motif of a mother eating her own child differs from other examples of parent-children relations, in the sense that it perverts the whole concept of motherhood. The point of these texts and motifs is to illustrate the humiliation of the suffering woman of Lamentations, and the historical experiences behind are those of Jerusalem and Judah's women during the mid-sixth century B.C. Babylonian conquest. As such, these text and motifs may have some appeal to contemporary readers with corresponding experiences from war or warlike situations, such as—for example—former, female child soldiers in northern Uganda. We will eventually come to them, but first some hermeneutical perspectives should be addressed.

Some hermeneutical perspectives

Contemporary biblical scholarship is increasingly acknowledging a responsibility for the ethical consequences and political potentials of its textual work. Interpreting the Bible is not an innocent activity, detached from the experiences and concerns of the interpretative communities, being that of so-called ordinary readers or that of biblical scholars. The latter, therefore, gradually realizes that it cannot any longer hide in the above-mentioned ivory towers and ignore the fact that its scholarship both reflects and may—or even should—be used by certain socio-political interests. Let me therefore address a couple of contemporary hermeneutical perspectives expressing this concern and relate them to the two texts from Lamentations discussed above, 5:11 and 4:10.

The first hermeneutical perspective I would like to address concerns the *ethical consequences* of academic biblical interpretation. What we choose to do as biblical scholars, and what we choose to neglect, has indeed ethical consequences. Two decades ago, the North American biblical scholar Elizabeth Schüssler Fiorenza addressed this topic in her Presidential Address in the Society of Biblical Literature—the world's leading organization for biblical scholars—arguing for no less than a paradigm shift in the ethos and rhetorical practices of biblical scholarship (Fiorenza 1988). Scholarly communities are not only investigative communities, but also authoritati-ve communities, she argues, as they possess the power to recognize and define what 'true scholarship' entails (ibid., 8). As far as biblical scholarship is concerned, therefore, she continues (ibid., 15): 'It must also include the elucidation of the ethical consequences and political functions of biblical texts and their interpretations in their historical as well as in their contemporary sociopolitical contexts.'

Fiorenza's point of view has received much support in the two decades that have passed, and few biblical scholars would today explicitly deny her concern, although many in practice continue to ignore it. Not least do we find such concerns about the ethical consequences and political functions of biblical texts and interpretations reflected in African biblical scholarship, with its preference for questions of relevance in relation to church and society (Holter 2008, 108-110).

Let us therefore relate Fiorenza's concern to our two texts from Lamentations, and to our context, the project on reintegration into society of female, former child soldiers. The major interpretative consequence of her concern, I would tend to argue, is a need for sensitivity with regard to the current and challenging situation of the former child soldiers. Two groups of women are to meet, one from sixth century B.C. Jerusalem and another from twenty-first century northern Uganda. Both have indeed experienced oppression. Moreover, both presumable also long for a better future; the young women in northern Uganda express their hope by leaving the bush, trying to return to a more normal life, whereas the suffering Jerusalemites express their hope verbally (cf. Lamentations 3:19-23):

> I remember my affliction and my wandering, the bitterness and the gall.
> I well remember them, and my soul is downcast within me.
> Yet this I call to mind and therefore I have hope:
> Because of the Lord's great love we are not consumed, for his compassions never fail.
> They are new every morning; great is your faithfulness.

An interpretation of—the texts on—the experiences of sixth century B.C. Jerusalemites from the perspective of the twenty-first century northern Ugandans should therefore try to establish an intertextual dialogue with comparative textual voices promoting freedom from oppression and hope for the future. And those who seek such comparative, textual voices of freedom and hope will find. There are admittedly central Old Testament voices that interpret the sixth century B.C. Babylonian conquest of Jerusalem in terms of an unavoidable consequence of previous generations' misdeeds (cf. e.g. 2 Kings 24:20; cf. also Jeremiah 19:9 and Ezekiel 5:8-10). But there are also Old Testament voices that would seem to reject the idea of trans-generational punishment, and rather invite their readers—here and now—to meet a merciful God. An illustrative example is attested in early sixth century B.C. prophets like Jeremiah and Ezekiel:

> In those days people will no longer say, 'The fathers have eaten sour grapes, and the children's teeth are set on edge.' Instead, everyone will die for his own sin; whoever eats sour grapes—his own teeth will be set on edge. (Jeremiah 31:29-30; cf. Ezekiel 18:2-4)

The second hermeneutical perspective I would like to address concerns the *political potentials* of academic biblical interpretation, again a perspective acknowledged by Schüssler Fiorenza (cf. above). What we choose to do as biblical scholars, and what we choose to neglect, has obvious political potentials. This has especially been acknowledged by explicitly ideological approaches to biblical scholarship, such as for example liberation or feminist/ womanist hermeneutical approaches. These labels cover a broad range of perspectives; some scholars find the problems in colonial and patriarchal interpretive traditions, others find the problems in the biblical texts themselves. Nevertheless, what these approaches to biblical scholarship have in common is a determined will to take sides in ideological and political struggles, and then let their scholarship serve certain oppressed groups and their fight for justice.

Explicitly ideological approaches to biblical scholarship are attested globally, and they have not least played—and continue to play—crucial roles in African theology and biblical scholarship (Martey 1993; Holter 2008, 23-26, 43-46). An example from a liberation hermeneutical perspective is provided by the Cameroonian theologian Jean-Marc Ela. The God proclaimed to Africans during colonial times, Ela argues, is a God who commanded adaptation and submission to the existing (colonial) order of things. Against this background, Ela points out the central role of the exodus motif in the Old Testament, and he argues that the God of the exodus—the God who hears the cry of his people—is also the God of the masses of Africa (Ela 1991, 264):

> In any community, village or city neighborhood, the prime interest in reading the Book of Exodus is to rescue the majority of African Christians from ignorance of the history of liberation. After all, this text is about nothing else. Moses is not sent to

Egypt to preach a spiritual conversion, but to lead Israel 'out of the house of slavery.' In this escape God is revealed as the unique, matchless God. In today's world changes do result from liberation movements, and Africans must not be kept from knowing that, in our age, living communities are struggling for their rights.

Another example—this one from a womanist perspective—is provided by the South African biblical scholar Madipoane Masenya. In an analysis of the poem of the ideal woman in Proverbs 31:10-31, she approaches the text from the perspective of African-South African women's experiences of a double suppression: subjugation and subordination in colonial and apartheid South Africa, but also patriarchal domination from pre-colonial times in South Africa (Masenya 2004, 6):

> (...) I hope to interrogate the text to see if the text is really useful to African women in South Africa. Can the text empower them and thus contribute towards their liberation? Will it help them recover their positive self-image as African Christian believers, an image which has been destroyed, amongst others, by the way their culture has been interpreted for them by Whites?

The consequence of this concern for an interpretation of the two texts from Lamentations—in a context of reintegration into society of female, former child soldiers—is then again, I would argue, to establish an intertextual dialogue with textual voices of freedom from oppression and hope for the future. And such contexts prove easy to find. It is a central point of liberation and feminist/womanist approaches to biblical scholarship that God has a special preference for the oppressed and marginalized, and the Exodus narrative provides a key paradigm here, such as it is highlighted in Exodus 3:7-8:

> The Lord said, 'I have indeed seen the misery of my people in Egypt. I have heard them crying out because of their slave drivers, and I am concerned about their suffering. So I have come down to rescue them from the hand of the Egyptians and to bring them up out of that land into a good and spacious land, a land flowing with milk and honey.'

A couple of practical perspectives

Let me sum up so far. In an attempt to draw some attention to academia's double role as far as interpretation of classical religious texts is concerned—not only asking what the texts meant historically, but also asking how they may be used today—I have asked how Old Testament texts and motifs that describe oppression of women in war and warlike situations can be used in the reintegration and healing processes in today's situation in northern Uganda. I started with pointing out some Old Testament texts that are relevant to the experiences of the female child soldiers, texts about rape and starvation, that is texts expressing women's particular vulnerability. Then I proceeded to relate these texts to a couple of central hermeneutical perspectives in contemporary biblical scholarship, one is the interpretative community's responsibility for the ethical consequences of its textual work, and the other is the political potentials of the textual work. I have now come to the third and final part, where I will relate these texts and hermeneutical perspectives to a couple of practical perspectives.

First, we should acknowledge the complexity that obviously will characterize any encounter between the female, former child soldiers and (for example) socially engaged Ugandan biblical scholars aiming to use their scholarship to serve this particular group. The relationship between the two—when they meet to read the Bible together—is a complex one, as far as power relations are concerned. The South African biblical scholar Gerald O. West has worked with similar encounters, in his case between socially engaged biblical scholars and local communities of poor and marginalized people. According to West, the interaction between the two tend to end up with the scholar falling into one of two ditches, either an uncritical 'listening to' or an arrogant 'speaking for' (West 1999, 37):

> Both an uncritical 'listening to', that romanticizes and idealizes the interpretation of the poor and marginalized, and an arrogant 'speaking for', that minimizes and rationalizes the interpretation of the poor and marginalized, must be problematized.

Rather than 'listening to' or 'speaking for,' West argues that—in relation to a biblical text or motif—the interpretative interaction between the biblical scholar and the ordinary, poor and marginalized reader is that of 'reading with.' The two should find ways of meeting on equal terms, so that the subjectivity of both can be taken seriously, and they can be allowed to interact with their respective resources, categories and contributions (West 1999, 53).

Second, in our case, a joint 'reading with' of the two Lamentations texts may hopefully enable the two interpretative communities—biblical scholars and female, former child soldiers—to use their respective experiences to expose the ancient texts and see them as being relevant for both, here and now. It is a question of experience, with lived lives and read texts. Experiences of suffering, from rape and starvation. And experiences of survival and hope. But also experiences with texts. Texts about rape and starvation. And texts about survival and hope. A 'reading with' may enable the biblical scholars to share the insights of their exegetical and hermeneutical training, and thereby let them pay back to society some of what has been invested in them. But it may also enable the female, former child soldiers to verbalize their own experiences, and through a broader selection of biblical texts see that God is not necessarily on the oppressors' side.

Who will then, eventually, benefit from a twenty-first century northern Ugandan interpretation of our two Lamentations texts? Perhaps some female, former child soldiers, who are able to see their own experiences in relief against Old Testament texts with similar experiences, canonical and thereby authoritative texts that did not stop there and then, but continued into future and hope. And certainly some members of the guild of scholarly interpreters, who were able to see that their scholarship made a change for fellow human being, change for the better.

References

Anum, Eric. 2000. Comparative readings of the Bible in Africa. In *The Bible in Africa: Transactions, trajectories and trends*, ed. Gerald O. West and Musa W. Dube, Leiden: Brill, 457-473.

Berges, Ulrich. 2002. *Klagelieder*. Freiburg, Basel, Wien: Herder (Herders Theologischer Kommentar zum Alten Testament).

Berlin, Adele. 2002. *Lamentations: A commentary*. Louisville, London: Westminster John Knox Press.

Brueggemann, Walter. 1997. *Theology of the Old Testament: Testimony, dispute, advocacy*. Minneapolis: Fortress.

Ela, Jean-Marc. 1991. A black African perspective: An African reading of Exodus. In *Voices from the margin: Interpreting the Bible in the Third World*, ed. Rasiah S. Sugirtharajah. Maryknoll: Orbis Books, 256-266.

Fiorenza, Elisabeth Schüssler. 1988. The ethics of biblical interpretation decentering biblical scholarship. *Journal of Biblical Literature* 107:3-17. Reprinted in Elisabeth Schüssler Fiorenza, *Rhetoric and ethic: The politics of biblical studies*. Minneapolis: Fortress (1999), 17-30.

Holter, Knut. 2002. *Old Testament research for Africa: A critical analysis and annotated bibliography of African Old Testament dissertations, 1967–2000*. New York: Peter Lang (Bible and Theology in Africa, 3).

Holter, Knut. 2008. *Contextualized Old Testament scholarship in Africa*. Nairobi: Acton Publishers.

Keefe, Alice A. 1993. Rapes of women/wars of men. In *Women, war, and metaphor: Language and society in the study of the Hebrew Bible*, ed. Claudia V. Camp and Carole R. Fontaine. Atlanta: Scholars Press, 79-97 (Semeia, 61).

Martey, Emmanuel. 1993. *African theology: Inculturation and liberation.* Maryknoll: Orbis Books.

Masenya, Madipoane. 2004. *How worthy is the woman of worth? Rereading Proverbs 31:10-31 in African-South Africa.* New York: Peter Lang (Bible and Theology in Africa, 4).

Renkema, Johan. 1998. *Lamentations.* Leuven: Peeters (Historical Commentary on the Old Testament).

Stone, Bebb Wheeler. 1992. Second Isaiah: Prophet to patriarchy. *Journal for the Study of the Old Testament* 56: 85-99.

Thistlethwaite, Susan Brooks. 1993. 'You may enjoy the spoil of your enemies': Rape as a biblical metaphor for war'. In *Women, war, and metaphor: Language and society in the study of the Hebrew Bible*, ed. Claudia V. Camp and Carole R. Fontaine. Atlanta: Scholars Press, 59-75 (Semeia, 61).

West, Gerald O. 1999. *The academy of the poor: Towards a dialogical reading of the Bible.* Sheffield: Sheffield Academic Press (Interventions, 2).

15

Authentic Reading of the Bible

By Magnar Kartveit
School of Mission and Theology, Norway

Abstract

The Lord's Resistance Army (LRA) in Uganda presupposes acknowledgement of the Bible's authority inside this armed rebel group, as well as in the larger society. In the preceding articles, three strategies have been adopted to counter the "LRA way" of reading and using the Bible. Helen Nambalirwa shows that the story of Sodom and Gomorrah is neither properly understood nor adequately applied by LRA. Knut Holter appeals to a dialogue with contexts of hope. Marta Høyland Lavik recognizes that an adequate understanding of Psalm 137 confronts us with a message that we cannot endorse for hermeneutical and moral reasons. In a society where religious authority is fundamental, these strategies may prove audacious because religious personnel who discuss the contents of religious literature runs the danger of destabilizing the system altogether. Yet, is there a way to avoid abuse of the Bible without questioning its authority?

It is all in the Bible!

On Sunday, May 3, 2009 the Norwegian Public Television, NRK, in its evening newscast reported on the current situation in Mexico after the outbreak of the flu caused by the H1N1 Influensa A virus. The reporter interviewed, among others, 80-year-old Maria Flores Pena from the village of Actopan, who made the following comments on the situation: "As for me, I don't know. They all say that it is in the Bible that it all has to happen. We can only hope for the benevolence of God, who is the only one who can know everything, right?"[1]

In these terse sentences we encounter a deep conviction: God knows everything, he is omniscient, and he is the only one capable of total knowledge. His plan is revealed in the Bible, and what is written there, has to happen. Maria Flores Pena dispenses of her own authority, relies upon common opinion, and surrenders herself to God's benevolence. On this account, the Bible constitutes the highest authority in the world, as it reveals God's plan. Man can only succumb to Biblical authority.

The authority of the Bible is undisputed in many parts of the world, in many groups and in many segments of society. In the case of Maria Flores Pena, she refers as common opinion that the Bible is the source for knowing what has to happen. This is a view of the Bible shared by many: it contains a message about the present or the future, perhaps hidden, but accessible to the interested reader. But the Bible may be accorded status on different grounds, for instance as providing directions for action. If we extend the question of authority to encompass other religious literature or traditions, and if we take Maria Flores Pena's conviction to represent whole societies, then we are dealing with a type of authority that may not be very visible in society, but without which society cannot be properly understood. For example, if the status of religious personnel is high in a society, this may reveal that the actual worldview has a religious basis.

The challenge for Biblical scholars and other religious personnel is to advocate a nuanced and balanced understanding of the Bible (or other religious literature) without loosing the attention of members of the community or of whole communities. This article will suggest that an "authentic reading" of the Bible may be considered as a method in this connection. The challenge for every reading proposed by religious personnel is to be heard and accepted by other Bible readers. Religious personnel stands a chance as long as people are willing to listen without retracting to parochial thinking, and barring themselves behind closed doors. If there is an opportunity for communication between religious personnel and other Bible readers, it has to be seen and taken. With an "authentic reading" of the Bible, religious personnel may be able to preserve and undergird the authority of the Bible without opening it for abuse.

The suggested method will become visible against the backdrop of some contributions in this volume, and some brief comments on them.

Helen Nambalirwa's approach towards the Bible reading of Lord's Resistance Army

The authority of the Bible in the case of the Lord's Resistance Army in Uganda is of a similar nature to that of Maria Flores Pena. As reported by Helen Nambalirwa in her article in this book, the LRA presupposes acknowledgement of the Bible's authority inside the Army, and in the larger society. Without such an acknowledgment the Bible would not be interesting as a point of reference for Joseph Kony or his followers. In this case, the Bible is not important for foretelling the present or the future, but as prescribing action and providing legitimization for violence. Even after they left the LRA, people referred to the story of Sodom and Gomorrah and to others as proof that their violent actions are justified. These stories serve as evidence for the principle that God destroys his enemies, and similar destruction was carried out by the LRA. The authority of the Bible is not derived from loyalty to Kony, but has an existence of its own. It can be referred to in connection with LRA's plan, which appears as a part of God's plan on earth and where the LRA are only human agents for the divine plan.

The strategy adopted by Nambalirwa to counter this use of the Bible by the LRA is to show that the story of Sodom and Gomorrah is neither properly understood nor adequately applied by them. In this process she makes many observations about Gen 18–19 that are accurate and relevant from a scholarly perspective. According to her, there is almost no fundament in the Bible for the type of Biblical interpretation and application demonstrated by the LRA. The challenge for her is to receive the attention her criticism deserves. What are the chances for this to succeed?

As encouragement for this kind of work, it can be mentioned that in 1998 the Norwegian School of Theology convened a seminar on the Faith Movement. A hundred people discussed different aspects of this movement, which stems from Kenneth Hagin of Tulsa, Oklahoma. Among the topics addressed was his use of the Bible, which was found lacking in several respects, much as Nambalirwa asserts for the LRA use of the Bible (Kartveit 2000). After this seminar, and other initiatives taken in its wake, it is my impression that the character of the movement changed in our country. One can no longer see invitations or books making the same promises as before.

Biblical scholars have too often neglected the task of addressing the popular use of the Bible, much to the detriment of our own work and church work in general. This is perhaps not so much negligence as the result of a deliberate choice, since we often harvest derogatory characteristics for such endeavors. We may be termed unbelievers, liberal scholars, etc. and such labels are not to be counted among our blessings, and they may persuade us to cultivate fields that promise to yield more tasty fruits. Nambalirwa is one of the scholars who have the courage to enter the battlefield.

Her efforts are also dependent upon acknowledgment of the authority of the Bible, only that she advocates a reading that is qualified by professional insights into the understanding of ancient literature. Such an approach presupposes that she herself is acknowledged as an authority in society—as one type of religious personnel acting on behalf of the supreme authority. This endeavor shows the challenge as it emerges on a personal level. The person who at the same time is a religious authority and a Biblical scholar emerges as the epitome of the problem: she or he needs to preserve communication, with her/his insights integrated in the message. The situation is precarious and continuously runs the risk of jeopardizing communication, which would be a loss to both sides.

There is therefore a need for a language that opens up for communication, and that keeps this openness intact in the whole process. The idea of an "authentic reading" comes in as a possibility here. It will appeal to all parts by being authentic, and as a "reading" it is not authoritarian.

Knut Holter's approach to the Bible reading of the Lord's Resistance Army

The same assumption of religious authority underlies the contribution by Knut Holter in this book. First, he presents Biblical texts that will tell oppressed and abused women that they are not alone in the world: there have been others before them suffering the same fate, and there may be some comfort in common tragedy. In addition, he appeals to a dialogue with contexts of hope; canonical, authoritative texts that enable, for instance, former female child soldiers to see their own experiences in relief against OT texts with similar experiences. These canonical and thereby authoritative texts did not stop with tragedy but continued into future and hope. If the scholarly community reads these texts together with female, former child soldiers this may bring about a change for the better.

In this model, the role of the religious personnel is that of providing material for comfort and hope, and the role of the former girl soldiers is that of discovering new insights that can create a positive change. Under the assumption that the Bible has authority and that the scholar has some derived authority, this model of "reading with" may work. The idea of "authentic reading" takes this "reading with" one step further, and introduces a program for the reading, by indicating the aim of the reading. It is supposed to reach out for the text itself, its essence, its core. Still, one wonders which elements might disturb the process, by, for instance, destabilizing the negotiated balance of authority.

Marta Høyland Lavik's approach to the Bible reading of the Lord's Resistance Army

One such element is addressed by Marta Høyland Lavik, in another contribution, where she discusses Psalm 137 and finds that it propagates the use of violence.

In the West, this psalm is perhaps best known through the version presented some years ago by the group Boney M: "By the Rivers of Babylon". Here, the whole of v. 1, parts of v. 2, and much of v. 3 were used, and this was combined with Psalm 19:14, slightly altered: "May the meditation of our hearts and the words of our mouth be acceptable in your sight, O Lord." In this version, the harsh contents of Psalm 137 were transformed into a lament over the present situation and a prayer for help. What Høyland Lavik sees as the part of the psalm offering a modern reader consternation, is left out in the Boney M version, and a well-known prayer from another psalm is introduced in order to make the result acceptable to a modern mind.

Such a strategy in dealing with OT texts has been very common. But the Biblical text is here with us, and from time to time the violence contained therein resurfaces. Høyland Lavik faces the violence described in the text, and denounces it. Her study ends with recognizing that an adequate understanding of Psalm 137 confronts us with a message that we cannot endorse. "...although an ancient holy text opens up for killing babies in the name of God, this does not automatically mean that it is an act that should be pursued" (p. 203 in this volume).

In a society where religious authority is fundamental, this strategy may prove audacious. If religious personnel flatly rejects the contents of religious literature, one runs the danger of destabilizing the system altogether. Maria Flores Pena would be left without the authority she relies upon. Or, the derived authority of the personnel would be rejected in favor of the higher authority of the text. From European history we know what upheavals such enterprises have occasioned, and we know that it took centuries to come to terms with a Bible bereaved of an all-encompassing divine authority, but accorded a type of authority acceptable in societies where authority is constantly renegotiated.

The suggestion to "read together" may eventually reach the point where the insights presented by Høyland Lavik become part of the common reading, if it is seen that this is in fact what the text is all about, if this is what an "authentic" understanding of the text brings forth. Her reading of Psalm 137 is important in the discussion and, if presented in the framework of "reading with," it has a fair chance of being heard. The next thing that might happen is that Joseph Kony and his likes will make such a reading their own, and act accordingly.

Does the Bible justify violence?

John J. Collins addressed the issue in his presidential lecture at the SBL Annual Meeting in Toronto 2003, now published under the title *Does the Bible Justify Violence?* (Collins 2004). He discusses several Biblical texts that seem to justify violence, and their subsequent use in new historical situations, and ends with the following statement: "The Bible has contributed to violence in the world precisely because it has been taken to confer a degree of certitude that transcends human discussion and argumentation. Perhaps the most constructive thing a Biblical critic can do toward lessening the contribution of the Bible to violence in the world is to show that such certitude is an illusion" (ibid., 32f).

How this can be done, is not addressed in the paper. One might think that it presupposes a society where authority is allowed to be scrutinized, and that it will work poorly in a society not prepared for such scrutiny. If it is tacitly presupposed that the whole Bible contains the thoughts of God without restrictions, the idea of severing the bonds between the Bible and human action is preposterous. Only religious personnel with a high authority will eventually be allowed to interpret the Bible in a way leading away from violence, if violence is the message found in the Bible. Even then, Maria Flores Pena would feel uncomfortable faced with the assertion that "such certitude is an allusion." Where would she then turn?

Nambalirwa's strategy is to purify Biblical interpretation against the abuse. Success for this endeavor depends upon her authority, and I hope this can be ascertained in the relevant contexts. Holter focuses instead on material in the Bible apt for creating a change for the better—a project not subject to establishing an authority alongside the Bible, and thereby avoiding the issue of a secondary authority. But on the other hand, it is vulnerable to the kind of texts discussed by Nambalirwa and Høyland Lavik. These texts confront us with violence as recommended by the text, and we have to consider if it is immoral and outdated. Høyland Lavik's reading of the text may be welcome with the LRA, but her rejection of it threatens to shake the fundament of the communication in society. One would not be astonished to see that she immediately will be confronted with a question of where she finds her standards. A Christian theologian will try to find them inside the Bible, and the problem is then to draw the line between authoritative and non-authoritative material there. In the West, the strategy has been to draw a line inside the Bible between, for example, reliable and less reliable material, even if there has been a discussion on the legitimacy of drawing such lines inside the Bible.

To Maria Flores Pena and many others this is no issue at all. They confer absolute authority to the Bible as the revealed word of God, and a discussion about it would be seen as irreverent, close to blasphemy. It is not easy to convince her that the question has to be addressed and that a simple trust in the Bible will lead into trouble, in some cases meaning violence.

The authority of the Bible and of religious personnel

Authority is something of a social and psychological nature and cannot be dealt with on a hermeneutical basis alone. We need the help of anthropologists and psychologists for understanding what goes on: who are in need of authority, who is able to create authority for themselves or for Scripture, and how this whole process functions.

If we recognize that the issue of religious authority has to be addressed, we soon enter into the field of methods in Biblical study, and not only hermeneutics. As a contribution to the discussion, let me suggest that the common template of understanding texts either with historical or literary methods is not helpful. Most critics use both synchronic and diachronic methods, and Louis Jonker has suggested to use all methods together (Jonker 1996). This may be helpful, if the proponents of the different methods agree that this is possible.

We might, however, consider the term of an "authentic reading" of the Bible. This expression is lent from the science of music and drama, and describes a performance intending to come close to the original setting for a musical score or drama or opera, by using original or imitated instruments, costumes, ways of singing, speaking etc. It clearly recognizes the limitation to the project: the performers and the audience are set in their time and age and cannot move to a different setting. An authentic performance is therefore a limited project, but nevertheless an attempt worth trying. It fully acknowledges its limits and therefore is self-conscious enough to test out its possibilities. There is not room here to discuss this idea at length, but let me clarify some of the relevant issues in my thinking on this topic.

In a society where religious authority is taken for granted, the Bible will take on a self-evident authority when introduced. As the word of God it immediately assumes a place in society, even to the extent that it is treated as a holy artifact. Holy books are handled with reverence; they are not placed on the floor or thrown around. The case of LRA makes it clear what such reverence may lead to; and indeed this is not the only case in history. Collins mentions a few more, and historians will have more of the same kind to tell us. It is of meager comfort that the Bible, taken "literally," has led to so much humanitarian effort, struggle for human rights, diaconal work etc., since it also constitutes a reservoir of texts supporting destruction, violence, and murder.

To take the Bible "literally" means to accord to every sentence, whether promise, statement, admonition, command or other, the same authority, and this attitude opens the field for self-defined Biblical authorities who choose to employ select texts for a specific purpose. On the whole, people tend not to do this, and we may be grateful for that, but there are enough examples of the contrary procedure to alert us. And it should alert every Bible interpreter, including those who profess to read the text "literally." The reason why the community of Bible interpreters and users has not done this with one voice, and some even rally around the "biblicist " or "literal" option, is a topic for reflection. Perhaps they have not read the Bible "literally," but used different interpretative strategies according to the demands of the text? One such strategy was applied by Boney M: to pick parts of a unified text and add elements from another setting, thereby creating in fact a new text. One cannot term this an authentic reading, as it concentrates on sentences that seem to be immediately applicable in a modern society, and ignores elements that are there in the text.

Another strategy has been to interpret passages allegorically. The allegorical method has a long standing in history, and in the interpretation of the Bible it has been used to gloss over inconvenient passages of every kind. This procedure is very common in circles pretending to read the Bible "literally." As soon as a literal reading is incomprehensible or inconvenient, the interpreter resorts to allegory—quite often without admitting to do so, and possibly without realizing that this is what happens.

For a number of years, a literary reading of the Bible has been in vogue, and this method has often been embraced by the "literally" inclined Bible readers. The enthusiasm for a literary reading may, however, evaporate with the realization that the new method is only interested in the text as text, and not in its possible references in the world. To a "literal" reader the reference in the world is the essential thing, without which the text remains words and not life. To the literary reader, on the other hand, the text is non-referential (Barton 1984, 182).

An authentic reading of the Bible

John Barton has recently reiterated the need for a historical reading of the Bible, taking seriously its historical nature and language, culture etc (Barton 2007). His approach is quite convincing, and an authentic reading comes close to his program. The title of his book, *The Nature of Biblical Criticism*, may however be subject to misunderstanding and disapproval by some of his audience. I refer to those who are not aware of the scholarly use of "criticism" as "analysis," "investigation," and misunderstand it in the sense of being judgmental and disapproving. This misunderstanding has given Biblical scholars much bad press, and at the outset one is intent on finding expressions that do not block the communication before it has started. So my suggestion is the expression "authentic reading," in the hope that it will convey the aim of every Bible reader: to come close to the text, learn from the text, listen to the text and tune in to its wavelength.

In the actual reading, differences in the practice of listening and learning from the text may become visible, but at least we may agree upon a goal: being authentic, and each time differences appear in the actual application of the method of Bible reading, there is the possibility to return to the beginning and start the process anew. Communication is not precluded by what some may consider bad language at the beginning, and the "reading with" stands a chance of succeeding.

Authentic reading involves approaching the text in the original language, at least in principle, and on this point the participants must consent, even they who do not have the necessary language training. To practice this can be done without any condescending attitude from those who have undergone such training, as there is always a possibility to enter deeper into a language and few will consider themselves well enough trained. We are speaking of dead languages, where none of us have the command native speakers will have.

Further, this reading means using the whole repertoire of methods in order to grasp the original meaning, form analysis, literary analysis, sociological and historical analysis, and so on. Common textbooks on method are available in different languages and there is no need to repeat titles here. If the aim is authenticity, participants will, hopefully, be open to these methods.

Authenticity builds upon self-consciousness on the parts of the readers. This is a point of some concern to the present writer, and it means to keep in mind the contingency of both reader and text. We approach the text in the full conviction that we are modern readers who dress up for the occasion, knowing that the text, incapable of approaching us with the help of such change, retains its originality and strangeness. The notion of strangeness has been discussed by Bård Mæland in a paper at a conference in 2005 (Mæland 2007). His descriptions of the reader as a foreigner over against the text and the text as a stranger to the modern reader correspond to the point made here. Communication depends on a meeting between the foreigner and the stranger—in fact this encounter is necessary for communication. Without the recognition of foreignness and strangeness, communication will not take place. Only when the roles are seen, can one participate in the process.

To speak of "authenticity" would have the chance of winning the approval from lay and professional readers of the Bible. A Bible reader will probably by her- or himself entertain the idea to read the texts authentically, "correctly," in accordance with the intention, meaning etc. of the authors. Even if such a purpose is not explicitly stated, on second thoughts many Bible readers will agree that this is the aim of their work with the Bible and their use of it.

To speak of an authentic reading of the Bible would have the chance of evading negative sentiments associated to the traditional terms, as it will carry with it positive connotations. The idea will be conscious of its limitations, and still draw near to the text on the text's terms. It does not imagine obtaining a fusion of horizons, as in the program of Gadamer (Gadamer 1975/1989), but has a more limited goal: approaching the text in the full awareness of this being a meeting between strangers (Mæland 2007).

Is the "authentic reading" only a new expression for things well known? I do not think so. It entails a program for the process, succinctly stated in the terms chosen, and not all methods have made clear such a program. Further, even if the mere outcome is that the name is changed, this is no small achievement, since the very name for understanding the Bible is important if this may open up for communication and contribute to maintaining that communication.

The hermeneutical process has not come to an end with a method for Biblical study. The result of this work is a Bible propagating violence simultaneously with words of comfort, hope and reconciliation. The hermeneutical task is to handle the material brought forward by the study of the Bible, and this is no small task. But a hermeneutical activity may be undertaken in the framework of an "authentic reading," since it means "reading with" texts that are disparate. By putting them together, the texts start to communicate with each other, even if they are strangers and foreigners to each other. Only then has the "authentic reading" come to its goal. The method has the advantage of reading the Bible in the way suggested by Nambalirwa, Holter and Høyland Lavik, and then addressing the concomitant hermeneutical issues for applying the text. But it will take a lot of persuasion to bring Maria Flores Pena onboard.

References

Barton, John. 1984. *Reading the Old Testament: Method in Biblical study.* Philadelphia, PA: Westminster.

Barton, John. 2007. *The nature of Biblical criticism.* Louisville, KC: Westminster John Knox.

Collins, John J. 2004. *Does the Bible justify violence?* Minneapolis, MN: Fortress Press.

Gadamer, Hans-Georg. 1975/1989. *Truth and method.* Second, revised version. New York/London: Continuum.

Jonker, Louis C. 1996. *Exclusivity and variety: perspectives on multidimensional exegesis.* Kampen: Kok Pharos (Contributions to Biblical exegesis and theology, 19).

Kartveit, Magnar. 2000. Bruken av Bibelen i trusrørsla. /The Use of the Bible in the faith movement. *Tidsskrift for teologi og kirke* 71:251-266.

Mæland, Bård. 2007. Interpreting strange texts: Hermeneutics as distance overcoming. In Knut Holter (ed.), *Interpreting classical religious texts in contemporary Africa,* 35-44. Nairobi: Acton.

Note

[1] In her vernacular, as transmitted on television: "Pues yo no sé. Todos dicen que está en la Biblia que todo está tener que suceder. No da mas esperamos la voluntad de Dios, qu'es l'unico que puede saber todo, verdad?"

PART IV

16

Moral Principles and

Participation in Practice

Ethical and Methodological Issues in

Research on Formerly Recruited Children[1]

Kjetil Fretheim
MF Norwegian School of Theology, Oslo, Norway

Abstract

Research on children associated with armed forces or armed groups represents a field where ethical considerations are not only imperative, but are also complex and full of dilemmas. In this article I highlight some examples of the challenges and 'ethical and methodological puzzles' implicit in qualitative and participatory research on formerly recruited children. Addressing participants' consent and freedom, their right to protection and to have their voices heard, as well as the issue of payment for research participation, I point out the need to combine ethical absolutism with ethical situationism. I argue that there are some moral principles researchers must respect and adhere to, but also acknowledge that the interpretation of how to do this must be based on a considered judgement in and on the given context.

Introduction

The many and brutal atrocities committed during the wars in the Democratic Republic of Congo, Sierra Leone, Uganda and elsewhere, and the recruitment of children into armed groups and forces in these conflicts, have been met with widespread condemnation from the international community. Such recruitment is a reminder of the drastic means that people are willing to use in times of war and conflict. It also inspires and obliges the academic community to address a wide range of issues, including children's rights, the ethics of war and ways of reintegrating formerly recruited children into civilian life.

In approaching these issues the academic community is equipped with a set of moral principles that should guide the aims set and methods used in its research activities (Graue and Walsh 1998; Oliver 2003). Such principles include respect for persons and their right to privacy, informed consent and avoiding doing harm (Hammersley and Atkinson 2007, 209), and some would add maximising benefits and local participation (Mertus 2007, 180). In addition various 'codes of ethics' add to these general principles some more specific recommendations regarding research on children. For instance the *Norwegian ethical guidelines for social science, law, the humanities and theology* includes a separate section on 'Children's right to protection' (NESH 2006, 16; see also Alderson and Morrow 2004; Farrell 2005).

To be of relevance in a given research project, these guidelines need, however, to be translated from abstract to applied principles. To do this both a discussion of the contents and implications of general ethical principles, and a clarification of the specific challenges the researcher might encounter, are important. This applies to all kinds of research, but becomes especially relevant when doing research on formerly recruited children. The very phenomenon of children associated with armed forces and armed groups and the reality of war and conflict challenge the academic community to reflect on how abstract principles should be interpreted and applied in such contexts and circumstances (Edmonds 2003; Hill 2005, 65).

Writing from the perspective of ethnography, Martyn Hammersley and Paul Atkinson distinguish between four different ways of understanding ethical issues in the research setting: ethical absolutism, ethical situationism, ethical relativism and Machiavellianism (Hammersley and Atkinson 2007, 219-220). In the following I will not address the latter two positions, as they either reject any discussion about right or wrong in a universal sense or make this a purely pragmatic issue of 'what works' or suits the researchers' interests. I believe ethics should at least include a universal perspective, and certainly not only be limited to pragmatic considerations. Accordingly, what follows will consider ethical absolutism and ethical situationism. While the first refers to a position where abstract principles are interpreted as strict rules that should be followed at all times, the second puts a much stronger emphasis on 'judgement in context' and an 'assessment of the relative benefits and costs of pursuing research in different ways' (Hammersley and Atkinson 2007, 219). Both of these perspectives seem highly relevant when doing research on formerly recruited children. As Jo Boyden remarks:

even though it is important to develop agreed standards in relation to ethnographic enquiry, especially with regard to research methods and ethics, these will inevitably be transformed by context. While the researcher may aspire to certain terms and conditions, war will always involve compromises in ethnography and it is impossible to ensure these in practice (Boyden 2004, 256).

In other words, and although the perspective in the following is not limited to ethnographic research, the underlying assumption will be that research on formerly recruited children represents a field where ethical considerations are not only imperative, but are also complex and full of dilemmas. Some abstract principles must be regarded as strict rules that must be followed (ethical absolutism), but this must necessarily be combined with a judgement in and on the given situation or context (ethical situationism).

Research on formerly recruited children can be done in a wide range of academic fields and may focus on research questions approached through numerous different methodologies. Research methods associated with the social sciences are, however, often adopted. A review of the literature in the field (Tonheim 2009) reveals that many studies are qualitative (Vlassenroot and Raeymaekers 2004; Shepler 2005; Corbin 2008) or rely on a combination of quantitative and qualitative methods and material (Porto, Parsons and Alden 2007; Mazurana and Carlson 2004). Many are interview studies (Keairns 2003; Gislesen 2006), and several of these are based on interviews with children or young people (Brett and Specht 2004), while others rely on focus group discussions (Verhey 2001; Veale and Stavrou 2003; Honwana 2006; Denov and Maclure 2006). Despite this growing body of research and literature, however, Mats Utas argues that '[m]ethodology is a rather neglected topic in studies of under-age combatants' (Utas 2004, 209). This short-coming calls for a renewed discussion on the aims and methods within the field, and it is partly as a result of such discussions that several scholars now call for, and adopt, participatory research strategies in research on formerly recruited children (see for example Christensen and James 2008 and Tonheim 2009).

Participatory approaches refer in this context to research strategies where the informants not only provide the primary material or supplementing information for the benefit of the principal researcher, but that they also act as co-researchers. They take part in the analysis of the material in question, maybe even in the (re)formulation of research questions, structure of argument, conclusions and recommendations (see for example Eyber and Ager 2004). Increasingly adolescents and children are allowed to play this participatory role also in the field of research on formerly recruited children. Jason Hart and Bex Tyrer argue, for example, convincingly in favour of including children's participation in the research process, and link this to the United Nations Convention on the Rights of the Child (UNCRC; Hart and Tyrer 2006, 13). They see children's participation in research as 'a means to improve the quality and relevance of the data *and* [their emphasis] make children themselves more visible within a particular community or within the broader society' (Hart and Tyrer 2006, 15). Similarly, Myriam Denov and Richard Maclure argue that the inclusion of 'adolescent researchers would enhance the richness of the discussions and therefore the quality of the data' (Denov and Maclure 2006, 766). Alcinda Honwana favours what she calls a 'bottom-up rather than a top-down approach—in other words, an approach that entails greater community participation in protecting children from conflict and in enforcing their human rights' (Honwana 2001, 123).

Michael Goodhart raises, however, important questions and critical concerns regarding the participatory approach. He argues:

> [t]here is potential tension between allowing the community to shape and direct the research and conducting research that gives voice to the oppressed children and mothers, a tension amplified in the case of mothers who internalize the community's attitudes and become oppressors of their own children. The problem is not just that researchers must be extra cautious in such cases, but rather that the easy harmony between their personal and humanitarian value commitments might slip into discord. [...] But bluntly, participatory research works best when the roles of victim and oppressors are clear; when those roles are blurred, ethical and methodological puzzles arise (Goodhart 2007, 193).

In the following I want to highlight some examples of such challenges and 'ethical and methodological puzzles' implicit in qualitative and participatory research on formerly recruited children. This is a field where practical solutions and compromises must be found, but it is also easy to agree with R. Charli Carpenter, in that '[t]he fact that there will be methodological and ethical tradeoffs, as in all research, should not preclude attempts to gather information but should instead generate particular care and sensitivity with respect to research design' (Carpenter 2007, 216). The following is meant as a contribution in generating such sensitivity by entering into dialogue with recent contributions in this field of research.

I begin by drawing attention to the very concept of 'child soldiers,' which is a frequently used, though criticized, term for children associated with armed forces or armed groups. In this way I address the issue of who the potential participants in participatory research on formerly recruited children are and how they can be perceived. In the next section I address the issue of participants' consent and freedom, two key research ethical concerns, and how they might be applied in this context. This leads in turn to a discussion on how the issue of protection becomes an important concern when formerly recruited children participate in the research endeavour, and how the participants' voices should be represented in the research report. Finally, the relationship between the researcher and the research participants is addressed, highlighting the issue of research and politics, as well as the issue of reward or payment of informants/participants. I conclude by calling for continued discussions and innovation when conducting participatory research, as the research community searches for new and creative ways of dealing with its potential problems and challenges.

Children and soldiers

Approaching the research field, the researcher brings with her a set of assumptions about this field, its characteristics, problems and power relations. This is a necessary precondition for being able to articulate the initial research interest and research question. Assumptions about the field constitute the resources scholars make use of when contemplating what it is they want to explore, investigate or assess. The terms and labels used for the research field or the phenomenon the researchers are interested in, will have, however, connotations attached and guide the subsequent study in a given direction. This does not and should not exclude the possibility of having these assumptions revised and adjusted in the course of the research process, but it becomes an ethical imperative to seek transparency and awareness of such connotations, admitting the limitations implied in such self-reflective exercises.

In the context of research on children associated with armed forces or armed groups, how the concept of a 'child' and of being 'associated' with armed forces or armed groups are understood, is, of course, of fundamental importance. Malcolm Hill argues that 'for too long, the developmental paradigm has portrayed children as deficient adults rather than competent human beings in their own right' (Hill 2005, 62), but it seems now to be widely agreed that 'children need to be studied as an analytical category in themselves', rather than viewing them as 'proto-adults or future beings' (Honwana 2001, 134). This does not, however, close the discussion, as different ideas about what formerly recruited children are, still abound. This is highlighted for instance in the ongoing discussions about the roles and functions of members of this group, and the terminological question of how to 'label' these children (Honwana 2005; Utas 2005 and Wessells 2006, 3). They are called soldiers, fighters, abducted children, recruited children etc.

Girls are referred to as both bush wives and sexual slaves, and they are regarded as combatants on the one hand and as 'associated' with armed forces on the other. Awareness about these discussions is highly relevant, as the terminology used—whichever is chosen—has ethical implications. I will in this paper use the term 'formerly recruited children' as emphasis here is primarily on research on children who have been involved in armed groups or forces. Much of the relevant literature uses, however, the term 'child soldier.' This latter label risks, however, not only stigmatizing the children concerned, but also blurs the different ways children are recruited and the various roles they might have played in the armed groups or forces. Still, the term 'child soldier' highlights two perspectives that deserve closer consideration: the individual in question can be viewed both as a child and a soldier. Depending on how the nature of childhood is perceived, a 'child' can, on the one hand, be considered as someone who is particularly vulnerable and who deserves special attention. On the other hand, she can also be regarded as expressive and independent. In this perspective the formerly recruited children's autonomy deserves protection. Viewed as 'soldiers' formerly recruited children are, however, members of a group others deserve to be protected from. There is thus an implicit ambiguity in the term 'child soldier', and it makes sense to claim that formerly recruited children can be both victims and perpetrators at the same time (McKay and Mazurana 2004, 121).

Mats Utas contends that the approaches used in research on formerly recruited children 'normally yield responses in victim modes and tend to conceal many important aspects of lived experiences' (Utas 2004, 209). Similarly, Boyden argues that the 'focus on children's rights and protection has brought with it a concern to treat the young as especially deserving victims, as opposed to conscious agent, of political conflict' (Boyden 2004, 248). The participatory approach in research on formerly recruited children can be seen as a response to these issues, in that the formerly recruited children's agency and own perceptions and experiences here are emphasised. The conflict between a concern for children's rights and viewing them as conscious agents might, however, be exaggerated. Rather, precisely because formerly recruited children are conscious agents, their rights need to be acknowledged. A concern for children's rights must be understood as a concern to protect their agency. Accordingly, there is in this perspective no inherent contradiction between a concern for human rights (ethical absolutism) and the participatory approach and its contextual character (ethical situationism).

Further, it is important to underline the difference between being a 'child' and being a 'soldier.' The recruited children can remain soldiers or their service in military or guerrilla troops can come to an end. In either case, he or she still remains a child. Put in philosophical terms, the primary ontological status is that of being a child, not a soldier. In this sense, the status of 'child' has priority over that of being a 'soldier.' This too has ethical implications. While the actions of formerly recruited children (and others) can be assessed as right or wrong, moral or immoral, the understanding of the persons committing these actions does not rely on their actions alone, or of their culpability. The 'inherent dignity ...of all members of the human family' (from the Universal Declaration of Human Rights, see Hayden 2001, 353) is not erased through actions that must be condemned. The distinction between the person and his or her actions is in other words fundamental. The fact that some children become associated with armed groups or forces can be considered to be contrary to this very dignity and their related 'inalienable rights', and in this sense formerly recruited children must be considered victims of human rights violations.

Participants' consent and freedom

It is a basic requirement in the social sciences that those being researched are sufficiently informed about the research topics and aims, and that they consent to their participation in this. Informed consent is often achieved by, for example, asking interviewees or others to sign a declaration of consent before the research process starts. In research on formerly recruited children many use written forms to state the affirmation of informed consent for the interviewees (Keairns 2003, 21), or they rely on verbal consent when the interviewees can not read or write (Burman and McKay 2007).

The notion of 'informed consent' raises, however, the question of how such consent should be understood. The underlying assumption is that this consent should be a result of the interviewees' own considerations, and not be forced on him or her in any way. This assumes, however, that consent is given under circumstances where no pressure or power mechanisms are at play. As is widely acknowledged, such conditions exist only in ideal theory. Power is everywhere, also in the encounter between researcher and informants/participants in the field. Regarding the issue of consent in research on formerly recruited children, Julie Mertus notes that 'the psychological distress that they [children born of rape and their mothers] have suffered may cloud their judgement and perceptions, thus interfering with their ability to choose to enter into and to participate freely in a research project' (Mertus

2007, 182). Similarly, Boyden argues that informed consent 'is not a free value but one that is bound up in a highly complex web of expectations, norms and meanings and as such can be hard to achieve in practice' (Boyden 2004, 243; see also Christensen 2004). Clearly, individual choice is often strained by a number of social, cultural, economic and other factors, and informed choice is especially difficult in context of uncertainty, fear and rapid social change.

Such power relationships in the field are, however, complex, as is the relationship between researchers and informants. On the one hand, the researcher is in the privileged position as she knows more about what she wants and the aims and issues involved in the research project. In addition she often, though not always, enjoys the respect that follows with being part of the educated academic community. On the other hand, portraying the potential informants or co-researchers in the research project as powerless in their relationship with the principal researcher and her team would not be fitting. Interviewees can be both reluctant and make their own demands. In a study from Ethiopia Angela Veale writes:

> The women were initially reluctant to be involved and the women presented a list of questions outlining their concerns about the research before agreeing to participate in the study. They wanted to know about the purpose and objectives of the study, and if it would contribute to bringing any changes or identifying solutions to problems faced. They wanted the researcher to understand their political commitment and they would not participate in anything that would be politically undermining of what they had fought or stood for (Veale 2003, 21).

Most importantly, the interviewee is in a position to say 'no.' He or she may simply refuse to cooperate with the researcher, and may withhold information and consequently limit the value of, and insights provided through, the research process.

It is of course the obligation of the researcher to highlight and clarify this option to her potential informants or co-researchers and explain what involvement or participation will imply, what topics will be raised and what effects their research intervention will have. This is, however, also problematic, as the researcher at the outset cannot be fully aware of where this research process will take her. Accordingly, the prospective research participants cannot be fully informed about the research process, the empirical findings, the analysis and the conclusions to be drawn. Thus, and as pointed out by Malcom Hill, '[a]n inherent tension exists between the desire to give maximum information and ensure choice is freely given, and the wish to maximize participation in the field' (Hill 2005, 69).

The issues of informed and free consent become even more complicated when it is children who are approached as potential participants in a research project. Can children be informed about, and accordingly understand, what being part of a research project implies? If the answer to this question is negative, the 'informed consent' criterion effectively blocks any research on children based on interviews, observation or other kinds of field work (ethical absolutism). If the answer is positive, however, this only raises new issues. How can children be informed about the implications of the research project and their participation in it? This must at the very least involve a kind of communication which is suitable for and adapted to the level of development and knowledge of the children in question. Further, the power relations between adults and children are also such that the notion of free consent must be reconsidered in this context (ethical situationism). Informed consent could be perceived as the informed consent of both parents and child. This would pose new challenges, however, in cases where the interests of the parents or guardians and the interests of the child are conflicting.

The ethical issues involved in this kind of research are, however, not limited to considerations about how to initiate the research project or individual research interviews. They include issues regarding how one should conduct such interviews. This relates to the issue of informed consent in the sense that by giving his or her consent, the interviewee has given the researcher(s) a green light and in this sense has accepted that questions will be asked and declared a willingness to answer these questions. It seems unreasonable, however, to regard this as permission to ask any kind of question or to argue that the interviewee is obliged to any question. The condition that the interviewee is allowed to withdraw from the research project and interview at any time is precisely such an escape clause. This raises yet another question: What kinds of questions can morally be asked in a research interview? While the researcher can refer to the principle of academic freedom and thus pose whatever research question she finds relevant and of interest (ethical absolutism interpreted as Machiavellism), it seems necessary to consider this freedom against 'common decency' and respect for the interviewees when specific questions in the interview are to be considered. In other words, moral principles concerning informed consent and the participants' freedom must be combined with considered contextual judgements.

Protecting participants

Research on formerly recruited children often takes place in areas with ongoing confrontation or that are in the process of disarmament and/or reintegration and responsible researchers must accordingly consider closely the possible harm the research intervention might have on the children involved. Both the researcher and the researched find themselves at risk and must seek ways of protecting themselves and others.

The primary method used for protecting informants in social science research projects, is to ensure the confidentiality and anonymity of the informants. Confidentiality refers in this context to the relationship between the researcher and the interviewee/participant and that what is said between them remains between them. Confidentiality is achieved through anonymity, meaning that the empirical data is de-contextualised in a way that it cannot be linked to or traced back to identifiable persons. Researchers are compelled to implement the necessary measures to protect their informants from potential protection threats. The issue of confidentiality is, however, not only a matter of finding ways in which to write the research report, but relates also to the question of who should be included in the research process and given access to the collected data. Researchers in this field often rely on intermediate contacts such as local community leaders, development workers or others to get in touch with the formerly recruited children (Veale and Stavrou 2003; Honwana 2006, 21-25; Coalition to Stop the Use of Child Soldiers 2008, 37). Explaining her approach in fieldwork in Mozambique, Honwana highlights the benefits of such cooperation:

> I decided to work through this NGO because the program was designed specifically for girls who had lived in military camps and addressed the systematic sexual violence they had endured. Had I attempted to conduct such research elsewhere, it would have been very difficult to find any young women who were willing to admit their involvement in the war and share their stories with me (Honwana 2006, 22).

To these contact persons, the identity of the research participants might be well known, and this fact implies a specific challenge in protecting their anonymity. The researcher (and translator and others involved in the research team) should for this reason sign (and comply with) a declaration of anonymity. So should other people present at the interview. However, the greater the number of people involved, the more difficult it will be to protect the formerly recruited child from any breach of confidentiality. The very presence of parents or guardians might even represent a breach of the confidentiality promised.

These considerations highlight the complexities and difficulties that arise when considering 'children's right to protection' (NESH 2006, 16) in actual research of this kind (Hill 2005, 75-77). Responding to such difficulties, Michael Wessells seeks to outline a 'potentially useful model for protecting the girls' well-being before, during, and after the interview' (Wessells 2006, 20). He describes three main steps in this model:

> Its first step was to select the participants by working through community networks of trusted informants who can identify whether girls can talk, which girls are in a position to participate, and where and how to conduct the interviews in a girl friendly manner. Next, the interview session had present a trained social worker or other person who can provide psychosocial support if necessary. After the interview, the social worker also made follow-up visits to the participant for purposes of psychosocial support (Wessells 2006, 21).

The challenges involved in conducting such interviews 'in a friendly manner' are particularly demanding due to the sensitive issues such interviews will often address. Responsible research must find ways to avoid—at least minimize—psychological harm both in terms of how they interact with their informants and by providing adequate psychosocial support. This relates, however, also to the issue of protection, as 'research pursued with this agenda could lead to the revelation by children of information that runs against the interests of certain adults, thus putting those children at risk' (Hart and Tyrer 2006, 16-17). This applies not only to the individual interview, but to the whole research process. As Boyden notes, 'the ethical codes that typically guide research tend to ignore the agency of respondents who may take advantage of, manipulate, or possibly even actively abuse research, sometimes with adverse consequences—intended or unintended—in terms of security' (Boyden 2004, 245).

This does not imply, however, that this kind of research is impossible, nor that it is not appreciated. Several research projects on formerly recruited children receive a positive welcome in the field. It seems many formerly recruited children have a 'desire to testify to and archive the atrocities and losses they have endured' (Boyden 2004, 246). Denov and Maclure maintain that 'it appears that the overwhelming number of girls who participated in interviews and focus groups for this study found the experience to be something of a catharsis' (Denov and Maclure 2006, 83). Similarly, Honwana shares that people 'appreciated our effort to investigate local beliefs and practices and to learn from elders, chiefs, and traditional healers' (Honwana 2006, 24), but also makes clear that

> [s]ome were not willing to talk about what had happened to them at war, however. Even in this supportive setting, it was extremely difficult for younger women to talk

about the sexual abuse they had suffered and for older women to discuss the girls'
experiences. People hardly talk about such taboo subjects within the family, let alone
to strangers (Honwana 2006, 22).

These difficulties must be acknowledged when doing this kind of
research, and be considered from the perspective of protecting the
participants. There is some truth in Wessells' comment that there are 'myriad
ways in which well intentioned research can inadvertently violate the
humanitarian imperative Do No Harm' (Wessells 2006, 4) and the issue of
inflicting harm can be challenging. Chris Coulter writes how she 'frequently
felt anxious about asking them to talk about what had happened to them or
what they had done during the war', and found that she "had to end many
interviews or steer them away from sensitive topics' (Coulter 2006, 56).
However, respondents also take some responsibility in this respect. Boyden
notes that '[s]ince they often have insights into the dangers they confront and
ways of dealing with them, respondents can frequently be relied on to steer
conversations away from hazardous topics' (Boyden 2004, 245). This
indicates how participatory approaches not only raise new ethical dilemmas,
but also enable morally sensitive and considered investigations to take place.
While protecting the participants remains a moral imperative (ethical
absolutism) its implications must be considered carefully in the actual
research practice.

The participants' voice

Scholars in this field of research seek not only to explain the phenomenon of
formerly recruited children with reference to background variables or macro
political factors, but also to understand the phenomenon as it is perceived by
those affected by their actions, by those recruiting them, as well as by the
formerly recruited children themselves. Empirical and participatory methods
are well suited to gaining such understanding. Such studies set out to explore
data identified through various methods (interviews, participant observation
etc.) and use these in the subsequent analysis. In other words, understanding
is sought on the basis of empirical data and analysis.

This takes us from the issue of whether or not informants are willing to
talk to what it is they actually say. Researchers have experienced how
'informants would alter or add previously unknown or even contradictory
information' (Coulter 2006, 55) over the course of the fieldwork. Honwana
shares how she finds participants might have 'exaggerated their stories', but
still maintains that 'the narratives told by these young women did not appear
unrealistic' (Honwana 2006, 22). Similarly, Denov and Maclure write:

As with all self-report data, of course, particularly in light of some of the violent events that these young people experienced and undoubtedly participated in, it is conceivable that occasionally they may have concealed, altered or exaggerated some aspects of their stories. Yet a number of factors minimized such tendencies and helped to ensure our overall confidence in the authenticity of their personal narratives (Denov and Maclure 2007, 248-249).

This optimistic, possibly naïve, assessment of the interview material, needs, however, to be tempered by a critical awareness of what Mats Utas has termed 'victimcy,' a strategy or 'tactical manipulation' employed by the respondents whereby they represent themselves as 'powerless victims' (Utas 2004, 209). This kind of strategy must be considered part of 'a political response to real security threats, as well as an economic strategy in relation to humanitarian aid projects' (Utas 2004, 209; see also Utas 2005), though it may also have psychological sources.

One key element of the research report is to give a reliable description of the empirical data, for example to render quotes from the interviews in a detailed and conscious manner. While it is important to acknowledge that every description represents an interpretation of the empirical data, and also that the empirical data at hand represents a reduction and a selection of data from a larger reality, a detailed and nuanced description of the empirical data that constitutes the primary material is of vital importance to the later assessment of the research report by the extended research community. Further, in a qualitative study based on participatory methodology, an important element of this description will be to convey the perceptions and interpretations of the informants and participants in the research field. The researcher's task will be to analyse and contextualise these interpretations in light of a given perspective or set of theories.

Not only *how* this is done but also *that it is done*, is of vital ethical importance. This becomes evident when the perspectives and interpretations articulated by the interviewees are of a morally dubious character. If the description of the empirical data includes explicit racist attitudes, detailed instructions on how to run a terrorist organisation or commit suicide, this represents morally problematic attitudes or suggestions. As pointed out by Hammersley and Atkinson, it is a 'fallacy' to assume 'that the researcher and the people studied will usually see the research in the same way' (Hammersley and Atkinson 2007, 219). A related issue is how the researcher should deal with information that might prevent further killing. Clearly there is an "obligation to avoid injury and severe burdens" (NESH 2006, 12), but the implications of this obligation can in concrete cases be difficult to discern.

There are certainly ethical reasons for focussing on and making controversial voices not only the object for one's studies, but also letting them be represented in the final report. Only by understanding the thoughts and ideas of racists, terrorists or committed soldiers, can one also counter them. In this way representatives of such groups are also held responsible for their ideas (and actions), and are forced to engage in a conversation with others, including their potential 'enemies.' However, it is a characteristic of good research that one distinguishes between one's own political, ideological and methodological convictions and that of one's research objects. The researcher should in other words not render the viewpoints of terrorists and racists in a way too coloured by his or her own viewpoints. This would make it impossible for the reader to distinguish between the two and to understand what the issue is all about.

In participatory research, however, this distinction between researcher and the researched is blurred. Thus, the ethical research standards need to accommodate the specifics of this approach (ethical situationism). Still, seeking understanding cannot mean accepting any kind of notions. Although it is important to understand what these attitudes and suggestions imply, it is equally morally important to challenge them. In other words, such viewpoints should not be the only voices heard in the research report. It remains a moral imperative to morally assess the voices represented in the material in the subsequent analysis (ethical absolutism).

Paying participants

Considering the contexts where formerly recruited children are found, researchers in this field will also often find themselves in settings characterized by poverty and human suffering. In such contexts the researcher will most often not only be an outsider to the field, but also be in a privileged position both financially and in terms of political rights and protection. What is the responsibility of the privileged when doing research in such contexts? Should research on formerly recruited children be regarded as an enterprise independent of the efforts to end the use of children in armed conflicts and to reintegrate them in their communities? Is research separated from values and/or politics or is it a tool to achieve normative and/or political aims? (for further discussion of this, see Tvedt 1998)

Some scholars in the field are explicit about their limited ambitions. Hammersley and Atkinson argue that 'social research is not inevitably, *and should not be* [their emphasis], political,' as 'the only value which is intrinsic to the activity of research is truth' (Hammersley and Atkinson 2007, 209). They admit, however, that

> there can be exceptional occasions when a researcher should stop being a researcher and engage in action that is not directed towards the goal of producing knowledge. There is in fact always much action engaged in by ethnographers in the field that is not directly concerned with knowledge production (Hammersley and Atkinson 2007, 228).

Similarly, Goodhart points out that 'academics are, after all, supposed to remain neutral and objective as we pursue our research' (Goodhart 2007, 188), but he too adds:

> Yet the urgency of the questions posed (...) cannot be grasped without a deep appreciation of the injustice underlying them. Fortunately, we also possess tremendous capacities to hope, to empathize, and to effect social change. (...) One role of socially engaged research is to marshal empirical evidence in providing analytic and normative guidance that can inform such efforts (Goodhart 2007, 188).

Acknowledging that 'exceptional occasions' are common when doing research on formerly recruited children, as well as the privileged researchers' actual capacity 'to effect social change' others favour a much more activist and ambitious understanding of the research project. Accordingly, some researchers explicitly aim to assist, for example, aid agencies in their work, 'maintaining that it is not ethical to conduct research during conflict unless there is an intention to act on the situation and ameliorate suffering' (Boyden 2004, 247). Some scholars call this as a 'rights-based approach,' referring to a commitment to promote and protect international human rights standards.

While it is necessary to be clear about how the role of the researcher is distinct from warring parties, aid agencies, the local government etc, the privileged researcher will form ties to those participating in the research project. As such, she should not relate to her informants merely as a means to an end, i.e. instrumental sources of information, but as ends in themselves, as persons. This Kantian maxim becomes an imperative also in this context (ethical absolutism). For this reason, and as discussed above, the privileged researcher must ask her informant or co-researchers for their permission to ask questions, observe and enquire into their lives in various ways. The prospective research participant might, however, also ask: What is in it for me? What do I get in return? Often, and reasonably so, the obligation to convey research results represents a minimum ethical obligation on part of the researcher(s) towards research participants, informants and their communities, although this might imply considerable practical difficulties. Informants might, however, have other (and even more demanding) expectations. Informants in Nepal are reported to have said: 'Why don't you give us your research dollars?' (Kumar, Gurung, Adhikari and Subedi 2001, cited in Hart and Tyrer 2006, 21), and there is an implied comparison in this question: How much money should be spent on research purposes while children are starving? And further: What would be the implications if research interviews are turned into offers you cannot refuse and commodified on line with commercial products or services? How should the individual researcher respond to the informant who also has become a friend, when she asks for a bit of support for herself and her family in times of need?

As also mentioned above, researchers often cooperate with NGOs in order to facilitate their research and gain access to the field. Wessells notes that 'in a situation of severe poverty and deprivation, there is a natural tendency for local people to think that outsiders who work for an NGO have many resources and will provide help if they are treated well' (Wessells 2006, 8, see also Hart and Tyrer 2006, 22). This creates expectations of different kinds. For this reason Wessells argues that

> researchers should work to manage local peoples' expectations and, more important, to connect their research with practical action and steps that will assist formerly recruited girls. One way to achieve this is by partnering with an international NGO or other agency that seeks to support girls' reintegration (Wessells 2006, 21-22).

This relates to the issue of the relationship between research and politics, and the role the researcher sees him- or herself playing in the larger picture and in the relationship to NGOs and others involved in (activist) political or (practical) development work. It is, however, also an issue that relates to how the researcher relates to individual informants and/or participants in the research project.

One key aspect of such researcher–co-researcher relationships is the issue of payment or compensation. This issue can be dealt with in a number of different ways from not offering or giving any kind of reward, via a compensation for costs and/or loss of income, to an agreed upon payment. If offered, the reward or compensation may be in the form of material goods, cash or other forms. But there are still further questions that need to be raised: Should payment be announced when recruiting participants to the research project, or should it rather come as an unannounced reward? Should it be a token of thanks, a compensation for time and lost income or travel expenses? (see Hill 2005, 71). Opinions on this issue vary.

One approach is, as mentioned, to reject any kind of reward: 'No inducements were offered to the respondents prior to interviews that might have influenced their willingness to participate' (Mazurana and Carlson 2004, 34; McKay and Mazurana 2004, 132). Coulter arrives at the same conclusion:

> While working with my informants I was often reminded of the fact that I had nothing to offer in exchange for their stories. I have no professional knowledge of how to deal with suffering and violence, I am not backed by an NGO with education or training, I could offer my informants nothing save for a few cups of rice once in a while, and my time. I did not pay informants to talk to me (Coulter 2006, 666).

This practice seems reasonable also in light of the effects compensation might have on the data collected and the quality of the material the research project is based on. Reward will represent an incentive to offer one's services to and participate in research projects, but becomes also an incentive to make oneself attractive to those doing research. Consequently, there is a risk that informants say what they think the researcher wants to hear, and they explain their actions in ways adapted to the assumed expectations of the outsider. In this sense, the needs of the research community require that such incentives are avoided or at least kept to a minimum. Indirectly, however, since research in the long run should serve the communities and people living there, it could be argued that the needs of the research community should not be considered entirely distinct from the needs of society. Only by providing research of good quality, can the research community offer good quality analysis and recommendations for society as a whole.

There are, however, also reasons to choose the alternative: to reward, compensate or pay informants and others for their participation in research projects. This option is also chosen by some researchers. Veale writes that in one of her studies, 'participants were given a small cash amount as a reimbursement for their time' (Veale 2003, 22), and Hart and Tyrer make recommendations in the same direction:

> In situations where children and their families are faced with a severe struggle simply to survive, the issue of payment for research becomes particularly acute. Where there is expectation or a clear responsibility to reward certain individuals this should be done in a manner that avoids fuelling tension amongst the community. Attempts to offer rewards secretly may backfire, badly confirming suspicions and fuelling resentment. It may be safer to make transparent the criteria for participation and the reasons for payment/reimbursement of particular individuals. Even if there is no expectation of material reward, attention must be paid to the possible loss of income and the cost involved for participating children. At the very least transportation and other incidental costs should be reimbursed and refreshments or meals provided to participants (Hart and Tyrer 2006, 21).

One primary concern that points in this direction is that of recruiting informants. Interviewees and others are not necessarily simply sitting waiting for researchers to come along, but have work to tend to, families to feed and other commitments. There are costs involved when researchers travel to meet their informants, and there are similar costs involved when it is the informant who has to travel to the researcher. While the researcher is on the job during the research interview, that might not be the case for the interviewee. In order to make it possible for the latter to participate, a kind of compensation for loss of income or to cover costs involved seems to be a reasonable strategy. Rachel Brett and Irma Specht write:

> Although at the conclusion of the interview you might present participants with a small gift, that gift is only a token of appreciation in the fullest sense of the word token: to say thank you and to mark the conclusion of that part of our interviewing relationship (Brett and Specht 2004, 156).

Against this background the main issue with regard to the issue of gifts or payments seems to be the question of what is 'appropriate', which necessarily has to be answered relative to the context in question (ethical situationism) and which cannot be answered on absolute terms once and for all (ethical absolutism). The conclusion is often that 'much depends on circumstances' (Hammersley and Atkinson 2007, 218). It is worth noting, however, that this kind of transaction is an integral part of the researcher's interaction with informants and participants in the field. The very fact that someone has been singled out by the research team and been given their special attention, can represent a type of social capital that strengthens not only self-esteem, but also his or her standing in the local community.

Conclusion

Research in social settings will be shaped, adjusted and challenged by various factors in the very context in which it takes place, and it is in these contexts that abstracts principles need to be applied. This is the case for all kinds of research, but becomes acute when doing research on children and in war and war-like settings. These contexts pose both methodological and ethical challenges for both professional academics and other research participants.

In this paper I have discussed some of the challenges that arise in qualitative and participatory research on formerly recruited children. Addressing participants' consent and freedom, their right to protection and to have their voices heard, as well as the issue of payment for research participation, I have pointed out the need to combine ethical absolutism with ethical situationism. I have argued that there are some moral principles researchers must respect and adhere to, but also acknowledged that the interpretation of how to do this must be based on a considered judgement in and on the given context.

Participatory research strategies have some specific challenges, and some of these have been highlighted here. These are, however, challenges, and not obstacles that should make the academic community reject such and other new and innovative methods in this kind of research. Rather, these challenges should inspire new and creative ways of dealing with them.

Reference list

Alderson, Priscilla and Virginia Morrow 2004. *Ethics, social research and consulting with children and young people*, Ilford: Barnardo's.

Boyden, Jo 2004. Anthropology under fire: Ethics, researchers and children in war. In *Children and youth on the front line: Ethnography, armed conflict and displacement*, ed. Jo Boyden and Joanna de Berry 2004: New York: Berghahn Books.

Brett, Rachel and Irma Specht 2004. *Young soldiers: Why they choose to fight*, Boulder, Colo.: Lynne Rienner.

Burman, Mary and Susan McKay 2007. Marginalization of girl mothers during reintegration from armed groups in Sierra Leone. *International Nursing Review* 54:316-323.

Carpenter, R. Charli 2007. Protecting children born of war. In *Born of war: Protecting children of sexual violence survivors in conflict zones*, ed. R. Charli Carpenter 2007: Bloomfield, CT.: Kumarian Press.

Christensen, Pia Haudrup 2004. Children's participation in ethnographic research: Issues of power and representation. *Children & Society* 18:165-176.

Christensen, Pia and Allison James 2008. *Research with children: Perspectives and practices*, New York: Routledge.

Coalition to Stop the Use of Child Soldiers 2008. *Returning home: Children's perspectives on reintegration. A case study of children abducted by the Lord's Resistance Army in Teso, Eastern Uganda*. London: Coalition to Stop the Use of Child Soldiers.

Corbin, Joanne N. 2008. Returning home: Resettlement of formerly abducted children in Northern Uganda. *Disasters* 32 (2):316-335.

Coulter, Chris C. 2006. *Being a bush wife: Women's lives through war and peace in Northern Sierra Leone*, Uppsala, Department of Cultural Anthropology and Ethnology, Uppsala University.

Denov, Myriam and Richard Maclure 2006. Engaging the voices of girls in the aftermath of Sierra Leone's conflict: Experience and perspectives in a culture of violence. *Anthropologica* 48:73-85.

Denov, Myriam and Richard Maclure 2007. Turnings and epiphanies: Militarization, life histories, and the making and unmaking of two child soldiers in Sierra Leone. *Journal of Youth Studies* 10 (2):243-261.

Edmonds, Casper N. 2003. *Ethical considerations: When conducting research on children in the worst forms of child labour in Nepal*. Geneva: International Labour Organization (ILO).

Eyber, Carola and Alastair Ager 2004. Researching young people's experiences of war: Participatory methods and the trauma discourse in Angola. In *Children and youth on the front line: Ethnography, armed conflict and displacement*, ed. Jo Boyden and Joanna de Berry 2004: New York: Berghahn Books.

Farrell, Ann 2005. *Ethical research with children*, Maidenhead: Open University Press.

Gislesen, Kirsten 2006. *A childhood lost? The challenges of successful disarmament, demobilisation and reintegration of child soldiers: The case of West Africa*. Oslo: Norwegian Institute of International Affairs.

Goodhart, Michael 2007. Children born of war and human rights: Philosophical reflections. In *Born of war: Protecting children of sexual violence survivors in conflict zones*, ed. R. Charli Carpenter 2007: Bloomfield, CT.: Kumarian Press.

Graue, Elizabeth M. and Daniel J. Walsh 1998. *Studying children in context: Theories, methods, and ethics*, Thousand Oaks, California: Sage.

Hammersley, Martyn and Paul Atkinson 2007. *Ethnography: Principles in practice*, London: Routledge.

Hart, Jason and Bex Tyrer 2006. *Research with children living in situations of armed conflict: Concepts, ethics & methods*. Oxford: Refugee Studies Centre, University of Oxford.

Hayden, Patrick 2001. *The philosophy of human rights*, St. Paul, Minn.: Paragon House.

Hill, Malcolm 2005. Ethical considerations in researching children's experiences. In *Researching children's experience: Methods and approaches*, ed. Sheila Greene and Diane Hogan 2005: London: Sage Publications.

Honwana, Alcinda 2001. Children of war: Understanding war and war cleansing in Mozambique and Angola. In *Civilians in war*, ed. Simon Chesterman 2001: Boulder, Colo.: Lynne Rienner Publishers.

Honwana, Alcinda 2005. Innocent & guilty: Child-soldiers as interstitial & tactical agents. In *Makers & breakers: Children & youth in postcolonial Africa*, ed. Alcinda Honwana and Filip de Boeck 2005: Oxford: James Curry.

Honwana, Alcinda 2006. *Child soldiers in Africa*, Philadelphia, Pa.: University of Pennsylvania Press.

Keairns, Yvonne E. 2003. *The voices of girl child soldiers*. New York: Quaker United Nations Office.

Kumar, Bal KC, Yogendra Bahadur Gurung, Keshab Prasad Adhikari and Govind Subedi 2001. *Nepal situation of child Ragpickers: A rapid assessment*. Geneva: ILO.

Mazurana, Dyan and Khristopher Carlson 2004. *From combat to community: Women and girls of Sierra Leone*. Hunt Alternatives Fund.

McKay, Susan and Dyan Mazurana 2004. *Where are the girls? Girls in fighting forces in Northern Uganda, Sierra Leone and Mozambique: Their lives during and after war*, Montreal: Rights & Democracy, International Centre for Human Rights and Democratic Development.

Mertus, Julie 2007. Key ethical inquiries for future research. In *Born of war: Protecting children of sexual violence survivors in conflict zones*, ed. R. Charli Carpenter 2007: Bloomfield, CT: Kumarian Press.

NESH 2006. *Guidelines for research ethics in the social sciences, law and the humanities*, Oslo: National Committee for Research Ethics in the Social Sciences and the Humanities.

Oliver, Paul 2003. *The student's guide to research ethics*, Maidenhead: Open University Press.

Porto, João Gomes, Imogen Parsons and Chris Alden 2007. *From soldiers to citizens: The social, economic and political reintegration of UNITA excombatants*, Pretoria: Institute for Security Studies.

Shepler, Susan 2005. The rites of the child: Global discourses of youth and reintegrating child soldiers in Sierra Leone. *Journal of Human Rights* 4 (2):197-211.

Tonheim, Milfrid 2009. *Reintegration of child soldiers: A literature review with particular focus on girl soldiers' reintegration in the DRC.* Stavanger: Centre for Intercultural Communication (SIK).

Tvedt, Terje 1998. Some notes on development research and ethics. *Forum for Development Studies* 2:211-227.

Utas, Mats 2004. Fluid research fields: Studying excombatant youth in the aftermath of the Liberian civil war. In *Children and youth in the front line: Ethnography, armed conflict and displacement*, ed. Jo Boyden and Joanna de Berry 2004: New York: Berghahn Books.

Utas, Mats 2005. Agency of victims: Young women in the Liberian Civil War. In *Makers & breakers: Children & youth in postcolonial Africa*, ed. Alcinda Honwana and Filip de Boeck 2005: Oxford: James Currey.

Veale, Angela 2003. *From child soldier to ex-fighter: Female fighters, demobilisation and reintegration in Ethiopia*, Pretoria: Institute for Security Studies.

Veale, Angela and Aki Stavrou 2003. *Violence, reconciliation and identity: The reintegration of Lord's Resistance Army child abductees in Northern Uganda*, Pretoria: Institute for Security Studies.

Verhey, Beth 2001. *Child soldiers: Preventing, demobilizing and reintegrating.* World Bank.

Vlassenroot, Koen and Timothy Raeymaekers 2004. *Conflict and social transformation in Eastern DR Congo*, Gent: Academia Press Scientific Publ.

Wessells, Michael G. 2006. *Child soldiers: From violence to protection*, Cambridge, Mass.: Harvard University Press.

Note

[1] The author wants to thank the editor, referees and participants at the conference in Stavanger May 2009 for their comments on an earlier draft.

17

Are Psychosocial Interventions for War-Affected Children Justified?

Ragnhild Dybdahl
Norad, Oslo

Nermina Kravic
Tuzla University, Bosnia and Herzegovina
Department of psychiatry, Clinical Center Tuzla

Kishor Shrestha
Tribhuvan University, Balkhu, Kathmandu

Abstract

In spite of the human ability to cope in adverse circumstances, there is overwhelming evidence that many children suffer physically, psychologically and socially during times of armed conflict and for years afterward. There is agreement that children need to be supported in order to promote their well-being and recovery, but the type of intervention is subject to much debate, especially regarding psychological and psychosocial interventions. The authors argue that the lack of strong evidence poses fundamental challenges regarding the ethics of response, particularly when one takes into account the need for solid research and culturally appropriate indicators and interventions. Do no harm issues are discussed and related to the lack of a strong evidence base. Different approaches to, and content of, support to children affected by armed conflict are discussed, as well as some of the challenges related to such interventions and research.

Introduction

Children have been exposed to the horrors and hardships of conflict and its aftermath throughout history. During and after armed conflicts, children are deprived of many of their rights to protection, provision and participation. Psychosocial issues and mental health are now an important part of public health in conflicts, disasters and complex emergencies. In this chapter we will discuss some of the challenges of psychosocial interventions, and whether, and under what conditions, these interventions are justified. Psychosocial interventions have potential to do good as well as to do harm, and therefore interventions are not in themselves justified, but must be viewed in terms of evidence and ethics.

There is no doubt that experiencing losses, dangers and injuries can seriously affect people's well-being and alter their world view, (e.g. Barenbaum, Ruchin, and Schwab-Stone 2004; Mollica, Lopes Cardozo, Osofsky, Raphael, Ager and Salama 2004). Van der Kolk and Mc Farlane express some of the challenges of trauma well when they state:

> Experiencing trauma is an essential part of being human, history is written in blood…. Despite the human capacity to survive and adapt, traumatic experiences can alter people's psychological, biological, and social equilibrium to such a degree that the memory of one particular event comes to taint all other experiences, spoiling appreciation of the present (1996, 3).

In addition to attention to trauma responses and psychosocial support as a cross-cutting issue, it is important to remember that people with severe mental disorders are particularly vulnerable and the needs that are specific for this group are often neglected in complex emergencies (Jones, Asare, El Masri, Mhanraj, Sherief and van Ommeren 2009).

The consequences of conflict and complex emergencies can be serious and long-long lasting, also for children, for example on their physical health, on their education, and on their social and psychological wellbeing. Although most research on psychological effects of potentially traumatizing events have been carried out in industrialized countries, there is now a substantial body of evidence from non Western settings showing that adults and children who have been exposed to severe complex emergencies, danger and traumatic loss are at increased risk of negative consequences for their health and development (e.g. Lustig, Kia-Keating, Grant-Knight et al. 2004) A recent multi-disciplinary review of reported findings regarding the relations between political violence, mental health and psychosocial wellbeing in Nepal identified 572 studies, of which 44 were included in the review, illustrating this large, and growing, body of literature (Tol, Kohrt, Jordans et al. 2009).

Following disasters and conflict situations, humanitarian agencies have increasingly focused on mental health and psychosocial support programmes. These types of programmes have been the subject of much debate (e.g. Bracken, Giller and Summerfield 1995; Jones 2008; Summerfield 2000), but that debate is not the focus of this chapter. However, questions related to a psychological symptom focus versus indigenous ways of coping and whether a Western construction of personhood and psychiatry is universal, underlie some of the challenges discussed here, inter alia why interventions needs to be justified.

As in other potentially traumatizing conditions, people in complex emergencies show great ability to cope and demonstrate resilience and dignity. They may live through even severe hardships without suffering serious or long-term physical or psychological injuries, and people's ability for self-recovery is high (e.g. Bonanno 2004; Bonanno and Pancini 2008; Jones 2008; Masten 2001, 2009). The degree to which children are vulnerable or resilient varies considerably between individuals and contexts. Whether children suffer long-term consequences depends on a range of individual and contextual factors and has been subject to much research. These factors include what children experience and how they experience it, the presence or absence of protective factors in the family, community and culture, availability of social support and individual hardiness.

For helpers and researchers, the dichotomy of vulnerability and resilience continue to be a challenge. We must become able to better accept and understand both human resilience and the potentially devastating impact of trauma, as well as the presence of suffering and changes in people's lives that are not best labeled as psychiatric or trauma disorders.

While we build on the human wish to contribute to the alleviation of suffering, we argue that we must use our best scientific methods and take as our starting point the principle *do no harm*. These challenges are the topic of this chapter. There is no disagreement that war causes suffering to children, also in terms of social, psychological and existential well-being. There is also agreement that affected children need support from their families, communities and in many instances the larger society. In this chapter we describe types of interventions and available guidelines and try to integrate the perspectives of resilience and vulnerability. The discussion of whether psychological and psychosocial interventions are justified is closely linked to available evidence for the effect of these programmes. We will also raise some of the challenges of this type of support and research, particularly related to ethics and sociocultural context.

What are the consequences of conflicts for children?

Life in war conditions involve people experiencing and witnessing direct war activities such as shooting, shelling, mines and other violence, separations, displacement, poor shelter, and the presence of abuse, torture and sexual violence. There has also been an increased attention to the indirect consequences of war, such as poverty, disease and malnutrition, poor healthcare and schooling, lack of infrastructure and normal everyday life as well as threats to culture and customs. Increased levels of violence and substance abuse are also part of the more indirect types of consequences that will affect children and their community. One recent study from Uganda (Blattman and Annan 2009) reported widespread and persistent effects of conflict on education and economy. Overall only a minority reported that they had psychological problems, and psychological problems were most frequent among those who had been exposed to the highest levels of violence, and more frequent among former combatants than others.

Traditionally, research on psychological effects of war was carried out on adult combatants, but in the last decades civilians have increasingly been participants in research efforts. Much attention has been devoted to women and children affected by conflict, including children associated with armed groups, whether carrying arms themselves, used as porters, messengers, for sexual purposes or forced into marriages. Thus, there is now a substantial body of literature on children and armed conflict and terrorism from all continents.

The consequences of conflict for children are diverse. Conflict may affect their health directly though injuries and indirectly through the spread of diseases and lack of adequate health care. Family separation, risk of labour and sexual exploitation are other serious consequences for many children, Children's and families' socio economic situation, opportunities for education, training and work may have serious long-term consequences. The impact of aggression and changes in roles and interpersonal relations in families and communities may change life and customs. There is a stereotype that hardships bring people together and promote support and unity. However, the experience of inability to support each other sufficiently, and even betrayal, is sometimes part of reality. Existential issues and challenges to moral development, including guilt, shame, stigma and isolation have been less studied but may have long term consequences not only for the individual, but for society.

Conflicts bring with them losses of people, homes, belongings, relationships and dreams, and the grief may be devastating. Experiencing multiple hardships and losses as is often the case in times of conflict, tend to predict more severe problems, also psychological problems. For example, in a study from northern Uganda, former child soldiers abducted by LRA (N = 301, mean age when abducted 12.9) were found to have experienced a mean of 6 traumatic events, including killing someone (39%). However, death of parent (especially mother) was a predictor of greater problems (Derluyn et al. 2004). Some studies (e.g. Dyregrov, Gjestad and Raundalen 2002; Hasanović, Sinanović, Selimbašić, Pajević and Avdibegović 2006)) report severe long-term psychological problems, mainly depression and post-traumatic stress symptoms, while others report less psychopathology (e.g. Angel et al. 2001). Prevalence from 20 % to 77 % has been reported in studies in a variety of countries (e.g. Dyregrov, Gupta, Gjestad and Mukanoheli 2000; Sack, Him and Dickson 1999; Qouta, Punamaki and El Sarraj 2003). In general, smaller and less well-controlled studies report higher prevalence of psychological problems. There are a number of reviews of the effects of war and refugees status on children (e.g. Barenbaum, Ruchkin and Schwab-Stone 2004; Lancet, 2002; Lustig et al. 2004).

Both studies from Western and non-Western contexts have shown that children who have experienced the consequences of conflict and disaster, particularly multiple hardships, interpersonal violence and loss and separation from their parents and family, are at heightened risk of experiencing depression, anxiety, impaired cognition, physical and social signs of distress and behavioural problems (Morris, van Ommeren, Belfer, Saxena and Saraceno 2007). The interaction between psychological, physical, social, and spiritual processes can be referred to as "psychosocial" (Wessells 2006).

Many positive changes and developments may also arise and follow war and disaster, including changes in the political, legal and education systems and on an individual level in term of post-traumatic growth. The realization of the immense resilience of individuals and communities may also bring about new strengths and is one of the important bases on which to build understanding and interventions.

Special attention has been on children and youth who are associated with armed groups (e.g. Honwana 2006). In spite of the growing body of literature, the effects of being associated with armed groups, whether as a combatant or in other capacities, are uncertain. The dominant view used to be that these children were traumatized and violent. Research in the last few years has shown a much more nuanced picture, finding that resilience is common (e.g. Shepler 2005; Wessells 2006) and that for many children and youths life with armed groups has been perceived also to have a protective and positive sides. However, in a recent study from Nepal, 141 former soldiers were compared with 141 never-recruited children (mean age= 15.8) (aged 6-16 at time of conscript). Former soldiers had greater mental health problems, and the difference remains for PTSD and depression even after controlling for trauma exposure and covariates (Kohrt et al. 2008). This highlights the need for vulnerability and resilience perspectives to co-exist. People's resilience must never be a reason to neglect human suffering or ignore violations of human rights.

Why justify interventions?

In spite of the solid evidence of children's resilience and ability to cope in adverse circumstances, there is overwhelming evidence that many children suffer because of war and there is a need to provide help. There is ample evidence that many children who are affected by conflict have serious and long-term problems related to their health and wellbeing. The United Nations Convention on the Rights of the Child (1989) states that children have the right to rehabilitation. When we argue that interventions need to be justified it is not because we doubt the seriousness of suffering or children's right to provision and rehabilitation. Rather, the reasons why are in view of the seriousness of the suffering. Firstly, because of the nature of psychosocial problems, psychosocial support often need to be justified or explained—e.g. compared to a child who has suffered psychosocial trauma, it is easier to see that a child who has been physically injured needs help and rehabilitation. Both experience and research have shown that the invisible scars and long-lasting effects of conflict are grave, and this knowledge can be used to justify psychosocial intervention. Secondly, psychosocial intervention needs to be justified because of doubts about what types of interventions work—and which cause harm—for whom under what conditions. Thirdly, what types of interventions are available in various contexts is a matter of concern. All of these reasons are real and serious.

Both findings from different disciples and experience from the field provide examples that mental health and psychosocial problems can be serious not only to the individuals and families affected, but also to communities and peace processes. However, there is a need for better documentation and understanding of these types of effects.

Consequences of conflict and emergencies may be due to already existing problems, problems caused by the disaster, and problems caused by humanitarian assistance (see Guidelines on Mental Health and Psychosocial Support in Emergency Settings, IASC 2008).

In order to justify interventions, evidence showing that interventions provide adequate support to address the pre-existing problems and those caused by the conflict, and to avoid causing harm, is needed. In order to provide such evidence, solid research is required, i.e. empirical studies using reliable and valid methodologies, while at the same time being culturally valid and ethically sound. These types of studies are often resource intensive. The question of whether it is justifiable to spend these types of resources on research when action is urgently needed, or whether it is indeed possible to carry out this type of research in a conflict context often arise.

There is no doubt that carrying out high quality research in a context characterized by power differences, poverty, fragility of state, and conflicts is extremely difficult and pose a number of ethical challenges (Dybdahl 2001; Tol and Jordans 2008). However, as good quality research is being produced in very challenging and varied contexts in Sudan, Afghanistan, Uganda, Rwanda, Palestine, Somalia and many other areas—often as partnerships between local, national and international researchers and participants, our confidence that such research is possible should be growing. One good example of such research is a controlled study comparing creative play interventions that was not intended to be therapeutic to interpersonal therapies for adolescents in Northern Uganda (Bolton, Bass, Betancourt et al. 2007). Other examples are recent studies on mental health in Afghanistan (e.g. Dawes and Flisher 2009; Miller, Omidian, Quraishy et al. 2009), a controlled study in Indonesia (Tol, Komproe, Susanty et al. 2008) and Mocellin's (2006) study from Somalia on the reintegration of former combatants.

While the resources and risks that are needed continue to be a challenge, failing to provide solid evidence of the harm and good caused by interventions, pose even larger challenges of continuing implementing interventions of which we do not know the effects, with the potential of wasting valuable resources that could have been spent better. Even more seriously, psychological and psychosocial interventions can have powerful effects, and also hold the potential to cause serious harm to individuals and communities.

What type of interventions?

For some purposes it may be useful to distinguish between psychosocial and psychiatric paradigms (Betancourt and Williams 2008). A psychosocial approach includes everyone who is affected by conflict and concerns the need to recreate physical and social environment, normality, predictability, justice, economic opportunity and cultural and spiritual support.

A psychiatric approach on the other hand focuses on the prevalence of mental health problems and promotion of mental health, and on those in need of help, including those who already had mental health problems before exposure to current stressors. There may be a danger of ignoring the contribution of stressful social and material life conditions. Cultural validity is a particular challenge within this approach as psychiatric diagnoses and treatment tend to be Western, although it should be noted that there are branches of psychiatry and approaches that take culture seriously. Different understandings of psychopathology need to be understood, but should not be an excuse for not responding to people who are seriously disturbed. Psychiatric patients are a particularly vulnerable group, not least in times of scarce resources and break down of infrastructure and social support.

Preventing psychiatric problems and promoting mental health may be challenging, but is cost-effective and prevents much suffering, also to families and communities. Mental health is an integral part of health. Integrating these two perspectives is important (Betancourt and Williams 2008), and in line with the main guidelines for mental health and psychosocial support in emergencies, such as the Guidelines of the Inter-Agency Standing Committee (IASC 2008) on mental health and psychosocial support in emergency settings. These guidelines describe the need for multiple layers of support, starting with the first layer of basic services and security necessary to ensure the well-being of all people, then the emergency response for a smaller number of people who will ber able to maintain their well-being if they receive help in accessing community and family supports, then the third layer representing focused, non-specialised supports for a still smaller number of people, and finally, at the top of the pyramid additional support required for the small percentage of the population, including psychological and psychiatric services. Miller and Rasmussen (2009) seek to bridge the divisive split between the psychiatric or trauma-focused approach and a psychosocial approach to addressing mental health needs in conflict settings by focusing on the role that daily stressors play in mediating direct war exposure and mental health outcomes.

Many organizations and agencies have developed guidelines and manuals for mental health and psychosocial interventions (e.g. WHO 2003). The Inter-Agency standing committee (IASC) was established in 1992 in response to a General Assembly resolution calling for strengthened co-ordination of humanitarian assistance and is formed by the heads of many UN and non UN humanitarian organizations.

In summary, basic principles for psychosocial support in disasters are Human rights and justice, participation, the principle of *do no harm*, integrated services, and the need to build on existing resources and capacity. A holistic approach with integrated services is generally stressed as important and involves health and nutrition, education, prevention and treatment of disabilities, repatriation, personal liberty and security, legal status, preserving and restoring family unity and psychosocial support/intervention. These are now well-accepted principles, but in practice adhering to them can pose a number of challenges.

The general Principles for engagement in fragile states (www.oecd.org/dac/) are also useful in this regard. The first principle emphasizes the need to take context as a starting point and avoid the idea of blueprints or *one fits all*, which is not least relevant regarding psychosocial support. Each conflict is different, and each child and family is different. "Even in the face of one disaster, children in the same family will respond differently and have different needs." (Jones 2008, 292). However, awareness of the crucial role of context does not mean that systematic approaches are not necessary. Flexible and context dependent (or adjustable) guidelines or manuals may be a useful way of applying accumulated knowledge and allowing for systematic evaluations and transparency (e.g. Bolton, 2003, Bolton, Bass, Betancourt et al. 2007, Dybdahl 2001; International Child Development Programmes 1997; Tol et al. 2008; War Child Foundation, see http://www.childrenandwar.org).

As part of these guidelines and manuals, a plethora of recommendations about what children in and following conflict need, and how to enhance their mental health exist (e.g. Ager 2002; Mollica et al. 2004; WHO 2003). Generally, knowledge about context is emphasized, as are relevant risk and protective factors, and the importance of a holistic approach (see also Ehntholt and Yule 2006) and it is "almost always a combination of psychological and non-psychological interventions that address issues of care, shelter, family connection, justice and reconciliation that may in the long run be the most helpful to the child" (Jones 2008, 292).

Moreover, there is an emphasis on respect for traditions and culture as important to secure acceptability and accessibility, and to increase the chances of success. Symbolic acts such as dances, songs, cleansing, and rites of passage and other rituals, special meals and traditional customs are assumed to contribute to protection, resilience and healing. It is recommended that normal cultural and religious events are maintained, including grieving and funeral practices and ceremonies. Meaningful activities, structure, continuity, predictability, normality, formal and informal schooling, play, being with peers, and in some circumstances also psycho educational activities are recommended. Social context, not least the significance of keeping the family and community together, is emphasized, also by UNICEF and the Child Convention.

Recommendations often focus on activities that aim to strengthen social support, especially for isolated persons such as separated children, child combatants and the elderly. Individuals with pre-existing psychiatric disorders should continue to receive relevant treatment, and plans should be made for a more comprehensive community based psychological interventions following protracted disasters. Recommendations to promote mental health in emergency settings also involve the availability of information and the importance of the community's ownership and involvement.

These and other recommendation are summarized and described in what are now well-established guidelines for interventions, such as Inter-Agency Standing Committee (IASC) *Guidelines for Mental Health and Psychosocial Support in Emergency Settings*, the Sphere Project, *Humanitarian Charter and Minimum Standards in Disaster* (2004), and the Inter-Agency Network for Eucation in Emergencies (INEE) *Minimum Standards* (2008).

The intervention pyramid from *IASC Guidelines on Mental Health and Psychosocial Support in Emergency Settings* (2007) underline the need for a holistic approach from basic services to specialized services. The model proposed by Miller and Rasmussen (2009) not only integrates the trauma and psychosocial approach, but also is in line with these priorities. Similarly, Ager (1997) pointed out the following hierarchy of interventions:

- Ensure that assistance causes minimal disruption of intact protective influences
- Reinstitute protective influences
- Compensatory support
- Targeted therapeutical intervention
- Multiple levels of needs

Most guidelines include an emphasis on need and resource assessment. Conducting needs and resource assessment can be difficult, but all the more necessary in order to achieve a coordinated process that avoids multiple assessments and that engages the community and promotes activity and ownership. The summary by Jones (2008) emphasizes coordination, combined quality and quantitative methods and involvement. It is in line with Inter-Agency Standing Committee (IASC) *Guidelines for Mental Health and Psychosocial Support in Emergency Settings* and provides a practical and sound example of steps in emergency needs assessment.

However, many psychosocial intervention programmes around the world do not follow the guidelines outlined here, and are neither built on solid evidence nor followed up by sound evaluation that allow for the possibility of detecting possible harm caused to children or their families. Many types of "trauma counseling" and expressive short- or long-term therapies where children talk, draw or in other ways express their experiences and feelings are carried out. Many activities encourage children to act out or talk about their experiences example using drama techniques, and when the sense of safety that is seen as crucial when recovery from trauma is not given sufficient weight, effects may resemble prematurely verbal retelling of a trauma and be harmful (see Paardekooper 2002; Morris et al. 2007). Too often interventions are carried out by people with little training and expertise, or with limited understanding of the context, without long-term supervision, lacking sustainability when experts leave and are part of programmes that fail to integrate the needs of the participants and be integrated into existing education and health care systems (see Jones 2008). This is a serious concern, and the awareness of minimum standards and quality need to be raised. When therapeutic approaches that have been effective in Western settings (or other settings) are introduced in new contexts, they should be evaluated using sound methodology and high quality research design.

In order to support children, it is likely that also parents, family and community should be supported as they potentially are their children's best sources of continuity, support and healing. In many countries the extended family and the local community play a major role in all aspects of life, and the public welfare system is limited. Programmes that focus on children without taking into consideration the concerns and needs of families and communities are unlikely to be sustainable, and there is a risk in causing harm by creating a divide between the child and its family.

Do interventions work?

The number of systematic evaluations of the effect of psychosocial interventions for children in conflict and post-conflict situations is still low, but growing (see Bolton et al. 2007; Dybdahl 2001; Gupta and Zimmer, 2008; Layne, Salzman and Poppelton, 2008; Mohlen, Parzer, Resch and Brunner, 2005; Mollica, Cui, Mcinnes and Massagli; 2002; Morris et al. 2007; Paardekoper 2002; Thabet, Vostanis and Karim 2005; Tol et al.; Woodside et al. 1999).

The evidence or indications of whether various interventions have effect, i.e. do harm or good, are of various quality and levels. There is a large body of literature describing intervention efforts and their effects, but most of these are reports from practice and anecdotal rather than systematic, and the reliability and validity often difficult to establish. More systematic studies exist, but again the quality of many is questionable because the instruments and methods used often lack in content and cultural validity. In a recent child centered review Morris and colleagues summarized four levels of evidence: expert opinion, anecdotal, quasi-experimental and randomised controlled trials. This review of the evidence for each of the interventions described as indicators for the Sphere standard on mental and social aspects of health suggests some, but limited, support for each of them (Morris et al. 2007). Most recommendations for mental health and psycho-social interventions in guidance documents are based on expert opinion rather than research. Consequently, interventions are being implemented without sufficient understanding of their potential benefit or harm.

Betancourt and Williams (2008) published a review of eight evaluation studies showing that interventions are found to have many positive effects. Most evaluations of psychosocial interventions show some positive effects, e.g. an interesting study in Eritrea (Farwell 2001) indicated that a relatively structured educational programme had positive effects and Akombo (2009) discusses how musicians in Africa consider music therapeutic. Unfortunately, most evaluations and reports of practice (even if called "best practice") are based on very limited data and are often carried out by people with invested interests (for example evaluating their own work), and very often more or less entirely based on self report.

An impressive study from Gaza found that expressing emotions and learning about stress symptoms had no effect (Thabet et al. 2005), and this type of research should be commended, as the result is important. Paardekooper (2002) compared a control group and two different programmes (psychodynamic versus a contextual programme focusing on everyday life) for Sudanese refugee children in Ethiopia. The context programme gave most improvement, whereas children in the psychodynamic programme got worse in certain areas, also worse than the control, group.

There are numerous accounts of rituals, spiritual cleansing and various culturally embedded activities that are carried out in order to provide healing and social acceptance (Agger 2001; Honwana 2006; Kostelny 2006). For example, in an article in Le Monde, Emery Brusset is cited to emphasise traditional Acholi ceremonies of purification as ways of helping villagers to accept the return of former child soldiers in the Gulu district of Uganda (Le Monde 4 October 2009). There are moving and powerful accounts of their effects, but these are largely anecdotal, extremely small-scale and based on self-report, and rarely systematically studied. The potential harm of such rituals and acts are seldom studied or reported, although anecdotes and witnesses of such negative effects exist. However, in an article addressing the many criticisms of western trauma therapy and questioning of the usefulness of Western approaches in other contexts, Dyregrov, Gupta, Gjestad and Raundalen (2002) discuss limitations and harmful practices of local and traditional practices, and argue that both western approaches and local healing practices may be needed and can supplement each other.

Jones (2009) notes that one of the reasons for the neglect of people with severe mental disorders in humanitarian settings is the prominence of at traditional healing systems, where the problem is perceived as being caused by evil spirits, witchcraft, or ghosts. She also points to the importance of building a respectful relationship between traditional and modern healers and the use of cross referrals, joint clinics and including traditional healers in treatment plans with the family which gives opportunities to identify and make suggestions for correcting inappropriate practices, and discussing the use and misuse of physical restraint.

In his Le Monde article by Michel Arsenault on demobilizing child soldiers, Radhika Coosmarawamy emphasises bringing the child back to his or her family and village and help them accept the child. She claims that it indeed the family who is in need of psychosocial support, because it is the family that must heal the child (Le Monde, 4 October 2009). In a randomised controlled study in a different context, psychosocial support was provided to mothers in an intervention programme implemented in Bosnia aimed at supporting mothers by combining trauma approaches and mother-child interaction programme (Dybdahl 2001). The children, whose mothers took part in the twice weekly intervention, were found to improve more than a control group on a number of physical and psychological indicators, including a significant weight gain. One possible working mechanism for this effect could be that the mothers' mental health, social networks and/or self confidence improved through taking part in the groups. A recent study carried out in kindergartens in Gaza (Massad, Nieto, Pari, Smith, Clark and Thabet 2009) also highlighted the importance of maternal health and education in affecting children's mental health.

In sum, the body of evidence of effects of various types of interventions in different contexts is growing, but we still have an urgent need for better understanding and better evidence in order to avoid doing harm and use resources more effectively. Not least is this the case regarding reintegration and rehabilitation of children or youth who have been associated with armed groups, in spite of the large body of literature on this group. In an interview by Michel Arsenault (le Monde 4 October 2009, UN supplement) posing the question how to demobilize child soldiers, Emery Brusset states "We are still trying to learn what to do—we are still not even able to define the success of an intervention."

Ethical challenges

One very real topic which need to be addressed when the question of whether psychosocial interventions are justifiable, is the topic of ethics. When resources are scarce and needs urgent, Is it ethically justifiable to prioritise psychosocial interventions and research? On condition that these are of good quality and cost-effective, it has been argued elsewhere (Dybdahl 2002, 29-32) that there are good reasons to do so. Firstly, there is an ethical obligation to evaluate interventions so that resources are used to maximum benefit and harm is detected and avoided. Secondly, activities should be described and shared in order to be the subject of scrutiny and learning of others. Thirdly, psychosocial health is important in itself, and in addition it has been found to impact on many other issues such as child rearing, nutrition and economy, and is also likely to have implications for peace and reconciliation.

However, in line with the guidelines proposed by Leaning (2001), in very difficult circumstances only studies that are vital to the health and welfare of the participants should be undertaken and the study design should impose a minimum of risk. We agree with Leaning's (2001) guidelines for research in refugee and internally displaced populations studies should be restrict to those that would provide important direct benefit to the individuals recruited to the study or to the population from which the individuals come. Moreover, the well-being, dignity, and autonomy of all participants should be promoted in all phases of the research.

Basic principles of research ethics apply in complex situations, and include such issues as research must benefit the affected populations, should not cause harm, and should be of high quality, but also other general ethical principles for therapy and research e.g. competence, respect for other's rights and dignity, fairness, informed consent and institutional approval, confidentiality and providing participants with information (Dybdahl 2002). Permissions to carry out research and store data should be obtained, following the laws and norms that go with being a researcher, for example through the health authorites or the national office for research permissions. In cases where one decides to avoid obtaining permissions for research, the reasons should be made explicit and advice sought from other competent bodies. The highest standards for obtaining informed consent should be used, and in some settings also the informed consent of the head of household, clan or village should be sought (Leaning, 2001).

Research with vulnerable populations always poses ethical challenges, and in conditions characterized by conflict and scarceness of resources, these become extremely important. Children are agents and their right to participation is no less in situations of conflict and disaster. When research is carried out in a setting that is culturally different from that of the researcher or funder, and where there is marked differences in power the issue becomes even more challenging (Dybdahl, 2002; Hart and Tyrer 2006).

In vulnerable situations, it is easy to skimp on quality as well as and ethics. These are related as "bad science makes for bad ethics" (Rosenthal 1999, p. 408). Study participants should be selected on the basis of scientific principles without bias introduced by issues of accessibility, cost, or malleability (Leaning 2001). The complex setting may also involve putting colleagues and participants at risk and both imperative of quality and ethics demand that researchers know the context and setting well so as to take all possible measures to avoid this. Procedures to assess for minimise, and monitor the risks and for their future security should be instituted (Leaning 2001).

Research in and following conflict is also likely to mean that one will face massive breaches of human rights, and ways to cope with this issue need to be considered. This includes how to deal with what should be called human rights abuse simply gets labeled psychiatry. In addition, when researching such inhumane acts as torture, there is a need to be aware that any findings from the research can, and will be used by its practitioners, and scientists must therefore approach torture with caution (see Miles 2009).

Although there are many ethical challenges, there is likely to be some ways to address these. These ways may involve exactly using a human rights' perspective as a tool and guideline, as well as collaborating with colleagues and others around the world who know the context well or have made valuable experiences in other settings, as well as the people the intervention and research aim to support.

Conclusion and future research

A large body of literature on children affected by armed conflict now exists. In this chapter it has been argued that psychosocial intervention can be valuable, important and justified, and that research of high quality is necessary. Much of what is labeled psychosocial support and mental health interventions is not built on best available knowledge, and is not subject to sound evaluations and research. Even interventions and recommendations that are in line with guidelines and supported by evidence, is to a large degree based on anecdotal evidence and experts' opinion. This means that the work to strengthen our knowledge, understanding and critical research should continue, but that our standards should become increasingly higher, not least regarding cultural validity, research quality and ethics.

The topics of research must be chosen with care. There is no need for more research to show that war is bad for children (Cairns and Dawes 2001). Research on the effects of war on children is already reviewed critically and questions of what new knowledge the research brought, whether no harm was inflicted on the participants of their community, or how the research benefitted the participants are frequently asked, e.g. in a letter by McKay and Wessells (2004) responding to the study by Derluyn and colleagues (2004). Like-wise, research must be of benefit to the participants, and it is high time to ask their opinions and involve children and communities in research questions and dissemination of results. Methods used must be chosen carefully, so that the design and instruments correspond to the questions asked. Longitudinal and controlled studies are still needed. There is a role for interdisciplinary studies, not least integrating physical and mental health with cultural, religious and existential issues.

We still need better understanding of the needs of young children and adolescents in fragile situations and emergencies, also implementation research and studies of effects of interventions. Holistic approaches that integrate the various aspects of health, including grief, and economic and existential topics are still scarce. It is important that the progress on producing systematic and innovative research which takes culture, family and community context seriously continues (see Elbedour, Bensel and Bastien 1993; McKay and Wessells 2006).

A developmental perspective is of particular use as it informative of the changing risks, needs and potentials of children in their contexts. The youngest children are often neglected by the researchers, aid agencies and governments. In fact, early human development is an area where the world is furthest from reaching the United Nations' millennium development goals. The youngest children are at particularly high risk of death and illness in times of war and disaster, and 200 million children under the age of 5 in developing countries do not reach their developmental potential (Engle, Black, Behrman et al. 2007). Perhaps the greatest threat to a young child's well-being is that the familiar caregiver(s) may be unable to meet the child's needs for care and support, which highlights the need to consider not only the child but its family and community (Massad et al. 2009).

In this chapter we have given a number of examples of studies that show that it is possible to carry out research even in very complex settings, but that the practical and ethical challenges are serious, and the need for collaborations and support amongst colleagues and across geographical and disciplinary boarders is needed.

References

Ager, Alistair. 1997. Balancing skills' transmission and understandings: A conceptual framework for planning support for trauma recovery. In Dean Ajdukovic (Ed.), *Trauma recovery training: Lessons learned,* 73-82. Zagreb: Society for Psychological Assistance.

Ager, Alistair. 2002. Psychosocial needs in complex emergencies. *Lancet* 360:43-44.

Akombo, David Otieno. 2009. Music and healing during post-election violence in Kenya. *Voices: A World Forum for Music Therapy.* http://www.voices.no/mainissues/mi 40009000267.php (accessed 26 January, 2010).

Barenbaum, Joshua, Vladislav Ruchin and Mary Schwab-Stone. 2004. The psychosocial aspects of children exposed to war: practice and policy initiatives. *Journal of Child Psychology and Psychiatry* 45:41-62.

Betancourt, Theresa and Timothy Williams. 2008. Building an evidence base on mental health interventions for children affected by armed conflict. *Intervention* 6:39-56.

Blattman, Chris and Jeannie Annan. 2009. The consequence of child soldiering. *Review of Economics and Statistics* (March).

Bolton, Paul. 2003. Assessing depression among survivors of the Rwanda genocide. In: *The Psychological Effects of War on Civilians: An International Perspective,* ed. Teresa M. McIntyre and Stanley Krippner, Greenwood Publishing Group, Westport, CT.

Bolton, Paul, Judith Bass, Theresa Betancourt, Liesbeth Speelman, Grace Onyango, Kathleen F. Cloughterty, Richard Neugebauer, Laura Murray and Helen Verdeli. 2007. Interventions for depression symptoms among adolescent survivors of war and displacement in northern Uganda: A randomized controlled trial. *Journal of the American medical Association* 298 (5):519-527.

Bonanno, George A. 2004. Loss, trauma and human resilience: Have we underestimated the human capacity to thrive after extremely aversive event? *American psychologist* 59 (1):20-28.

Bonanno, George A. and Anthony D. Mancini. 2008. The human capacity to thrive in the face of extreme adversity. *Pediatrics* 121:369-375.

Boothby, Neil, Jennifer Crawford, and Jason Halpern. 2006. Mozambique child soldier life outcome study: Lessons learned in rehabilitation and reintegration efforts. *Global Public Health* 1(1):87-107.

Bracken, Patrick, Joan Giller and Derek Summerfield. 1995. Psychological responses to war and atrocity: The limitations of current concepts. *Social Science and Medicine* 40:1073-1082.

Cairns, Ed and Anthony Dawes. 2001. Children: Ethnic and political violence – a commentary. *Child Development* 67(1):129-139.

Dawes, Andy and Alan Flisher. 2009. Children's mental health in Afghanistan. *Lancet. Sep 5, 374 (9692):766-7.*

Derluyn, Ilse, Eric Broekart, Gilberte Schuyten and Els De Temmerman. 2004. Post-traumatic stress in former Ugandan child soldiers. *Lancet* 363:861-863.

Dybdahl, Ragnhild. 2001. Children and mothers in war: an outcome study of a psychosocial intervention program. *Child Development* 72:1214-1230.

Dybdahl, Ragnhild. 2002. Bosnian women and children in war: Experiences, psychological consequences and psychosocial intervention. Dissertation for the Doctor Psychologiae degree. Department of Psychology, Faculty of Social Science, University of Tromsø.

Dyregrov, Atle, Leila Gupta, Rolf Gjestad and Magne Raundalen. 2002. Is the culture always right? *Traumatology* 8 (3):135-145.

Dyregrov, Atle, Leila Gupta, Rolf Gjestad and Eugenie Mukanoheli. 2000. Trauma exposure and psychological reactions to genocide among Rwandan children. *Journal of Traumatic Stress* 13 (1):3-21.

Dyregrov, Atle, Rolf Gjestad and Magne Raundalen. 2002. Children exposed to warfare: A longitudinal study. *Journal of Traumatic Stress* 15 (1):59-68.

Engle, Patrice, Maureen Black, Jere Behrman, Meena Cabral de Mello, Paul Gertler, Lydia Kapiriri, Reynaldo Martorell, Mary Eming Young, and the International Child Development Steering Group. 2007. Strategies to avoid the loss of developmental potential in more than 200 million children in the developing world. *Lancet,* 369: 229-42.

Ehntholt, Kimberly and William Yule. 2006. Practitioners review: Assessment and treatment of refugee children and adolescents who have experienced war-related trauma. *Journal of Child Psychology and Psychiatry* 47 (12):1197-1210.

Elbedour, Salman, Robert ten Bensel and David Bastien. 1993. Ecological integrated model of children of war: Individual and social psychology. *Child Abuse and Neglect* 17:805-19.

Farwell, Nancy. 2001. "Onward through strength": Coping and psychological support among refugee youth returning to Eritrea from Sudan. *Journal of Refugee Studies* 14 (1):43-69.

Gupta, Leila,and Catherine Zimmer. 2008. Psychosocial intervention for war-affected children in Sierra Leone. *The British Journal of Psychiatry* 192 (3):212-216.

Hart, Jason and Bex Tyrer. 2006. *Research with Children Living in Conflict Situations: Concept, Ethics and Method,* Working Paper no. 30, University of Oxford: Refugee Studies Centre.

Hasanović, Mevludin, Osman Sinanović, Zichnet Selimbašić, Izet Pajević and Esmina Avdibegović. 2006. Psychological disturbances of the war-traumatized children from different foster and family setting in Bosnia and Herzegovina. *Croatian Medical Journal* 47 (1):85- 94.

Honwana, Alcinda. 2006. *Child soldiers in Africa.* University of Philadelphia, PA: Pennsylvania Press.

IASC. 2007. Guidelines on mental health and psychosocial support in emergency settings.

IASC. 2008. http://www.humanitarianinfo.org/iasc/ (accessed 12 November 2008).

International Child Development Programmes Oslo & Program on Mental Health. (1997). *Improving Mother/child Interaction To Promote Better Psychosocial Development in Children* Geneva: WHO

Jones, Lynne. (2008). Responding to the needs of children in crisis. *International review of psychiatry* 20:291-303.

Jones, Lynne, Joseph B Asare, Mustafa El Masri, Andrew Mohanraj, Hassen Sherief and Mark van Ommeren. 2009. *Severe mental disorders in complex emergencies* 374 (9690):654-661.

Kanagaratnam, Pushpa, Magne Raundalen, and Arve Asbjørnsen. 2005. Ideological commitment and posttraumatic stress in former Tamil child soldiers. *Scandinavian Journal of Psychology* 46:511-520.

Kohnt, Brandon A., Mark J.D. Jordans, Wietse. A. Tol,, Rebecca A. Speckman, Sujen M. Maharjan, Carol M. Worthman, and Ivan H. Komproe. 2008. Comparison of mental health between former child soldiers and children never conscripted by armed groups in Nepal. *Journal of the American medical Association* 300 (6):691-702.

Kostelny, Kathleen. 2006. A culture-based integrative approach. In Boothby, Neil, Alison Strang and Michael Wessels (eds.). *A World Turned Upside Down: Social Ecological Approaches to Children in War Zones,*19-38. Bloomfield, CT: Kumarian Press.

Lancet. 2002. Psychosocial needs in complex emergencies. Vol. 360, Suppl. 1, Dec, s43-s44.

Layne, Christopher M., William R. Saltzman and Landon Poppleto et al. 2008. Effectiveness of a school-based group psychotherapy program for war-exposed adolescents: A randomized controlled trial. *Journal of the American Academy of Child and Adolescent Psychiatry* 47 (9):1048-1062.

Leaning, Jennifer (2001). Ethics of research in refugee populations. *Lancet* 357:1432-1433.

Lustig, Stuart L., Maryam Kia-Keating, Wanda Grant-Knight, Paul Geltman, Heidi Ellis, Dina Birman, J. David Kinzie, Terence Keane and Glenn N. Saxe. 2004. Review of child and adolescent refugee mental health. *Journal of the American Academy of Child and Adolescent Psychiatry* 43:24-36.

Massad, Salwa., Nieto, F. Javier, Mari Palta, Maureen Smith, Roseanne Clark, and Abdel-Aziz Thabet. 2009. Mental health of children in Palestinian kindergartens: Resilience and vulnerability. *Child and Adolescent Mental Health* 14:89-96.

Masten, A. S. (2001). Ordinary magic: Resilience processes in development. *American Psychologist* 56:227-238.

Masten, A. S. (2009). Ordinary Magic: Lessons from research on resilience in human development. *Education Canada* 49 (3): 28-32.

McKay, Susan. & Wessells, Michael. 2004. Post-traumatic stress in former Ugandan soldiers. *Lancet* 363:1646.

Miles, Steven H. 2009. Profane research versus researching the profane: Commentary on Basoglu (2009). *American Journal of Orthopsychiatry* 79 (2):146-14.

Miller, Kenneth E, Patricia Omidian, Abdul Samad Quraishy, Naseema Quraishy, Mohammed Nader Nasiry, Seema Nasiry, Nazar Mohammed Karyar, and Abdul Aziz Yaqubi. 2006. The Afghan Symptom Checklist:

A culturally grounded approach to mental health assessment in a conflict zone. *American Journal of Orthopsychiatry* 76 (4):423-433.

Miller, Kenneth and Andrew Rasmussen. 2010. War exposure, daily stressors, and mental health in conflict and post-conflict settings: Bridging the divide between trauma-focused and psychosocial frameworks. *Social Science and Medicine.* 70 (1):7-16.

Mocellin, Jane (2006). Reintegrating demobilized militia and former combatants: Lessons learnt in Somalia. In M. Fitzduff and C. Stout, (eds.), *Psychology of resolving global conflicts: From war to peace, Vol. 3,* 216-241. Westport, CT: Preager.

Mohlen, Heike. Peter Parzer, Franz Resch and Romuald Brunner, 2005. Psychosocial support for war-traumatized child and adolescent refugees: Evaluation of a short-term treatment program. *Australian and New Zealand Journal of Psychiatry* 39:81-87.

Mollica, R.F., X. Cui, K. McInnes and M.P. Massagli. 2002. Science-based policy for psychosocial interventions in refugee camps: A Cambodian example. *Journal of Nervous and Mental Disease* 190 (3):158-166.

Mollica, RF., B. Lopes Cardozo , H.J. Osofsky, B. Raphael, A. Ager and P. Salama. 2004. Mental health in complex emergencies. *Lancet* 364 (9450):2058-2067.

Morris, Jodi, Mark van Ommeren, Myron Belfer, Shekhar Saxena and Benedetto Saraceno. 2007. Children and the Sphere standard on mental and social aspects of health. *Disasters* 31:71-90.

Paardekooper, Brechtje. 2002. Children of the forgotten war: A comparison of two intervention programmes for the promotion of well-being of Sudanese refugee children. Amsterdam: Vrije Universiteit, Academic Proefscrift.

Sack William H., Gregory N. Clarke, Chanrithy Him et al. 1993. A six-year follow-up study of Cambodian refugee adolescents traumatized as children. *Journal of the American Academy of Child and Adolescent Psychiatry* 32 (2):431-437.

Qouta, Samir, Raija-Leena Punamäki and Eyad El Sarraj. 2003. Prevalence and determinants of PTSD among Palestinian children exposed to military violence. *European Child & Adolescent Psychiatry* 12:1018-8827.

Rosenthal, Robert. 1999. Science and ethics in conducting, analyzing, and reporting psychological research. *Psychological Science* 5 (3):127-134.

Shepler, S. A. 2005. *Conflicted childhoods: Fighting over child soldiers in Sierra Leone*. Berkeley, UC Berkeley.

Sphere Project. 2000. Humanitarian charter and minimum standards in disaster response. Oxford: Oxfam Publishing.

Sphere Project. 2008. http://www.sphereproject.org (accessed 12 November 2009).

Summerfield, Derek. 2000. War and mental health: A brief overview. *British Medical Journal* 22 July, 321:232-235.

Tol, Wietse A. and Mark J. D. Jordans. 2008. Evidence based psychosocial practice in political violence affected settings. *Intervention* 6 (1):66-69.

Tol, Wietse A, Ivan H. Komproe, Dessy Susanty, Mark J. D. Jordans, Robert D. Macy, Joop T. V. M. De Jong. 2008. School-based mental health intervention for children affected by political violence in Indonesia: A cluster randomized trial. *The Journal of the American Medical Association* 300 (6): 655-662.

Tol, Wietse A., Brandon A. Kohrt, Mark J. D. Jordans, Suraj B. Thapa, Judith Pettigrew, Nawaraj Upadhaya and Joop T.V.M. de Jong. 2010. Political violence and mental health: A multi-disciplinary review of the literature on Nepal. *Social Science & Medicine* 70 (1):35-44.

Thabet, Abdel-Aziz, Panos Vostanis and Khaled Karim, K. 2005. Group crisis intervention for children during ongoing war conflict. *European Adolescent Psychiatry* 14:262-269.

Van der Kolk, Bessel and Alexander McFarlane. 1996. The black hole of trauma. In: Bessel van der Kolk, Alexander McFarlane and Lars Weisæth (eds.), *Traumatic stress: The effects of overwhelming experience on mind, body and society*, 3-23. New York: Huildford Press.

Wessells, Michael. 2006. *Child soldiers: From violence to protection*. Cambridge, Harvard University Press.

WHO. 2003. *Mental health in emergencies: Mental and social aspects of health of populations exposed to extreme stressors*. Geneva: Department of Mental Health and Substance Dependence. WHO.

Woodside, Donald, Joanna Santa Barbara and David G Benner. 1999. Psychosocial trauma and social healing in Croatia. *Medicine, Conflict and Survival* 15:355-367.

18

Interviewing Formerly Abducted Children as Informants in Research

Some Methodological and Ethical Considerations

Thor Strandenæs
School of Mission and Theology, Stavanger, Norway

Abstract

This article raises some methodological and ethical considerations which researchers must pay attention to when interviewing formerly abducted children who have been associated with armed forces or armed groups, and who are in the subsequent process of disarmament, demobilization and reintegration (DDR) into civil society. The study argues that one must consider carefully where *in this process the formerly abducted children are, and apply appropriate ethical and methodological guidelines accordingly. It particularly highlights the need to be aware of and reflect the spatial and geographical location where the formerly abducted children are at, and their social, physical and psychological conditions at the time when interviews are conducted.*

Where are the formerly abducted children? Two relevant questions

I shall attempt to address two questions in this paper—two *'wheres'*. Both questions prompt some methodological and ethical considerations which researchers must keep in mind when interviewing formerly abducted children who have been associated with armed forces or armed groups, and who are in the subsequent process of disarmament, demobilization and reintegration (DDR) into civil society.[1] The Paris Principles (2007, 2.9) define child reintegration as the process through which children transition into civil society and enter meaningful roles and identities as civilians who are accepted by their families and communities in a context of local and national reconciliation. Sustainable reintegration is achieved when the political, legal, economic and social conditions needed for children to maintain life, livelihood and dignity have been secured. This process aims to ensure that children can access their rights, including formal and non-formal education, family unity, dignified livelihoods and safety from harm.

There are also other ethical and methodological issues concerned when doing research on such formerly abducted children which I am unable to deal with here. Some of these considerations have been dealt with elsewhere in this book, particularly by Milfrid Tonheim, Ragnhild Dybdahl, Kjetil Fretheim and Gerd Marie Ådna. The two questions I shall focus on both start off with 'where' and are prompted by the fact that, more often than not, authors do not reveal *where* in the process of DDR, chronologically and geographically or spatially, their informants were at the time when the interview took place.[2] Nor do they normally describe (fully) to their readers *where* in the process of social, physical and psychological rehabilitation the interviewees were during the interviews.

The first concern may be expressed by the question, '*Where, physically*, in the process of disarmament and demobilization, in rehabilitation camps and formal and material rehabilitation in society does the interview with the informant take place?' This question involves aspects relating to geography, location or space in the process.

The other question is, '*Where* are the ex-child soldiers in the *process* of social, physical and psychological rehabilitation and reintegration into society when they share their stories?' This question involves time related and material aspects of the process.

The point I wish to make here is that, in the process of reintegration of former child soldiers, their *whereabouts* (that is, their geographical location and stage in the DDR process) as well as *where* they are in the social, physical and mental rehabilitation process will influence the type and amount of information they share with the interviewer as well as what they, consciously or subconsciously, keep back. The interviewer must therefore keep this in mind when preparing for and conducting the interview (and follow-up interviews), since such awareness is both ethically and methodologically relevant. In the following I shall therefore elaborate on why the two 'wheres' are important. I will show how the whereabouts and the stage which the former child soldiers have arrived at in their social, somatic and psychological healing and rehabilitation process are likely to affect them. Three considerations are also important for dealing adequately with the two 'wheres', and I shall start by addressing these.

Three Considerations

Ways of documenting and relating the stories of ex-child soldiers

In her journalistic account of the so-called Aboke Girls—the children who were abducted from a boarding school in northern Uganda in December 1998—Els De Temmerman (2001) has tried to establish *facts* in the form of an historical account of the events. Since her objective was to establish documentary facts, proving that the abductions had taken place, in order to create abhorrence and political awareness about them, and stimulate action that might put an end to this and other abductions, she has interviewed the informers with a view to checking the accuracy of the girls' stories and the stories of the others:

> Everything in this book was checked with a second and often a third source. Ellen's story was verified with Grace's and Caroline's (...). Sarah's testimony was checked with Justine (...). The five girls were then confronted with each other in order to sort out any differences or contradictions (De Temmerman 2001, Preface 3).

De Temmerman interviewed children at the World Vision reception centre in Gulu as well as children "at different places in northern Uganda" (ibid.). Two questions are not reflected in her book, however. How does the place in which the former child soldier lives or stays during the interview affect them and the stories they tell—both the ones they include and (consciously or subconsciously) exclude? Second, how does the social, physical and emotional stage in which the ex-child soldier is at the time of the interview affect his or her information or reflections and his or her way of presenting them?

Having first given an example of fact-finding accounts I shall next deal with accounts of autobiography. Different from information obtained through interviews is the information given by ex-child soldiers on their own initiative, such as that given by Grace Akallo (McDonnell and Akallo 2007) or in autobiographies by children who are affected by war (e.g., Loung Ung 2000, China Keitetsi 2004, and Ishmael Beah 2007). These accounts are usually written by persons who have been more or less fully rehabilitated. Although they may not necessarily reflect consciously on their mental or emotional state during the different stages of the DDR, they are able to tell their story as a whole, and we get a comprehensive picture—not a fragmented or unfinished one. Most often also these persons are able to describe very clearly the mental and emotional reactions during the different episodes which they recall. Thus the story told by Grace Akallo in *Girl*

Soldier: A story of Hope for Northern Uganda's Children (in McDonnell & Akallo 2007) is told by a person who—as far as it is possible for the reader to discern—is both formally, functionally and emotionally reintegrated into society. Hence her story is the story of 'one who has managed to come back' in the full sense of the meaning.

A third type of account is the one where researchers use qualitative, semi-structured interviews to obtain information from informants. Here the focus is on what the individual has experienced, and what his or her feelings are (or have been) with regard to this experience. In such interviews the researcher does not (at least officially) cross check the information. It is, however, possible for him or her to record some common *tendencies* in the information given by several informants. Many of the interviews made with ex-child soldiers are based on or follow this type of approach (e.g., Brett and Specht 2004; Briggs 2005; Wessells 2006). The two 'wheres' which I address here obviously have bearings on all three types of accounts—fact finding, autobiographical, and qualitative, semi-structured interviews—since the informant will be influenced by both geographical or spatial and time aspects relating to his or her process of reintegration.

There is, of course, a difference between the first two types and the last type of accounts. In the latter type the acquired information must, for ethical and safety reasons, be kept anonymous. Since the information which the ex-child soldiers give is sensitive, and may in turn be used against them or their families in retribution, place names and the identity of the interviewee(s) must remain known only to the researcher. Hence the children must not be identified by their real names but by fictive ones. Also place names which are mentioned by the informants, as well as the exact location(s) where the interviews were given must remain a secret and are not to be published. Thus, both when preparing and conducting interviews, when interpreting the data, and when conveying the data and the interpretations thereof in publications, the researcher must abide by the principle of *identity or privacy protection*.[3] This, however, neither implies that the researcher looses the authentic voice of the informants, nor that the interpretations become invalid. It rather means that, in the entire process, the researcher must constantly ask himself or herself the following question, "Can my quotations and interpretation of data cause retributions and reprisals to the children because my informants can somehow be identified?" If the answer is 'yes', the researcher must handle the material in a different way.

Informants or hosts?

I have chosen to use the pair 'interviewer' and 'interviewee(s)' (or 'informant(s)') when referring to the researcher and the formerly abducted child(ren), respectively. It is also possible, as some scholars have opted for in recent years, to make use of another pair, namely 'host' and 'guest'.[4] The latter pair ('host' and 'guest') invites the researcher to be conscious of the role he or she plays in his or her meeting with the formerly abducted child; the interviewer is, after all, a guest in the other person's life. Although the interview may have come about upon the request of the researcher, he or she is nonetheless the guest of the ex-child soldier. Added complexity arises here because the interviewer typically enters villages or centers through the 'appropriate channels.' In villages, the local chief may give permission for the interviews, making him the actual host. This raises questions about informed consent—if the chief has welcomed this outsider into the village and given permission to talk with young people, how could a young person refuse? Hence the guest must conduct the interview in such a way that he or she shows respect for the host. While I prefer using the first pair ('interviewer' and 'interviewee(s)'/'informant(s)') this does not imply that I think the interviewer can neglect his or her status as guest of the other or of the village (chief) or centre (official). After all, the interview could not have been conducted without the hospitality shown by the formerly abducted child.[5] Also, whether one makes use of either of the two pairs ('interviewer' and 'interviewee'/'informant' or 'host' and 'guest) this does not alter the fact that the information which is gathered in interviews is negotiated, and that both parties—researcher and formerly abducted child—are involved in the construction of meaning. Moreover, a village chief or a centre official may by the way in which they approve for the interview to take place influence this negotiation of meaning.

The nature of the interviews

By addressing the two 'wheres' I am *not* implying that the interviewees are less authentic than informants in qualitative interviews at one of the places, times or stages of the DDR process than at others. What I wish to stress, is that the stage of the process which the informant is at, will influence his or her recollection and reflection, and either restrict or assist him or her with regard to sharing information. I am also not implying that such interviews are invalid because they have been or are conducted without paying attention to the two 'wheres'. The key point is that when interviews are conducted with conscious attention paid to the two 'wheres' the interviewer is more likely to pay due respect to the ethical and methodological considerations related to either and both of these.

Where are they? Awareness of spatial and geographical location

During disarmament and demobilization, soldiers—including abducted children—normally undergo some kind of debriefing or interrogation. During these stages rumours are spread and create uncertainty about what will next happen to the (former) soldiers. They do not know whether they ought to fear or to take comfort, and whether or not they are likely to receive any kind of punishment or retribution. In such situations former child soldiers are likely to think carefully about what kind of information they are willing to give, and the extent of it. If they suspect that their information will subsequently be used against them, they are likely to say as little as possible and use self-censorship. On the other hand, if they trust that their information will not lead to reprisals or punishment, they are more likely to be open and share information. And, if the (former) child soldier believes that he or she may be rewarded for generous sharing of information, he or she may even tell lies or construct a reality which is only in their own minds in order to obtain a reward.

As already mentioned I am not questioning the authenticity of the testimony of the (former) child soldier, be he or she fully or only partially rehabilitated. My intention is rather to create awareness on behalf of researchers that place, state of mind, as well as stage of emotional and social rehabilitation within which the former child soldier is, are likely to affect the information he or she gives.

A person who is interviewed while he or she is still in detention, in a situation of disarmament or demobilization (DD) *may (purposely) withhold essential information.* This is due to the fact that he or she is likely either to be suspicious about the nature and purpose of the interview, notwithstanding the positive affirmation from the researcher, that the information which is given

- will remain anonymous,
- is for research purposes only,
- will not be used to betray the informant, by for instance passing on information to those who abducted and/or enrolled him or her as child soldiers, or to the national or local courts.

Also their information *may be consciously edited and/or given with a hidden or obvious purpose*, such as that of achieving benefits or an early reintegration. After all, children are often interrogated or debriefed during the DD-process. During the DD-process in particular—but also afterwards—researchers can therefore easily be perceived as being associated with the national armed forces or the political regime in control, rather than with a scientific environment. Hence the interviewer must show critical awareness of how both the informants and their information are conditioned by the stage within which they are in the DDR process as well as by local circumstances.

This point is closely connected to the *different roles and identities* which child soldiers live with and have lived with. In her article, "Innocent and Guilty: Child-Soldiers as Interstitial & Tactical Agents", Alcinda Honwana (2005) shows how child soldiers can go in and out of different roles and identities. They can understand themselves in the roles of both victim and perpetrator (cf. Cock 1991; Utas 2005). And, as Honwana (2005, 48) concludes,

> Should we consider child combatants to be passive victims, empty vessels into which the capacity of violence has been poured? Or are they active agents, fully culpable and accountable for their actions? There is no easy answer, because the extenuating circumstances and internal emotional states of children vary from case to case. Nevertheless, their actions in the war are complex, and certainly transcend, in my view, the often simplistic and moral analysis that depicts them solely as victims. Certainly they are victims, but they also became more than just victims. The process in which they became involved transformed them into something else—an oxymoron—that, as I stated in the title of this article ["Innocent & Guilty"], brings together this ambiguous association of *innocence* and *guilt*. While they cannot be, on the one hand, considered fully responsible for their actions, they cannot, on the other hand, be completely deprived of agency.

In soldiery the children have developed and exercise what Honwana (2005, 49) refers to as "tactical agency." By this she means "a specific type of agency that is devised to cope with the concrete, immediate conditions of their lives in order to maximize the circumstances created by their military and violent environment. Their actions, however, come from a position of weakness. They have no power base (...) and act within the confines of a 'foreign territory.'"

Depending on their stage in the DDR process they may continue to exercise their 'tactical agency' also after the war and (subconsciously or consciously) choose the most opportune role during debriefing, interrogation and interviews—that is, the role which is likely to give them fewest problems. The researcher must therefore pay attention to which role(s) the interviewee adopts during the interview. It is particularly important to discern why a particular role is chosen in his or her discourse, and to observe how he or she makes use of it when negotiating meaning and relating experience. Only with such awareness may the researcher adequately contribute to construction of meaning.

In both the 'wheres' which I have identified here, consecutive interviews with the same former child soldiers are to be encouraged. The trust (or lack of such) which (supposedly) has been built up between informant and researcher in the first interview will normally have bearings on the next interview(s). When they meet on the second or third occasion the added familiarity between them may help to open up for a more in-depth exploration of the matters related. Also there is the added value that the personal reflection (on behalf of the ex-child soldier), which he or she has normally engaged in after the last interview, will often enable him or her to present new or supplementary information when host and guest meet next time.

A reflection on how the interviews are conducted is relevant here. I have elsewhere proposed some general guidelines for dialoguing with children, and where—amongst other topics—the need to be aware of the power which adults hold in such dialogue has been highlighted (Strandenæs 2004, 508-511). Many of these guidelines will also prove relevant to follow when interviewing or dialoguing with formerly abducted children but will not be reiterated here. Here I shall focus on the *mode* of interviewing such children. Many of them will find it difficult to respond to an interview which is conducted in a question-answer mode. Such interviews may easily remind them of interrogation or debriefing sessions. If, when interviewed, the child is still in a DD situation, he or she may find it easier to respond if they are asked to tell their story, to make drawings and subsequently interpret them, or even to act out their story by role play or songs. Some children may be more ready to respond if the interview is conducted in groups, while others in individual conversations. The place where the interviews are conducted must also be regarded as fairly comfortable and safe by the interviewee. Since many are still young and vulnerable, the researcher must also make sure that he or she is accompanied by a staff or a guardian who the ex-child soldier has trust in. When preparing for the interviews the researcher should therefore consult the relevant camp staff or a guardian, so as to provide for maximum safety and comfort on behalf of the interviewee(s).

Where are they in the process of reintegration? Social, physical and psychological aspects

Social, physical and mental aspects

McConnan and Uppard (2001, 91) have given the following definition of reintegration of former child soldiers: "Reintegration is a long-term process that aims to give children a viable alternative to their involvement in fighting forces and help them to resume life in the community." They go on to describe the process (ibid., 91f) that may involve:

- supporting children to make a break with military life and to prepare for life in civil society, with their family (or other carers) and in the community
- finding alternatives if returning to the family is impossible...
- providing education and training...
- devising a strategy for economic and livelihood support that is based on proper analysis of the local situation...

To this one may also add work on reconciliation, health and spiritual dimensions, as are also reflected in The Paris Principles (2007, especially in ch. 2. "Definitions", ch. 3. "Overarching Principles" and ch. 7 "Release and Reintegration").

What has not been included among the four points of McConnan and Uppard, but by others (e.g. Wessells 2006), are the physical, mental and emotional rehabilitation and healing which may be, and ought to be, an integral part of the reintegration process. Also in The Paris Principles (2007, ch. 7) these are reflected. As for Wessells (2006, 94-97), he first deals with health hazards during war that are experienced by girl soldiers in particular (e.g., sexual violence) and child soldiers in general.[6] Then, when dealing with the transition to civilian life (ibid., 181-207) he goes on to describe the process of healing and psychosocial support (ibid., 189-202) that must be part of the reintegration process. Also McConnan and Uppard (2001) deal with health care in connection with demobilization (ibid., 103, 117, 122f) and in the transitional period between demobilization and returning home (ibid., 145, 155). But the long term needs for continued health care, such as physical and psychological treatment, are not paid attention to by them as an aspect of the reintegration process.

Cohn and Goodwin-Gill (1993, 105-115) have identified a number of the psychosocial, physical and social consequences which children suffer as consequence of participating as soldiers in war. I include two of them here:

The traumatic experiences have psychosocial outcomes. They have executed and experienced violent acts, and have been exposed to chronic fear and anxiety. Many of them host a desire for revenge. Generally they harbour fear of retribution and related feelings of guilt.

The children have suffered all manners of physical injuries. Some of these can be healed. Other children have become handicapped and with visible scars that they will never get rid of.

Wessells (2006, 127f) also makes two observations about the mental implications which participating in war have had on these children: First, that war does not affect the child soldiers in the same way—some have a traumatic reaction, others not. And, secondly, that the children suffer from the war long after their soldiering has ended.

He goes on to say that the effects "vary significantly in regard to the nature, duration and severity of their war experiences, and equally important, in their postwar situations, which differ along the lines carved by gender, disability, and their access to social support." (ibid., 127). Wessells (ibid., 199-202) also finds that former child soldiers may be classified in three distinct groups:

- A group of approximately 70 % "function well and will benefit from work, play, attending school, and general improvements in economic, political, and social conditions" (ibid., 199f).
- A group of 20 % "includes children living on the streets and children with disabilities" (ibid., 200f).
- A group of approximately 10 % "is severely affected and unable to function in a culturally appropriate manner" (ibid. 201).

Hence, for children who have been serving as soldiers in war and have had traumatic experiences, such experiences can for some lead to post-traumatic stress disorder (PTSD), and they may continue to suffer from these over a long time. (Singer 2005, 194) PTSD also has secondary effects, such as "learning difficulties, lowered ability to concentrate, changes in memory, and greater intellectual inflexibility. Physical manifestations include sleep disorders, severe headaches, and stomach pain, which are all common psychosomatic disturbances" (ibid., 195). Singer also names other comorbid problems, which are not reactions to PTSD per se: "Depression, anxiety, higher levels of aggression or introversion, extreme pessimism, limited capacity to accept frustration, and a lack of personal mechanisms to resolve conflict are all common among former child soldiers going through rehabilitation" (ibid.).

For the researcher it therefore becomes pertinent to be aware of *where* in the process of rehabilitation and possible healing the informant is—socially, physically, mentally and emotionally—and how the informant has been able to cope with traumatic experience in and after war. Otherwise one may miss out on important information shared by the ex-child soldier. There is a large literature attesting to the problems of memory that are associated with PTSD.[7] And since these problems have important implications for the analysis offered in this paper the researcher must study the relevant literature prior to engaging in the interviews.

There are also three other reasons why such awareness is important. Since the role of the researcher is not that of a therapist, questions must not be formulated in a therapeutic way. Also, the interview must not be conducted in such a way that the informant feels that he or she is subject of interrogation. Finally, awareness of where the informant is in the process of rehabilitation and possible healing will enable the researcher to avoid questions which irritate or trigger anger and resent.

Implications for researchers doing qualitative (semi-structured) interviews

Although qualitative interviews, when conducted for the purpose of research, are not intentionally part of the healing process, some of them may have the additional effect of contributing toward it. Some of the informants find that telling their stories to a person they can trust help them to 'get the ghosts out of the closet.' Others, however, find it painful to talk about their past experiences. Repeated interviews or opportunities for telling their stories may even have the negative effect of slowing down or interrupting the healing process. This is particularly true if the researcher probes difficult experiences (even gently) that can pick people open and leave them more vulnerable. Also, if the young person believes himself/herself to be spiritually contaminated and has undergone a cleansing ritual, talking is viewed as reopening the door to the angry spirits, as Honwana (2006, 104-134) has clearly demonstrated. This means that the researcher has to be alert to either of these possibilities. Hence the stage in which the child is in his or her rehabilitation and reintegration is important to identify. The more successful the process of rehabilitation has been, and the further progress the informant has made, the more likely is he or she to be able to cope with the interview situation. Under such circumstances they are also likely to be able to convey a more comprehensive story of the past. If, however, the former child solider is early in the process, he or she is more likely to bring a fragmented picture, leaving out some of the most painful parts of the past war experience. The latter is part of the mechanisms of survival and pattern(s) of coping in daily life which the person has adopted. In either case the interviewer must by no means put pressure on the informant to relate more information than he or she is prepared to give voluntarily. The researcher should therefore avoid phrasing questions in any interviews with ex-child soldiers in a way that puts pressure on them.

Understanding the situation of the children is therefore both pertinent if one shall avoid hurting the ex-child soldier and obtain adequate information from him or her. As has been reflected by McConnan and Uppard (2001, 145-149), understanding their situation involves assessment of what children in the DD situation want and do not want, assessing the situation to which children are returning, and their need for temporary care. Here relevant camp staff or (temporary) guardians may offer the researcher valuable background information which may prepare him or her adequately for meeting with the informant(s).

Different approaches to reintegration and how they influence the interviewees

In his chapter, "Turning a Soldier Back into a Child", Singer (2005, 183-207) deals with how *healing* is part of the process of integration and rehabilitation.

> The healing is not one step but is a process. It involves disarming and demobilizing the children, conducting an arduous process of rehabilitation, and then capping the transition back to childhood through reintegration with families and communities (ibid., 183).

In studying the reintegration of former child soldiers the distinctions made by the Norwegian sociologist, it is useful to draw on Reidar Grønhaug's (1979) distinction in his work on the integration of immigrants into Norwegian society. He has distinguished between *isolation* (minimal contact), *assimilation*, and *incorporation* in this process. His categorization of approaches may aptly be modified and employed in monitoring how children are reintegrated into civil society. When applying his three distinct approaches to the reintegration of ex-child soldiers, we may further describe the implications of each of them as follows, each approach having its obvious consequences for the re-socialization process:[8]

Isolation or minimal contact will imply a segregation, where the ex-child soldiers are kept apart from or isolated by the other members of society. The ex-child soldiers may, of course, also contribute themselves to this line of segregation, but the attitudes of the other members of society, especially their families and clans, will be most dominating as to whether minimal contact or segregation is the result. This is because conscious or unconscious choices are made by either party or both parties—the ex-child soldiers and their societies alike—but the community has a key role to play. In the case of *isolation*, the result is two cultures, developing side by side, one majority and one minority culture, respectively. Here there is little room for negotiation between the two, since they seldom meet and get to know each others' experiences and needs. Life is conducted in isolation. As a result, the attitude which the ex-child soldier encounters, is one of "come as you are, remain as you are." In the interview situation such informants are likely to express freely their true feelings, including hostility to the surrounding society. Those who feel that they were more powerful and in control during the time they were abducted may even regret having left the armed forces. Such reactions are possible since, in their isolation, they are normally free from direct sanctions from the majority culture due to views and opinions they hold.

Assimilation implies that the minority culture—in this case represented by the former child soldiers, who are less numerous—supplant their own culture and needs and adopt the majority culture—the one dominated by adults. The result is a *forced integration*, where the ex-child soldier must adopt the values in the adult culture, and grow to become like the adults as soon as possible. If not, they will feel like outsiders. Also here there is little room for negotiation, since the majority culture imposes its values and forms of expressions on the minority group—the ex-child soldiers. The latter have to follow the values of and standards set by the majority in the community. As a result, the attitude which the ex-child solider encounters, is one of "come as you are, but become like us." Even informants in this situation are likely to harbour resentment to the majority culture for not taking seriously their past experience, since they are made to adopt its life standards and values. Some informants will therefore be cautious not to give information about the atrocities they have committed but rather relate facts and incidents which can document their role as victims.

Incorporation, however, involves negotiation, since neither the majority nor the minority is forced to give up (all or most of their values or) their experiences. On the contrary, they enter and live their lives in community with their experience without loss of cultural identity. The result is a mutual openness, where both parties give and receive from each other, where they jointly contribute, and where both the ex-child soldiers and other members of community are enriched from the shared negotiations. As a result, the attitude which the ex-child soldier encounters is one of "come as you are, let us share together and see what we (have) become." Informants in this category are likely to feel free to relate both negative and positive experiences they have had, and to give information which may present them as either oppressors, victims, or both. This is because they do not (normally) fear sanctions from the other members of the community on their lives.

In the process of reintegration the ex-child soldier, the family, the clan, other bodies, and the wider society are all agents who contribute to its success or failure. Thus, if the former child soldier does not wish to be reintegrated, his or her social network meets with more obstacles than if he or she wishes for this to materialise. On the other hand, if the former child soldier wishes to become reintegrated but finds that his or her family, clan or the society at large wishes to prevent it, they face grave difficulties. Whereas both the individual and the society must cooperate in the process, obviously the latter carries the heavier responsibility, since it is the family or clan or extended society which identifies the means by which a successful reintegration may take place.

Further, although an ex-child soldier may have been *formally* reintegrated into his or her family (or clan) or the extended society, for example through ritual(s) (Honwana 2006, 104-134), *the type of integration* he or she experiences may nonetheless be either of the three above. If the ex-child soldier has been formally reintegrated, the researcher, when interviewing the ex-child soldier, must therefore try to identify *which type* of reintegration he or she has experienced, since either type of (re)integration is likely to affect the kind and amount of information which the interviewee is prepared to share with the interviewer, thus affecting the interview situation.

In the event of *isolation* the informant is segregated and left on his or her own and has not been healthily reintegrated. In the event of *assimilation* the informant is likely to have experienced that his or her past experience is considered of no value for the family or the wider community. If, however, a former child soldier has met a line of *incorporation*, he or she is aware that his or her past experience is solicited and used by the wider community, and vice versa. Although all three types may be the result of *formal* integration, the first two tend to perpetuate separation or segregation in daily life. Only integration understood as *incorporation* will effect a full reintegration of the ex-child soldier into society (clan or family). In the event that the informants are either isolated or assimilated, they may avoid relating experience which may put them in a bad light vis-à-vis the rest of society, although those assimilated may fear more the sanctions of other members of society than those who are isolated. For the researcher it is therefore paramount to make sure, that informants are either accompanied in interviews with persons whom they trust, or that they meet alone. Otherwise they may not be able to tell the whole story, fearing possible sanctions due to the information they give.

Summary and conclusion

I have identified some methodological and ethical considerations which must be kept in mind when doing research on former child soldiers, and in particular when using such persons as informants in interviews. I have related these considerations to two aspects of the process of disarmament, demobilization and reintegration of former child soldiers. When dealing with the first aspect I have emphasised that researchers must show awareness for the location where interviews take place, and how it may influence the interviewees and the kind of information they are able or prepared to give. When dealing with the second I have shown that researchers must be aware of where the informants are in the process of disarmament, demobilization and reintegration, socially, physically and psychologically, as also this may influence the interviewees and what kind of information they are able or prepared to give.

Two main points emerge from this analysis. *First*, as I have shown, the researcher must first and foremost keep in mind to protect the identity of the ex-child soldier, and his or her whereabouts. This is necessary so as to prevent that the information he or she obtains is later abused or used for reprisals against the ex-child soldiers by armed forces or legal courts. Equally important is for the researcher to set up and conduct the interviews in such ways as will secure maximum safety (and the feeling thereof) on behalf of the informants, and to enable them to share their experience in ways that are congenial with their situation, age and personal preferences. This means that ethical considerations must take precedence over methodological ones.

Second, methodologically the researcher must be aware of the fact that the place or phase where the former child soldiers are in their process of disarmament, demobilization and reintegration, as well as how they have experienced the process will influence the kind of information they are able or willing to share. The researcher must also be aware of the fact that, depending on what the interviewees consider as opportune for themselves in the situation, they may withhold, exaggerate or relate false data or information. Here the way in which they have been reintegrated—formally or functionally/materially—into family, clan or the wider context of society will equally influence what data and information they relate and how they do so. Further, if the atmosphere in which the interviews are conducted creates a feeling of safety on behalf of the informants, they are more likely to be frank and speak openly than if they feel insecure. Nonetheless the information will reflect *where* in the DDR process the interviewees are and *how* they have fared. This, then, prompts a methodological awareness and approach on behalf of the researcher which pays attention to both when and how he or she gathers and interprets data and information from the former child soldiers regarding their past (and present) experience.

References

Beah, Ishmael. 2007. *A long way gone: Memoirs of a boy soldier*. London: Fourth Estate.

Briggs, Jimmie. 2005. *Innocents lost: When child soldiers go to war*. Cambridge, MA: Basic Books.

Cock, Jacklyn. 1991. *Colonels and cadres: Women and gender in South Africa*, Cape Town: Oxford University Press.

Cohn, Ilene, and Guy S. Goodwin-Gill.1994. *Child soldiers: The role of children in armed conflicts*. Oxford: Clarendon Press.

Denzin, Norman K., and Yvonna S. Lincoln (eds.). 2003. *Collecting and interpreting qualitative materials*. Thousand Oaks, CA: Sage.

Eth, Spencer, and Robert S. Pynoos (eds.). 1985. *Post-traumatic stress disorder in children*. American Psychiatric Press, Inc.

Faris, Alexander S. et al.. 2009. Examining motivational interviewing from a client agency perspective. *Journal of Clinical Psychology* 65:1-16.

Fontana, Andrea, and James H. Frey. 2003. The interview: From structured questions to negotiated text. In *Collecting and interpreting qualitative materials*, eds. Norman K. Denzin and Yvonna S. Lincoln. Thousand Oaks, CA: Sage, 61-106.

Grønhaug, Reidar. 1979. Nordmenn og innvandrere: om etnisitet og klasse som to ulike forutsetninger for sosial deltagelse i Norge. In *Migrasjon, utvikling og minoriteter: Vandringen fra Asia og Middelhavsområdene til Nord-Europa*, ed. Reidar Grønhaug. Bergen/Oslo/Tromsø: Universitetsforlaget, 125-145.

Honwana, Alcinda. 2005. Innocent & guilty: Child-soldiers as interstitial & tactical agents. In *Makers & breakers: Children & youth in postcolonial Africa*, eds. Alcinda Honwana and Filip De Boeck. Oxford/Trenton/Dakar: James Currey/Africa World Press/Codesira, 31-52.

Honwana, Alcinda. 2006. *Child soldiers in Africa*. Philadelphia: University of Pennsylvania Press.

Keitetsi, China. 2004. *Child soldier*. London: Souvenir Press.

Masten, Ann S., Karin M. Best, and Norman Garmezy. 1990. Resilience and development: Contributions from the study of children who overcome adversity. *Development and Psychopathology* 2:425-444.

McConnan, Isobel, and Sarah Uppard. 2001. *Children not soldiers: Guidelines for working with child soldiers and children associated with fighting forces.* London: Save the Children.

McDonnell, Faith J. H., and Grace Akallo. 2007. *Girl soldier: A story of hope for Northern Uganda's children.* Grand Rapids, MI: Chosen.

Moradi, Ali R. et al.. 1999. Everyday memory deficits in children and adolescents with PTSD: Performance on the rivermead behavioural memory test. *The Journal of Child Psychology and Psychiatry and Allied Disciplines* 40:357-361.

Rapley, Tim. 2004. Interviews. In *Qualitative research practice*, eds. Clive Seale et al.. London: Sage, 15-33.

Strandenæs, Thor. 2004. Dialoguing with Children on Liturgy and Worship, *Swedish Missiological Themes* 93 (2):489-515.

Thabet, Abdel Aziz, and Panos Vostanis. 2000. Post traumatic stress disorder reactions in children of war: A longitudinal study. *Child Abuse and Neglect* 24 (2):291-298.

The Paris Principles: The Principles and guidelines on children associated with armed forces or armed conflicts. 2007. Geneva: United Nations, http://www.un.org/children/conflict/_documents/parisprinciples/ParisPrin ciples_EN.pdf) (accessed 7 January 2010).

Ung, Loung. 2000. *First they killed my father: A daughter of Cambodia remembers.* New York: HarperCollins.

Utas, Mats. 2005. Sweet battlefields: Youth and the Liberian Civil War (Ph.D. dissertation). Uppsala: Uppsala University.

Wessells, Michael. 2006. *Child soldiers: From violence to protection.* Cambridge, MA/ London: Harvard University Press.

Notes

[1]　Should one use 'DDR' or 'DDRR'? 'DDR' stands for the process of 'disarmament, demobilization, and reintegration.' Countries like Liberia have used 'DDRR', adding a second 'R', which stands for 'rehabilitation,' to describe the process (hence 'DDRR'). Most commonly now 'DDR' is used, such as in The Paris Principles (2007; Wessells

2006, 154f). This reflects the fact that, in the case of ex-child soldiers, reintegration is a long process which includes both formal and material reintegration. Formal reintegration may involve some degree of rehabilitation, as in the case of traditional rituals of cleansing and welcome. But only a lengthy process of material reintegration will enable the persons to become fully rehabilitated—if he or she ever reaches that stage of social and emotional healing. Wessells (2006, 154-180) has devoted a whole chapter (ch. 7) in his book to formal processes of disarmament, demobilization, and reintegration. He has outlined the processes, reviewed particular country programs, examined challenges that arise in situations of ongoing conflict, and suggested practical guidance for improvement. In The Paris Principles (2007, 24-40), an entire chapter deals with the release and reintegration and addresses twenty five different issues that are involved in the process. See Tonheim's article in the present book for research on the process of DDR.

2 Authors such as Honwana (2006, 182f) usually identify the village, town, region or country where interviews have been conducted but often fail to indicate where in the process of DDR the informants are at the time when interviews are conducted.

3 The principle of identity protection is reflected in, e.g., the legal and ethical guidelines for research of the Norwegian Social Science Data Services. Here the Privacy Ombudsman has a special responsibility for safeguarding identity protection and privacy in research. See http://www.nsd.uib.no/nsd/english/pvo.html (last accessed 22 October 2009)

4 The history of interviewing and a presentation of different kinds of interviews have been introduced by Fontana & Frey (2003). Other aspects of the collection and interpretation of interviews are covered in Denzin & Lincoln (eds.) (2003).

5 His or her role as 'guest,' however, does not imply that the researcher is not free to openly ask the questions which he or she needs answers to, only that the interviewer knows that he or she has entered the territory of the other and must accordingly show respect both for readiness to be interviewed, and for hospitality.

6 E..g., becoming wounded or disabled, infected by HIV and other sexually transmitted disease (107-125), as well as being affected by the invisible wounds of war (126-153).

7 E.g., Eth and Pynoos 1985; Moradi et al. 1999; Masten, Best and Garmezy 1990; Thabet and Vostanis 2000; Faris, Cavell, Fishburne and Britton 2009.

8 See Tonheim's article in the present book (ch. 2) for research on the contextual dimensions of reintegration.

19

The Interaction Between Interviewees and Interviewers:

Perspectives from Religious Studies[1]

Gerd Marie Ådna

School of Mission and Theology, Stavanger, Norway

Abstract

With formerly recruited children as its specific focus, this article addresses the question of what "techniques" are considered appropriate in interviews of children and emphasises in particular the need of including the religious and spiritual aspects of the children's worldview and experiences, as these have often been neglected or underestimated in research. The article refers to examples from a few handbooks on qualitative research compared to literature about youth that have experienced atrocities. Further, religious studies and examples of research on children's religiosity are presented and discussed in substantiating the need of addressing religious and spiritual issues in order to get a more comprehensive understanding of the children's world view and life in total. Whether there is a space between the interviewer and the interviewee and how to bridge it, is discussed by way of issues like language, small talk and gender.

Introduction

Two girls, 9–10 years of age, riding on a brown adult male horse with a flowing mane and tail on a sandy path in lovely spring weather. What a view of beauty, elegance and power! To me as a non-rider it creates admiration and anxiety. Admiration—because these girls can sit on horseback and ride with the most natural attitude I have ever seen. They are the very image of freedom and happiness. But also anxiety—because I, the onlooker, fear that

they will fall off around the next curve and up the steep hill where I cannot
see them. These girls have never been interviewed by me. Hence, their story
is only imaginative. My assumptions are formed in my mind and based on
my memory of a former bad experience back in my childhood as well as on
some narratives about children being too courageous and having challenged
the powers of strong animals. The result of such an accident with the horse
was for one girl a paralyzed body and a totally changed life. The feeling of
admiration is formed by my reading of Mary O'Hara's trilogy from 1941–
1946[2] about the relation between children and horses. Her generously
described children take responsibility and care for animals, which are big and
powerful. For me being a youth, these books brought me into the sacred and
fascinating "other" that had been closed to me before that time.

Although the skill of riding a horse is globally known, this is not an
activity that is practised by all children. Accordingly, our experiences differ
regarding these animals. Likewise, the person who tries to describe the horse
and its rider will probably easily expose her deficiency being a non-rider.

This is not a study on riding a horse. The introductory remarks and
reflections are simply intended as a thematic bridge between my own
experiences from a quite safe child- and adulthood in Norway and another
world that I have encountered in my reading of testimonies made by female
formerly recruited children from Acholiland in Northern Uganda.[3] Many in-
depth interviews with young women who had been utterly and violently
deprived of their lives were introduced to me. These interviews also confronted me with their not-yet-integrated new life in camps and villages. I could
hardly believe what I was reading; it was just too cruel and gruesome. The
helplessness and extreme concern that I have felt for the young girls—but
also for those who were listening to these violent stories—have been boring
into my mind ever since I began to read about them. I get the same feeling as
the one I experience while anxiously looking at the riders, a feeling of not
being able to do anything, either to help avoiding the danger or to repair
wounded bodies and souls.

On this background I ask myself: How can a scholar be able to
professionally distinguish between herself and the subject(s) she is interviewing or even only reading about? Further, there are many possible links of
interference between the two, which we may call *reflexivity*. In order to cope
with these extraordinary experiences and testimonies, I have had a strong
desire to be able to envisage hope in the interviews with formerly recruited
children as well as in the reports that have been written about children in war
zones on a more general basis.

Some authors have surely demonstrated that there are prospects of hope,
and as I discovered the technique and method described in *Testimony After*

Catastrophe by Stevan Weine (2006),[4] I was able to understand that there *may be* elements of healing for the young women in the process of giving interviews to and talking with for instance wise human beings capable of listening to them. In short, we may talk about what the guidelines presented by the so-called Market Research Society emphasise in research with children and youth: "To protect the researcher and client by publishing the necessary good practice required to meet their legal and ethical responsibilities" (MRS 2006, 2). Hence, it is utterly important that the researcher is conscious about these challenges and performs her interviews in an ethically responsible way with due respect for the legal rights of the interviewee. Such a practice will give more reliable results and will in fact be a protection of both the researcher and the client.

How can a researcher improve her ability in interviewing children and young women, and how can the interaction between the two become a fascinating and complex play of roles and attitudes, words and silence, experiences and learning? In this article I will try to combine experiences and valuable learning from different fields, from cross-field religious studies, from literature and psychology, and from such texts as those mentioned above, written by authors like Mary O'Hara (see note 2) and Gro Dahle (2001). All these contributing sources may bring interesting aspects into our concern, namely, to improve the understanding of the children, their adult associates and their interviewers, but even more, to visualize how interviews *may* have a healing effect on a person who is utterly damaged by political violence. At present, I am standing betwixt and between these two worlds, the so-called safe world of Norway and the very different, fascinating as well as frightening, world of female formerly recruited children.[5]

Victor W. Turner (1974, 232) describes this state of being in-between two conditions when it comes to rituals and their liminal phases. Simultaneously he describes the role of being betwixt and between *and* at the same time being an outsider "referring to the condition of being either permanently or by ascription set outside the structural arrangements of a given social structure." Obviously, this idea suits the double status of the female ex-child soldiers when they are staying in the bush, and upon their return in their home village when they reach a second phase of liminality, becoming outsiders even there. Furthermore, I will consider the *researcher*, being in the situation of the interviewer or the reader to exist in a similar outsider role.

Analogously to Turner, Edward W. Said's (1978) idea about *Orientalism*, may be used to compare the researcher or the reader of this research standing *outside* the door of the sacred Acholiland room and looking through the keyhole, into the totally *other* world of the LRA fighters and their appalling practices. For some, it is very exotic and it may pull them with its fascinating and irresistible attraction of suffering. However, were it not for the researcher's duty to read the texts by her PhD student, she would never endure standing there. Or, would she? Edward Said has taught us that the portrait drawn of *the other* tells us as much about the storyteller herself as about the focused subject. Hence, this is another example of *reflexivity* in humanistic research; the researcher writes about something that personally concerns and triggers her, and she influences the interpretation of the testimony given (Brown 1999, 350-353). So then, is research always inward-looking? Not at all, but this time it is necessary to include the condition of the interviewer. And I defend the need of such reflection and contemplation on oneself in order to be able to continue to read texts that are utterly disgusting. Actually, in order to endure and overcome the strains caused by such texts one might need an intellectual "time off", i.e. access to spaces or practices where the grief and emotional distress can be let out.

The following discussion will be directed by three main concerns of mine: First, how can researchers in Humanities improve their considerations of and abilities in seeing children and youth when they are interviewing them? Secondly, how can an outsider—the interviewer or the reader of an interview—understand and analyse what a child or young person has gone through without having been involved herself or, at least, having been an observer to the atrocities? Thirdly, how can interviews and, hence, testimonies from a war zone have a certain perspective of *hope* so that the interviewees *and* the interviewer can face a better future?

Appropriateness of interview "techniques" in relation to children and due consideration of religion

Examples from a few handbooks on qualitative research

In two of the most popular books about doing qualitative research, authored by Seale and Silverman, there are very few references to "children", as if they were non-existent in this sort of research. Some articles handle vulnerable situations and crises (for instance Fielding 2004, 236-248), but children are not explicitly addressed as a topic of their own (cf. Seale 2007). Silvermann (2005, 58-59; Seale 2007) touches children when writing about child abuse and about the interaction between a mother and her baby. But it is interesting—and quite astonishing to me—that children and youth are almost absent in two of the leading handbooks for doing research in social sciences. Still, these books are often used by researchers in anthropological and religious studies in the English speaking academic world.

In handbooks in the fields of psychiatry, pedagogics, and social work, where children and youth are explicitly the subject of the books, they are extensively discussed, which is not surprising. I will especially mention the books by Charmaine R. Brittain and Deborah Esquibel Hunt (2004) and by Ann Farrell (2005) in this respect, and I will return to some relevant issues from their research later. First, I will look at some findings by scholars in religious and anthropological studies.

Religious studies and examples of research on children's religiosity

Senior lecturer of History of religions at the University of Oslo, Nora Stene Preston, has in her doctoral thesis, *Angels in Platform Shoes: Religious Socialisation of Coptic Orthodox Children in London* from 2005 made a thorough foot print in children-related research in the Humanities, and has hence given children a strong voice within religious studies as well as in migration research. Preston's investigation of Coptic children in London is obviously different from doing research on children in other places, and especially in a war zone like Northern Uganda. But I claim that in spite of this it is possible to learn from Preston's methodological considerations.

According to Preston (2005, 21) three different levels have to be examined in order to understand children's religiosity: The child is a *family* member; second, the child is a *church* community member, and, thirdly, the child is a pupil in *religious education* classes. If the child is not examined and viewed in these three ways, it will probably not be understood fully as a religious individual and a social participant in the wider community. Preston interviewed and observed children during a period of one year in the mid-1990s. In her earlier master thesis (1991) she studied Coptic children in Cairo, and is therefore able to compare these two quite different contexts for Coptic religious formation and socialisation (Stene 2005, 49). Her main hypothesis is that "children have to be evaluated as independent religious actors who contribute to change and continuity in the religious group they belong to."[6] This leads us to Preston's criticism against some of the main actors in children research in Europe: She claims that some of them seldom discuss the role and place of the child *within* a religious community (Preston 2005, 354). The children are obviously listened to but are still being isolated in their religious world. Hence, I conclude, the picture drawn of them is an abridged one. It is not sufficiently understood *from within*. We can compare this practice to looking through a keyhole. The child is becoming the *other*, a fascinating stranger. This is an image and an approach that is similar to the above mentioned attitude of the *Orientalist* look.

Christopher Blattman and Jeanine Annan (2006, v) do maintain that the role of the family and the village is crucial for former child soldiers: "Family connectedness and social support appear to be the key protective factors for the psychosocial well-being of youth." The social frame is not forgotten in their research. Jo Boyden and Joanna de Berry (2004, xvii-xviii) underline the importance of the extended context, socially and politically, in order not to be too individualistically and psychologically oriented towards formerly recruited children. Still, a more concerned examination of religious elements of the family structure and support seems sometimes to be neglected.

Hence, my consideration is: In research on formerly recruited children there has been a focus on their experiences in the bush and on their return to the village. Therefore, their world view (implying religion and beliefs) has been examined, but still probably too one-sided. Consequently, it may be appropriate to ask whether these East-African children and youth have been studied and observed in settings that sufficiently *include* all important situations the children are a part of. For instance, it is relevant to ask whether their spiritual world view is fully acknowledged. In some reports only randomly chosen practical situations in a camp, an integration programme or similar seem to have been chosen.

In order to understand a formerly abducted child she should be seen in her totality as a child (1) within her family, (2) within her church or mosque, (3) within her learning environment, Sunday school or Qur'an school (*madrasa*), in addition to being observed living in the village setting surrounded by different group members from all generations. This communal element is referred to in the African saying: "It takes a village to raise a child." Only when all these three elements—or at least more than the interviewing situation in a certain setting often outside the village—are included, the child is understood in its own religiosity and for its community's sake.

Construction of childhood

Furthermore, Preston underlines how children and their operative context (Norwegian: "handlingsrom") are connected to certain comprehensions or constructions of "childhood." One of these underlying conceptions in her research is the Coptic Orthodox construction of children being "pure like angels" (Preston 2005, 354-359). Another sub-conception is the definition of the transitional age from childhood to youth. Preston's main informants are below 12 years of age, and she shows how the Middle Eastern and Egyptian-British communities maintain the age of *puberty* of approximately 12 years to notify the shift (Preston 2005, 15). In most research on formerly recruited children the defined transition age is 18 years. (Andvig and Gates 2007, 3;

McMahan 2007, 12)[7] In sub-Saharan Africa, childhood is normally viewed as ending when rites of passage (typically around 14–15 years of age) have been conducted or when a young person begins to perform typical work of an adult, but this is not always taken into consideration by scholars writing on formerly recruited children.

In consequence, I find it intriguing that in most texts where ex-child soldiers are discussed, the methodological and ethical challenges of interviewing *children* are mentioned in spite of the fact that most informants are *youth* and *young adults*. Most of them—in what I have read so far—are at the time of the interview no younger than 15 years of age. Supportive of my impression in this respect, Boyden and de Berry (2004, xiii) write, "In most cases the informants are adults—parents, teachers or others presumed to be in close contact with children." They also criticise the tendency of a research being too individualistic and based on too few interviews conducted over too short periods of time (2004, xiii-xiv). In Blattman and Annan's report *The State of Youth and Youth Protection* from 2006, none seems younger than in their early twenties. This means that this particular research on child soldiers predominantly discusses experiences of young adults and only indirectly children's experiences insofar as the these young adults also refer to experiences they have had during a long period including their childhood. As long as the information about formerly recruited children, acquired in interviews, is drawn from informants who are young adults, an inevitable implication is that these childhood descriptions, based on memory, also will have strong constructed elements. Hence, the childhood communicated and mediated to the interviewer has got *mythic* dimensions. Nevertheless, the testimonies of those who at the time of the interviews already have become young adults are to be respected in their own right, and it is essential that the researcher approaches them in such a way that they are evaluated as truthful in their own respect.

Interviews of children and adults

Nora Stene Preston associates herself with the tradition and practices developed by Kim Knott (1992), Sissel Østberg (1998) and Eleanor Nesbitt (2000) with regard to interviewing children in a migration context. This technique implies for instance an open question like: "If someone from your school came and stayed with you for a week, what do you think he or she should notice?" (Preston 2005, 47) Thereupon, the children told eagerly about their life at home and in church, and the researcher got a lot of information to sort out and analyse.[8]

The very notion that children can be main informants about religiosity has often been disputed in previous research, according to Preston and Anne Solberg (1994), even if we surely know of research with children in fields like psychology of religion.[9] According to Solberg (1994, 195), the crucial strategy is "ignoring age", which means that assumed and often culturally created differences between children and adults should be set aside and made irrelevant in the interviewing process. In this way, presupposed ideas about *what a child is*, are given little priority, and instead the child is considered able of doing "everything." If one starts an interview with the idea about what the child can do, the result will be limited. "Attention should be moved from the qualities of the child towards the research process in encounters between researcher and researched" (Solberg 1994, 160). In other words, Solberg and Preston conclude by maintaining that only minor distinctions vary with regard to the interviewing method, but there is a difference regarding the research *process* between children and adults.

In Jo Becker's report (2007, 15) we are told about a former soldier boy in Sri Lanka who was interviewed at the age of 16, and he mixed his soldier experience with a frightening experience of the burning of houses and the rape of his mother that happened when he was only three years old. This is how the human psyche can work. Another soldier's reason for joining a forced group was a former violent treatment of his family in the village when he was small. (Becker 2007, 16) It is not up to me to analyse these cases, but I do see the problematic gap between having become an adult at the time of being interviewed and the childhood past as the subject of this interview. Of course, youths have the right to tell *about* their childhood, but the researcher has to know that this unfolds in the shadow of what has happened in the transition from *childhood* to the formation of becoming *youth*. The interviewer has also to consider "forgetfulness" due to for example psychological or other communal mechanisms.[10]

Weine (2006, xiii) has developed an important element of trust in his work on testimonies, stating that they "have three defining characteristics: they are personal, truthful, and ethical." This is also how we have to characterize the testimonies from formerly recruited children. Otherwise, the interviewees may be called "liars", and no trust is identified between them and the interviewer. The British anthropologist Jo Boyden (2003, endnote 9; cf. 2004, xi) in her studies on children with war experiences in several countries declares, "There are many reasons why adults' recollections of childhood may not adequately represent the perspective and feelings of the children they once were, not least because human resilience partly involves blotting out memories as, for example, in the grieving process." Hence, truthfulness must to a greater extent be addressed to the interviewer than to the interviewee.

Religion

"Religion" is a term that Blattman and Annan (2006) do not mention in their report; the same applies to McMahan (2007) in his paper about ethical considerations. Moreover, neither "ritual" nor "world view" is used by these scholars. Blattman and Annan (2006, iv-v), however, do consider the "spiritual world" and children being "haunted by the spirits" (*cen*), and how some are helped by witch doctors or prayers. When Andvig and Gates (2007, 11-15) write about how children are recruited for soldierhood, they mention religion, but only once as a factor for creating identity, never for bringing sincere motivation or help into their lives. This seems strange to me when I have in mind the multiple references to religion that is found in transcripts of interviews with young adults in Acholiland. It is even more remarkable that the *Paris Principles* (2007) do not mention religion or spirituality to be one of the necessary conditions for becoming a reintegrated child or youth in society. According to these principles, human rights, justice, and social and economical relations should be taken into account, but no specific religious or spiritual values are brought up. Alcinda Honwana (2006, 18-22; and former books) is, however, one exception who has comprehensively descri-bed the role of religion in communities in Mozambique, which became arenas for employing children as soldiers and after the end of the civil war in 1992 for healing processes where spiritual rituals where included.

Ninian Smart's eight dimensions of religion (1968)[11] are often pointed at for scholars and students in religious studies. These dimensions, respectively aspects, of religion do not say anything specific about interviewing people (including children) about religious issues. However, Smart's listing of dimensions is a reminder for the interviewer so that she may become more observant and alert to the manifold variety of religious expressions among individuals and in the community. Therefore, I would let them assist me when trying to find out more about the spiritual world that children and youth in war zones like Northern Uganda are a part of, especially the dimensions that concern the emotional and mythical aspects (2 and 3).

I will follow up Smart's eight dimensions of religion and point to the idea of the anthropologist Clifford Geertz (1973, 127), who states: "Belief systems express a worldview, that is, a culture's picture of the way things in sheer actuality are, their concept of nature, of self, of society. It contains their most comprehensive ideas of order." In other words, there are hundreds of understandings or conceptions of *order* and *meaning*s to explore in religious studies. I assume that the idea of religion as "social order" and religion as "cosmos contra chaos" also covers some of the understandings of "religion" in Northern Uganda and for its children. Hence, more questions about religious and spiritual issues should be asked to the children and young adults in order to get a more comprehensive understanding of their world view and life in total.

The space between the interviewer and the interviewee and how to bridge it

Language

In her thesis Preston discusses challenges connected to interviewing children. Her dialogues were both in English and Arabic, two languages which the researcher speaks fluently. Thus, she did not need any translator and/or distorting factors but could converse freely with her informants (Preston 2005, 46). Religious language is to a high extent strongly symbolic and rich in metaphors. It is complicated to understand any poetry or language with many allusions, even more so if this language is not your mother tongue. Excuse me for probably being unfair to some, but I cannot hide that I am sometimes unconvinced about research undertaken in a language not mastered sufficiently by the researcher.

There are many pitfalls in the world of translations and translators. Tim Rapley (2007, 18-19), in his very interesting chapter on interviews, does not seem to reflect on the condition of using a translator at all. The same seems to apply to Farrell (2005); she gives the impression of considering neither the very troublesome necessity of using translators nor the problem of being a weak speaker of the interviewee's native language. Hence, I frankly ask whether these authors consider translation as a bridge or a pitfall, or as any challenge to the dialogue at all. Researchers in religious studies are by no means any better than social scientists regarding language skills, but perhaps some of the anthropologists and those with missionary or any other language trained background can be more proud in this respect.[12]

Small talk

The Norwegian author Gro Dahle wrote in 2001 a small book *Loop* about life and language. Because the title *Loop* has the addition *A logbook*, it may be seen as a diary about how to become the very best user of the right words in particular situations. Alternatively, it may be regarded as Dahle's autobiography that tells her own creation story from childhood to womanhood. One of her texts is called "All these small words" (In Norwegian: *Alle disse småordene*; 2001, 54). She discusses words like *excuse me* and *poor you* and *in a way*; short phrases that we use all the time. Dahle sometimes gets tired of these words and she will discipline herself to avoid them. This style may express little and is often superficial, she argues. But she and we know that these small words are indispensable for a fluent conversation in any language.

From learning a new language, though, it is well known that such phrases constitute its most difficult component to get under your skin and tongue. When you are able not only to understand but to use such words, you feel *included,* you are one of *them,* you have become an *insider.*[13] Similarly, the formerly abducted children who speak Acholi, know their small talk and terms. According to internal rules and customs these words mean a lot more than the interviewer with little or no knowledge can grasp. The outsider in language may become an outsider and an onlooker in her very concern of getting to information from the informant.

In another text, Dahle describes her developed ability to talk about many issues that demand more knowledge than needed for daily conversations and about how she can *show off* her readings of books and encyclopaedias. "I can tell that the blue colour [used for a painting] of Virgin Mary's coat was the most expensive colour at that time" (Dahle 2001, 55, my translation). A *show off* attitude from the interviewer's side can destroy and suppress information from the informant. But as Dahle demonstrates, she uses her skills in art and religious studies positively and modestly even if she seldom directly touches these issues in her texts. Still, she writes extensively about *aesthetics* and *meaning* often linked to children's way of thinking, their fears and joys. She shows that she understands how certain children think and express themselves. Her approach is that of an artist author more than a researcher but sometimes I wonder whether she could have been a better interviewer and reader of interviews than I and my colleagues are. She is able *to rub off the dust* so that we understand the words of the child and young person, the small talk and the solid information alike.[14]

The courage to endure the "empty room"

In art history and art analysis one of the most essential issues is how space *between* elements in a certain frame is constructed. By looking at a painting one may ask the important question: What could be *taken away* without losing the substantial meaning of the artist's intention? There are millions of over-crowded paintings. When do we have the courage to leave the "empty room" empty, the courage to open up for unexpected interpretations? In speech communication these breaks or empty pockets are called *silence*. The good artist and the skilled interviewer have some abilities in common: they leave some room for something I will call an intuitive under-standing for complicated issues that cannot necessarily be explained in words.[15] From both a religious studies and a socio-pedagogical point of view I see this "empty room" as crucial to create dialogue with the interviewee and a dialogue with the reader of the current research. In Preston's representation it seems clear to me that she "opened up" and gave room for silence and interpretation. Only in this way the children trusted her and gave her their secrets.

Interviewing highly traumatized children and young adults requires this ability of giving space and letting the interviewee be heard in all facets in their lives. What really happens in the break or space between the informant and the interviewer's questions and comments may be compared to a new liminal phase, filled with anxiety and grief. "Literary artists and philosophers help us realize that although testimonies give accounts that are bound to what has been destroyed, lost, or damaged, testimonies remain—precisely because they are stones—a valued part of life as hopeful energies of living history," Weine (2006, xiv) underlines. According to his view, the interviewer has to be a supporter and modestly help the traumatized to pass the threshold to a better future (Weine 2006, 120). He calls this help "creative understanding" that "provides a vision on how testimonies may build knowledge that is linked to efforts for peace and reconciliation in the broader field of culture" (Weine 2006, 120). As Mary O'Hara helped me create hope and new ideas, artistic and wise interviewers and readers can contribute to a better frame-work and understanding where the children's words, acts, sighs, tears and silence become bricks for the walls of a new room after they have left the liminalities of the bush and sometimes of the village that rejects them.

"Knowledge as positioned"[16]

This phrase, stated by Solberg, takes us back to my introductory story about myself looking at two children riding a horse. Is the (inter)viewer free from her background and experience encountering the children in speech and observation? Probably not. There is previous knowledge that may well be called "expectation." What does the researcher *want* to hear from the child? We are all aware of the power relation between the two (Ryen 2007, 223). Blattman and Annan (2006, 2, 18) even discuss the desire for sensation on the interviewer's side. One may even recall *manipulation* to be a possible consequence. Child and adult are in an asymmetric hierarchical position to each other. Preston sets aside this hindrance and is perhaps too optimistic, stating that she "tried to decrease the social distance" between herself and her informants, in order to establish contact and create trust (Preston 2005, 51).

Additionally, a dialogical way of interviewing children (and adults) corresponds to ideas known as Hans-Georg Gadamer's "hermeneutic circle," where it is noted that pre-knowledge and prejudices have influence on our understanding of a certain topic, and the prejudices themselves are being a target for change in the dialogical process. Further, of importance for our topic is Gadamer's insight into the notion that a certain understanding is a part of a whole and cannot be understood fully without this knowledge.[17]

Armi Pekkala (2007, 177) emphasises with examples from his valuable research that the atmosphere of trust between the researcher and the informant is crucial. He describes how he went back to his informants and told them what he had written. "Without exception, they listened very carefully, and after I had finished they agreed, but started to tell me all over again how things really were. From their need to start telling me their life once more I concluded that I had not got all the important details they wanted emphasised." This very idea of feedback and some sort of compensation is crucial to the outcome of Pekkala's research, and he continues, "Reciprocity means that the subjects can maintain self-control, autonomy and authority while interacting. It is a question of human dignity and respect—equality" (Pekkala 2007, 177).

The creative tension between the two main actors in an interview leads us to a topic that has been discussed in religious studies for many years. Who can be recognised as a religious insider and who is an outsider? My hypothesis is that the formerly recruited child is a definite insider in her world. Hence, she is very powerful. In her world the interviewer is the outsider. Consequently, my notion above about the asymmetric relation must be questioned. To be in the position of expressing, "You are the outsider!" is traditionally a very powerful one. One aquires the right to *define* and, hence, to *control*. It belongs to the role of an *expert*. In this sense, the child or young adult from Acholiland is really the powerful expert from the soldier bush. Still, there will in many cases be opportunities for *sharing power*. We may call them *negotiated spaces*.

Boyden and de Barre (2004, xiv) problematise this issue on children affected by war even more and write:

> The reality is more complex in that some young people assume a voluntary role in combat even while others are abducted and or otherwise cajoled into taking up arms. Moreover, children and adolescents can be very active in defining their own allegiances during conflict, as well as their own strategies for coping and survival.

This implies that the prevailing dichotomy between adult as active perpetrator and child as passive victim needs challenging.

Hence, there exists a challenge in times of war but also in times of post war when interviews, memories and negotiation of space and power are at stake. That Boyden (2003) even speaks of a "paradigmatic shift" that "involves thinking about children as agents of their own development who, even during times of great adversity, consciously act upon and influence the environments in which they live" is an additional emphasis of the attention and respect by which the interviewer must encounter the child.

The issue of gender

A criticism against the valuable research about the Nuer people in Sudan and Western Ethiopia of the late Evans-Pritchard (1940), is his *under-representation* of female Nuer voices. Being a male, Evans-Pritchard obviously had easier access to male than to female informants. He was also a child of his age, and hence, not as alert as he should have been according to contemporary standards regarding the valuable and useful information to be collected among the Nuer women. Only with their voices their world and life would have been described and understood. Evans-Pritchard is only one among many researchers who have brought to us a *partial* truth of one group's religion and life. Feminist research in theology and religious studies has analysed many misconceptions of this kind.[18]

In field research in Muslim communities the issue of gender is often discussed among researchers, however not very commonly considered in written texts. I remember the American Islamic scholar Valerie Hoffman telling about her studies among female *sufi* practitioners in Cairo. With herself dressed very traditionally in a long dress and scarf she was admitted access to so-called closed or secret rituals for healing (*zar*) and remembrance (*dhikr*). She told that her visits became even more successful and that she was more welcome when she, after some time, brought her baby girl. An adult male person would have been totally denied access to such a setting. One's gender may be an essential condition for receiving certain information. Likewise, Virginia Morrow (2005, 159-169) discusses this issue and considers herself receiving more information from girls than from boys, and more from those who look upon her as a 'mother figure' than from those who are sceptical and suspect her of being like an authoritarian and controlling man.

Final comments

My article draws to a close. I have tried to dive into some aspects of cross field religious studies in order to create a more observant attitude regarding to what extent and how religion is a part of the venue in for instance Northern Uganda. In recent research on religion in Europe and the United States institutional religious boundaries towards the social context are described as "permeable."[19] When it comes to children and societies in Uganda, this European result of secularization may not be of any help. Still, it seems to me to be a change in- and outside religious institutions in Uganda. If the religious world(s) of each child and their families and villages shall be understood, the altering institutions as well as the total operative context of the child and young adult must be analysed.

I have in this article mainly used the stories of others. Nora Stene Preston's religious studies are valuable. Her informants were *seen* and *listened to*. The encounters also affected her, I think. The formerly recruited children in Eastern Africa deserve to be seen and heard. Their testimonies may have had a healing effect on them and created hope against hope. The world needs to hear a variety of stories from and about children, such as narratives like *The Catcher in the Rye*[20] but from a Ugandan background, as well as the more idyllic stories like *My Friend Flicka* from the United States or Norway. My yearning is that scholars can write about the child and the young adult in their complex and holistic diversity. This is exactly how I, the (inter)viewer or the reader, want to be characterised, not as one-dimensional but as truthful and generous in all my analyses and interpretations of children's experiences. Hence, we have the need for the reciprocal attitude that both Stevan Weine and Armi Pekkala stand for.

I cannot and will not do away with the feeling of disgust and fear when confronted with the heart-breaking testimonies of formerly abducted children, but still, by now, I think that I can better cope. Around the next curve there is perhaps a dangerous hill but also possibilities for a different life. My own research process must contain humbleness towards a huge field of not-yet-known-to-me narratives and experiences. I cannot act *as if* I understand. I have to be modest and listen. And to fetch hope that the interviewees are supported with hope on their way towards a better future.

References

Ammerman, Nancy Tatom (ed.) 2007. *Everyday religion: Observing religious lives.* Oxford: Oxford University Press.

Anderson, Priscilla. 2005. Designing ethical research with children. In Farrell 2005, 27-36.

Andvig, Jens Christopher, and Scott Gates. 2007. *Recruiting children for armed conflict.* Available at http://www.isn.ethz.ch/isn/Digital-Library/Publications/Detail/?ots591=0C54E3B3-1E9C-BE1E-2C24-A6A8C7060233&lng=en&id=45788 (accessed 7 March, 2010).

Assmann, Aleida. 2008. The religious roots of cultural memory. *Norsk Teologisk Tidsskrift* 109:270-292.

Assmann, Jan. [1992] 2005. *Das kulturelle Gedächtnis. Schrift, Erinnerung und politische Identität in frühen Hochkulturen.* München: C.H. Beck.

Becker, Jo. 2007. *Child recruitment in Burma, Sri Lanka and Nepal.* Human Rights Watch.

Blattman, Christopher and Jeanine Annan. 2006. *The state of youth and youth protection: Findings from the Survey of War Affected Youth.* UNICEF reports = SWAY

Boyden, Jo. 2003. Children under fire: Challenging assumptions about children's resilience. *Children, Youth and Environments* 13(1). Available at http://colorado.edu/journals/cye (accessed 4 March, 2010)

Boyden, Jo, and Joanna de Berry (eds.) 2004. *Children and youth on the front line: Ethnography, armed conflict and displacement.* Studies in forced migration, Vol.14, New York: Berghahn.

Brittain, Charmaine R. and Deborah Esquibel Hunt (eds.) 2004. *Helping in child protective services: A competency-based casework handbook.* 2nd edition. Oxford/New York: Oxford University Press.

Brown, Karen McCarthy. 1999. Writing about 'the other'. In Russell T. McCutcheon (ed.), *The insider/outsider problem in the study of religion: A reader.* London/New York: Cassell, 350-353.

Dahle, Gro. 2001. *Loop: En loggbok.* Oslo: Cappelen.

David, Tricia, Jo Tonkin, Sascha Powell and Ceris Anderson. 2005. Ethical aspects of power in research with children. In Farrell 2005, 124-137.

Farrell, Ann (ed.) 2005. *Ethical research with children.* Maidenhead: Open University Press.

Farrell, Ann. 2005b. New times in ethical research with children. In Farrell 2005, 166-175.

Farrell, Ann. 2005c. New possibilities for ethical research with children. In Farrell 2005, 176-178.

Fielding, Nigel. 2004. Working in hostile environments. In Seale [2004] 2007, 236-248.

Geertz, Clifford. 1973. *The interpretation of culture: Selected essays.* New York: Harper Torchbooks.

Hansen, Stig Marker. 2009. Reconciliation as a paradigm in Uganda's post-conflict reconstruction. University of Copenhagen: Centre of African Studies. Available at http://www.teol.ku.dk/cas/research/publications/ africapapers/2009/CAS_Africa_Papers__November_2009__Stig_Marker _Hansen.pdf/ (accessed 7 March 2010).

Honwana, Alcinda. 2006. *Child soldiers in Africa.* Philadelphia: University of Pennsylvania Press.

Knott, Kim. 1992. *The changing character of the religions of the ethnic minorities of Asian origin in Britain.* Leeds: University of Leeds, Department of Theology and Religious Studies, final report of the Leverhulme Project, research paper no.11.

McCutcheon, Russell T. (ed.). 1999. *The insider/outsider problem in the study of religion: A reader.* London/New York: Cassell.

McMahan, Jeff. 2007. *Child soldiers: The ethical perspective.* Available at http://www.isn.ethz.ch/isn/Digital-Library/Publications/Detail/?ots591= 0C54E3B3-1E9C-BE1E-2C24-A6A8C7060233&lng=en&id=45682 (accessed 7 March 2010).

Morrow, Virginia. 2005. Ethical issues in collaborative research with children. In Farrell 2005, 150-165.

MRS. Conducting research with children and young people. March 2006. Available at http://www.mrs.org.uk/standards/children.htm (accessed 10 July, 2009)

Nesbitt, Eleanor. 2000. *The religious lives of Sikh children: A Coventry based study.* PhD diss., Leeds: University of Leeds: Department of Theology and Religious Studies.

O'Hara, Mary. *My friend Flicka* (1941), *Thunderhead, son of Flicka* (1943) and *Green grass of Wyoming* (1946), all originally published by Lippincot; 1992. New York: HarperPerennial.

Østberg, Sissel. 1998. *Pakistani children in Oslo: Islamic nurture in a secular context.* PhD diss., Warwick, UK: University of Warwick.

The Paris Principles: The principles and guidelines on children associated with armed forces or armed conflicts. 2007. Geneva: United Nations, http://www.un.org/children/conflict/_documents/parisprinciples/ParisPrin ciples_EN.pdf) (accessed 7 January, 2010).

Pekkala, Armi. 2007. Persuasion or coercion? In Bente Gullveig Alver, Tove Ingebjørg Fjell and Ørjar Øyen (eds.) 2007, *Research ethics in studies of culture and social life.* Helsinki: Academia Scientiarum Fennica, 167-191.

Penn, Helen. 2005. *Understanding early childhood.* London: Open University.

Preston, Nora Stene. 2005. *Engler i platåsko: Religiøs sosialisering av koptisk-ortodokse barn i London.* Diss, nr. 221, Department of Culture Studies and Oriental Languages, University of Oslo.

Rapley, Tim. 2007. Interviews. In Clive Seale et al. [2004] 2007, 15-33.

Ryen, Anne. 2007. Ethical issues. In Clive Seale et al. [2004] 2007, 218-235.

Said, Edward W. 1978. *Orientalism.* New York: Pantheon.

Seale, Clive, Giampietro Gobo, Jaber F. Gubrium and David Silvermann. [2004] 2007. *Qualitative research practice.* London: Sage Publications.

Silvermann, David. 2005. *Doing qualitative research: A practical handbook.* 2nd edition. London: Sage Publications.

Simones, Asbjørn et al. 1995. *Møtet med barnet i sorg og krise.* Oslo: Samlaget.

Smart, Ninian. 1968. *The world's religions: Old traditions and modern transformations.* Cambridge: Cambridge University Press.

Solberg, Anne. 1994. *Negotiating childhood: Empirical investigations and textual representations of children's work and everyday life.* Diss. Stockholm: Nordic Institute for Studies in Urban and Regional Planning (diss. No. 12).

Stene, Nora. 1991. *"Fordi barn er som engler...": En religionshistorisk studie av barn i den koptisk-ortodokse kirken i Egypt.* Master's thesis, Department of Culture Studies and Oriental Languages, University of Oslo.

Turner, Victor W. 1974. *Dramas, fields, and metaphors: Symbolic actions in human society.* Ithaca: Cornell University Press; partly reprinted in Joan Vincent (ed.) 2002. *The anthropology of politics: A reader in ethnography, theory, and critique.* Malden, Mass.: Blackwell, 96-101.

Weine, Stevan. 2006. *Testimony after catastrophe: Narrating the traumas of political violence.* Evanston, Illinois: Northwestern University Press.

Notes

[1] I want to express my thanks to the participants in the Child soldier conference at the School of Mission and Theology in Stavanger, Norway, 13–15 May, 2009, for inputs and questions that were given to my paper during those interesting days. Personally, I have for the first time in my life and professional career been directly exposed to the issue of child soldiers and their dire situation as a participant in the research group "Reintegration of Former Child Soldiers in Uganda and the Democratic Republic of Congo" at the School of Mission and Theology. In this context I have a role as supervisor for a PhD student who has performed interviews with female ex-child soldiers. Being no expert with regard to interviews of individuals who have suffered severe traumas, my intention and ambition has been to bring in insights from the field of religious studies and, combined with further reflections based on general human experience, attempt to make them relevant for the challenging task of performing interviews with severely abused children, *in casu* female ex-child soldiers in Uganda, and of assessing the answers given in such interviews.

[2] *My Friend Flicka* (1941), *Thunderhead, Son of Flicka* (1943) and *Green Grass of Wyoming* (1946), all published by Lippincot; see http://en.wikipedia.org/wiki/My_Friend_ Flicka (accessed 26 April, 2009). These books were all translated into Norwegian and also published in the popular book club "Bokklubbens Barn" (Stabekk: Den Norske Bokklub-ben) in the early 1970s.

[3] I will not bring any direct references to the PhD student's interviews in this paper, but will take my examples from published books and articles.

[4] I am grateful to my friend Reverend Annette Rodenberg, Bavaria, for her notices on the practice of testimonies as a healing method (August 2009).

[5] Victor W. Turner (1974) uses the term "betwixt and between" to describe the liminal phase in a rite of passage; see Vincent (ed.) 2002, 96-101.

[6] My translation, from a summary of Preston's thesis; http://wo.uio.no/as/WebObjects/frida. woa/wo/0.Profil.29.25.2.3.15.1.2.3 (accessed 1 May, 2009).

[7] According to the guidelines from MRS (2006, 14) on conducting research on children, the divisional age for being interviewed without parental permission is usually 16 years.

[8] This was strongly emphasised by the opponent Sissel Østberg in Preston's doctoral defence on 2 February, 2005, at the University of Oslo.

[9] For instance Penn 2005 and Simones et al. 1995.

[10] See Stig Marker Hansen's (2009, 17) remarks on "Social forgetting." Cf. Jan Assmann [1992] 2005 and Aleida Assmann 2008.

[11] Ninian Smart. [1968] 1989. *The World's Religions: Old Traditions and Modern Transformations.* Cambridge: Cambridge University Press, 12-25. 1: The Practical and Ritual dimension, 2: The Experiential and Emotional dimension, 3: The Narrative or Mythic dimension, 4: The Doctrinal and Philosophical dimension, 5: The Ethical and Legal dimension, 6: The Social and Institutional dimension, 7: The Material dimension, 8. The Political dimension.

[12] I have had no opportunity to check what has been done regarding these issues in the field of linguistics, but I am confident that a number of scholars must have reflected and written extensively on this topic.

[13] The academic field *Intercultural communication* has many useful terms for this issue that I will not mention here.

[14] Gro Dahle's ability to recapture the world of children is discussed in newspapers and literature programmes every time when she publishes a new book for children.

[15] Cf. the contribution of Bård Mæland in this volume.

[16] Solberg 1994, 196 and 196-201; cf. reference in Preston 2005, 50.

[17] http://plato.stanford.edu/entries/gadamer/#3 (accessed 1 May, 2009).

[18] Ursula King (ed.) 1987. *Women in the World's Religions: Past and Present.* In: God, the Contemporary Discussion Series. New York: Paragon House; Ursula King. 1989. *Women and Spirituality: Voices of Protest and Promise.* In Women in Society Series. Basingstoke: Macmillan Education; Ursula King (ed.) 1995. *Religion and Gender.* Oxford: Blackwell; Ingvild Sælid Gilhus and Lisbeth Mikaelsson. 2001. *Nytt blikk på religion: Studiet av religion i dag.* Oslo: Pax.

[19] Nancy T. Ammerman. 2007. *Everyday Religion: Observing Religious Lives.* Oxford: Oxford University Press, 7: "The modern 'functional' notion that social institutions operate discretely has become increasingly implausible, and we carry the insight into our study of religion. We expect institutional boundaries to be permeable, and that allows us to ask how and to what effect."

[20] J.D. Salinger. 1951. *The Catcher in the Rye.* One of the most discussed books in USA, about sexuality and anxiety in youth culture after the Second World War.

Bible & Theology in Africa

The twentieth century made sub-Saharan Africa a Christian continent. This formidable church growth is reflected in a wide range of attempts at contextualizing Christian theology and biblical interpretation in Africa. At a grassroots level ordinary Christians express their faith and read the bible in ways reflecting their daily situation; at an academic level, theologians and biblical scholars relate the historical traditions and sources of Christianity to the socio- and religio-cultural context of Africa. In response to this, the Bible and Theology in Africa series aims at making African theology and biblical interpretation its subject as well as object, as the concerns of African theologians and biblical interpreters will be voiced and critically analyzed. Both Africans and Western authors are encouraged to consider this series.

Inquiries and manuscripts should be directed to:

> Professor Knut Holter
> MHS School of Mission and Theology
> Misjonsmarka 12
> N-4024 Stavanger, Norway
> knut.holter@mhs.no

To order other books in this series, please contact our Customer Service Department:

> (800) 770-LANG (within the U.S.)
> (212) 647-7706 (outside the U.S.)
> (212) 647-7707 FAX

Or browse online by series:

> www.peterlang.com